Eighth Edition

BEST

in

LEIS   s

JANET TICE AND JANE WILFORD

INSIDERS' GUIDE®

GUILFORD, CONNECTICUT
AN IMPRINT OF THE GLOBE PEQUOT PRESS

INSIDERS' GUIDE®

Text design: Mary Ballachino

ISSN 1536-6170
ISBN 0-7627-3861-8

Manufactured in the United States of America
Eighth Edition/First Printing

The prices and rates listed in this guidebook were confirmed at press time. We recommend, however, that you call establishments to obtain current information before traveling.

TO FABIANA AND SYKES,
WHO FIRST PROVIDED THE INSPIRATION,
AND TO PAUL AND SARAH,
WHO CONTINUED THE ADVENTURE.
OUR WONDERFUL CHILDREN
AND OUR BEST FAMILY TRAVEL CRITICS!

Eighth Edition

100
B E S T

Family Resorts
in North America

a photo essay

Wild Dunes Resort

 Grand View Lodge

The Broadmoor

 Fairmont Le Chateau
Lake Louise

Fairmont Le Chateau
Lake Louise

 The Mount Washington
Resort at Bretton
Woods

Snowbird Ski and
Summer Resort

 C Lazy U Ranch

Angel Fire Resort

 The Tyler Place
Family Resort

Skytop Lodge

 Mohonk Mountain House

The Broadmoor

 Wild Dunes Resort

CONTENTS

PREFACE

"Best" is a curious adjective, one that is entirely subjective. So let us define our sense of best—both what it does and what it doesn't mean.

Best is not necessarily the fanciest, the biggest, or the most expensive.

Best is not always the sleekest, the poshest, or the newest.

Best, in the context of this book, is what is best for families.

Best is variety in setting and atmosphere.

Best is variety in recreational interests and in prices.

Best is variety in geographical location. A broad selection allows you to have choices whether you want to travel far or near.

We searched for the most extensive children's programs, yet balanced this with an interest in presenting a good cross section of North America. If we have overlooked your favorite, let us know. Please write to us in care of The Globe Pequot Press, P.O. Box 480, Guilford, CT 06437.

Janet Tice
Jane Wilford

INTRODUCTION

Although traveling with children is not a new phenomenon, many Americans these days are viewing the traditional family vacation in a different light. In past decades family vacations most frequently have been determined by the needs and wants of the children. Planning the entire vacation around the kids often left Mom and Dad feeling that they had not had a vacation at all but, rather, a trial by fire. The only option was to leave Junior behind in the care of grandparents or close family friends while the parents ventured off on their own. In an attempt to share experiences with their children, many parents, seeking middle ground, are adjusting the focus of their leisure-time plans.

Vacations these days often mean shorter and more frequent jaunts. Increasingly, they involve flying rather than loading up the family car and driving. Minivacations are becoming popular and are frequently planned to coincide with one or the other parent's business trips. On the philosophical side, current trends in child care emphasize the importance of a parent's presence, especially for the first three years, and many parents are reluctant to leave their infants and toddlers for extended periods.

The intent of this book is to identify those places where adults and children can enjoy interesting and age-appropriate activities. Babysitting services for infants, a ski school for three-year-olds, and a supervised recreational program for older children are some of the possibilities explored. In selecting resorts, we have taken into consideration different styles, price ranges, and diverse geographic locations. It is a representative sampling rather than an all-inclusive listing. Often we have been limited by lack of space

and lack of information. This book does not highlight every Disney and Six Flags Over Somewhere establishment in the United States. While these certainly serve an important educational function in a pleasant and exciting atmosphere for children, therein lies the catch: They are directed primarily toward children. But parents deserve vacations, too—adult vacations with grown-up activities.

This is not, then, a book about vacations *for* kids. Rather, it is a book about vacations *with* kids, about family adventures in which adults can be adults and children can be children and in which there is common ground for sharing. Our original concept of "time together and time apart" remains valid.

In general we are pleased with the progress we've noted in the resorts we have chosen from our previous editions. They are not resting on their laurels but seem to be enthusiastic and dedicated to making more and more improvements and providing better and better facilities and programs for families. In addition, new resorts developing exciting programs are constantly entering this family-oriented market.

If we've left out your favorite family spot, or if you own a resort and feel slighted, please write to us in care of The Globe Pequot Press. We're always glad to know of places where families find special treatment.

Costs and Caveats

Prices are noted throughout the book in the accommodations section of each resort's description. They are current as of 2005. But, just like the new car that depreciates the minute you drive away from the showroom, prices have to be adjusted for inflation the minute they're stated. Keep this in mind if your travel plans do not materialize right away but instead are put on the back burner for a couple of years. Inflation takes its toll simultaneously and universally; however, the prices quoted here can serve as a basis for comparison among resorts regardless of the year in which you consult this guide.

The problem most commonly caused by prices is sorting out just what a given price includes. In the travel industry, various pricing schedules are frequently used to identify the relationship between lodging and meals. For example:

European Plan means the rate quoted is for lodging only.

Modified American Plan means two meals a day (usually breakfast and dinner) as well as lodging are included in the daily rate.

Full American Plan means three meals a day and lodging are covered in the daily rate.

All-inclusive means that all meals, generally all activities, and other extras are included in one price.

The extent of what else is included in the daily room rate, such as use of the recreational facilities, varies widely from one resort to another. Every effort has been made to identify the extras for which no additional charge is required. If "complimentary" or "free" is not clearly stated for a service or activity, you can safely assume that there is a fee.

Certain other things may come as a shock when you check out, so be sure to investigate beforehand. For example, we have not included taxes in the rates. This varies from state to state and will be 7–17% additional. Sometimes occupancy taxes are also added, based on the room or on the number of people.

Recently, it's become a common practice for hotels to add a "resort fee" or "amenity fee" of $5.00 to $15.00 per night. This fee covers things that previously were "free" or included in the rate: in-room coffee and tea, daily newspapers, Internet access, or telephone charges for local or toll-free numbers, etc. Often, resorts will add this fee to include "use of the facilities"—fitness rooms, swimming pool, beach chairs—any number of things. Or it may include room gratuities. We've tried to identify these charges, but they're not always easy to find. You'll want to read the fine print, so to speak, and ask, ask, ask. No one wants a nasty shock at the end of a lovely vacation.

Although we've already discussed rates, it's a complicated issue and bears repeating, so please forgive us if you already know this. The rates that we list will not be exact. Sometimes they may be more; often they may be less. Rates depend on many things—size of the room, day of the week, location and view, season of the year, number of adults and children—the list goes on and on. Especially now that technology is so prevalent, hotels are following the airlines' examples and using yield management techniques. This simply means that a hotel will look at its past booking patterns and its current occupancy rate (how many empty rooms are sitting there) and adjust its rates accordingly, sometimes day by day. And competition is fierce: A resort may lower or raise its rates based on what its neighbors are doing. Also, many resorts, again like the airlines, are putting lower rates on the Internet. While we often give a sample package rate in the descriptions, there may be more packages available. Sometimes it may not be labeled a family package, so don't limit yourself. The resort may be marketing the spa or other recreation, with very good rates.

Besides lodging, prices are specifically noted for children's programs. As a well-seasoned traveler, you already have a ballpark idea of the prices of lift tickets for skiing and greens fees for golf. Emphasis here is on costs of the children's activities because now you're trying to become well seasoned as a traveling parent.

Most children's programs, even if it's not stated in the descriptive entry, require children to be potty-trained. Those programs specifically for infants and toddlers, of course, do not. However, they usually do require parents to supply diapers and baby food or formula.

Reservations, reservations, reservations!! Again, we may not always list this in the entry, but it's safer to assume that reservations are required. If staffing is limited, the program may fill up—many parents plan months in advance via phone or Internet. Most resorts plan their staffing ahead of time, and if no children are signed up, there may be no program. Another caveat: Many hotels are now charging a fee if you cancel your child within twenty-four hours. Illness might not count, but capriciousness would. Advance planning may limit the spontaneity, but ultimately makes life, and certainly vacations, smoother.

PLANNING FAMILY VACATIONS

How This Book Can Help You

As your vacation rolls around, you start weighing the pros and cons of bringing the children along. You feel that you desperately need exclusive time for adult conversation with your spouse or other grown-ups. Yet you wonder if following through on that idea is fair to your kids. Vacations need not be an either/or proposition—either resigning yourself to a week or two of nonstop "Sesame Street" activities with no relief in sight or excluding the children from the few leisure weeks you have away from a demanding career. The former scenario almost always requires relinquishing your own interests, while the latter is complicated by worry and guilt over little Johnny or Susie left behind at Grandma's as you're off footloose and fancy-free. It is possible, however, to have a vacation that is fair to both you and your children.

So you're ready to plan a vacation with the kids. Though this sounds like what parents have been doing for generations, you're different from previous generations. You're better educated and fairly well traveled; you've delayed getting married and having children until your career was launched; and most likely you're older as you reach this phase of family life than were your parents. In addition, you probably have different expectations for both yourself and your children, expectations that influence how you want to spend your leisure time. While you're devoted to your children and conscious of the importance of your input into their intellectual, emotional, and social growth, you also realize that part of being a good parent is tending to your own physical and psychological well-being. You imagine that it must be feasible to share a pleasurable vacation experience with your children without denying your own interests and concerns. Well, it is!

When you've made the decision that the kids should come along this time and you know that one more carousel or one more pair of Mickey Mouse ears just might drive you crazy, then let this book help you discover the perfect vacation spot, where the whole family can be happy together.

Whether you are considering a few relaxing days at a country hideaway or a week of fun in the sun on a beach, rest assured that there are accommodations with facilities and activities that will delight both you and your children. A family vacation doesn't have to mean settling for renting the same house at the nearest beach each season for the next several years or the proverbial visit to Grandma's house year after year. Variety can be found, and if you're itching for a good game of golf, you don't have to fret over whether your three-year-old can manage walking eighteen holes or what antics he'll perform along the way. These concerns can be resolved by choosing the proper surroundings and conditions.

When a young parent once inquired about children's activities at one resort, the staff member gave her a bottle of bubbles. That would last about thirty seconds, right? Thank goodness many resorts are more enlightened, and you'll find those here.

Explore in the following pages a selection of hotels and resorts that offer conveniences to accommodate the needs and wishes of both adults and children. So that you can gratify your diverse and periodically changing geographical interests, you will discover that this guide includes establishments throughout the United States, with a few in Canada. The United States is at the forefront of the new approach to family vacations.

In compiling this collection, several criteria were considered: attractive surroundings; good dining facilities, including comfortable lounges and bars; babysitting services; and recreational activities for both parents and children. Needless to say, some of the establishments listed here meet more of the criteria or meet them better than others. But then, your wishes and requirements may vary from one trip to the next: One year you may need just a competent babysitter to stay in your hotel room with your infant while you enjoy an elegant, leisurely dinner, and the next year you may need a complete day-care center/nursery school for your energetic toddler while you spend the day out on the slopes. This book does not rank resorts on how well the criteria are met; it simply describes them and all their available services. You can then pick and choose according to your personal preferences and current needs.

To make it easier to find your ideal vacation spot, the descriptive entries are grouped by geographical location, then alphabetically within these divisions; addresses, telephone numbers, and Web sites are included in the descriptions.

Following the descriptions is a standard alphabetical index of resort names to help you pull out the perfect place that a friend recently mentioned at a dinner party, the location of which eludes your recollective powers. We've also included an alphabetical index by state and province. This arrangement should afford you easiest access to the required information regardless of your perspective when designing your vacation.

Finally, a special categories index is given that lists resorts by the seasonal schedule of the children's programs.

While probably the foremost concern for your next trip is simply to make that perfect match between your personal circumstances and the most suitable resort, you may occasionally feel a bit nervous about some of the practical logistics of traveling with kids. The next section, on helpful hints when traveling with children, may forestall a few inconveniences that can arise when away from home; the medical information should allay some fears about illnesses and emergencies; and the segments on educating yourself and the advantages of a good travel agent may assist in ironing out the details of your vacation arrangements. In any case, they will stimulate you to analyze your own and your children's habits so that you can anticipate some of the problems and joys of traveling with youngsters.

So you're off. Good luck and have a happy vacation!

Helpful Hints for Traveling with Children

It can be a joy to travel with children. Sure, sometimes the preparations may seem exhausting and spurts of parental anxiety en route may be tiring as well, but the excitement and wonder of children as they encounter new experiences are worth the price of admission.

On the following pages you'll find some helpful hints for traveling with kids. Many of these suggestions may seem incredibly obvious, but stating the obvious is not always a disadvantage. And a little repetitive reinforcement may help you react more quickly or think better on your feet. One easy-to-read and practical resource book is *Trouble-Free Travel with Children: Over 700 Helpful Hints for Parents on the Go* (Book Peddlers,

2004) by Vicki Lansky, author of more than twenty-five books for new parents.

Preparation, preparation, preparation! The first trick to traveling with kids is preparing them for the adventure. Talk to your child in advance; advise her where you're going and what you'll be doing. Infants (in spite of the mounds of diapers you must tote) are very portable. Even toddlers whose whole world revolves around Mom and Dad are happy as long as familiar faces are near at hand. But as a child's world expands to include friends and a wider realm of belongings, verbal preparation becomes very important. Sometimes it's easy to assume that your youngster will pick up on things by osmosis, but children don't always assimilate information about vacation plans that floats around the house in chitchat. It's necessary to explain directly to them what is in store.

Many families like to spend time together planning vacations. Encouraging participation from all family members and allowing children to help plan the trip makes them feel like "shareholders," creating cooperation and increasing satisfaction for everyone. Books and maps about your destination and route can be shared; even for very young children, maps translate the excitement of travel into a tangible form. Participation easily continues throughout the vacation when you assist children with keeping a "journal" (drawings, pictures, flowers, poems, ticket stubs, whatever!); allow them their own camera (inexpensive, of course); or encourage them to collect postcards, badges for their backpack, or follow any theme that appeals to them.

Besides detailing the fun of this new experience, reassure your child that you'll be returning home; that although your daughter may not bring along every Barbie doll and Raggedy Ann, her dolls will still be here when she gets back; and that even though your son may miss his best friends, they won't forget him. Even three and four year-olds can "write" postcards along the way as a means of staying connected with friends back home.

As an experienced traveler, you know the ropes of appropriate packing for trips. As a conscientious parent, you are most familiar with what your child will want or need away from home. The standard rule of thumb—don't overpack—applies just as well for children as it does for adults. The length of the trip adjusted for the dirt factor of your own child (how many outfits can he go through in a day?) should give you a reasonable handle on the amount of clothes to pack. Laundromats are never that far away, many hotels have laundry services, and kids' clothes (just by virtue of their size) are fairly easy to hand wash in a hotel bathroom. And don't take along what your child isn't happy with. No matter how much time dear Aunt Josie spent crocheting that sweet little dress, if your daughter doesn't like it, if it's uncomfortable, it will be nothing more than an unnecessary bulge in your suitcase. We've developed a couple of packing "rules" over the years. Rule #1: Take half as many clothes and twice as much money as you think you need; and Rule #2: Pack your bag and then walk around the block with it to test it before departure!

If your child uses a bottle, a trip may not be the best time to nudge him out of it; a bottle may provide a bit of security in unfamiliar surroundings. Just be sure to pack a bottle brush: If a bottle gets lost at the bottom of a travel bag for a day or two, mysterious molds blossom, or new life forms may be discovered.

Toys, too, have to fall under the "don't overpack" rule. Remember that for children, seemingly mundane objects in new surroundings often provide considerable amusement. It's a good idea to stash away a couple of new attention-getters, but don't forget the tried and true. A cuddly doll, even if it is beginning to look somewhat old and ratty, or a special pillow is often very comforting for a little one sleeping in a strange bed for the first time. Age-appropriate books, a small ball, crayons, coloring books, scissors, construction paper, a bean bag (remember them from when you were a kid?), and small games such as a pint-size checkerboard are all packable items. Even blocks like Duplos or Legos, if arranged in one compact cube, can be packed fairly easily. Some parents cherish a Fisher-Price tape recorder or a Walkman (with earphones, please) as something akin to a gift from the gods. Terrifically totable and accompanied by a selection of tapes (anything from Disney stories to old radio shows to historical accounts of George Washington and Benjamin Franklin are on the market now), a tape recorder can effectively hold a child's attention.

For the preschooler or older child, consider investing in a backpack. Set down the rules with your child when packing: She can bring along whatever fits in the pack, and she has to carry it. This way you give your child a sense of participating in the preparations and obviate the almost inevitable whine about something Mom didn't include. And you can sneak in a little lesson in responsibility practically unnoticed. Just make sure enough room is left for new additions along the way.

A "surprise box" is a fun way to keep children interested and amused. Without divulging details, prepare "surprises" such as snacks, small toys, or other things you know your child will like. Then watch the fun as he delves into the goodies when the vacation adventure begins. A surprise box can entertain your youngster anywhere from two minutes to two hours; if you're clever, you'll be on the upper end of the spectrum.

When making plane reservations, try to secure seat assignments at the same time. Indicate the age of your young traveler, and request the bulkhead seats. These seats afford a little extra leg room and can be padded with blankets and pillows if your child decides to snooze (lucky you!). It may mean that your feet will be struck by paralysis if little Janie nestles down on her pillow and curls up on your toes, but it is an improvement over having her elbow in your drink. Also, without passengers in front of you in this seating arrangement, you won't fret over a rambunctious child's kicks disturbing other people.

If two parents are flying with a lap child (under two years old), try to reserve an aisle seat and a window seat. Regular air travelers never request a center seat, so if the plane is not full, you'll wind up with that third seat in which to spread out; if a stranger does venture into your row, it's simple enough for one parent to move over a notch. Often parents opt to purchase a ticket for the child, bringing their own safety seat.

In the past, airlines stocked onboard activity packs, and even special meals for their younger travelers. These days, you need to pack your own. Bringing a mostly disposable picnic lunch onboard can keep the whole family happy. Do take advantage of the early boarding airlines provide for families with small children—it helps to "settle in" before the crowd arrives.

Airplanes pose additional problems: Small children often have greater difficulty than adults in adjusting to altitude changes. During takeoffs and landings, infants should be encouraged to nurse or drink a bottle; the sucking action combats blocked ear and painful sinus problems. Older children can use the same techniques as adults—yawning and chewing gum or candy.

If you plan to rent a car during your vacation, be sure to request a car seat for a child four years old and younger. While many rental agencies take this in stride, the number of car seats is usually limited, so it's important to make a reservation for this accessory in advance. Whether your mode of transportation is your own car or a rental, plan frequent stops. Cramped legs and fidgetiness set in fast for youngsters. These factors are not unknown in air travel either; even a walk down the aisle of the plane to the bathroom is a change of pace for a child.

In car travel, a small ice chest in the back seat can be a real boon. Filled with milk, juice, and fruit, it provides a source of ready refreshment and relieves frantic searches for a fast-food stop or a corner grocery. Even when traveling by air, if your luggage allotment permits, check a small ice chest (empty) along with your other bags. Once you arrive at your hotel, it can be filled with ice and drinks and can be taken along in a rental car on side trips. Or, upon arrival at your destination, make one of your first stops at a grocery, drug, or discount store and pick up an inexpensive Styrofoam cooler that can be left behind. Many accommodations include small refrigerators in the rooms, and some are equipped with kitchens, but if not, you've solved a problem before it arises. It's much easier to dig into an ice chest for a drink than to track down juice somewhere in the hotel facilities at nine o'clock at night. But if this seems too cumbersome and your child desperately needs something late at night, remember the hotel bar—it is the best place to hit, for it always has orange juice (for Screwdrivers), tomato juice (for Bloody Marys), and milk (for White Russians). It may be more expensive, but can you really afford to count pennies when Johnny refuses to go to sleep without his nightly cup of milk? It's an investment in your peace of mind.

When stocking up on drinks, buy the variety in cardboard cartons. Since they are unbreakable and need no refrigeration, they can be squirreled away in a suitcase or even tossed into a purse. On an airplane, the flight attendants never seem to pass by soon enough or often enough to satisfy little ones.

For edibles, small boxes of raisins, granola bars, and individually wrapped cheese chunks such as La Vache qui Rit (what child can resist a silly laughing cow in a red net bag?) make good nourishing snacks. Good old clever Mom can rack up some kudos when she pulls one of these treats from her bag before Susie even thinks about getting antsy.

Once you arrive at your destination and settle into your hotel, turn over an area, even if just a corner, to your child. Having his own space filled with his own stuff may mean a lot in terms of a sense of belonging, and with a bit of prodding, you may avoid having toys strewn all about.

Collecting souvenirs on a trip can be a time-consuming process or maybe even cause a headache or two. Either Joey wants everything in sight or he chooses the most inappropriate piece of junk you've ever seen. Sure, certain limits on buying have to be set, but who cares if he chooses the made-in-Japan pencil sharpener in the shape of a cannon during a visit to Valley Forge? Just as a cookbook containing three wonderful meat-pie recipes from Nova Scotia or an artistic ceramic tile made in the Southwest is something that you must have, there are special reminders of a trip that a child feels he needs. They're just different. A few neat rocks and a couple of sticks may be the only things Joey wants to show off to his best buddy back home. Or if your little girl wants to take home a shiny red coin purse to her best friend, she doesn't care (and neither does her friend) that the same item is on the shelves in every chain store across the country, so why should you? A smattering of understanding and patience can go a long way.

Recreational activities in your new surroundings must be evaluated with a clear head and a sharp eye. Most of the resorts included here offer organized children's activities or babysitting services, so it may not be necessary to drag kids along on every adult event you want to investigate. Antiques hunting and long museum visits are usually not first-rate attractions for members of the kiddie league. Plan on a babysitter or a group activity for an afternoon that you want to spend on a grown-up outing.

And for those days that are devoted entirely to being together, alternate grown-up pursuits with juvenile ones. Remember that a child's attention span is not as refined or sophisticated as an adult's; variety is more than the spice of life—it's the key to sanity in some cases. Climbing on the cannons at an old fort is much more fun for a child than reading every historical marker; a mixture of both keeps everyone happy. All day on the beach may be too much for a three- or four-year-old, and you can take ten-to-one odds that he won't be content following your lead to relax and soak up the sunshine. Bargain with your child: a run on the beach and a few splashes in the waves, then quiet time building a sand castle; an hour of shopping or sightseeing for two hours in the swimming pool.

Many resorts have lodging with fully equipped kitchens so that you can cook family meals in a homelike setting. Many resort restaurants make an attentive effort to please children; a special dining hour for families or a children's menu certainly helps make life more pleasant. And when you grow weary of dining in restaurants, a picnic may be a reasonable alternative. Many hotels can prepare box lunches, or you can pick up some cold cuts at a small grocery for a do-it-yourself picnic. Ordering a meal through room service is often a special treat for a child.

As you skim the descriptive entries of the resorts that follow, you'll realize that most are self-contained vacation spots. Each offers a place to sleep, a place to eat, and something to do. This is intentional, as children seem to function best staying in one place. Establishing a home base, exploring the setting, and taking afternoon side trips are often preferable to being on the road constantly. Besides negating all the packing and unpacking of a traditional road trip (remember, this is not the newest rock star promoting his latest album that you're traveling with!), having a home base helps a child develop a sense of security as the new surroundings become familiar.

With a few tricks up your sleeve, some understanding, and forethought, traveling with kids can be a fun-filled family adventure. Your well-considered plans make the whole process workable and buy a lot of happiness for both you and your child. With solid preplanning there's space for spontaneous "happenings" that make a vacation memorable.

Medical Information

Unless you can take your own family doctor or pediatrician with you, the best advice to follow is the old Girl Scout motto "Be Prepared." Keep in mind: (1) this adventure you're about to embark upon is not a trek along the shores of the East Siberian Sea, and (2) you are not the sole custodian of Band-Aids. As amazing as it may seem, doctors and pharmacies do exist out there in that twilight zone called family vacations.

Before starting your trip, consult your pediatrician for advice; she may even be able to supply names of colleagues where you'll be visiting. If you fear that your child is coming down with something as you depart on your vacation, or if he's particularly accident-prone, you can check with the resort staff upon arrival about the location of the nearest hospital and pharmacy and the availability of doctors and nurses (many resorts have medical personnel on call). Sometimes the best recommendations come from other parents, wherever you may find them. If the need is immediate, don't hesitate to ask a likely looking parent working in a car rental agency, a restaurant, a shop, or the airport. And without seeming alarmist, look up the telephone number of the local poison control center; anticipating the slim chance of ever needing it, you'll be gratified that it's handy should your child ingest a handful of your brightly colored vitamin pills. It is also a good idea to check with your medical insurance provider before you leave home for out-of-state or -country authorization/billing procedures.

Pack a medical emergency kit and try to envision the unexpected. If your child scrapes a knee at a playground or develops an earache in the middle of the night, you won't want to take time tracking down a drugstore to relieve his discomfort. You can purchase a ready-made medical kit that fits compactly in a car's glove compartment or carry-on bag, or you may prefer the do-it-yourself variety. The following list is merely suggestive; review your own medicine cabinet to fill in the gaps.

- vitamins and medications your child normally takes
- a thermometer
- children's Tylenol
- children's cough syrup
- adhesive strips
- nose drops (though most kids hate them)
- a decongestant
- an aspirator

- ear drops
- suppositories and antidiarrheal medicine (change in water and altitude or sheer excitement can affect a child's system)
- Desitin, A&D, or calendula ointment
- antibiotic ointment or spray (for cuts and scrapes)
- tweezers and a sterile needle (to remove splinters)
- ipecac (to induce vomiting if your child overdoses on peculiar substances)
- Q-Tips and cotton balls
- sterile gauze pads (for applying direct pressure to cuts)
- insect repellent
- Band-Aids (of course)
- sunblock

Though this list seems long, the items take up very little space in a suitcase. Remember, you don't have to pack a lifetime supply of any of these things. A small supply will meet the immediate need and buy you time to find a drugstore.

Knowing What Questions to Ask

Sometimes it seems as if there are almost as many pricing schedules, package plans, and special programs as there are stars in the sky. There are EP, MAP, FAP, golf and tennis packages, weekend specials, and midweek discounts. Depending on geographical location, high season is winter at one resort and summer at another. Even the seasons are defined arbitrarily. Summer may be the end of June through Labor Day or, perhaps, Memorial Day through Labor Day. Christmas season starts December 15 at some places and a week later at others. All the jargon and variations on a theme can make you feel like a babe in the woods when contacting a resort about your plans. To avoid arriving someplace and getting halfway through your stay only to find out that you should have taken advantage of some special offer, you have to be savvy in the possibilities and the vocabulary. Even if you aren't familiar with the latest buzzwords, just knowing that different vacation configurations exist puts you a leg up; you can at least ask, "Are there any family discounts or package plans for _____ (fill in the blank—golf, tennis, skiing, etc.)?"

At some resorts, you walk in and pay one price. At others, every hour on the tennis court or every bicycle ride around the block is charged separately. Both approaches have redeeming aspects. To some folks, it's downright annoying to have to constantly reach for a wallet. After all, this is a vacation and they don't want to be troubled with mundane monetary matters. On the other hand, some people would rather pay as they go, laying down the cash for only the services they use. If you've had aquaphobia since childhood and don't care to be within 10 feet of a lake, much less out in the middle rocking a canoe, free boating privileges are worthless. As long as you're in the know as to a resort's practices and policies beforehand, you'll suffer no surprises and no aggravation or disappointment during your visit.

Much of a resort's terminology is self-explanatory, and acronyms may or may not be a mystery to you. The most commonly used abbreviations are EP for European Plan, meaning lodging only; MAP for Modified American Plan, which includes two meals a day in the room rate; and FAP for Full American Plan, which includes three meals a day.

Knowing a resort's designation of low and high season is also crucial to your planning. If you're not absolutely wedded to certain dates and you can juggle your schedule on the home front, you might land in the low season simply by altering your plans by a week.

Moving to more detailed information, you may want to ask a resort certain specific questions. The questions outlined here can be used on the resorts described in this book for elaboration on particular points, or you can test them out on places that you discover on your own.

Lodging

Are the accommodations hotel rooms, condominium units, or cottages with kitchens?

If they are hotel rooms:

- Are there connecting rooms?
- Is there a refrigerator in the room? (This is handy for chilling juice and milk and keeping snacks fresh.)
- What is the range of prices, and is there a reduced rate for children?
- Is there a charge for a crib or rollaway bed?

Dining

What types of dining areas are there? Is there a spot to get the kids a hot dog and a place that tantalizes more refined taste buds?

Is there a dress requirement? (What a disappointment to venture into a tempting restaurant only to learn that gentlemen are required to wear jackets and you packed nothing but golf shirts!)

Is there a meal plan? Is it mandatory or optional?

Kids

Is there a supervised program for children?

- What are the planned activities, and what are the ages of the children who participate?
- When is it held—times of the year, days of the week, and hours of the day? (The level of specificity may seem a little overboard, but consider a Monday-through-Friday-morning program: It's not going to be much

help if you pull in at 1:00 P.M. on Friday and leave at 10:00 A.M. Tuesday.)
- What is the daily or hourly fee?

Is there a playground or game room? (Even if you're doing the supervision, if there's something amusing for the kids, they can release some energy and you can sit on the sidelines and read the newspaper.)

Are babysitting services available?
- Who makes the arrangements—you or the resort staff?
- What is the average rate? (You may linger a bit longer over that fine cabernet if your babysitter receives $6.00 an hour rather than $15.00 an hour.)

And if you're skittish about your kid's health or proclivity toward disaster, inquire about local medical facilities.
- Is there a doctor or nurse in residence or on call?
- Where are the nearest hospital and pharmacy?

For You
If you're investigating a resort or have chosen it as a vacation destination, you no doubt have an inkling as to its recreational facilities. You're looking at it because of its beach, golf course, tennis center, or ski mountain. Besides its main attraction, you'll also want to know what secondary diversions are possible. You can't play golf sixteen hours a day—not even Tiger Woods does that. So ask:
- Is there a jogging path? Parcourse fitness trail? Hiking trails?
- Is there a spa or exercise room? Sauna, steam room, whirlpool?
- Does the tennis complex also house racquetball courts? Indoor courts?
- For golf, tennis, and fishing, is it

possible to rent equipment, or is it necessary to bring your own?
- Are there any concerts, lectures, or classes?

Your interests will determine which questions to ask. Once you get a handle on what to ask, you'll find planning a vacation a lot more fun and a lot less time-consuming. You don't have to have all the answers; just being able to pose a few intelligent questions sets the ball in motion and can generate maybe even more information than you thought you wanted. As a knowledgeable consumer, you can pursue plans on your own or you can work quite effectively with a travel agent. In either case, a little self-education can certainly enhance the preparation and the end product: your leisure time.

Information, Please

Travel, like so much else today, has become increasingly complicated. Since the deregulation of the airlines, the proliferation of airfares has been phenomenal. Any given pair of cities has up to one hundred different fares, with as many rules and regulations. While this ultimately benefits the pleasure traveler, it also creates a certain amount of chaos. On a trip from New York to San Francisco, for example, the same seat in the airplane can cost anything between $299 and $1,499, depending on how far in advance you book, how long you're staying, and the promotional needs of the air carrier. When one adds other factors such as the day of the week, certain airports, one-stop versus nonstop flights, or whether you're wearing polka dots, more complications arise. While airlines generally give you their own lowest fares, they do not necessarily tell you about a competitor who may have even lower fares or more convenient flights.

The Internet provides what seems like an unlimited amount of information, as well as a direct and efficient system for travel suppliers to market their wares. Airlines constantly evaluate their "load factors"—how many empty seats remain on each flight. Once that airplane takes off, each empty seat is "dead" and has earned no revenue. The same is true of hotels—an empty room cannot be profitable. Therefore, more and more, airlines are offering last-minute flights, particularly on weekends, in an effort to fill those seats. They are also offering lower fares, additional frequent-flier miles, and other incentives to encourage travelers to directly book online. Hotels and car-rental companies are following suit and wooing travelers with free nights, upgrades, and special offers. Developing "brand loyalty" has long been a goal of travel suppliers; the advent of the Internet has intensified that process.

Incredible amounts of information exist in cyberspace. You can get lost for hours, sometimes pleasurably, sometimes not. Most airlines, hotels, car-rental companies, tour companies, and cruise lines have their own Web sites. Tourist offices in many states and countries offer virtual tours. Newsletters, chat rooms, and articles abound. A search for "travel with children" quickly gets you started. Each entry in the book has an Internet site listed, on which you'll find photos, detailed descriptions and hours, and the latest prices and packages. It's an invaluable adjunct to planning.

Not comfortable with surfing the Web? Ask your ten-year-old to help! Start with Family Travel Forum (www.familytravel forum.com, 888–FT–FORUM), a comprehensive site for family travel information. The site offers lots of news, deals, and ideas for free; flexible membership plans begin at $3.95 a month for "armchair travelers" and include savings and discount coupons from family-friendly suppliers. Encourage your children to share their travel experiences by submitting articles to FTF for publication on their affiliate site, www.kidtravels.com. Another affiliate site, www.tinytravelers.net, lists tips and articles on trips, health, gear, and keeping baby safe.

Family Travel Network (www.familytravel network.com) is another extensive site for talking online with other parents and kids, finding tons of information, hot deals, and travel tips—all free.

Dorothy Jordon, one of the acknowledged pioneers of family travel, offers advice and a quarterly newsletter, *Family Travel Times,* at www.familytraveltimes.com. The site is fairly simple, and Jordon's approach is straightforward and no-nonsense. As she says, "an honest publication—written by parents, for parents—based on first-hand research." Subscription information is found on the Web site or call (212) 477–5524.

This is the age of information overkill; managing this information, sorting through the myriad possibilities, can be mind-boggling. Working with a professional travel agent can add several dimensions to this information process. An agent is a bountiful source of books, brochures, and maps; but more important are the agent's personal experience, the client base that gives feedback on pros and cons of trips, and close contact with colleagues in the travel agency who have traveled extensively. Even something as seemingly straightforward as a hotel reservation can be complicated by weekend specials, golf or tennis packages, seasons, midweek, and family offers. A good agent is a whiz at interpreting brochures and deciphering the fine print. "Ocean view" does not mean on the beach; in fact, you may have to hang over the balcony with a pair of binoculars to see the ocean. "Secluded" may mean private, or it may mean you have to go 10 miles to find any other signs of life. Finally, you can capitalize on an agent's knowledge of the fares and facilities that each airline provides for children and of any special family-travel offers, such as "kids fly free" and discounts for spouses. A good agent can pull all of this together, analyze your needs, and help make your vacation dream become a coherent reality.

Travel agents provide a service. In the past there was no charge to the traveler for booking airline flights, or reserving hotel rooms and rental cars, as the travel suppliers paid commissions to travel agents. In recent years the airlines have ceased to pay commissions to travel agents. While hotel, cruise lines, and car-rental companies still pay a 5–10% commission to travel agents, many agencies maintain they cannot survive without charging service fees. It has become an accepted practice for agencies to charge for each service they provide. The cost varies according to the services provided—from $10 for issuing an airline ticket to $100 per hour for planning and researching a more complicated trip. If you decide to work with a travel agent, it is vital to establish the charges up front. If the agent books a hotel abroad, do you have to pay fax or phone charges? If you change your plans, what are the change or cancellation fees? Don't be afraid to ask.

Travel agents are dealers in dreams—in charge of that very precious event, your vacation. You should pick your travel agent as carefully as you would your doctor—or your auto mechanic! It's very nice to go to your Aunt Nelly or your neighbor's first cousin, but a smart consumer considers more substantial factors. A number of people prefer to go to the travel office and talk with the agent face to face. Others are comfortable with a telephone relationship, or even with booking online, perhaps with an agency that specializes in family travel. It's

important to identify your own particular preferences and to honor them.

Regardless of which method you choose, certain considerations are basic. What are their policies on service charges, refunds, and payments? Are they an appointed agency of the airlines, Amtrak, and the cruise lines? Airline appointments indicate a certain basic financial investment and preparation and the ability to write airline tickets. Agencies are computerized and have the capability to scan quickly for the best fares and most convenient flights, make seat assignments, and request special meals. Ask if they hold your money in an escrow account until your travel date. What insurance do they provide? What is their responsibility to you if the hotel/cruise/tour reservation is canceled or not properly delivered? In short, be proactive. This is your vacation; you should feel comfortable and ask questions—even the same one repeatedly and especially the ones you're afraid may sound dumb.

Whether you use a travel agent or do it yourself, the higher your level of involvement in planning, the more satisfaction you stand to gain from your trip. A good agent should be able to determine the broad outlines of your trip, to respond and listen to your ideas and needs, and to fill in with specific suggestions. The agent should have an idea of your lifestyle, your ideal vacation, and your budget. Your agent should ask, or you should volunteer, what seems to be personal information: How do you like to spend your days? Is shopping important to you? If you have a beach, are you happy? Will you die if you have no evening entertainment, or do you prefer a quiet stroll and a good book? What are your hobbies or special interests? Again, do not be afraid to discuss financial expectations. This can avoid a few nasty surprises—such as having to ransom one of the kids to pay for the trip!

No one knows your expectations as well as you, so assume some of the legwork for detailed information yourself. Check with the tourist offices of the state or country you plan to visit for brochures and information on special events and attractions. The American Automobile Association (AAA) is an excellent resource for maps and detailed information if you're a member and are driving for part or all of the trip. Travel books and articles are fun for the family and often have good advice on extras or little-known attractions in the area; check your local library for these. Chinaberry Book Service, in San Diego, California, is committed to conscious parenting and has well-selected general books and tapes catalogued for various ages and interests (800–776–2242, www.chinaberry.com). Also, talk to your friends who have been there, for those real inside tips.

Several tour operators specialize in family travel, working with both travel agents and individual clients. In Chevy Chase, Maryland, Grandtravel does escorted tours for grandparents and grandchildren, both in the United States and abroad (800–247–7651 or www.grandtrvl.com). In San Francisco, California, Rascals in Paradise (800–U–RASCAL or www.rascalsinparadise.com) offers resorts and tours all over the world. Many local agencies are becoming aware of the family market and are beginning to specialize in this field; check your local parents' paper or the travel section of the local Sunday paper for agencies in your area. Several agencies are listed on Family Travel Forum's Web site, www.familytravelforum.com.

Finally, close your suitcase, lock the door, and take off—secure in the knowledge that your advance planning, plus professional help, will make this the best trip ever!

NEW ENGLAND

Maine
Massachusetts
New Hampshire
Rhode Island
Vermont

THE BALSAMS
GRAND RESORT HOTEL

In the fine tradition of grand old hotels, The Balsams, a 15,000-acre private estate located high in the White Mountains, has been graciously welcoming guests since 1866. The three main buildings are interconnected and quite impressive, with their white facades and red-tiled roofs. Two date from the late 1800s—the Dixville House and The Balsams Inn—and the "new" wing, the Hampshire House, was added in 1917. At the foot of three very precipitous mountains—almost entirely surrounded by steep, 1,000-foot cliffs with the Notch Road the only way in or out—and overlooking Lake Gloriette, The Balsams offers a relaxed escape in a charming atmosphere. In summer Dixville Notch is a refreshing mountain retreat; in winter, a delightful getaway for skiers.

The Balsam's all-inclusive American Plan adds all the amenities for a fun-filled vacation in a worry-free atmosphere. Golf, tennis, swimming, hiking, mountain biking, lawn games, children's day camp, fine dining, and nightly entertainment are available and—an increasingly rare practice these days—at no additional charges for use of any of the facilities. Spring and fall seem to be the seasons for groups and conventions, while the Summer Social Season (late June to early September) and winter (mid-December to late March) are geared toward individuals and families. Winter activities include on-site skiing, snowboarding, snowshoeing, and skating. Your needs are tended to, your interests can be pursued, and your cares dispelled. The resort is open from mid-December until early April, reopening for the summer season from late May to mid-October.

Accommodations: There are 204 rooms at The Balsams, many with views of the mountains or the lake. Select family suites (connecting bedrooms with one bath), and parlor suites (sitting room and bedroom) offer ample room for youngsters; these are quite popular, so early booking is advised. Rates are based on two adults, plus $12 times the age of each child, with a minimum of $195. The Hampshire House is configured to provide convenient adjoining rooms for family accommodation but is substantially higher in cost. All the rooms have been restored, creating a comfortable ambience. Rates depend on the size of the room, its location and view, and the time of the year. Summer rates, per person double, range from $234 to $289 per night. Winter rates range from $175 to $225 per person and do not include lunch. During Christmas season (December 19–January 2) rates increase to $189 to $309. During Presidents' Week, rates increase further to $249 to $289. In all holiday periods, lower rates are offered depending on the length of your stay; i.e., longer stays receive lower daily rates. Rates for children sharing a room are on a graduated scale, calculated at $10 per night multiplied by the child's age, with a minimum charge of $40. So, infants to four-year-olds are $40 per night, and so on. These rates are based on a Full American Plan (Modified American Plan in winter) and include unlimited access to all the facilities and activities. Cribs are provided.

Dining: The main dining room serves breakfast, lunch, and dinner during the summer season, breakfast and dinner only during the winter season. And, of course, meals are included in the rates. The summertime luncheon buffet is a sumptuous display of hot and cold entrees, cheeses, fruit, and desserts; you might sample the fried Maine shrimp or the Atlantic salmon. A menu luncheon is available at the Golf Clubhouse. The dinner menu offers an entirely different selection every evening, featuring seafood dishes as well as Long Island duckling, beef, and chicken. At the dinner hour jackets for men are required. Parents are advised to bring appropriate dinner clothes for older children as well.

In the summer you might try The Panorama Golf Clubhouse or the poolside bar for refreshments; both offer delightful views and a chance to soak up the beautiful scenery. In the winter enjoy light fare between noon and 6:00 P.M. at the Wilderness Lounge, or après-ski, warm up with a cup of cider or hot buttered rum in La Cave. Also in winter you'll be shuttling over to The Balsams/Wilderness Ski Area, where breakfast and lunch are served at the base lodge. Evening entertainment means cocktails and floor shows in the Switzerland of America Ballroom or dancing in the Wilderness Lounge; both are in the hotel.

Children's World: The Balsams is interested in providing excellent service for its younger guests as well as its adult visitors. For children this translates into a busy schedule of fun activities. Camp Wind Whistle is available from late June through Labor Day, seven days a week; here children four through ten–plus meet with counselors in The Balsams Playroom for sports, games, picnics, swimming, nature walks, arts and crafts, fishing, farm visits, and movies. Outdoor activities are emphasized. Children have lunch with their counselors and then, after linking up with Mom and Dad around 4:00 P.M. to share their day's experiences, they can rejoin their young group for dinner

at 6:30 P.M. There is no charge for this service. Age groups are divided as follows: four to six years, seven to nine years, and ten and above, with age-appropriate activities.

The outdoor children's area features a state-of-the art fiberglass and stainless steel play structure. The indoor game room (supervised) has an array of board games, and video games, and table tennis and pool tables. Open daily from 9:00 A.M. to midnight, the game room is a popular spot for youngsters to gather and make friends during both summer and winter seasons.

In winter children ages three to five can enroll in the Wee Whistle Ski School. Older children have their own morning and afternoon lessons. The cost is approximately $40 for 1 to 1½ hours. Wintertime room rates for children at The Balsams include ski privileges, but not lessons.

From December through March a well-equipped nursery/play area in the Alpine Base Lodge welcomes children ages six months to five years. The experienced staff amuses children with a selection of games and toys from 9:00 A.M. to 4:00 P.M.; parents may want to join their children for lunch. This service is provided gratis to children of hotel guests. Individual babysitters (usually off-duty hotel employees) can be arranged at reasonable rates; sitters should be requested when lodging reservations are made.

Recreation: At The Balsams you can spend busy days of back-to-back events from morning to night or just relax, set an unhurried pace, and enjoy the peace and beauty of the mountains. Five major garden areas with over 35,000 flowers and plants please both guests and local hummingbirds.

Two golf courses await golfers. The Panorama, an eighteen-hole championship course, was designed by Donald Ross, a Scottish golf course architect famous during the early twentieth century. Set in the mountains, the undulating terrain can be challenging and the views truly stunning. The nine-hole executive course, the Coashaukee, is just right for beginners or those who haven't tested their clubs in a while. There are pro shops at each course, putting greens, a practice fairway, and a pro staff on hand to help you polish your swing. The Centennial Golf School operates in June and features individualized coaching by PGA professionals. The Balsams is the only resort in New England to be named "One of the Nation's Finest Golf Courses" by *Golf Magazine*.

Tennis enthusiasts can choose to play on either red-clay courts (three) or all-weather courts (three). Improve your skills at the Tennis Tune-Up and Tennis Camp clinics, sign up with the pro for group or private lessons, and stop by the tennis shop to pick up those indispensable accessories.

Swim a few laps in the Olympic-size heated swimming pool overlooking Lake Gloriette. With the mountains in the background, this is an idyllic spot for sunbathing. You might try a refreshing dip in the lake or a relaxing excursion in a paddleboat, canoe, or rowboat. Fish in a crystal-clear mountain stream, hike in the wilderness (solo or with a guided group), or take a nature walk with the staff naturalist. The hotel's natural-history program combines tours, hikes, and discussions for a good introduction to the flora and fauna of the area. The mountain biking trails are well marked and offer fun at every level. Mountain bike rentals and repairs are available.

Lawn sports include badminton, horseshoes, croquet, volleyball, and shuffleboard; when you head indoors, there are billiards, table tennis, bingo, an aerobic-exercise room, and a movie theater. Take to the library/card room to snuggle up with a good book or play a few hands of bridge, or view wide-screen films in the movie theater. To track down that essential souvenir, drop in at the gift shop, craft shop, gallery, balloon store, and fashion boutique.

In the wintertime this wonderland is draped in snow, and The Balsams/Wilderness Ski Area (located on the property) is just a short shuttle ride from the hotel. There are sixteen tree-lined downhill trails and 95 kilometers of packed and groomed trails for cross-country, ranked among the top ten in North America. Wintertime also means ice-skating, snowshoeing on dedicated trails, and riding in horse-drawn sleighs. Like to stay inside? Enroll in the three-day culinary cooking class and prepare a sumptuous four-course meal for family and friends.

Nearby attractions include a "Watchable Wildlife Corridor" along Route 26 with viewing stations for watching moose and peregrine falcons; an American bald eagle nesting site on Lake Umbagog; the Poore Family Homestead, a farm dating back to the 1820s; the 45th Parallel, marking the latitude equidistant from the North Pole and the Equator; and Magnetic Hill, where cars facing downhill seem to mysteriously roll backward up the hill. You may also find a visit to the Ballot Room interesting. Here the first-in-the-nation voters cast their ballots at midnight in all presidential primaries and general elections.

Whether you're seeking an escape from city crowds or want an active sports-oriented vacation, The Balsams makes it all possible.

**Dixville Notch, New Hampshire 03576
(603) 255–3400, (800) 255–0600,
(800) 255–0800 (in New Hampshire)
www.thebalsams.com**

HIGHLAND LODGE

Greensboro, Vermont

A family-owned country inn, and cross-country skiing in Vermont—it sounds so romantic and wholesome. A lovely old white-frame building with a comfortable front porch, the lodge is set on 160 acres bordering Caspian Lake. Open from Christmas to mid-March, the lodge facilities make it easy to enjoy wintertime sports; open again from Memorial Day weekend until mid-October, the lodge is a perfect spot for viewing the fall foliage colors or for enjoying a summer trip of swimming and boating. Step back in time, relax, and enjoy.

Accommodations: Choose one of the eleven guest rooms in the lodge or one of the ten cottages on the hillside just behind the main building. Tastefully decorated with nice furnishings and old-fashioned wallpaper, these accommodations can house approximately sixty guests. The cottages feature a living room, porch, bath, and one to three bedrooms; nine cottages include kitchenettes. Based on a Modified American Plan and double occupancy, room rates are $222 to $280. One- to four-bedroom cottages range from $255 to $530 per night. Children sharing a room or cottage with their parents are charged according to their ages: Infants are free (cribs provided), toddlers (two to four years) are $35, four to seven years are $60, eight to eleven years are $70, twelve to fifteen years are $75, and sixteen to twenty years are $90.

Dining: Included in the rates, breakfast and dinner are served in the dining room, overlooking either garden or lake. A la carte lunch is also available in the summer and fall, except on Mondays. On summer Mondays, guests enjoy a beach cookout. At dinner, an elegant four-course meal is served; for entrees you may select fresh fish, lamb, duck, veal, or prime rib with vegetables from a local farm, and sample the homemade soups and breads, but be sure to save room for what the staff boasts are sinful desserts. You might sit near the fireplace in the dining room or by the large windows to take in the view; weather permitting, dining tables are set up on the porch. Children's portions and special items for youngsters tempt the pickiest palate. Box lunches may be requested.

Children's World: A swing set and a sandbox stocked with toys attract little ones. There are tennis and hiking for older children. For children of all ages, swimming at the private beach is a great way to spend the afternoon. After a busy day kids may settle into the children's library, where they'll find books, games, and puzzles. A separate room with table tennis and foosball is a popular spot for kids to "hang" and socialize. In the mornings during July and August, youngsters four to nine link up with the Play Lady, who devises programs of crafts, games, and nature hikes; this is free of charge to guests. Two or three times weekly the inn arranges special programs for ages six and up in the afternoon; perhaps a children's hike or nature or art programs. There's a nominal charge (from $5.00) for these activities. In addition, the staff can make arrangements for individual babysitters.

Recreation: Thirty miles of groomed cross-country ski trails meander through fields and forests and across frozen lakes. You can line up a guided tour or pick up a little instruction. Bring your own equipment or rent the necessary paraphernalia at the ski/snowboard shop. Sledding, tobogganing, and snowshoe trails wind through the property.

Enjoy the sights and sounds of nature in both summer and winter with a resident naturalist on guided nature walks. In warmer weather hike or jog in the adjoining Barr Hill Nature Preserve, walk the lodge's nature trail, rent a bicycle, or take to the water: swim at the beach or head out on the lake in a canoe, kayak, sailboat, or paddleboat provided by the lodge. The lake also means good fishing, particularly in early summer and fall; set your line for salmon, trout, or perch.

Back on land, challenge another guest to a tennis match on the clay court and then round up a game of badminton, volleyball, or croquet on the lawn. The nearby Green Mountains and White Mountains lure guests into afternoon driving and hiking excursions. Or simply sit on the wide verandah and let it all come to you.

Caspian Lake
1608 Craftsbury Road
Greensboro, Vermont 05841
(802) 533–2647
www.highlandlodge.com

KILLINGTON SKI AND SUMMER RESORT
Killington, Vermont

Killington is the largest ski area in the eastern United States, and its vital statistics are indeed impressive: 200 runs on six interconnected mountains, plus Pico Mountain at Killington; more than 3,000 vertical feet; and a ski season that starts in mid-October and continues to June. Killington boasts an average annual snowfall of 250 inches. To ensure it has the earliest opening date and latest closing date in the East, sophisticated snowmaking techniques assist Mother Nature. Thirty-three lifts, including an eight-passenger heated gondola, get you quickly to the top.

A year-round resort, Killington is cradled in the Green Mountains of central Vermont, a setting whose beauty does not wane with the melting snow; in late spring and summer, the lush green landscape is the backdrop for tennis and golf holidays; in autumn the fall foliage colors take over.

Accommodations: There are almost 200 properties at Killington, ranging from small inns and lodges to condominium complexes and private houses. Killington Central Reservations (800–621–6867) lists more than 115 of these and publishes helpful, descriptive information clearly outlining the many package plans available. Ski-in locations include Trailside Lodge, with standard rooms/bunk beds; Trailside Village; Sunrise Village; and Spruce Glen condos. Rates are lower in summer and higher at holiday periods. Call or check the Web site for the latest rates.

Killington Resort Villages (800–343–0762) offers hotel-style and one-, two-, and three-bedroom condos, some within walking distance of the slopes, plus several other condominium complexes. The Grand Resort Hotel is 50 yards from the lift, while Sunrise Mountain Village in Bear Mountain Base Lodge has its own lift and trails.

Condominiums not within walking distance but right at the base of Killington Mountain include Edgemont, Whiffletree, Highridge, Mountain Green, and Pinnacle. Studio to four-bedroom units have fully equipped kitchens and fireplaces. Some condominiums have special features, such as indoor pools or spa/exercise facilities (if you don't get enough on the slopes!). Shuttles run every fifteen to twenty minutes in winter.

Lodgings near the Snowshed Base Lodge may be the most convenient location for families, as this is one of the main lodges for adult lessons/activities and is also located across the street (connected by an underground passageway) from the Rams Head Base Lodge, where children's activities and day care are held.

Dining: In addition to the half dozen cafeterias at the bases of and on the mountains, in the area you'll find Italian, Chinese, Mexican, and German restaurants, or sample French country dinners at the Red Clover Inn, typical New England dishes at the Vermont Inn, or Continental cuisine at the Casa Bella. Especially fun for families is Casey's Caboose, where model trains circle the room, and dining is done on the floor, in odd nooks and crannies, or up a ladder in a boxcar. Pepper's, Peppino's, the Skybox Grill, and Santa Fe Steakhouse are also options. For that romantic, haute cuisine dinner for adults only, Hemingway's is the place. Pubs and nightclubs provide late-evening entertainment in winter and summer.

Children's World: Whether your child is six weeks old or twelve years old, a first-time skier or a veteran, he or she will find a niche at Killington's Children's Center. Friendly Penguins Day Care provides for infants six weeks to twenty-three months at the Ramshead Base Lodge Family Center from 8:30 A.M. to 4:00 P.M. Monday through Friday (from 8:00 A.M. on weekends and holidays). Cost is $65 for a full day and

$50 for a half day (from 11:30 A.M.). Half-day option is not available during holiday periods. Daycare is also available for ages six weeks to six years at the Grand Hotel. Rates and hours are the same, and full day includes lunch. Choose morning or afternoon half days, and include lunch and an extra half-hour for $6.00. Program includes indoor/outdoor play, stories and art, free play, movies, nap, and snacks. Parents are not encouraged to "drop in" as this disrupts the children, but may check at any time with the counselors. The First Tracks program combines the Friendly Penguin daycare with outdoor on-snow sessions to introduce toddlers to skiing and is customized to each child's developmental levels and enthusiasm in one or two one-hour sessions, with lift tickets, equipment, and lunch included. Prices range from $95 for a full day with two sessions ($80 for one session) to $65 for either half day session. Four- to six-year-olds enjoy the Ministar (skiing) and Lowrider (snowboarding) programs from 8:30 A.M. to 3:30 P.M.; indoor play and two-hour outdoor sessions including lunch and lift tickets are $90 for full day and $65 for half day. The Superstars Program groups experienced seven- to twelve-year-olds by ability for a full day of ski or snowboard play. Full-day fees ($69 for first day, $60 each consecutive day) include lunch; half-day sessions ($45 for first day, $30 each consecutive day) are available. Camp Free Ride is a new program geared toward those kids with skill enough to be ready for a new adventure and to hang out with Killington's best free-ride pros; no formal lessons, just new school skiing and riding. Cost is the same as for Superstars. Ages seven to twelve who are first-timers can join the new Learn-to-Ski or Ride one-day program. SnowZone, for ages thirteen to eighteen, is designed to engage teens in on-snow learning while providing opportunity for them to interact with their peers. Costs are the same as for Ministars/Lowriders, but lift tickets and equipment are not included. The winter children's program runs from November through the first week of April.

A summer kids' program in July and August for ages two to ten years is offered at the Grand Resort Hotel from 8:00 A.M. to 4:00 P.M.; cost is $50 per day. Children enjoy indoor and outdoor activities such as arts and crafts, music and movement, volleyball, Frisbee, hiking, and water play. Lunch and two snacks are included.

Recreation: Start your visit with a Meet the Mountain tour; skiers are grouped by ability and guided through a complimentary two-hour introduction to Killington's mountains. All seven mountains are accessed by the same lift ticket. All have beginner runs from their summits so that even novices can enjoy top-of-the-mountain views. From long lazy runs (one beginner's trail is 10 miles long) to steeply pitched expert terrain, every skier finds the appropriate challenge. This goes for ski and snowboard clinics too, from classes for the newest beginner to workshops in racing for the advanced skier.

Après-ski activities include movies in the village, ice-skating, rock climbing, snowmobiles, puppet and magic shows, and ice-cream socials. Or maybe most appropriate for the end of an active day is a quiet rest in a sauna or a massage at the Grand Resort Hotel.

Summertime brings golf on an eighteen-hole course (actually, there are 270 holes of golf in the area); tennis at the Killington School for Tennis; fishing, hiking, mountain biking, and horseback riding in the mountains. Killington's Adventure Center specializes in—you guessed it—adventures; try water slides, a skateboard park, and climbing wall for starters. Another center at Pico adds minigolf, an Alpine Slide, and the Bungee Thing. There's something for everyone, from scenic chair rides to art and antiquing.

4763 Killington Road
Killington, Vermont 05751
(800) 621–MTNS
www.Killington.com

THE LIGHTHOUSE INN
West Dennis, Massachusetts

An old-fashioned country inn, The Lighthouse Inn sits on the shores of Nantucket Sound. It was originally constructed in 1854 as a lighthouse called the Bass River Light, which was operative until 1914. In 1938 the Stone family purchased the Lighthouse property, and three generations later they still own and operate the inn. After being dark for 75 years, the light was relit in 1989, and is the only privately

owned, privately maintained working lighthouse in the country, now recognized by the Coast Guard as the West Dennis Light. The classic Cape Cod-style main house provides a beautiful view of the ocean; sprawling out behind are nine secluded acres with additional accommodations and recreational facilities.

Accommodations: A wide selection of accommodations exists: rooms, family suites, and oceanview and oceanfront cottages with one to three bedrooms. The Main House, Lookout, and Carriage House offer family suites; rates, based on two people and including full breakfast, are $280 daily in the summer season. Cottages begin at $310 (one-bedroom or oceanfront). Mid-may through June and early September to mid-October, deduct $40 per person from all rates. Children sharing a room or cottage with their parents are charged a graduated rate depending on their ages: ages three through twelve, $40 per child, per day; thirteen and older, $45 a day. The daily rate for children includes breakfast. Dinner is $10 additional for younger children; $25 additional for teens. For adults, dinner is approximately $50 more per day and is also available a la carte.

Dining: The dining room in the Main House entices guests with a varied menu, including fresh fish and lobster dinners and lovely views over the water. Outdoors, the oceanside deck is the setting for a la carte lunches. A snack bar adjoins the pool, serving light lunches and beverages during July and August. Once a week a poolside cookout is planned.

A really nice touch is that all children are welcomed to a special InnKids Dinner offered each evening from 5:30 to 8:30 P.M. They may order their favorite meal in advance, eat, and play with their peers—all in a separate area from the more formal Main Dining Room, where proper attire is requested, and parents can tarry over a relaxed dinner. Evening entertainment in the Sand Bar ranges from boogie-woogie piano to jazz saxophones.

Children's World: Games, swimming, arts and crafts, sand-castle building, kite flying, miniature golf, and nature walks fill the days for InnKids. Three- and four-year-olds participate from 9:30 A.M. to noon, while children ages five and older carry on until 3:00 P.M. In the evening both groups are invited to get together from 5:30 to 8:30 P.M. for dinner and entertainment; perhaps a movie, a magician's show, puppets, clowns, and sing-alongs. Children under three are welcome to participate if accompanied by a babysitter. The InnKids program runs from late June through August and is included in the fees for children noted above. Individual babysitting is available on request.

Recreation: Enjoying the soft ocean breezes may be all the activity you want during your first couple of days at The Lighthouse Inn. Renewed and refreshed, you can then jump into the swimming pool, splash in the gentle waters of Nantucket Sound, and stroll along the beach. The outdoor tennis court awaits you when you turn energetic, go golfing at one of five nearby eighteen-hole courses, or fishing can be a pleasant morning outing. You can also play table tennis, pool, and shuffleboard or pursue quieter interests in the library/game room. The inn is also in a great location for exploring Cape Cod. And, as the old song by Patti Page says, "If you're fond of sand dunes and salty air, quaint little villages here and there, you're sure to fall in love with old Cape Cod."

---

1 Lighthouse Inn Road
West Dennis, Massachusetts 02670
(508) 398–2244
www.lighthouseinn.com

MOUNT SNOW

West Dover, Vermont

Over fifty years ago, Walter Schoenknecht decided that music, barbecues, and outrageous special events would liven up his ski area. Since other resorts weren't even serving food, he was deemed rather eccentric. But sure enough, old Walt was right, and today that same infectious, creative spirit is not only encouraged, it's one of the core values of the resort.

A very popular New England ski resort, Mount Snow is situated in the beautiful Green Mountains of southern Vermont. Much of its popularity is, no doubt, due to its accessibility and proximity to major Northeast metropolitan areas: A four-and-a-half-hour drive from New York and two and a half hours from Boston make this a very manageable weekend trip for residents of these cities. But Mount Snow's size and variety also account for its appeal. From gentle beginner and broad intermediate slopes to some of the steepest expert runs in the Northeast, 145 trails in all drop down from a 3,600-foot summit for 1,700 vertical feet, served by twenty-three lifts. The average annual snowfall is about 166 inches. It is supplemented by sophisticated snowmaking that covers 76% of the skiable terrain; the ski season runs from about early November to late April.

Accommodations: Lodging runs the gamut of possibilities in atmosphere, style, price, and location. From modern condominium complexes to quaint country inns, more than fifty options are within 10 miles of the mountain base. The lodging bureau (800–451–4211) will help you choose the right spot, and various package plans for lodging and lift tickets are offered.

A full-service hotel at the edge of a small lake with grand views of the mountain, Snow Lake Lodge runs free shuttles to and from the slopes. With its own restaurant, game room, and spa, it's also walking distance to evening entertainment at the Snowbarn. Two-day weekend rates range from $318 to $398 with continental breakfast. Seasons and Snow Mountain Village are condominiums near the base, where two-bedroom units start at $1,198 for a two-day weekend. These units have kitchens and fireplaces; some have balconies and mountain views.

The 200-room Grand Summit Resort Hotel is located slopeside in Mount Snow's main base area and offers a variety of rooms, ranging from standard hotel-style rooms to multiroom suites with kitchenettes. Amenities include ski-in/ski-out accommodations, valet parking, a health club, spa and fitness programs, a year-round heated outdoor pool, Harriman's Restaurant, and more. A two-day weekend ranges from $698 to $1,530.

The many country inns around the area can add a distinctly New England flavor to a ski holiday. The charming Hermitage Inn, 3 miles from Mount Snow, maintains 40 miles of cross-country ski trails. The White House of Wilmington also has cross-country trails. Vacation Services (800–245–SNOW) books many of the inns and bed-and-breakfasts.

Dining: At the base of Mount Snow are ten cafeterias and restaurants along with eight bars/lounges; at the Summit Lodge, views over the mountains complement cafeteria-style lunches. Also near the base is the Lakeside Bar and Grill, in the Snow Lake Lodge. Most of the inns and lodges of the area have their own restaurants and feature a variety, from hearty home-style cooking to the Continental cuisine typical of the Hermitage and the White House of Wilmington. Dot's of Dover is reputed to have the best breakfast in town, while TC's and Two Tannery offer fine dining. Many restaurants have children's menus.

Children's World: Throughout the year, kids have a place at Mount Snow. Child Care, a quality program for ages six weeks to six years, is located in the heart of the main base area. The program is fully licensed by the state of Vermont and is designed to be interactive, fun, and developmentally appropriate for each child's needs. Playrooms are designated as Baby Bears (six weeks to twelve months), Magical Forest (thirteen months to twenty-three months), Furry Friends (twenty-four months to thirty-five months), and Bears Den (three years and up). Child Care is open weekdays from 8:30 A.M. to 4:30 P.M.; weekends and holidays, 8:00 A.M. to 4:30 P.M. Reservations are required (800–889–4411). A full day is $70; snacks and lunch are provided, but you must supply diapers and infant food. A list of babysitters is available through Child Care.

Cub Camp allows three-year-olds to experience the thrill of skiing through fun and games, combined with Child Care programs. A morning or afternoon 1½-hour on-snow session, including equipment, costs $59; Child Care add-on is $45. For children four to twelve, Mount Snow offers Perfect Kids ski and snowboard clinics. Snow Camp is divided into full- and half-day sessions and is designed especially for children four through six years of age. Children are placed in small groups based on their age and ability levels, and groups ski, take breaks, and have fun together. Full-day programs include lunch and child lift ticket; cost is $89 for one day, $169 for two days. Half-day sessions include snack and lift ticket, $59 one session, $111 for two sessions. Multiday rates are available. Mountain Camp and Mountain Riders is for

seven- to fourteen-year-olds; rates are $77 for a full day with lunch and $42 for half days. Rental equipment is not included and begins at $26 per day; junior lift tickets are also required. Children new to skiing or snowboarding can enjoy expanded, private learning terrain. All Perfect Kids programs are centrally located in the main base area.

Children five and under ski/ride free, while kids twelve and under ski/ride free when their parents purchase a three- to five-day nonholiday lift ticket. During "Kid's Adventure Weeks," three- to five-day vacation packages include lodging, lift tickets, and many fun family activities. The week is filled with games, activities, pizza parties, ice-cream parties, fun races, and free tubing. Mount Snow also offers a new lift-served snow tubing park open every day and weekend nights. The Galaxy Arcade is open daily in the main base area and features video games, recreational games, a penny candy counter, and a lounge area.

Summer is in full swing from mid-June through August with Mount Snow's Kid's Adventure Camps. The Child Care program is available Monday through Friday, again offering individual playrooms and programs for ages six weeks to five years. Activities include arts & crafts, water play, puppet shows, mini–nature hikes, gardening, games, and music. Special rest areas are also provided for quiet time. Mount Snow's Summer Kid's Adventure Camps offer children from age six to twelve years a variety of activities and hands-on exploration. Kids are grouped according to age, and enjoy swimming, hiking, mountain biking, creative arts and crafts, chairlift rides, and field trips around the Mount Snow area. Kid's Adventure Camps and child care are offered Monday through Friday from June 20 through August 26. Operation times are from 9:00 A.M. to 4:00 P.M. Rates for both programs are $50 per day ($200 for five days). Lunch is not included, and bathing suits are part of the "uniform." Reservations are required and can be made by calling (800) 889–4411 or (802) 464–4152.

On Wednesdays and Saturdays (4:00 to 5:00 P.M.) in July and August, Kid's Golf Clinics for ages seven to seventeen years can give a child a strong start in this popular sport. Cost is $15 per session, six or more for $10 each. Reservations are required (802–464–4254).

Recreation: Almost 50% of the runs at Mount Snow are ranked intermediate. The rest are just about evenly split between beginner and expert. The Main Mountain has forty beginner and intermediate trails, the North Face with its steeper terrain and moguls attracts advanced skiers, and the Sunbrook area with sunny southern exposure supports a couple of long lazy runs. Four terrain parks and a Super Pipe keep snowboarders happy. The teaching staff is prepared to show you the way to improved techniques, and you have your pick of packages for various combinations of lifts, lessons, and equipment.

For cross-country skiers, four touring centers are within 10 miles of Mount Snow at the Hermitage, Sitzmark, Timber Creek, and White House. Also within this distance are three stables—Beaver Brook, Flames, and Adams Farm—where you can arrange sleigh rides. Other winter sports include snowmobiling, a tubing park, and nearby snowshoeing and ice-skating. If your tastes run to being pampered, schedule a session at the Grand Summit Spa, or curl up in front of the fire with a hot drink.

When the mountains turn green, the big event is the Golf School, held on the championship Geoffrey Cornish course. More warm-weather activities include swimming, fishing, hiking, biking, and horseback riding. Sit back and enjoy the scenery from one of the scenic chairlift rides, or prowl through the unique shops that feature the crafts, pottery, wood carving, and antiques to be found only in Vermont. The whole family will love Adams Farm, a sixth-generation working farm, home to more than one hundred friendly farm animals that you can visit and interact with. Take a hayride, wander through the craft and quilt shops, or enjoy a bonfire and marshmallow roast.

Route 100
West Dover, Vermont 05356
(802) 464–3333, (800) 245–7669
www.mountsnow.com

THE MOUNT WASHINGTON RESORT AT BRETTON WOODS
Bretton Woods, New Hampshire

Majestic Mount Washington presides over this resort, a massive complex of lodging, dining, and recreational facilities on 2,600 acres of wooded New Hampshire countryside in the White Mountains. Voted a *Better Homes and Gardens* "Favorite Family Resort," the architectural gem and focal point of this New England resort is the gracious and stately hotel. Built in 1902 by the industrialist and railroad tycoon Joseph Stickney, the hotel began welcoming visitors to a lifestyle of classic elegance and soon claimed its status among prime vacation retreats of the Northeast.

International fame came to Bretton Woods in 1944 when the hotel hosted financiers from forty-four countries who created the World Bank and the International Monetary Fund and set the gold standard at $35 an ounce (ah—the good old days). In 1978 this fine old structure—with its wonderfully spacious verandah furnished with white wicker chairs and settees, and its 150-foot-long lobby—was added to the National Register of Historic Places. Since 1986 it has held the distinction of being a National Historic Landmark. With the purchase of Bretton Woods, Mount Washington became a year-round resort.

Accommodations: The 200-room hotel offers standard to deluxe lodging with a number of two-bedroom family suites. Nearly all have views of Mount Washington, the Willey-Rosebrook Mountain range, or the well-tended gardens. All guests in the hotel participate in a Modified American Plan, and per-person prices range from $185 to $525 for double occupancy. Children under age four stay for free, ages five to twelve are $35, and over twelve are $70. A family suite costs $570 to $1,600 a night and accommodates up to six persons. The thirty-four rooms and suites of the Bretton Arms Country Inn, also a National Historic Landmark, offer accommodations in the atmosphere of a Victorian inn. Guests here enjoy all the facilities of the main hotel. Bed-and-breakfast prices range from $65 to $199 per person per night; children's rates are $10 per night for ages four to twelve, and $20 for thirteen and older. The Bretton Arms is open year-round.

Also open year-round, The Lodge at Bretton Woods, located across from the hotel's entrance, offers contemporary accommodations at rates of $99 to $199 per night, with continental breakfast included.

For an economical alternative, the Townhomes at Bretton Woods provide ample space for parties of two to twelve people; situated on the mountainside, these one- to five-bedroom units (with full kitchens) run from $199 to $899 per night, accommodations only, depending on the size of the unit and the season. All guests have access to all resort recreational facilities at established guest rates. Cribs are complimentary, and cots are available at $10 a night. Inquire also about special seven-day vacation packages.

Dining: With all the different dining arrangements, your biggest problem will be deciding where to pick up your napkin. From casual, light meals to gracious, formal dinners, it just depends on how the spirit moves you. The opulent four-diamond main dining room of the Mount Washington Hotel is a large octagonal space (heaven forbid anyone should be relegated to a corner!) glimmering with crystal chandeliers and stained-glass windows. The menu changes nightly and features Continental cuisine and regional American dishes. In this elegant setting, with orchestra music and views of Mount Washington, guests are invited to regard dinner as a dress-up affair; jackets are required for men, and ladies and children should dress appropriately. Sumptuous breakfasts are also served in the dining room.

The Bretton Arms dining room is also open year-round for breakfast and dinner; here the evening meal features classic New England cuisine. For lunch and seasonal dinner, Stickney's Restaurant (located on the lower concourse of the hotel) has a cafe atmosphere with indoor and outdoor seating and specializes in lighter fare—salads, sandwiches, and light entrees; afternoon cocktails are also served here. Darby's Pizzeria in the lodge serves seasonal dinner; guests enjoy family dining in a warm, rustic atmosphere, along with scenic views of the mountains and the hotel. For sandwiches, Italian fare, and seafood, Fabyan's Station is open year-round for lunch and dinner. A restored railroad depot from the Victorian era, Fabyan's is near the base of the ski area about a mile from the hotel. The base lodge at the ski area offers full lunch at Slopeside. Quick breakfasts and lunches cafeteria-style for those eager to hit the slopes can be found at Lucy Crawford's Food Court. The midmountain Top O' Quad restaurant serves lunch with spectacular mountain views in winter.

For sipping cocktails, you may want to linger at Stickney's, the Conservatory, the Princess Lounge, or the Verandah. Try the unique Rosebrook Lounge, set behind the grand staircase and serving on the porch and verandah, weather permitting. The Cave Lounge, located in the lower lobby of the hotel, offers a speakeasy atmosphere and nightly live entertainment. The Pool Bar offers refreshments on warm summer days.

Children's World: Late June through Labor Day, and on holiday weekends/weeks, the hotel sponsors Kids Camp for children four to twelve. Enroll your child for a full- or half-day program with adventures like hiking in the woods, treks to the stables, swimming, tennis, "Cooking with the Chef," "Putting with the Pro," and crafts sessions. The program is from 9:00 A.M. to 3:00 P.M., and is complimentary for hotel guests. For resort guests not staying in the hotel, the cost is $40 for full day, $25 for a half day. Lunch is available for $10. There's also an evening program ($25 per child for non-hotel guests and includes dinner) from 6:00 to 9:00 P.M. so that parents can dine quietly alone. Teen Scene for ages thirteen to sixteen features activities and a chance to interact with peers from 7:00 to 10:00 P.M on selected evenings. In summer, two-hour programs on Wednesday and Saturday evenings provide socialization; cost is $25 for non-hotel/resort guests. Babysitting can be arranged for children under the age of

four. The resort charges a $10.00 processing fee; rates are $8.00 per hour, plus $2.00 per hour for each additional child. Reservations are required for all programs (603–278–8869).

In the wintertime, the Babes in the Woods nursery at the ski area lodge takes children from two months to five years for an indoor program costing $69 full day or $45 half day. Open 8:00 A.M. to 4:30 P.M., hourly rates ($12) are also an option. Children ages four to twelve participate in the Hobbit Children's Ski and Snowboard School; however, snowboarding is only for ages six to twelve. Rates for lifts, two lessons, equipment, and lunch are $89 a day. Half days are $69 (no lunch). Those children under age five and toilet trained, who are new to the slopes, can join a snow play and ski-readiness program at the same rates.

In 2002, *Ski Magazine* rated Bretton Woods number two in North America for family programs, and in 2003, number one in New Hampshire for family programs.

Recreation: All room rates at the Mount Washington Resort at Bretton Woods include an array of complimentary features. Summer offers court time, putting green, full use of Bretton Woods Sports Club, family lawn games, guided walks and mountain bike tours, and introductory clinics in golf, tennis, and fly-fishing. In winter enjoy ice-skating (with skates available), snowshoe tours, and ski clinics. Year-round enjoy music, culinary demonstrations, arts and crafts, and admission to special events. Check with Recreation, and ask for the special discounts on other activities.

You'll never be at a loss for things to do at Bretton Woods; your only dilemma may be trying to fit in all the activities. You may start your day jogging on one of the many marked trails ranging from 1 to 11 miles in length and graded by levels of difficulty.

Then stroll over to the first tee for a match on the eighteen-hole Donald Ross–designed championship golf course or the challenging nine-hole Pleasant Course and take in the rolling terrain and mountain views, or sharpen your skills on the putting green and driving range. The Golf Club Pro Shop can meet all your needs for equipment and accessories (including attire) and can assist in scheduling lessons.

There are two heated pools at the hotel (one outdoor and a smaller indoor one) and another indoor heated pool at the lodge; both locations have a sauna, and the lodge facility includes a Jacuzzi as well. Or you can take a refreshing dip in the Ammonoosuc River.

Tennis buffs can head over to one of twelve well-groomed red-clay courts or join the tennis program for instruction (group and private lessons) at all levels of expertise.

The horseback-riding stables mean good fun for those who want their exercise sitting down. Set in an old Victorian building, the stables offer lessons and guided trail rides on the 50 miles of picturesque trails in the woods and fields. The woods are captivating whether you choose horseback riding or hiking (maybe you'll link up with a guided tour or a nature walk).

Other diversions include trout fishing; a game of badminton, croquet, volleyball, or horseshoes; an afternoon of bicycling; a sunset carriage ride; or an hour in the game room for billiards, table tennis, and video games (particularly big with the seven- to fourteen-year-old group). Your interests may take you to a night at the movies, a fashion show, an aerobics class, a bridge tournament, or a presentation of fine culinary techniques (these often include a bit of wine, sampling a dish, and a tour of the kitchen). The activities staff is on hand full-time to plan interesting and varied events. For some private, quiet time, wander into the library or relax under the nimble fingers of an expert massage therapist.

Kids love an excursion on the Mount Washington Cog Railway, the original "little train that could." Built in 1869, it was the world's first mountain-climbing cog railroad, and it remains the only one still powered entirely by steam. The (breathtaking!) round-trip takes about three hours, and you can visit the mile-high park and observation center at the top.

Wintertime explodes in skiing events at Bretton Woods. The Bretton Woods Touring Center, housed in a Victorian-style building, is one of the finest cross-country skiing complexes in the East. There are approximately 100 kilometers (60 miles) of beautifully groomed trails among the firs and birches of the scenic countryside and the White Mountain National Forest; three different trail systems are ranked in difficulty. Head out on your own, enroll for instruction, or join a daytime guided tour or a moonlight trek. Alpine skiers and snowboarders are delighted with the expansion done in the past decade. This once modest ski area now boasts a 1,500-foot vertical drop, 101 trails, a terrain park, and nine lifts. The addition of West Mountain makes Bretton Woods the largest ski area in New Hampshire, and it's set to become even larger with the planned addition of Mount Stickney. The ski season lasts from late November to early May; the average annual snowfall is 200-plus inches, and 92 percent of the trails are covered by snowmaking equipment to assist Mother Nature.

Add snowmobiling, snow tubing, ice-skating, snowshoeing, sleigh rides, and winter hiking trails, and there's enough to keep you busy for two vacations.

Route 302
Bretton Woods, New Hampshire 03575
(603) 278–1000, (800) 258–0330
www.mtwashington.com

SMUGGLERS' NOTCH RESORT

Smugglers' Notch, Vermont

The Green Mountains of Vermont are not just about beautiful foliage colors in the autumn and skiing fun in the winter. Smugglers' Notch Resort makes sure there's much more to enjoy all year long. This is our idea of a true "family resort." Tucked in the rolling hills and mountains of northern Vermont, Smugglers' Notch is a self-contained resort village with sports facilities and getaway relaxation potential for the whole family. In winter, when Mother Nature blankets the region in snow, skiing on the three interconnected mountains is the primary activity. Tennis, hiking, swimming, and horseback riding are favorite pastimes when the weather warms. Any time of year one can explore the natural beauty and charm surrounding this mountain village and experience family fun—guaranteed! Yes, the resort guarantees families will have fun or it refunds the activity portion of their stay. Maybe that's why, for six years in a row, Smugglers' Notch has been voted the number one family resort by *Ski Magazine,* and the number one family resort in the Northeast by *FamilyFun,* a Disney publication, for three years.

Accommodations: Almost 650 condominium units are arranged in clusters of two- and three-story, modern but rustic buildings. From these all the amenities of the village are accessible by foot or free shuttle service. Most of the units have fireplaces and private balconies, and all have completely equipped kitchens or kitchenettes. Size varies from studios to five-bedroom apartments.

The Club Smugglers' package plans cover lodging and most of the recreational activities. For example, the summertime FamilyFest program for seven days and seven nights includes accommodation in a one-bedroom condo (which sleeps four), full-day programs for children three to seventeen, guided walks and hikes, swimming and water sliding, evening entertainment for both families and adults, and much more; from $1,759 to $2,985 (rates based on dates of stay). A winter five-day package in the same type of lodging costs $99 to $195 per adult per day and $79 to $179 for youths three to seventeen years, depending on the time period. This includes lift tickets, lessons (Nordic, Alpine, snowboard, cross-country, telemark, and shaped skis), ski camp, outdoor ice-skating, welcome parties, swimming pool, sauna, and après-ski activities. A crib or extra futon cot for two- to seven-year-olds can be provided for $20 for the entire stay.

Dining: Though you may opt to cook in your condo, there are several restaurants in the village when dining out seems better than facing a skillet. The Green Mountain Deli serves home-baked breakfast treats and hot lunches with fresh-roasted specialty coffees. The Mountain Grille is open for all three meals, including light fare available well into the evening and a special buffet for children. At the Hearth & Candle, parents enjoy nouveau cuisine, and at Riga-Bello's all ages savor the ever-popular Italian favorites—pizza, calzones, salads, and beverages—to eat in or have delivered to their condo. For ice-cream treats, there's Ben and Jerry's Scoop Shop, or choose refreshing drinks at Bootlegger's Lounge, with its big-screen TV.

The Mountainside Cabana is a relaxing summertime spot for lunch and cocktails.

And teenagers even have their own club-houses, the Outer Limits and Teen Alley, open daily from 5:00 P.M. to midnight, serving juice and soda. For extras, snacks, and wines stop by the Village Country Store.

Children's World: The Smugglers' Just for Kids program operates from early December to the beginning of April. Discovery Dynamos' three- to five-year-olds join their ski host for morning and afternoon ski lessons, tractor rides, movies, and arts and crafts. Skiers and boarders ages six to ten meet with the Adventure Rangers Ski or Snowboard Camp for lessons, snow soccer, and races. The Notch Squad, for ages eleven to fourteen, increases the adventure with more emphasis on improving skills. Après-ski activities include a daily bonfire at 3:30 P.M. with hot chocolate for parents and children. With lunch included, the daily rate for these programs, 9:30 A.M. to 4:00 P.M., is $95, or $69 on a Club Smugglers' package.

For teens fifteen to seventeen, Mountain Explorers offers challenging instruction and techniques, racing development, and a great way to make new friends. With the Outer Limits and Teen Alley teen centers and scheduled daily activities at 7:00 and 9:00 P.M., teenagers have plenty to do.

Treasures Child Care Center is the fully certified, $1 million facility for children ages six weeks and older, with special features like giant fish tanks in every room, one-way mirror viewing for parents, 5,400 square feet of indoor space, and over 4,000 square feet of outdoor playground.

Located in a quiet, sunlit slopeside area of the resort, Treasures offers ten rooms of real state-of-the-art facilities. There are kid-size bathrooms, a complete kitchen, an infant "crawler room" equipped with mirrors and soft-sculpture gym, a separate crib room for naps, a closet of costumes, radiant floor heating, and an indoor jungle gym. Open from 8:30 A.M. to 4:30 P.M. during ski season, it's staffed with professionals and boasts a ratio of one caretaker to four children.

Rates are $66 per day, or $15 per hour for up to three hours. If you prefer, individual babysitters are available in your condo at $10.00 per hour for one child, $1.00 per hour each additional child, plus a finder's fee. Smugglers' has a great understanding of kids of all ages, and more options than it's possible to list. Check the Web site for all the details and watch your kids get super-excited.

During the summer season, from mid-June through Labor Day, days and nights are filled with fun events: outdoor games, fishing, arts and crafts, hiking, treasure hunts, and swimming. At the playground are swings, climbing equipment, and a sandbox. The day camps are included in the price of the FamilyFest vacation ($45 per day, regular rate). Summer Fun University allows kids to major in fun and minor in a variety of other activities like arts and crafts, nature and hiking, sound and stage, or adventure and games. So, they'll get the same great activities always offered in the all-day camps, plus a special focus of their own choosing. They'll join the Discovery Dynamos (ages three to five), Adventure Rangers (ages six to ten), The Notch Squad (ages eleven to fifteen), or Mountain Explorers (teens sixteen to seventeen); all from 10:00 A.M. to 4:00 P.M. daily. Teen Alley (ages thirteen to fifteen) and the Outer Limits (ages sixteen and older) provide gathering centers with all those things dear to teens—video games, Internet access, music and dancing, and no parents! Optional programs, for extra fees, include tennis and golf camps; overnight hikes; "Wheels," clinics in mountain boarding (blending snowboard and skateboard) and "diggling" (a cross between a mountain bike and snowboard); and Video

Camp, where kids learn the basics of camera operation, make their own video, and enjoy watching their directorial debut weekly at Smugglers' Vermont Country Fair. The fair is a taste of a small New England fair, with cotton candy, entertainers, and lots of family games and contests.

And talk about entertainment—try the Friendly Pirate Breakfast, where the pirate sings, tells jokes, and swashbuckles with the kids (cost of breakfast only). Another nice feature is Kids Night Out, when children ages three to eleven are invited to dinner and a fun evening from 6:00 to 10:00 P.M. The cost is $25 per child, and it operates on Tuesday, Wednesday, Thursday, and Saturday.

The fun doesn't end in the fall. For families with children under five, AutumnFest packages provide morning programs for children six weeks to five years (all day on Wednesday and Thursday) with family fun in the afternoons, amidst that gorgeous Vermont foliage—and at the lowest rates of the year.

Recreation: A network of seventy-eight trails on three interconnected mountains is the focus of wintertime play. The ski season runs from Thanksgiving to mid-April, and the average annual snowfall of 286 inches is supplemented by snowmaking equipment covering 62 % of the terrain. The three mountains fall more or less into novice, intermediate, and advanced runs, but each mountain offers skiing for all levels of expertise. The total vertical drop is just over 2,600 feet making it Northern Vermont's biggest. For the cross-country skier, 14 miles of trails roam through the mountains. Lessons in cross-country skiing, downhill skiing, and snowboarding can help you learn as a beginner or improve your skills. Smugglers' has four Learning and Fun Parks, geared from rank beginner to expert. You might also try ice-skating with the kids or snowshoeing, an

increasingly popular sport. Experience the winter woods on your own two feet, with dedicated snowshoeing trails, guided family tours, or for the more adventurous, a lift ride up the mountain, and a walk down.

Turning indoors, you can enjoy the benefits of the Mountain Massage Center. The FunZone offers indoor play for all ages: inflatables, rolling in the ball slides, table tennis, basketball, and jousts (very popular with teens), and even a little minigolf. Also in winter, the large, heated swimming pool is covered with a bubble, so pack your swimsuit along with your ski sweater.

In summer the bubble comes down. There's a water slide called the Flume, a baby wading pool, and a seventeen-person outdoor hot tub. Free swimming instruction is provided as part of the day-camp program, and adults can join the Aqua Aerobics class for a good workout. Lots of family activities are balanced by some evening adults-only programs, including improv comedy and Marco's Hypnosis.

Notchville Park, Smugglers' newest water playground, encompasses three acres with three pools in a unique, tiered hillside setting. In addition to 5,000 square feet of water, the park includes Raven's Roost Climbing Tower, Catbird's Croquet Court, Sand Swallow's Volleyball Court, Peregrine's Picnic Pavilion, and the Half-Moon Bath House. The Twister is the most recent addition and has 360-degree turns and twists, covering two swimming pools—not for the faint of heart.

The Mountainside Pools is a third, separate water facility that includes a turtle slide (for children ages three to eight years), the Little Smugglers' Lagoon (a large splash pool with waterfall, tunnels, fountains, and a lazy river ride), a lap pool, and every parent's delight, the Giant Rapid River Ride—306 feet of twists and thrills on an inner tube beginning 26 feet up in the air. Bathhouse, snack bar, and lounging deck with gorgeous mountain views help one recover.

Also a favorite with families is Rum Runner's Hideaway, a beautiful swimming lake tucked in the mountains, a short hike or drive away from the village. Access is free to resort guests for swimming, fishing, picnicking, and relaxing; canoes and paddleboats are available for rent. It's a great way to relive the old days and introduce your kids to the joys of summer days at the ole swimmin' hole.

In addition to two indoor tennis courts, there are eight outdoor clay courts; six are lighted for evening play. The Ten Pro Tennis School, which has videotape review, just about guarantees improvement in your game.

For those who can't possibly leave home without their golf clubs, courses in nearby Stowe and Morrisville are open to Smugglers' guests, or take a practice time with instruction on Smugglers' own driving range.

Hiking and biking are popular ways to enjoy the mountain countryside, or try jogging on one of the cross-country trails. Head to a mountain stream for perch, pike, and trout fishing. Outdoor lawn games include Frisbee, basketball, volleyball, soccer, and shuffleboard. Disc golf is quickly becoming a family favorite. If your inner artist is seeking expression, take a painting or sculpting workshop. And don't forget Vermont! Stowe is just across the Notch, and the surrounding area is filled with antiques, country shops, glorious scenery, and even the sound of music, as the Von Trapp family settled nearby.

4323 Vermont Route 108 South
Smugglers' Notch, Vermont 05464-9537
(802) 644–8851, (800) 451–8752
www.smuggs.com

STRATTON MOUNTAIN RESORT
Stratton Mountain, Vermont

Lessons, lessons, lessons! At Stratton Mountain Resort you can have instruction and training in several major sports. Whether your interests lead you to golf, tennis, swimming, racquetball, cross-country skiing, downhill skiing, telemark skiing, snowboarding, or snowshoeing, you can participate in classes for an introduction to a new sport or for polishing existing skills and techniques.

And where could you find a better place to get into shape and sharpen your sports expertise than in southern Vermont? Stratton Mountain Resort is set on 4,000 acres in the beautiful Green Mountains of Vermont. Since its opening in 1961, the resort has expanded a number of times to enhance the facilities and to attract sports-minded visitors to return again and again.

Accommodations: At Stratton, you can choose varied types of lodging, all within 500 yards of both village and lifts. The Inn at Stratton Mountain has 119 rooms and suites, and also houses a restaurant, fireplace lobby, and pool/sauna; winter rates range from $99 to $349, summer rates begin at $69. Liftline Lodge offers fairly basic motel-type rooms and a restaurant; winter rates are $79 to $250 and summer rates begin at $49. Rates are per room, and vary depending on date and day of the week; children under seventeen stay free in the room with parents. For condominiums, Landmark, in the heart of the village, is newly renovated and offers two- and three-bedroom units ranging from $399 to $749 in winter; Long Trail House is quite popular with families, with studio rates beginning at $199 and the 5-bedroom penthouse going for $2,500. Stratton Condos range from $219 to $799, and the newest addition, Rising Bear Lodge, has units ranging from $299 to $849. Summer rates begin at $110 for a studio. Check with Stratton for exact rates, as their condominium policy is based on number of adults per room. Also inquire about the Kids Stay and Ski Free weeks (after Thanksgiving and before Christmas), and various two- to five-night Lifts and Lodging packages for even greater economy; package rates begin at $59 to $101 per adult.

Dining: The Stone Chimney Grille at the Inn at Stratton Mountain serves hearty breakfasts, seasonal lunches, and New England cuisine dinners; savor cranberry duck or rack of lamb and pick up the recipe for your favorite dish, graciously shared by the chef. Also at the Inn is the Bear Bottom Pub, a cozy spot to sip a hot toddy or your favorite cocktail and sample hearty pub fare. Tenderloins is the restaurant and lounge at the Clubhouse on the golf course, open for summer lunches.

In the winter start your day with breakfast at the base lodge, also fine for a quick lunch; try the Cafe on the Corner in Liftline Lodge or the Partridge in a Pantry deli in the village. The Mid-Mountain Restaurant (at 2,700 feet) is perfect for those who don't want to be off their skis long. Mulligan's is a great spot for families, with a good kids' menu, fireplaces, and live music, and Mul-

berry Street serves up a taste of Little Italy. For terrific entertainment, head back to the base lodge for live music at Grizzly's bar/restaurant. Or stroll through Stratton Village and discover restaurants from casual pizza to fine dining, such as Verde, or Luna (at the Stratton Mountain Club).

Children's World: The ski season lasts from mid-November into April, and during this period youngsters are well cared for and find lots of entertainment. Seven- to twelve-year-olds join the Big Cub group for full-day supervision, lunch, lift ticket, and ski lessons, at $140 a day. Little Cubs takes in ages four to six years for indoor games and fun as well as ski lessons (8:30 A.M. to 4:00 P.M. daily); the fee is $110 a day, including lunch; a half day is $65. And real tiny tots gather at the Stratton Childcare Center, a certified day-care facility for children six weeks to four years old. It operates from 8:00 A.M. until 5:00 P.M. and offers indoor and outdoor activities. Winter rates are $95 for a full day; $50 for half-day sessions. The Stratton offers Saturday night activities for ages five to twelve including pizza and a movie plus some outdoor fun; cost is $55.

The fun continues in summer with day-camp programs offered seven days a week during July and August. Kids between three and twelve years old spend from 8:00 A.M. to 5:00 P.M. busily engaged in art classes, swim and gymnastics lessons, group games, and field trips. Little KidsKamp (three to five years), Big KidsKamp (six to eight years), and Adventure Camp (nine to twelve years) offer age-appropriate activities and the freedom of the mountain. The cost is $59 per day or $150 for the week for all camps. Kids Kare entertains ages six weeks to three years for the same hours and rate, including lunch. The Gunterman Tennis School at Stratton was ranked among the top twenty-five in the world by Tennis Resorts Online 2004 Readers Poll. An intensive tennis camp for ages six to fifteen focuses on lessons and tournaments but breaks up the day with hikes, games, and swim time. Two- and three-day Junior Golf Camps help kids from seven to fourteen improve their skills on the green ($250 to $499). If your child is wild about horses, the Sun Bowl Ranch (802–297–9210) offers four-day Junior Riding Camps ($440), riding lessons, and pony rides.

Recreation: Skiing at Stratton Mountain is a big event. Thirty-seven miles of trails add up to ninety-two runs for all levels of downhill skiers. Mother Nature drops an average annual 170 inches of snow on this mountain—at 3,875 feet, the highest peak in southern Vermont—and is nudged along by rather sophisticated snowmaking equipment, covering 80% of the skiable terrain.

The Stratton Ski School holds classes for every level of ability. It prides itself on a full-day learning experience—five hours with an instructor. The Stratton Touring Center offers instruction in cross-country skiing for treks through the tall evergreens and across quiet meadows. Ice-skating is another favorite winter sport.

If you're more inclined to warm-weather sports, enroll in the Stratton Golf School. Meet fellow students and your PGA instructors in a twenty-two-acre outdoor classroom where all playing conditions can be simulated, then head to the Stratton Mountain Country Club for a round on the twenty-seven-hole championship course.

Attend the Stratton Tennis School for private lessons or a group clinic. There are seventeen indoor and outdoor tennis courts at the Stratton Sports Center.

At the Sports Center you can take classes in swimming and aquacise in the 75-foot indoor pool, join aerobics classes, use Nautilus equipment, play tennis, or use one of the racquetball courts. During a recess from classes, sneak into the steam room or the whirlpool for some solitary relaxation. In addition, an outdoor pool, a sauna, and two whirlpools are located at the inn. Fishing equipment, kayaks, and mountain bikes can be rented. Nearby Sun Bowl Ranch lets you enjoy trail rides and even overnight rides. Two skateboard parks are within twenty minutes of the resort.

And don't forget to make time to poke around the beautiful Vermont countryside. Hike in the hills and breathe that fresh clean air, jog or bicycle (rentals available) down country roads along fields of wildflowers, horseback ride on mountain trails, or try mountain biking from the summit. When you've had your fill of exercise, join bargain hunters at a local antiques auction or crafts fair. Stratton Mountain Village, with the flair of an Alpine village, has lots of quaint shops, so finding the right memento of your trip will be an easy task.

Stratton Mountain, Vermont 05155
(802) 297–2200, (800) STRATTON
www.stratton.com

SUGARLOAF/USA

Carrabassett Valley, Maine

Traditional New England reserve seems to be missing at Sugarloaf/USA. The prevailing attitude is friendly, upbeat, and casually welcoming. While mainly associated with skiing and winter, Sugarloaf is fast becoming an all-season destination, with golf predominating in summer. All access is via Portland or Bangor, and once in western Maine, just about all roads lead to Sugarloaf. Route 27 is the main road to the ski area, and from the Carrabassett Valley, Sugarloaf literally stands out. You can distinguish the peak from 20 to 40 miles away, and once you leave the valley floor and start to climb, the panorama just gets better and better. Locals and repeat visitors have dubbed one particular spot "Oh-my-gosh corner," because it is so stunning as you round the corner and suddenly see the front of this impressive mountain with its 133 trails and an Alpine village set on the slope.

Accommodations: Sugarloaf has the capacity to sleep approximately 7,000 people on the mountainside. Nine hundred–plus condominiums are set in various clusters of two to twenty-eight units and offer a wide selection of design. Styles include hotel rooms, studios, lofts, and up to five-bedroom, three-bath complexes. The forty-two–room Sugarloaf Inn and the Sugarloaf Grand Summit Resort Hotel's 120–plus rooms and suites complete the lodging options. Custom packages are planned for each family's needs. Packages generally include a health club pass and group ski lessons. A complimentary shuttle system gets you around the resort with ease.

Rates range from $128 to $678 for a hotel room, from $135 to $745 for a one-bedroom unit, and from $370 to $870 for a four-bedroom condominium. Cribs and roll-away beds are provided at a daily charge of $5.00.

Sugarloaf was one of the first ski areas to introduce the ski-in/ski-out concept; in fact, most accommodations are slopeside or within walking distance of a lift. This is great for older children, as it gives them a sense of independence and it gives everyone a sense of freedom. If you want to sleep late or linger over coffee, others in your party need not delay their skiing. Gondola Village, the largest condominium and the heart of the development, is where you will find the nursery.

Dining: Dining in the Sugarloaf area is a fun adventure that is taken quite seriously. With fourteen on-mountain restaurants, you can have everything from burgers to bouillabaisse to full meals.

Gepetto's is a slopeside restaurant with salad, pasta, soup, and steaks; a greenhouse addition; and a mini-arcade. The Seasons Restaurant at the Sugarloaf Inn offers fresh Maine lobster every night and innovative American cuisine in a relaxed atmosphere. The Double Diamond Steakhouse at the Grand Summit boasts good food, great drinks, and entertainment. For après-ski the Widowmaker Lounge offers cocktails and music you can hear yourself talk over. Upstairs at the base lodge, Avalanche provides a nonalcoholic teen center with lots of action. One of the more recent additions to Sugarloaf/USA is the Shipyard Brewhaus, located just at the base of the Birches slope. It serves fine Maine microbrews on tap, lunch daily, and pub fare after 2:00 P.M. During the summer six restaurants remain open, so there's still a wide choice.

Children's World: Sugarloaf has a terrific winter child-care program. A state-licensed child-care center at the base of the mountain accepts children from ten weeks to five years of age. Hours are from 8:30 A.M. to 4:00 P.M. Advance reservations are a must (207–237–6804). The charges are $52 for a full day or $32 for a half day. The night nursery is available from 6:00 to 9:00 P.M. on Thursday and Saturday for $25, $10 per additional sibling. A fenced-in outdoor play area adds to winter fun, and inside are toys, movies, story time, circle time, and arts and crafts—a developmentally appropriate program provided by caring professionals. The nap area is separate, with individual cribs, cots, and mats. A hot lunch is served, and snacks are given during the day.

Mountain Magic teaches skiing to children ages three to six years and stresses independence, safety, and fun. The Perfect Kids system teaches walking on skis, wedge stops and turns, side-stepping, falling, and, of course, getting up. In fact, most first-timers will be skiing under their own power after the first day. Half- ($49) and full-day ($65) programs are available. The full-day program includes lots of skiing, indoor activities, a snack, and a hot lunch. Lift passes and rental equipment are included in both sessions. For three-year-olds, the morning half-day Mooseketeers session is recommended. This allows your youngest to acquaint themselves with skiing at a comfortable pace. Mountain Adventure is a program for ages seven to fourteen, where skills are perfected. These programs run from 8:30 A.M. to 3:00 P.M.; half-day ($42) and full-day programs ($57) are available. The full-day program includes lots of skiing/riding, a snack, and a hot lunch. Mountain Teen provides group clinics for ages fifteen to eighteen. Lift tickets and equipment are not included for these age groups. Evenings offer free supervised activities for five- to twelve-year-olds six nights a week. Included in the offerings are game nights, Movie Night, Wild Card Night, and Turbo-Tubing. Reservations are required.

Summertime brings flowers and traditional July-to-mid-August day camps. A six-week program provided by Carrabassett Valley begins in the second week of July. Kids ages four to thirteen enjoy lessons in swimming, tennis, golf, and fly-fishing, and an extensive arts program. Weekly themes cover environment, ecology, nature, and weather. At $125 for five days or daily rates of $30, it's a great deal. For little ones, Sugarloaf offers summer child-care Monday through Friday from 8:00 A.M. to 4:00 P.M. for ages ten weeks to five years. Reservations are required (207–237–6804), and the cost is $40 per day.

Recreation: The most impressive aspect of skiing Sugarloaf is that you are skiing a big mountain. It is a traditional mountain in that it begins gently, goes to intermediate in the middle, and gets "durn hard at the top," as a local might say. Sugarloaf has the most continuous vertical drop in the East. It is possible to come almost straight down the 2,820-foot vertical drop (and even do it in an upright position if you're good) having taken only two lifts. A good beginner or low intermediate skier can take Tote Road, a 3-mile trail from the top that follows the ridge and comes safely to the base, but gives that exciting feeling of skiing at the top of the world and surviving it. A Super Pipe, Half Pipe, and three terrain parks add to the thrill. The Pipeline boasts hits so big you can see your house from there. At the Outdoor Center, cross-country skiers can explore 100 kilometers of trails, including some lighted for night skiing, or relax at the warm, comfortable lodge.

Other winter fun includes ice-skating, snowshoeing, turbo-tubing, and hockey. The three Family Theme weeks offer additional family activities, and Holiday Weeks are chock-full of entertainment opportunities, such as a free sleigh ride through the woods. At the foot of Sugarloaf/USA, the Carrabassett Valley Antigravity Recreational Complex is a 20,000-square-foot facility that boasts Maine's largest indoor skate bowl, trampolines with harness rigging, an indoor rock-climbing wall, and a multipurpose court with a running track, along with weight training and aerobics facilities.

Come summer, when there is no snow on the ground, the Sugarloaf Golf Club opens. Designed by Robert Trent Jones Jr., this course is one of the best for wilderness golf and is one of the top one hundred to play in the United States, according to *Golf Magazine*. Every tee has a spectacular view, and the mountain air is always cool. Tennis is limited to outside play, with two courts on the mountain and four in the town. The village has indoor racquetball courts, a sauna, hot tubs, a steam room, tanning beds, a climbing wall, and two swimming pools. But probably the most exciting summer sport is white-water rafting on the Kennebeck River. Sugarloaf also has a concentrated mountain biking program, environmental programs, and guided adventures for the whole family.

RR 1, Box 5000
Carrabassett Valley, Maine 04947
(207) 237–2000, (800) THE–LOAF
www.sugarloaf.com

THE TYLER PLACE
FAMILY RESORT
Highgate Springs, Vermont

Tucked away in the northwestern corner of Vermont, on Lake Champlain and just minutes away from the Canadian border, Tyler Place Family Resort rightly boasts of its beautiful setting and family-friendly atmosphere. The Tyler Place was one of the first resorts to devote itself entirely to families. The original owners, Mr. and Mrs. Edward Tyler, developed a concept that includes family time as well as time for parents to rejuvenate as a couple. And for over seventy years, the Tyler family (second and third generations) has continued to carry on the resort's family philosophy. Open from late May to early September, it's the kind of place that families return to again and again. Parents and even grandparents who came here as children now bring their own kids.

Accommodations: The inn is the hub of activity, with its recreation rooms, main dining room, fireside lounge, deck, and glass-enclosed porches for visiting, relaxing, cocktails, and candlelight dining. Guest rooms—some are studios, some suites—are located in a separate wing. In addition, thirty cottages, most with a fireplace in the living room and two or more bedrooms, are situated on or near the lake; these have kitchenettes and can sleep up to eight people. Many of the rooms include sleeping lofts or bunk beds; with these special attractions, it may not be difficult at all to get a youngster to go to sleep in a strange place. Cribs and high chairs for infants and toddlers are available at no extra charge.

In total, Tyler Place accommodates approximately sixty families. Based on a Full American Plan, the daily per person rate for each of the first two lodgers in a unit is $161 to $299 from mid-June to Labor Day; children and teens are $101 daily. This rate covers lodging, all meals, sports, eight separate Toddlers to Teens programs, and most activities. Rates are $84 to $227 for adults and $66 to $91 daily for children and teens in late May, early June, and September. Stays generally run from Saturday to Saturday, although there are some half-sessions, and a special Memorial Day long weekend. If your dates don't match theirs, they'll make every effort to fit you in, space permitting. Infants and toddlers have programs or one-on-one Parents' Helper care; request their special leaflet and rates. The resort is closed the rest of the year.

Dining: The main dining room in the inn serves a semibuffet breakfast, lunch, and dinner. New American country cuisine is the kitchen's specialty, with fresh, locally grown foods, and since a Full American Plan is in effect, you have only to decide which delicious entree to sample. Children have earlier dining hours with their counselors, allowing parents to relax over evening meals. Share breakfast with your children in the family breakfast room or request a family picnic lunch basket at no extra charge.

Children's World: Outstanding, individualized, and flexible describes the children's programs at the Tyler Place Family Resort. During the entire season there's an extensive program of events geared to eight different age groups, plus infant care. From the youngest Junior Toddlers (twelve to eighteen months) to Senior Teens (fourteen- to sixteen-year-olds), children are well entertained with morning and evening activities led by energetic and enthusiastic college students. Children take meals with their group leaders, and the hours between breakfast and lunch and after supper are filled with arts and crafts, nature walks, songs, games, storytime, volleyball, swimming, hayrides, fishing, movies, treasure hunts, sailing, tennis, sailboarding, kayaking, indoor pool parties—one gets out of breath just listing the activities! Busy and active, your child will no doubt be happy as well, with no chance of being "kid-starved." Afternoons (1:30 to 5:30 P.M.) are devoted to individual family time, with activities available if desired. If you can drag the kids away from friends and counselors, the staff will help you plan a day of sightseeing or fishing and send you off with a picnic lunch.

For the very young (newborns to two and one-half years), the resort features one-on-one "Parents' Helpers" (from high-school-age to mature adult), who will care for your young child and even prepare meals. The standard fee is $5.50 to $7.50 per hour. This is a real vacation for Mom and Dad, a break from wet diapers and baby food. During Family Retreat Weeks, Parents' Helpers are available only in the evening. Mornings, the Infant Center provides care for the wee ones (with a 1:2 ratio), and toddlers are looked after in the Toddler Center (with a 1:3 ratio of caregivers to children).

During the first week of September, you're invited to bring a friend (ages six to fifteen) at no extra charge as long as the friend is in the same age group as your child.

Recreation: Beautiful Lake Champlain is the source of much of the recreation and relaxation of Tyler Place. Take off in one of the resort's sailboats, canoes, kayaks, pontoons, or sailboards. Try waterskiing (with instruction), windsurfing, guided canoe and bike trips, yoga, aerobics (step and water), and the workout facilities. Or bait your fishing line for bass and pike. The outdoor and indoor heated pools and Jacuzzi on the lakeshore provide hours of fun. Kids and adults both get a thrill from the "banana boat ride."

Retreats for the whole family, a popular addition, started in 1998. They feature hands-on activities for all ages, including such topics as gardening, nature and outdoor skills, lakeshore studies, rural and farm life, and family wellness.

On land, six tennis courts and a fleet of bikes (one-speed, mountain, children's, tricycle, and child seats, all with helmets) are at your disposal, and the nature trails beckon hikers and joggers. For a change of pace, challenge another guest to an old-fashioned game of horseshoes, or try your hand at archery. Maybe you'll join a soccer game or start up a tennis round-robin with the folks in the neighboring cottage. Golf privileges are available at three golf courses within a fifteen- to forty-five-minute drive of the resort. Recreation fees are applied only for golf, outboard motors for fishing, water-skiing, lake cruises, and mountain bikes.

Within an hour's drive you can get a taste of Europe by visiting cosmopolitan Montreal, or take a mountain hike and an aerial tram ride at Stowe or Jay Peak. Covered bridges, waterfalls, little New England towns, country auctions, and antiques shops are even closer. A plethora of working farms, state parks, and vineyards and wineries can make decisions difficult.

Nighttime brings other events, from dances and live jazz to guitar sing-alongs and Monte Carlo nights—pick your pleasure. What many guests like most is the hospitable atmosphere of the many and varied activities, with never any pressure to participate.

Box 1, Old Dock Road
Highgate Springs, Vermont 05460
(802) 868–4000
www.tylerplace.com

WEEKAPAUG INN
Weekapaug, Rhode Island

If you like lights, action, and lots going on, then just skip right over this entry. However, if you sometimes tire of the hectic, everyday insanity most of us call our ordinary lives, you may wish to read on. The story begins in 1899, when the Weekapaug Inn was simply another fashionable seaside resort, one of many strung along the length of the Atlantic Coast. Frederick Buffum, the original owner, built it because he thought that "the view was just too gorgeous not to share with friends." It comes full circle to the present, with owner Jim Buffum, the fourth generation of his family to run the inn, delightedly accepting the Forbes.com declaration that the 107-year-old Weekapaug Inn is one of

three best beach resorts in the United States and among the twenty-five best in the world. *Money* magazine ranked Westerly as one of the top twelve vacation spots in North America. What's the attraction here? Perhaps the beautiful beach, the view across water and more water to distant Block Island, the stately edifice, or a sense of serenity and tradition, of time suspended? Perhaps it's the feeling of retreating to a lovely old summer house? It's really hard to say. It's not an easy place to find, it's not on many maps, and even if it is, it's so small people often don't know they've arrived.

Weekapaug comes from a Niantic Indian word meaning "end of the pond," and that's exactly where it is. The mile-long expanse of sand is actually a barrier beach with the ocean on one side and saltwater ponds and marshes on the other. Rebuilt in 1938, after a major hurricane destroyed everything on the beach, as *Forbes* observed, "it has remained true to its original conception." After that hurricane, the Buffum family was instrumental in getting agreement from all the neighboring landholders to prevent any future development on the beach, so the view remains perfect. Weekapaug is at the western end of Quonochontaug Pond—easy to say, right?

Accommodations: The sixty-five rooms are clean and comfortable, but rather plain. There are no telephones and no television in the rooms; pay phones are available, and hotel policy allows "discreet use of cell phones in designated areas." A story from a book commemorating the One-hundredth anniversary of the inn tells of the early guest who was puzzled by the fact that the inn was full, even though "the furnishings were poor, the beds hard, there was no running water in the room and the bath is at the end of the hall." The senior Buffum thought for a minute and said, "Frankly, I don't understand it either." The guest returned every year. All rooms now have private baths (and running water) plus the claw-foot bathtubs have had showers added. The inn is open from the third Thursday in June through Labor Day. The room rates are all-inclusive; all meals, amenities, and activities are included in the per-person rates of $195 to $225 daily. Children are "about" $125 daily, depending on their ages and the room. The inn does not accept credit cards.

Dining: Upon arrival, each family is assigned a table, and like a cruise ship, that's your table for the duration. You get to know your waiter and your neighbors. Mostly college students, the fifty–plus employees live on-site, as does the owner's

family. Menus are mouthwatering, and anything but simple. For example, asparagus, Gorgonzola, and spinach strudel with yellow tomato coulis; smoked tomato risotto–stuffed calamari; coffee-crusted grilled filet mignon with a Venezuelan quasala sauce; roasted eggplant pancakes over a ratatouille sauce with garlic mascarpone cream; tandoori chicken; or poached salmon—and that is just a portion of the menu for one meal! It makes it worth getting dressed—tie and jacket are required for gentlemen and appropriate dress for women and children. Daytime attire can be "somewhat casual," but no bathing suits, please. Lunch is generally a buffet in the dining room; you may also order a picnic lunch delivered to the bathhouse. Sunday is a more elaborate buffet lunch, and a light dinner. Thursdays bring a casual cookout by the pond. Smoking is not permitted anywhere inside, and the inn does not sell alcohol. However, each room has an assigned cubby near the lounge for bottles, and self-serve ice and mixers are available for a small charge, on the honor system.

Children's World: The children's program is included in the rates and meets twice a day for ages three to ten years; from 10:30 A.M. to 1:30 P.M. and again from 5:30 to 8:30 P.M. Regular activities include playing at the beach, art, crafts, games, and nature hikes, and meals are taken as a group. Evenings bring movies or a theater excursion. The Children's Playroom has a television, but not for use during program hours. Babysitting can be arranged with twenty-four hours' advance notice.

Recreation: Bring all those books you haven't had time to read and correspondence you've been saving for the past year, as evenings are quiet and made for socializing or playing board games. There are two televisions but it's interesting how boring they are compared to what's happening around you. Sometimes storytellers or guest speakers are on the agenda, as are dancing or movies. If golf is your game, local courses are nearby. Two tennis courts are on-site, and lawn bowling, shuffleboard, and croquet are popular pastimes. Your croquet not quite up to speed? Complimentary lessons are offered every Tuesday by the Weekapaug Croquet Club. Bicycles are a lovely way to get around. Sailing, canoeing, kayaking, and rowing on the pond are great fun—sign up for a boat at the front desk. Guests may use the Weekapaug Yacht Club Bathhouse at the private community beach, with attendant on duty from 9:00 A.M. to 5:00 P.M. for towels, chairs, and umbrellas. Fenway Beach, also private but open to guests, is good for children as it has a more protected area with gentle, sloped access into the water. Clamming in Mud Cove delights children and may bring back memories of your own earlier summers.

---

25 Spray Rock Road
Weekapaug, Rhode Island 02891
(401) 322–0301
www.weekapauginn.com

EAST

New York
Pennsylvania

GOLDEN ACRES
FARM AND RANCH
Gilboa, New York

"Old MacDonald had a farm, ee-i-ee-i-oh. And on that farm he had a cow." Well, the Gauthiers have a farm too, with at least as wide a variety of animals as Old Mac did—horses, goats, sheep, ducks, chickens, and a number of baby animals for cuddling and petting. If you like, you can begin your day by milking a cow, collecting eggs from the henhouse, or feeding the animals. Since it opened in 1950, the farm has always been family oriented and prides itself on a genuine "down-on-the-farm" experience with modern comforts. This 800-acre farm/resort is located on top of a 2,000-foot-high knoll in the Catskill Mountains and is open mid-June to Labor Day only.

Accommodations: In the main house are the dining room, the nursery, an indoor playroom, and a teen lounge. Next door is a motel complex connected to game rooms, lounges, and the indoor pool and hot tub. Across the road (a short city block away) is Gilboa Ridge, with a farmhouse and farm cottage. There are ten connecting rooms and suites. Most rooms contain a double bed and a single bed, with space for rollaways or cribs ($25 per stay per crib). Also at Gilboa Ridge are twenty-six "you cook" vacation apartments with kitchenettes (you bring your own dishes, towels, etc.) and a campground area with water and electric hookups. The farm pays particular attention to single parents and has nondiscriminatory rates for one adult traveling with a child. Weekly rates for a one-bedroom in the farmhouse begin at $520 per adult, or $660 in the main complex, and include two meals. Infants under one year old stay free, and children/teens are priced by age, ranging from $155 to $335,

including three meals. Two-night packages range from $210 to $285 per adult and $65 to $100 per child. The U-Cook Apartments rates are based on the number of people, and range from $885 to $1,025 for a family of three, $1,025 to $1,135 for a family of four, with no meals. Everything is clearly outlined on the Web site, plus you can request a free video. Rates include meals as outlined, and all activities, equipment, and children's programs.

Dining: Only in the Catskills can you find fresh country meals that are also kosher. Children and adults have a joint menu and dining room for breakfast and dinner, but no adults are allowed at lunch; then the children and teens and their counselors eat all those things that are so dear to their hearts—pizza and hamburgers, along with a few fruits and vegetables. Jewish dietary laws are observed, as is Shabbos. Two snacks daily are included for the young set, and the selection at the Snack Bar hits the spot between meals. Food is fresh, locally grown, and hearty, and you can eat all you wish. The evening menu includes appetizer, salad, soup, choice of two meats or one fish entree, side dishes, and desserts. All breads and pastries are freshly baked daily in the farm bakery.

Evening activities center on the Skylite Room and the Ragtime Lounge and include happy hour, bands, and entertainment; folk and square dancing; night at the races; and other activities—some for everyone, some for adults only, and a teen lounge for special programs. After the early evening entertainment, live music and dancing continue in the Ragtime Lounge.

Children's World: The "Just Us Kids" program for children varies by age, takes advantage of the farm surroundings, and is offered from mid-June through the first week of September. For the under-four set, a complete nursery service is scheduled from 10:00 to 11:45 A.M., 12:30 to 5:00 P.M., and 6:30 to 7:45 P.M. Parents collect their children for mealtimes.

For four- to twelve-year-olds, it is nonstop action throughout the day. For teens, informal activities emphasize meeting others and sharing things while maintaining freedom of action. The rec room, with its jukebox and video games, is popular with this group. Experienced and enthusiastic counselors (most of whom are studying to be teachers) supervise the events. The staff is international, with many countries represented. It's great exposure for the children, who learn games and activities from around the world.

A typical day starts at 10:00 A.M. with a tour to feed the animals, collect eggs, or visit the gardens. Then come horseback riding (teaching beginners is a specialty here), swimming, lunch, and a rest period. Afternoon activities are geared to the children's interests—berry picking, frog hunts, hayrides, crafts, games, and perhaps an excursion to the caves or a hike and cookout in the woods. A snack of milk and cookies is followed by rounding up the cows for milking.

After a break for dinner and a quick hello to the parents, evening activities such as bonfires, talent shows, or cartoons start at 7:45 P.M. Kids have another snack, then head for bed about 9:00 P.M.—and well deserved it is! Parents can go out if they want, as a "check at your door" night patrol is on duty from 9:00 P.M. to 1:00 A.M., with a sign-in sheet on each room door. If you prefer, you can hire a babysitter from either the staff or local listings at approximately $7.00 an hour.

Recreation: There is no charge for any of the activities. After catching your limit of fish, you might take off to one of the two tennis courts, the archery field, either of the two swimming pools, or the exercise room, followed by the spa hot tubs. The boats and floating docks at the lake make for a relaxing afternoon, or join a group for softball or volleyball. And grown-ups, too, can partake in the farm activities—feeding the animals, horseback riding, hopping aboard a hayride. A less active afternoon might include a class in macramé, copper enameling, pottery, or stained glass, or a stop by one of the recreation rooms for table tennis and pool. If the weather is uncooperative, there's an indoor riding arena, five playrooms for rainy-day activities including nine-hole miniature golf, and a complete workout room for adults. One nice feature at the Golden Acres is the policy of allowing an early check-in and late use of the facilities when checking out.

Local sites of interest include Howe Caverns, Secret Caves, Hunter Mountain, game farms, and bird sanctuaries. Cooperstown, home of the Baseball Hall of Fame, is nearby, as is the Oneonta Soccer Hall of Fame. Golden Acres is in the center of numerous auction barns, flea markets, and roadside vegetable stands.

The addition of a nearby 400-acre farm with a thirty-five-acre lake and a ten-acre island including a land bridge to the island from shore provides hours of entertainment. You'll be able to discover and explore a beautiful site, just like the early settlers.

South Gilboa Road
Gilboa, New York 12076
(607) 588–7329, (800) 847–2151,
(800) 252–7787 (in New York)
www.goldenacres.com

MOHONK MOUNTAIN HOUSE

New Paltz, New York

The wholesome peace and serenity of Mohonk Mountain House are not merely by-products of its setting in 2,200 acres of the Shawangunk Mountains, 90 miles north of New York City. The resort was founded in 1869 by twin brothers, Albert and Alfred Smiley, who, following their Quaker upbringing, regarded drinking, dancing, smoking, and card playing as unacceptable activities. Rather, they emphasized spiritual renewal as evidenced by the nature walks or prayer meetings planned for their proper clientele.

The times have indeed changed, but the gracious, quieter way of life of a bygone era still prevails at Mohonk. No discos swing until dawn here. Instead, you'll find cozy conversation lounges furnished with Victorian antiques, verandahs lined with rocking chairs, miles of hiking trails, and extensive gardens. Open year-round, the rambling wood-and-stone Victorian structure appears almost like a castle, complete with turrets and towers, and sits on the edge of a clear mountain lake a half mile long. In fact, Mohonk means "lake in the sky" in Iroquois. Though physically isolated, guests want for nothing during a stay here.

Accommodations: The 251 guest rooms are spacious and tastefully and simply decorated with period furnishings. Some have fireplaces and private balconies overlooking the lake or looking across the valley to the mountains. Some connecting rooms share a bath. On a Full American Plan (mandatory), daily rates are from $408 to $698 for a standard double guest room. The special Victorian and tower rooms command higher rates. For children occupying a room with their parents, the charge is $139 a day for those over twelve and $78 a day for four- to twelve-year-olds; children under age four are accommodated free. There is no charge for cribs or roll-away beds. Weekly rates and package plans are available. Ask about the "kids stay free" events held throughout the year.

Dining: Breakfast, lunch, and dinner are included in the rates. The main dining room is large and elegantly simple with highly polished woodwork and paneling rising 30 to 40 feet. The kitchen specializes in American cuisine and ingredients indigenous to America. "Healthy Choice," vegetarian, and kosher menus are also available, and the spectacular natural setting adds to the dining experience. Jackets are standard attire for gentlemen age twelve and over at the evening meal. Cookouts and clambakes are occasionally planned; enjoy casual outdoor dining at Picnic Lodge or the Granary; and complimentary afternoon tea is served daily at 4:00 P.M. Refreshments are also available in the Ice Cream Parlor and Soda Fountain and the Tee Room on the golf course.

Children's World: On weekends and holidays throughout the year and daily from mid-June through Labor Day, Mohonk's Kids' Club divides children into three age groups: Tykes, two- to three-year-olds; Explorers, four- to six-year-olds; and Adventurers, seven- to twelve-year-olds. Groups have daily activities in the morning and again in the afternoon, after lunch with the family; and evening activities as well. Typical events on the agenda are hikes, nature walks, scavenger hunts, shuffleboard contests, swimming, pony rides, rock scrambles, and frog hunts. Movies, square dances, and campfires are frequently planned for evenings. During July and August, special activities for teens (ages twelve to eighteen years) are planned. From mountain biking, rock scrambles, tennis and golf clinics, and day-long hikes to just "hanging out" in the Teen Lounge for music, movies, and socializing, all activities are well-supervised. Winter brings ice-skating, snowshoeing, and hot chocolate. Kids' Club is a complimentary service for hotel guests. Babysitters can be hired for younger children, with advance notice, and there are planned activities for the whole family to enjoy together.

Recreation: Discovering nature's beauty is at the core of Mohonk's recreational activities; with the exception of horseback riding, carriage rides, weekend golf, and massage, recreation is complimentary. More than 85 miles of hiking trails wind through the woods and along the lake; dotting the paths are one hundred gazebos where you can sit to take in the views. Explore the grounds on horseback (Western and English style), or leisurely meander through the award-winning gardens and Victorian maze. Lake Mohonk has a small sandy beach at the west end and is stocked with trout; it is the location for swimming, fishing, and boating.

Traditional sports are tennis (lessons available) on the six courts (four clay, two Har-Tru) and the two platform tennis courts, and golfing on the 107-year-old nine-hole Scottish-design course and the eighteen-hole putting green. Tennis and midweek nine-hole golf are complimentary. There are tennis and golf pro shops for equipment and apparel. Lawn games include shuffleboard, croquet, and lawn bowling.

During the winter months, when the lake freezes, ice-skating is a favorite sport. Mohonk's Victorian Skating Pavilion is host to skating parties on a refrigerated ice rink in fall and winter. And Mohonk maintains more than 35 miles of marked trails for snowshoeing and cross-country skiing, also included in the rates.

Throughout the year lectures, concerts, nature shows, movies, and dancing are scheduled in the evening. Several three-day to weeklong themed programs are planned, covering topics such as bird watching and identification, gardening, photography, foreign languages, cooking, music, mystery and sleuthing, and stargazing; professionals in the respective fields conduct these programs.

The Spa at Mohonk Mountain House, opened in 2005, prides itself on sixteen treatment rooms, all amenities, indoor and outdoor pools, and a state-of-the-art fitness room.

Lake Mohonk
1000 Mountain Rest Road
New Paltz, New York 12561
(845) 255–1000, (800) 772–6646
www.mohonk.com

ROCKING HORSE RANCH

Highland, New York

"Giddy-up, ole paint" and, with a tip of your ten-gallon hat, off you ride into the sunset. Located only 75 miles from New York City with a Three-Diamond rating by AAA, Rocking Horse Ranch has been owned and managed by the Turk family since 1958. They take pride in treating their guests as family; in fact, more than 80% of the guests are repeat clients. The 500 acres easily accommodate up to 450 guests while permitting a feeling of "wide open spaces." With a stable of 120 horses, mainly quarterhorse stock, Rocking Horse stakes a claim to being one of the best family dude ranches in the East.

Accommodations: Rooms (120 in all) are located in either the main lodge or the Oklahoma Annex (motel-style units). The twenty-four connecting rooms and the ranchettes may be appropriate for large parties. The latter are similar to minisuites, with sitting areas and convertible sofa beds. Eighteen rooms have refrigerators. Summer daily all-inclusive package rates based on double occupancy are $230 to $310 per adult; children under four are free; ages four to fifteen are $105 for the first child and $100 for additional children. Less per day for longer stays! Weekly rates per adult are $1,150 to $1,345, first child is $550, additional children $515. Spring, fall, and winter feature weekend and midweek stays; during certain time periods, rates are further reduced by 10–25%. Winter weekend rates (Friday to Sunday) range from $330 to $395 per adult and $145 per child (ages four to fifteen years); midweek for a two-night package is from $222 to $258 each adult, and $84 for children. Spring and fall rates are comparable, and holidays are more expensive.

Dining: Meals and entertainment are included in the resort's rates. Choose from the Longhorn Dining Room, The Cactus Grill, or during summer, poolside parties and snack bar. Adults receive breakfast and dinner while children have all three meals, enjoying lunch with the counselors. Meals are five to six courses, prepared by graduate chefs from the nearby Culinary Institute of America. Dinner selections include roast prime rib, barbecued steaks, or fillet of sole brought in fresh from a local market, complemented by a huge salad bar. At the dessert bar the chocolate blackout cake is not to be missed. The Round-Up Room Nightclub has floor shows and a live band. Two other cocktail lounges, each with a fireplace and a conversation area, are also quite inviting.

Children's World: The Fort Wilderness playground area, with swings and climbing equipment and the animal farm where Chewbacca the Camel lives, is a favorite with kids. Year-round, children have a planned, supervised program seven days a week. The 9:00 A.M. to 5:00 P.M. schedule is filled with horseback riding, swimming, waterskiing, crafts, and games. In the evening the family fun continues with pizza parties, dances, and cookouts. On weekends during the winter, kids turn to skiing and snow tubing.

There is no charge for the day's events, which include lunch and snacks with the counselors for ages four to twelve. Children are divided into small groups (ages four to six, seven to ten, and eleven to twelve) with age-appropriate activities. The under-four set is the only group with an extra charge ($6 per hour) either in the nursery or with an individual babysitter. Teens have evening programs and mixers, and plenty of opportunity to "meet and mingle" during daytime activities.

Recreation: You might start your day with an early-morning horseback ride; invigorated by the sweet mountain air, lead your horse down a quiet trail through the woods. If you're a novice, you can link up with the experienced ranch staff for some basic instruction.

The rest of your day may be filled with waterskiing (instruction is free), enjoying more than 150 feet of water slide, swimming, fishing, and boating (paddleboats and rowboats) on the ten-acre lake. Play a game of tennis and hike or jog along the nature trails. A relaxing swim in one of three heated pools (two are outdoors, with one just for kids) can revive your spirits for a workout in the exercise room or a rousing game of volleyball, softball, basketball, or badminton. The climbing wall is a popular place. For an easier pace, try a round of croquet, shuffleboard, or horseshoes. An archery field and an indoor shooting range are available for aspiring marksmen, and the eighteen holes of miniature golf are fun for kids and their parents. New in 2005, a Giant Fun Barn features interactive foam ball play at Ballocity and an indoor climbing wall.

In the fall the social director plans hayrides and cookouts; in winter add cross-country skiing, snow tubing, and horseback riding in the snow. The 300-foot vertical ski slope is modest but has two new trails. At Rocking Horse over fifty activities are free; the horseback riding, the use of all the sports equipment and facilities, and the entertainment are all covered in the lodging rates.

Highland, New York 12528
(845) 691–2927, (800) 647–2624
www.rhranch.com

THE SAGAMORE
Lake George at Bolton Landing, New York

The notion of an island hideaway usually involves images of thatch-roofed huts or oceanside condominiums, palm trees waving in a gentle breeze, miles of sandy beach, and golf, tennis, sailing, and swimming. The Sagamore will take you by surprise, for it is an island resort, and it grants its guests opportunities for golf, tennis, sailing, and swimming—and then it deviates from the traditional image. You see, The Sagamore is on a seventy-acre island in Lake George in upstate New York. Surrounded by clear lake waters and the Adirondack Mountains, the tall evergreen trees and the clean mountain air set the stage here and Lake George and Bolton Landing are within the borders of the six-million-acre New York Adirondack State Park.

The Sagamore itself is different. Originally opened in 1883, it is part of another era, gracious and elegant. The main hotel building dates from 1930 and is listed on the National Register of Historic Places. After an extensive multimillion-dollar renovation, The Sagamore reopened as a year-round resort in 1985 and is a member of Preferred Hotels and Resorts Worldwide. The wings radiate from the main lobby and its semicircular, white-columned porch seems to embrace the lawns, gardens, and lake views. Down the wings are more porches for sitting, strolling, and catching a different view of the lake. In the center, topping off this Victorian showplace, is the bell tower.

Accommodations: Of the 350 rooms and suites, 100 are in the main hotel and another 240 are distributed among the island's seven modern lodges (don't worry, modern does not denote a disturbance to The Sagamore's ambience). The remaining ten suites are part of a business executive complex. You will find attention to detail and historical accuracy in the decoration of the rooms and throughout the hotel. You'll think "charming, quaint, elegant, reserved" when you see Adirondack Stick or American Country furniture. Perhaps your room will be in mahogany and you'll draw a Queen Anne–style chair up to the desk when writing postcards. Rocking chairs and quilted bedspreads complete the picture in some rooms. In others fireplaces or balconies capture a guest's eye. Even the bathrooms are special and true to a grand era, with their pedestal-base sinks and mahogany towel bars.

Rates vary within the main historic hotel and the lodges, depending on the season. Winter rates are the lowest, beginning at $180 nightly for a hotel room, or $285 for a suite. This rate goes from $410 to $525 from late June to early September, the Adirondack season. A one-bedroom family suite ranges from $230 in winter to $460 in the Adirondack season. Children to age seventeen pay only a service charge on the room, except in July and August, when there is a $50 charge per child. The Sagamore's rates do not include meals; you may dine a la carte or arrange a meal plan for everyone over thirteen; Mister Brown's Pub and the Club Grill offer children's menus.

Dining: For a casual afternoon by the pool, you can have a light lunch and beverages at the Terrace. The newly renovated, now family-friendly Trillium can transport you back through time; recipes for this restaurant have been carefully researched so that you can have an adventure in history as well as in dining. In between these options are the Sagamore Dining Room near the lake, where regional favorites are served at breakfast and seasonal dinner, and the Club Grill on the mainland, where views stretch out over the golf course and the lake. During the Adirondack season, The Pavilion offers outside dining on the lake for lunch, and a Wednesday through Monday evening Lakeside Lobsterbake. At the glass-enclosed Verandah, in the lobby, guests can enjoy tea and finger sandwiches in the afternoon, and nightcaps before retiring. Mister Brown's Pub serves light meals in a publike setting and provides evening entertainment. May through October, the 72-foot yacht *Morgan* cruises the lake during lunch and dinner, offering its diners constantly changing scenic views. It is suggested that you make your dinner reservations when you book your room.

Children's World: Under the cheerful and watchful direction of the activities counselor, Sagamore kids take swimming lessons, play lawn games, dance, do face painting, go on boat rides, see clown shows, and unveil their hidden talents in crafts classes. In this one area The Sagamore does not follow nineteenth-century practices, which were somewhat restrictive when it came to children. Instead, in keeping with modern philosophies, The Sagamore wants its energized children to have a fun, athletic, and creative visit. The authentic 16-foot tepee gives the program its name: The Tepee Club. It runs from 9:00 A.M. to 4:00 P.M. daily, July 1 through Labor Day for ages four through twelve; a modified program operates on Saturdays and holidays. Costs are $25 for a half-day session (no lunch) or $65 for a full-day session (with lunch). From 5:00 until 9:00 P.M., children can have dinner together, play, and enjoy games such as dress-ups or clown parties ($45 per session). A game room offers table tennis, a pool table, video games, and a television. Babysitting is available for $15.00 an hour for the first child, $5.00 each additional child, with a three hour minimum required. Children under four may participate in the programs, accompanied by a babysitter (not an older sibling).They pay program costs ($25 half day, $45 full day, and $35 evening) plus babysitting costs. Registration is required, and a $25 fee applies for cancellations within twenty-four hours.

Recreation: Just across the bridge from The Sagamore's island, Donald Ross designed an eighteen-hole championship golf course in the Adirondack foothills near the lake's edge, complemented by the restaurant and pro shop facilities at the course's attractive Tudor-style clubhouse.

The indoor swimming pool, tennis courts, and racquetball courts help guests stay busy and active year-round. The complete health spa offers its own form of indoor workout with its Nautilus equipment and then pampers with saunas, whirlpools, and massages. European-style spa packages include special diets, herbal wraps, and aromatherapy.

In warm weather swim in the beautiful, clean, freshwater lake; skim across its surface sailing, waterskiing, or sailboarding; or gently stroke the waters in a rowboat or fishing boat. Sailing clinics are available for teens, women only, and new sailors. Jog on the trails around the island or hike the foothills around the golf course. Take a horse out for an hour-long jaunt or stay close to home for a Sunday afternoon concert on the lawn.

In the wintertime Lake George freezes; hearty souls go ice-fishing, while others snuggle together during a horse-drawn sleigh ride. Ice-skate over the frozen lake or go tobogganing and cross-country skiing on the snow-covered golf course. Downhill skiers can take advantage of nearby Gore Mountain and West Mountain, ski areas to which the Sagamore provides free bus transportation.

Saratoga is about 30 miles away and in summer shares its Performing Arts Center with interested visitors. Tour historic Fort Williams, the setting for *The Last of the Mohicans;* walk along the lake boardwalk for shopping and dining; or visit Great Escape Amusement Park, boasting one of the country's top ten roller coasters, The Steamin' Demon.

---

110 Sagamore Road
P.O. Box 450
Bolton Landing, New York 12814
(518) 644–9400, (800) 358–3585
www.thesagamore.com

SCOTT'S OQUAGA LAKE HOUSE

Deposit, New York

A reader shared this gem of a family resort with us, and described it as "warm, friendly, hospitable, fun, down to earth, great for every age, and even enchanting." We tend to agree. Six generations of Scotts have created this lovely resort, beginning in 1869. Over the years the warmth of the welcome you receive and the sense of belonging to a family has not dimmed. Set on a clear, spring-fed lake amidst the hills and woods of beautiful New York State, it is truly run for families, by a family; Mom and Pop Scott (Ray and Doris) plus daughter Patty and her family all work in different capacities at the resort. Reminiscent of the Von Trapp family, the "Singing Scotts" even present a Broadway musical review! An all-inclusive policy (you never see your wallet during your stay) adds to the old-fashioned charm of this country resort—and there's no tipping! Scott's is open late May to mid-October, so stroll up the flower-lined walk to the main house and into everyone's memory of a summer house on a lake—somewhere.

Accommodations: One hundred thirty-five rooms are set in the main lodge, various buildings, and cottages; some with two doubles or two twins, a few with king-size beds; all are simple, clean, and comfortable. Rates are per person and include room, three full meals, all recreation and entertainment, kids program, and unlimited golf, tennis, waterskiing, and all other sports and activities. July and August are the high season, but rates are only about $10 more per day; single parents pay only $30 to $40 more. Based on double occupancy, per person rates range from $118 to $138; weekly rates are $690 to $844. Two-room suites are $158 to $176 daily per person. Children

under three are free; three to five are $54; six to twelve are $69; and thirteen to nineteen are $82.

Dining: Contrary to many times in our hectic lives, eating is a communal event here, showcased in the large dining room. Fresh, natural ingredients prepared simply and with care, shared family-style with fellow guests make it easy to slow down and appreciate life and good food. Choices abound, and kids may even eat their vegetables! Twice a week you can bus or hike to a sheltered pavilion for a lavish cookout, with live music and dance and a spectacular view.

Children's World: Long summer days spent swimming in a lake, or watching nature in the woods, lunch with friends, lots of adventures—it's great to give your kids a taste of a slower, relaxed time. Supervised activities from 9:30 A.M. to 12:30 P.M. and again from 2:00 to 4:30 P.M. provide just that, while keeping kids from three up busy and amused. Age groups are blended nicely, and it's secure enough for kids to strike out on their own yet still be safe. A large playhouse on the lakefront, which includes a nostalgic soda fountain, pool tables, table tennis, and some old-fashioned bowling alleys, provides a focal point for fun. Teens can "hang" here, and while they'll laugh at having to set up their own pins, they'll probably secretly get a kick out of it.

Recreation: You'll experience no shortage of activities here, as the resort's nearly 1,100 acres are packed with things to do. Anything even remotely connected with sports is yours for the asking—volleyball, softball, bocce, table tennis, pool, bowling, two scenic nine-hole golf courses, a nine-hole pitch-and-putt and a putting green, and one indoor and three outdoor tennis courts. On the water, row a boat, canoe, sail, take a speedboat ride, fish, or water-ski. In the water, swim, splash, or simply lie on the floating raft and soak up the sun. For a different water experience, go on a canoe trip down the Delaware River—all included! Colorful Adirondack chairs line the lake-front beach, perfectly conducive to contemplating the green mountains while everyone else does all of that activity. Hike, bike, walk in the woods, or dance—your choice of ballroom, square, line, country, or folk dancing, all on a 3,200-square-foot hardwood dance floor on the lakefront. Enjoy live shows and family entertainment nightly. Ride the *Show Boat,* a tradition on Oquaga Lake for years, and you provide the sing-along show! Most of all, experience summer as you like it.

Oquaga Lake, Box 47
Deposit, New York 13754
(607) 467–3094
www.scottsfamilyresort.com

SKYTOP LODGE
Skytop, Pennsylvania

The Pocono Mountains have long had a reputation as a romantic honeymoon destination. While this is certainly warranted, the Skytop Lodge will convince you that this area of northeast Pennsylvania is just right for a family vacation as well. Set on 5,500 acres of rolling hills, lakes, and rivers, the lodge is a large, rambling, stone building with a welcoming circular drive. Just 100 miles from either New York or Philadelphia, Skytop attracts many visitors with its relaxed atmosphere, hospitable charm, and recreational activities. One of the Historic Hotels of America, it is open year-round.

Accommodations: Most of the rooms in the historic stone manor house, the Lodge, have views of the gardens and grounds; some will accommodate a family of four. If a large-enough room is not available, or if parents prefer, children are given their own room during non-holiday periods for 50% of the regular rate; during holiday periods the reduction is $100. This applies to two children only; additional children are $45 each.

Based on double occupancy, Full American Plan high-season (May through October) rates begin at $535 per night; winter rates begin at $503. Children under sixteen sharing their parents' room pay $45.

Also available are ten cottages, each with four interconnecting bedrooms. Each room within the cottage can be occupied separately or together in suites from two to four. Midweek Family Fun packages, based on two adults in standard or cottage rooms, begin at $595 for one night, $983 for two nights, and include three meals, the children's program, and use of seasonal recreational facilities including golf, tennis, skiing, and ice-skating. May through October, rates change to $640 for one night, $1,113 for two nights. Midweek golf packages, including three meals, begin at $395 per night.

Dining: Skytop's Full American Plan includes a choice of meals in the Windsor Room in the main hotel and the Lake View at the Inn; both request that gentlemen wear jackets, although ties are not required.

Also available, but not included in the dining plan, is the Deli, a seasonal lunch spot in warm weather. The Pine Room, an elegant and inviting area of the lobby with floor-to-ceiling windows, is the site of afternoon tea (part of the dining plan) with musical entertainment in the summer and cozy gatherings near the fireplace in the winter. The Tap Room, offering food, cocktails, and entertainment/dancing, and the Tea Room, with light fare such as soups and sandwiches, are not included in the dining plan.

Children's World: Camp-in-the-Clouds is in session for four- to ten-year-olds daily from mid-June to Labor Day. The morning program runs from 9:30 A.M. to 1:30 P.M., the afternoon program from 1:30 to 4:30 P.M. Each session is $15, or $30 for the full day, and covers a program of swimming, boating, hiking, soccer, golf and tennis lessons, games, and crafts. Young children also enjoy the playground and the kiddie pool, while the older ones make the most of pool, table tennis, and video games in the Recreation Room. Saturdays bring picnics for everyone and an evening dinner from 6:00 to 8:00 P.M. for children. The weekly Saturday night "Grand March" has become a tradition at Skytop. A combination parade, quadrille, and snake dance, it becomes hilarious at times, and guests and staff alike anticipate the fun. At holiday times during the rest of the year, the staff plans activities, dinners, and movies for children. Individual babysitters can be arranged for $10.00 an hour; $1.00 each additional child. Reservations must be made prior to arrival.

Recreation: The Poconos make a lovely setting for sports activities. The eighteen-hole championship golf course is a combination of lush fairways and beautiful old trees on a rolling terrain. Putting greens and a pro shop round out the golfing facility. Tennis players are invigorated by the clean mountain air; of the seven outdoor courts, five are Har-Tru and two have all-weather surfaces. Private lessons and clinics are offered.

Skytop's Fishing and Shooting Center provides fishermen with a trout-filled stream and three lakes full of bass and pickerel; novices will appreciate the Orvis School fly-fishing instruction. Others take to these waters for swimming, boating, and canoeing. There's an outdoor swimming pool, and in cool weather swimmers enjoy the large indoor pool in its solarium setting.

You can work out in the exercise room, but outdoors you can have beautiful scenery *and* all the exercise you want. Try lawn bowling on well-tended greens (tournaments are held during the summer), or practice more conventional sports like badminton, croquet, archery, shuffleboard, softball, and miniature golf. The 30 miles of trails through the woods are perfect for hiking, biking, and jogging, and the gardens are suitable for relaxing strolls. Naturalists conduct tours of the local wildlife and vegetation. In the evening you might find a bridge game, play a little pool or billiards, take in a movie, or relax in the library.

In the winter Skytop has a few gentle slopes for downhill skiing. Two poma lifts and seven trails with a vertical drop of just 275 feet make it ideal for learning. A ski pro can help with lessons. Several well-groomed trails cover acres of attractive territory for cross-country skiing. Rental equipment is available for both types of skiing, and larger ski areas are nearby at Alpine Mountain (8 miles) and Camelback (15 miles). Tobogganing, sledding, and ice-skating are also wintertime favorites.

One Skytop
Skytop, Pennsylvania 18357
(570) 595–7401, (800) 617–2389
www.skytop.com

MID-ATLANTIC

Maryland
North Carolina
South Carolina
Virginia
West Virginia

FAIRFIELD SAPPHIRE VALLEY

Sapphire, North Carolina

The rolling foothills of the Blue Ridge Mountains provide the backdrop for Fairfield Sapphire Valley, a four-season resort community. The 5,700 acres, filled with the scent of pines and fresh mountain air, encompass three lakes, a golf course, a horseback-riding stable, and picturesque scenery for nature lovers and hikers. The serenity of a canoe ride on the lake, a relaxing afternoon fishing from the dock, or the rigors of a tennis clinic attract vacationers to this mountain setting tucked in the southwestern corner of North Carolina. Back in 1896, finding this place meant travel by wagon or train. Today, that serene and rustic lifestyle still exists, but it's a lot easier to get there!

Accommodations: Hotel rooms, efficiencies, one- to three-bedroom condominiums, and three- and four-bedroom houses boast spectacular mountain views or are nestled among tall pines. Most of these lodgings have kitchens, and all have sundecks or balconies where you can sit to watch the sunset. Condominium rates begin at $100 for a kitchenette or $175 for a one-bedroom and go to $285 for a deluxe three-bedroom with view. Off-season (November through March) rates are $10 to $35 less, and weekly rates are available. Housekeeping services (clean towels daily) are provided only for those units with no washer/dryer. There is a one-time linen fee from $10 to $30. Useful items you may want to pack include napkins, paper towels, salt and pepper, coffee and coffee filters, dish soap, and laundry detergent.

Dining: Many families prepare meals in their villas, but if your idea of a vacation does not include cooking, the restaurants can relieve you of this chore—although you'll definitely want to have breakfast items and snacks on hand in the condo. The Library Restaurant offers dinner in a casual atmosphere, while Mica's Restaurant has an old-world charm and serves lunch and dinner daily with a children's menu. Sunday brunch, karaoke twice a week, and live music and dancing on Saturday nights make Mica's the center of Sapphire social life. Jimmy Mac's is family-friendly with simple, mostly Italian fare, plus soups and sandwiches. The club for the Sapphire Mountain Golf Course also houses a restaurant, which is open for lunch. The resort is located in a dry township; while no liquor, beer, or wine can be purchased on-site, brown bagging is permitted and setups are available in the area restaurants. Venture to Cashiers (3 miles) or Highlands (12 miles) for more dining selections. A car is recommended to fully enjoy the area.

Children's World: The children's program operates Monday through Friday from 9:00 A.M. to 4:00 P.M., mid-June through mid-August. Enroll your child for a full-day session of events supervised by an enthusiastic staff. A full day with lunch is $40. The program is offered for ages five to twelve.

Swimming, boat rides, tennis, nature walks, fishing, and arts-and-crafts classes are on the agenda, as are an occasional puppet show and scavenger hunt. Video games are offered for the young computer whiz in your group. The recreation staff assists in making individual babysitting arrangements.

Recreation: An Amenities Card ($5.00 per person for ages fourteen and over) is required to access recreation facilities; a cardholder must accompany children under fourteen. There are modest fees for most activities.

The Sapphire Mountain Golf Course is an eighteen-hole championship course. Views of the beautiful Blue Ridge Mountains provide ample inspiration for your game. Water hazards on nine holes, including a waterfall, make it a memorable experience. If you're really serious about your performance, seek private instruction at the pro shop, which also accommodates your fashion and equipment needs.

Tennis enthusiasts enjoy the Tennis Center, which includes eight Har-Tru courts and two all-weather courts (two courts are lighted for evening play), as well as a well-stocked pro shop. The resident pro can assist in improving your swing in either private lessons or clinic programs.

For hikers and nature lovers, several trails wind around the lakes and through the woods; along the Fairfield Lake Trail, information plaques describe the plants and wildlife of the area. Trek around Whitewater Falls, at 435 feet the highest waterfall in the eastern United States. At the Equestrian Center you can engage a mount for a group-escorted trail ride.

For an unusual afternoon outing, you might consider gem mining. In the late 1800s the land was mined quite successfully—after all, that's where the name comes from. While you might not bring home a sapphire or a ruby, you'll no doubt have a fun excursion. Check with the Recreation Department for mining tips and equipment.

Swimmers can opt for a dip in one of the lakes or in the indoor and outdoor heated pools located at the Recreation Center. Lake Fairfield is also the setting for boating expeditions; canoes, paddleboats, rowboats, and fishing boats can be acquired on a rental basis. Fishermen head to the lakes or a quiet mountain stream for fine trout fishing. A North Carolina license is required; obtain one in Cashiers.

At the Recreation Center you'll also find basketball, volleyball, table tennis, swimming pools, miniature golf, a game room, an exercise room, Jacuzzi, and a sauna. In winter the Recreation Center Ski Lodge becomes the focus of snow activities. Two main trails, one for beginners and one for intermediate, are covered by snowmaking and lighted for evening skiing; group and private lessons are taught at the ski school. Snowboarding and tubing have been added for more variety.

Many visitors reserve time for sight-seeing in the area. The Biltmore House and Gardens, along with its winery, certainly warrant a side trip, as do the Great Smoky Mountain Railway or the Cherokee Indian Reservation. Monday through Friday the resort schedules van trips. Local mountain crafts can be purchased in Cashiers and Highlands.

The Community Center is open from 9:00 A.M. to 8:00 P.M. There are socials, television viewing rooms, a gift shop, trip and event reservations, table tennis, the nature center, board games, puzzles, book exchange, and area information. The Starlab Dome, a portable planetarium, allows you to view the stars and constellations, and then enjoy a laser show. Sapphire Valley is making an effort to add more evening activities and special events such as summer concerts and weekly comedy nights.

70 Sapphire Valley Road
Sapphire, North Carolina 28774
(828) 743–3441, (800) 533–8268
www.fairfieldsapphirevalley.com,
www.sapphirevalleyresort.com

THE GREENBRIER

White Sulphur Springs, West Virginia

The Greenbrier is a 6,500-acre estate in the beautiful Allegheny Mountains. Its history dates back to just after the Revolutionary War, when early settlers discovered the sulfur springs of this area. The grand Georgian architecture of The Greenbrier with its white columned porticoes, elaborate formal gardens, and friendly atmosphere sets the scene for a memorable experience of fine dining, recreation, and relaxation.

The only problem at The Greenbrier may be deciding what to do first. With a list of recreational and social activities a mile long, you may need a personal secretary to help you get organized. When planning events for your stay, though, save time for an escape to discover nature's charms along the enticing woodland trails, well marked for joggers and walkers alike. And pause among the twelve acres of formal gardens, tended meticulously from spring through fall. With a reputation that has attracted presidents and royalty, The Greenbrier provides a level of elegant service and comfort that ensures an unforgettable vacation. It is open year-round.

Accommodations: With rooms and suites in the hotel as well as guest houses and cottages, you have a wide choice of accommodations. The rooms are large and bright, with comfortable, elegant furnishings, and each one is unique in both decor and configuration. Based on a Modified American Plan, daily rates for a standard room are $237 to $324 (depending on the season) per person, double occupancy; larger rooms and prime locations command slightly higher rates, up to $398 for a junior suite. There is no per-person charge for children seventeen and under occupying the same room as their parents and breakfast and dinner are complimentary for children. However, all guests over the age of four pay a daily service charge of $28. The guest cottages include one to four bedrooms, a living room, and a porch or patio; many have fireplaces. Daily rates per person, in a one-bedroom, range from $316 to $436; two bedrooms are $264 to $362, Modified American Plan. Cribs are provided at no extra charge. With the Family Package, children seventeen and under may stay free (taxes and service charges apply) in the room or may have their own room at a special per room rate; adults pay the per-person daily rate, and up to four children may stay in the second room at one-half the cost of the adult room. Breakfast and dinner are always included for everyone. April 1 to October 31 is high season. Accommodations for single parents are well priced in spring and fall ($286), but rates rise sharply ($542 to $598) in summer.

Dining: The Greenbrier boasts exciting culinary experiences. Regional Southern specialties, such as spoon bread and fresh trout from the nearby mountain streams, as well as Continental dishes, make dining a special part of a visit here. The sumptuous breakfasts, featuring homemade biscuits and country ham, are a real treat. A Modified American Plan is required for all guests. A coat and tie are standard attire for gentlemen at dinner in the main dining room; live piano and violin music accompany dinner. Chef Peter Timmins is one of only fifty-nine certified master chefs in the world, so prepare your palate!

The main dining room serves breakfast and six-course dinners; for a la carte dining

April through October, the Tavern Room provides a sophisticated setting and gourmet dining, along with a wine bar. Sam Snead's at the Golf Club is a casual dining option to the elegant main dining room, showcasing panoramic golf course views and an open kitchen, where you can watch the food being prepared. It is included on the meal plan for dinner; lunch is a la carte. Slammin' Sammy's is a sports lounge (with ultralarge TV and pocket billiards) and good-time entertainment spot with a daytime a la carte menu. Both are open only in summer. The Rhododendron Spa Cafe, located adjacent to the indoor pool, offers a light, spa cuisine lunch menu, smoothies, fresh juices, and snacks. Drapers Cafe—especially popular for its homemade ice cream—is convenient for light meals, snacks, and pastries throughout the day. Complimentary afternoon tea is served daily with musical accompaniment. In the elegant and warm Old White Lounge, guests gather at 5:00 P.M. for cocktails and complimentary hors d'oeuvres and later for music and dancing until closing.

Children's World: From Memorial Day through Labor Day and at the holiday times of Thanksgiving, Christmas, and Easter, the Greenbrier Adventure Zone more than fills the days of three- to twelve-year-olds. During the summer elementary-school teachers and child-development specialists supervise full-day and evening programs for Discoverers (ages three to five), Explorers (ages six to eight), and Expeditioners (ages nine to twelve), combining intellectual enrichment with outdoor activities. Creative Classrooms, an innovative series of hands-on workshops designed with Carnegie Hall, West Virginia, include mask magic, puppet making, basketry, art history, and more; drama and stagecraft classes are taught by staff and performers of the Greenbrier Valley Theatre. Along with the usual swimming,

tennis, golf, nature hikes, and fishing, children can experience falconry, carriage rides, or visits to the stables and fire station. Full-day programs run from 9:00 A.M. to 4:00 P.M. The fee is $56 a day for your first child and $46 a day for each additional child.

From 6:30 to 10:00 P.M. for $46 first child, $31 each additional child, children ages six to twelve years old can join their counselors for dinner and an evening of bowling, board games, or movies. Babysitting services for younger children are also available at an average hourly rate of $8.00 for the first child, $2.00 each additional child. So it's possible for grown-ups to arrange an evening or two for wining and dining. Teens have the option of hikes, kayak trips, mountain biking, and even spa treatments designed especially for them.

Recreation: Avid golf and tennis players are well served at The Greenbrier. The Allegheny hills provide the beauty and the challenge of three eighteen-hole championship golf courses, one of which was redesigned in 1979 by Jack Nicklaus. The Greenbrier Sam Snead Golf Academy provides golfers of all skill levels the opportunity to improve their game. The academy provides professional teaching staff and state-of-the-art equipment and services.

The staff at the tennis pro shop can assist in finding partners on one of the five outdoor or five indoor courts. You may also confront the idiosyncrasies of your swing during instructional videotaped replays of your performance.

Kate's Mountain is the picturesque site of the Gun Club, with its four trap and skeet fields. Group tournaments can be organized, or perhaps you'll take in the action from the sidelines in the Clubhouse lounge. The Falconry Academy allows guests to interact with this exciting sport.

Fishing enthusiasts head for the well-stocked streams and lakes, while swimmers can work out in the indoor or outdoor pool or relax poolside. An exercise room is adjacent to the indoor swimming pool. The bowling center (eight lanes), table tennis, horseback riding, shuffleboard, horseshoes, croquet, bicycling, carriage rides, and movies offer additional diversions. The five hiking trails are graded by length and rise in elevation. One of the two jogging trails features twelve exercise stations. Winter brings snow hiking and sleigh rides. Downhill skiing is ninety minutes away at the Snowshoe Ski Resort.

And when the body wearies and the spirits droop, the only respectable place to be is the Spa, which pampers guests with mineral baths, massage, steam, and sauna facilities. It was the sulfur water with its medicinal and recuperative powers that first attracted visitors to this region. For shoppers, a fine selection of fashions, jewelry, handcrafts, and gifts is presented in the Gallery of Shops.

---

300 West Main Street
White Sulphur Springs, West Virginia 24986
(304) 536–1110, (800) 453–4858
www.greenbrier.com

THE GROVE PARK INN RESORT AND SPA

Asheville, North Carolina

The scenery and climate of the Blue Ridge Mountains have long attracted visitors to Asheville. The Grove Park Inn, located on the western slope of Sunset Mountain, opened its doors to guests in 1913 and gives a feeling of pure country in the midst of the city, with grand vistas of mountains and green golf courses. Built of granite from the nearby Sunset Mountain and dedicated to preserving a gracious early-twentieth-century atmosphere, the inn was added to the National Register of Historic Places in 1973. Its guest list over the years reads somewhat like a who's who: Thomas Edison, Henry Ford, Woodrow Wilson, Enrico Caruso, Béla Bartók, and President and Mrs. Franklin Roosevelt. History buffs will have a fine time wondering which room General Pershing slept in or if F. Scott Fitzgerald sat by the fireplace in the Great Hall sipping an after-dinner brandy. The

fireplace there, by the way, is so huge that an adult can walk into it!

The resort's country club (originally the Swannanoa Hunt Club that began in 1893) and the inn were renovated in the late 1980s. Two wings, which complement the architectural style and materials of the main building, were added. The four-diamond, three-star Grove Park Inn is open year-round.

Accommodations: Both the historic main inn and the wings house 510 guest rooms, all refurbished within 2003–2005; those offering panoramic mountain views enchant many a guest. There are theme suites and an exclusive club floor if your entourage warrants the space or additional amenities. In the historic inn rooms, a small refrigerator keeps children's drinks and snacks chilled and close at hand. Panorama Corner rooms are more spacious, with superb views, and are ideal for families. Rates range from $115 to $385 for a double room; a one-bedroom suite is $500 to $1,250. Value season is January through March, while June through October is peak season, with the highest rates. Rates are EP, although meal plans are available if desired. Various packages are also available; ask about rates. Children under sixteen stay free in their parents' room; cribs and rollaway beds are available at no cost.

Dining: A full range of refreshments, from snacks and sandwiches to full-course meals, is offered. Enjoy breakfast, lunch, and dinner in the glass-enclosed terrace of the Blue Ridge Dining Room. Casual during the day, collared shirts and long pants are requested in the evening. One of the South's most famous and popular outdoor dining verandahs, the Sunset Terrace offers majestic views and sunsets over the city skyline and mountains, serving prime rib and fresh seafood for lunch and dinner; in the evening dinner music and dancing are added. In the winter months, it simply moves inside, still with lovely views. Breakfast with a view of the mountains and Asheville skyline at the Magnolia Grill, and then have a casual lunch by the waterfall at the Spa Cafe or at the Pool Cabana, adjacent to the golf course and outdoor pool at the Country Club. Sample the award-winning gourmet cuisine at Horizons, a four-diamond-rated restaurant; jackets required. In the evening you can enjoy your favorite beverage in the old-world charm of the Great Hall Bar, along with hot hors d'oeuvres and live music nightly.

Children's World: Monday through Friday from Memorial Day through Labor Day, and on Saturdays year-round, the inn organizes children ages four to twelve in Cubs Adventure Camp, a fully supervised program. Full days are 9:00 A.M. to 4:00 P.M. ($55 including lunch); half-day camps

run from 9:00 A.M. to noon or 1:00 to 4:00 P.M. ($30 with snack or $40 with lunch). Usual activities include theme days, swimming, nature hikes, and arts and crafts. "Kid's Night Out" ($30) provides a "night out" for kids and parents alike from 6:00 to 10:00 P.M. on Monday through Thursday during summer. Available Fridays and Saturdays year-round, activities include dinner, night swimming (there's an indoor pool), organized games, face-painting, campfires, and movies for $35. If you prefer, the concierge desk will provide a list of individual babysitters, with varying fees.

Recreation: An eighteen-hole Donald Ross championship golf course meanders down the gentle mountain slope. Practice your backhand on one of the six tennis courts (three outdoor, three indoor). The staff in the tennis and golf pro shops can assist you with your playing and fashion needs. An indoor Sports Complex has racquetball and tennis courts, weight and exercise rooms, and a fully equipped aerobics room with professionally taught classes. There are also indoor and outdoor pools available for hotel guests. And remember to make time for a walk down the garden paths and nature trails, also suitable when the urge to jog hits you. The Grove Park Inn was created as an idyllic retreat, a place for total relaxation; the addition of the spa in 1998 simply enhanced that lofty goal. Beautifully designed, it is open to the sun, yet protected, while waterfalls and pools add to the serenity. Allow yourself to just stop—and enjoy. The access fee of $50 can be applied 100% toward services.

Nearby you can explore the lake or try your hand at fishing, horseback riding, cycling, mountain biking, white-water rafting, ballooning, or llama trekking. In the winter a day of skiing (cross-country or downhill) is a popular excursion. For souvenirs, you'll discover unique items at the resort's six gift shops as well as many crafts shops and potteries in the area. The Biltmore Estate is only 8 miles from the inn; an afternoon can be well spent discovering the art, antiques, winery, and formal gardens of this magnificent old estate. Strolling the streets and shops of Asheville provides hours of diversion.

290 Macon Avenue
Asheville, North Carolina 28804
(828) 252–2711, (800) 438–5800
www.groveparkinn.com

HIGH HAMPTON INN & COUNTRY CLUB
Cashiers, North Carolina

The verdant Blue Ridge Mountains provide a beautiful setting, and High Hampton Inn, located in the Cashiers Valley at an altitude of 3,600 feet, allows its guests an escape to clean, crisp air, clear mountain lakes, and tall pine trees. Some people like the ambience of a country inn—quiet, friendly, with rustic accommodations and good home-style cooking. Others like the atmosphere of a resort, with lots of activities and events and busy days and nights. Happily, High Hampton has managed to blend the best of both these worlds. Roam over the 1,400 acres and explore the beauties of nature in the southwest corner of North Carolina. Dating from the mid-nineteenth century, High Hampton was once the summer home of Confederate General Wade Hampton and remained in the Hampton family until the 1920s. The inn is on the National Register of Historic Places.

For more than seventy-eight years, under the continuing ownership of the McKee family, the inn has welcomed guests to an informal atmosphere for golf, tennis, swimming, fishing, and simple relaxing. The architecture of the inn is charming and rustic, blending with the natural surroundings. The wide porches filled with plants and the lobby's stone chimney with four fireplaces hint at the warmth and friendly spirit within. The inn is open only from mid-April to mid-November, with a famous Thanksgiving Houseparty to close the season.

Accommodations: The 117 rooms at the inn (some of which are suites) are simple, warm, and rustic; the knotty pine walls and mountain-style furniture echo the landscape and the crafts of the region. Many of the rooms have very pleasant views of the grounds and there are no telephones or televisions in the rooms. What a way to relax! Several cottages are nestled into the mountain landscape. Based on a Full American Plan, daily rates are $96 to $120 per person midweek, $102 to $130 on Friday and Saturday; children three and under are free; ages four to eight are $40 to $50; older children are $66 to $75. Cribs are available for infants and toddlers at no charge. A number of privately owned homes are also available; these are fully equipped, with fireplace, deck, laundry, and kitchen. Choose from two to four bedrooms with no meals, but with daily maid service, for $290 to $514 a day. If you choose not to cook, a Full American Plan is available for $45 per person per day, or $23 for children under nine years. For one-week stays a discount of 5% on daily rates is given.

Dining: The one dining room at the inn specializes in regional Southern cooking, and service is buffet style. Imagine down-home favorites like country ham, fresh local trout, cream of peanut soup, homemade biscuits, and vegetables fresh from the garden. The Overlook Cafe, next to the Pro Shop, serves light lunches, continental breakfast for early birds, and everyone's favorite—ice cream and sweets. Coats and ties are standard attire for men in the evening, as High Hampton clings to traditional ways. Afternoon tea is served daily in the lobby with cakes and socializing.

Wine and beer only are served in the dining room, but mixed drinks are served at the Rock Mountain Tavern, a popular spot to gather, listen to music, meet other guests, and line up partners for bridge or tennis; coat and tie after 6:30 P.M. Movies, lobby games, bridge, and mountain hayrides fill the evening. Small groups of guests may gather on porches to compare notes, sip their own drinks, and talk about the day.

Children's World: Kids have their own building at High Hampton, called Noah's Ark, where youngsters ages three to twelve meet with counselors for daily activities such as arts and crafts, games, tennis, nature studies, and hiking. Offered from June 1 through Labor Day, the program runs from 9:00 A.M. to 2:00 P.M. and includes lunch. After a free afternoon children can rejoin their group at 6:00 P.M. for dinner (sometimes a hayride and cookout!) and games, movies, and stories until 9:00 P.M. The fee is $3.50 an hour per child. Babysitters are available for wee ones and for nights after 9:00 P.M.

While there's no swimming pool, a restricted, shallow area of the lake with a sandy beach is especially designed for young children. The area includes a toddlers' playhouse, swings, seesaw, and jungle gym, keeping the little ones amused for hours.

Rather than a teen club, High Hampton has the Gathering Place. Here, the next generation can gather to socialize and enjoy the pool table, table tennis, and video games. Outdoor activities such as volleyball, boating excursions, and picnics or mountain hikes are planned and enjoyed by all.

Recreation: The mountain terrain and picturesque scenery make golf a challenge and a pleasure. The eighteen-hole course, designed by George Cobb, is carved on a gently rolling plateau, skirting lakes and weaving through white pine and hemlock. There are two putting greens and a practice range; lessons are available.

The tennis center encompasses six outdoor clay courts, a pro shop, and a practice area; clinics and private lessons are offered. You pay court fees and greens fees unless you are on a four- or seven-day golf or tennis package.

There are three mountain lakes, but the thirty-five-acre Hampton Lake is the center of activity, where paddleboats, canoes, rowboats, and sailboats can be rented. Blissfully, motorboats are not allowed. These clear waters are not just for invigorating swims and peaceful excursions. When the fishing mood strikes, you'll be happy to know that one of the lakes has rainbow and brook trout; bass and bream can also be lured from the waters.

Discover the rich natural beauty of these surroundings on one of the eight major hiking trails. Or take to the mountain trails—in 1½ hours you can climb to the 4,618-foot summit of Chimney Rock for absolutely spectacular views. Take the ten-station Fitness Trail to the base of Rock Mountain. Weekly guided half-day hikes with picnic lunch and walking sticks provide yet another diversion. In a more leisurely manner, lawn sports such as badminton, croquet, shuffleboard, and archery may attract you, or maybe you'll be drawn to the gardens for a stroll among the dahlias, mountain laurel, rhododendron, and azaleas.

The inn occasionally holds workshops in such diverse areas as bridge, fly-fishing, quilting, watercolor painting, and investments—what a pleasant way to glean helpful hints on a variety of topics! While proud of its facilities, the High Hampton Inn mostly boasts of its friendly atmosphere, its low-key pace, and the serenity and beauty of its natural setting. It is also proud that High Hampton "is not for everyone." But those who stay return year after year, and their children bring their own children. It's that kind of place.

P.O. Box 338, 1525 Highway 107 South Cashiers, North Carolina 28717 (828) 743–2411, (800) 334–2551 www.highhamptoninn.com

THE HOMESTEAD
Hot Springs, Virginia

Few classic institutions in the United States have captured the attention of vacationers for many centuries. With all its charm and grace, The Homestead ranks as one of these. Its fascinating history has roots in the 1700s, and yes, George Washington visited here (1755 and 1756), yet The Homestead has moved into this century with style, preserving an atmosphere of friendly Southern elegance. As with several fine old resorts in this country, the medicinal quality of mineral springs first attracted people to the site of The Homestead. In fact, the real history dates back to 7,000 B.C. when prehistoric peoples began using the famous springs. While The Spa is still a captivating diversion for guests, many recreational facilities have been developed over the years, with golf being the premier sport here.

The current hotel was built in 1902, with additions continuing into the late 1920s. Despite almost three decades of construction, The Homestead is a cohesive, majestic structure of red brick and white columns in Georgian style. At an elevation of 2,300 feet, the estate sprawls over 15,000 acres (yes—15,000!) of the Allegheny Mountains in western Virginia. It is open year-round.

Accommodations: The Homestead boasts almost 500 bright and spacious rooms, all recently renovated. Almost every room offers views of the surrounding Allegheny Mountains. Each wing of this National Historic Monument has its own theme. Sizes vary from traditional rooms to parlor rooms and suites; the rate is determined by the size of the room and its location. Based on a Modified American Plan, the rate for a superior double room from May through July and September through October is $239 to $275 per person per day; weekend rates are the highest. The rates are slightly lower November through March and August ($155 to $215), except during the holiday seasons. There is no charge for children under five and no additional charge for cribs and rollaways. Children ages five to twelve pay $47 each for meals and ages thirteen and over pay $70. The Modified American Plan rates include the room, breakfast and dinner daily, valet parking, swimming, afternoon tea, evening movies, hiking trails, and the fitness center. Separate fees are charged for all other activities, and family packages are available.

Dining: Dining at The Homestead is special. Imagine baked apples and kippered herring for breakfast; consider lunches and dinners that feature local favorites such as Smithfield ham, rainbow trout from nearby mountain streams, and fresh turnip greens, as well as fine international cuisine. The sublime creations of pastries, sorbets, and fresh fruit tarts should not be missed.

The Dining Room is open year-round and requests jackets and ties for gentlemen in the evenings. During the April through October season, the 1766 Grille features fine dinner dining with French and American cuisine in an intimate atmosphere. Jackets required, and a $20 per person surcharge applies. Four miles south of The Homestead, the seasonal Cascades Club Restaurant offers a casual lunch dining atmosphere for golfers just finishing their round. During warmer months, the Cottage Café serves lunch and sweets in a 1950s soda-fountain atmosphere. The Casino Club Restaurant, also seasonal, features a hearty lunch menu in a casual setting overlooking the swimming pool, tennis courts, and lawn game area. During the summer the Casino is also open on Friday and Saturday evenings for dinner. Sam Snead's Tavern serves history along with tavern favorites for lunch or dinner. Located across the street from the resort in a late-nineteenth-century building, it provides a bit of local color. In winter the Mountain Lodge Restaurant is a cozy getaway for skiers and nonskiers alike. Choose the elegant Presidents Lounge for pre- and post-dinner cocktails or The Players Pub for tuning in to all the sports action, darts, billiards, and dancing to Top 40 music while drinks and snacks are served continually. Or do both!

Picnic lunches can also be prepared if you choose to spend the day outdoors in the wooded mountains.

A time-honored custom at The Homestead is Afternoon Tea, served daily at 4:00 P.M. in the Great Hall. In an elegant setting graced by chandeliers and Corinthian columns, you can relax to soft piano music while sipping tea.

Children's World: Headquartered in their own Clubhouse on Cottage Row, The Homestead offers excellent daily year-round supervised activities for ages three to twelve. The Kids Club runs from 9:00 A.M. to 4:00 P.M. daily (only to 12:30 P.M. on winter Sundays); it is licensed through the Commonwealth of Virginia Department of Social Services and is a member of the National Association of the Education for Young Children and the Virginia Fine Arts Museum. "Learning through Fun" is the program's goal—kids love the "fun" aspect of the program, and parents (and kids!) like the "learning" part. Activities follow three areas: children's literary and storytelling, science and biology, and art and design. These themes weave through both indoor and outdoor activities and provide a seamless experience for kids.

The outdoor playground has been completely renovated, and children have their own fishing pond—great for kids of all ages. Other activities, even if children choose not to join Kids Club, include tennis on special minicourts, bowling, swimming, hiking, mountain biking, hand-led horseback rides, and exotic falconry demonstrations. In the winter, kids learn to ski at the Bunny School, and enjoy winter sports such as ice-skating, snowboarding, and snow tubing. Costs are $55 for a full day ($27 for additional children in the same family); $35 for a half day with lunch or $30 for half day with no lunch. On Friday and Saturday evenings in the summer (Saturday evenings only in the winter), Children's Dinner Programs are held from 6:30 to 10:30 P.M.; the cost is $25 per child on MAP plans, and $35 per child with no meal plan. Babysitting requires a two-hour minimum and is $12.00 an hour for the first child and $2.00 for each additional child in the immediate family. Club H caters to teenagers' desires for a "cool place to chill" in their own space, and has some activities if at least four teens can be corralled.

Recreation: Even golf and tennis have hundred-year-old histories at The Homestead. There are three eighteen-hole golf courses, and the fact that native son Sam Snead started his golfing career here adds a certain panache to the atmosphere and lends credence to the caliber of play. The Old Course was opened in 1892 and revamped in the 1920s when a second course, the Cascades, was added. Robert Trent Jones designed the third course, the Lower Cascades, which opened in 1963. All three courses weave through a picturesque wooded landscape. With a putting green, a practice fairway, a pro shop, and lessons available, you have all the necessary ingredients to improve your game.

Tennis also got under way here in 1892. Today The Homestead has six courts, including two Har-Tru courts and four clay courts. Two tiers of courts are laid out to give your game privacy plus a spectacular view of The Homestead tower and the mountain valley. Tennis lessons can be scheduled, and the tennis shop is well equipped.

The facilities at The Spa include massage, aromatherapy, mineral baths, skin therapies, aerobics classes, and indoor and outdoor swimming pools. The beautiful indoor pool, built in 1903, is fed by the naturally warm mineral water of the nearby hot springs. There may be no proven miraculous powers in the famous mineral waters, but the benefits of a spa regimen to both body and spirit are not to be questioned.

For fans of trap and skeet, there are four fields; instruction is offered so that even novices can try this sport. Other outdoor sports include horseback riding in the wooded countryside, canoeing and kayaking, trout and fly fishing in the Cascades Stream, and hiking or biking on the 100 miles of mountain trails. A guided hike through the Cascades Gorge is very popular. Or you may prefer to enjoy the scenery during a carriage ride in an old-fashioned buckboard or a surrey with fringe. The tractor-driven hayride to a secluded bonfire is a great family activity.

Some more-unique activities are paintball games for ages twelve and up, on a special course; mountain boarding; extreme golf; touring the unique caves in the area; a challenge course (see how much you trust your family members!); and falconry, with a history stretching back nearly 4,000 years. Lessons are available, and you even get a photograph with the hunting bird. Or opt for bowling, table tennis, billiards, or card and board games. In the evenings go dancing or take in a movie.

Winter sports are limited, but The Homestead does have ten downhill ski runs, open mid-December through March. With a vertical drop of just 700 feet, it cannot offer the diversity and challenge that a good skier or snowboarder seeks, but it may be a fun place for kids to learn, and it does provide an added dimension to a winter vacation. A ski school and bunny school get you started. Near the lodge, which houses a restaurant, the ski school, and ski shops, is an Olympic-size skating rink; skating lessons are offered. A snowboard park with half-pipe, jumps, and moguls as well as tubing, offers more fun in the snow. Cross-country skiers can explore acres of mountain meadows and trails, weather permitting, of course.

Nearby explore Monticello, home of Thomas Jefferson, and Montpelier, home of James Madison. George Washington and Thomas Jefferson National Forests are also in the area.

1766 Homestead Drive
Hot Springs, Virginia 24445
(540) 839–1766, (800) 838–1766
www.thehomestead.com

HYATT REGENCY CHESAPEAKE BAY
Cambridge, Maryland

Hyatt's Golf Resort, Spa, and Marina fit beautifully on the Choptank River on Maryland's eastern shore. This is the perfect spot for visiting wildlife refuges with two nearby, and the Heron Point Wildlife Refuge on the resort property. Cambridge is Maryland's second-largest deepwater port, and 1,700 miles of shoreline wind around the area. It's only an hour from urban Baltimore, but the 342 landscaped acres and the river make it feel like the country.

Accommodations: Four hundred luxurious rooms, including sixteen suites, all with balcony or patio area and minirefrigerators, and the style and amenities one expects from Hyatt. Winter is low season, when rates begin at $149; June to October rates range from $225 to $405. Packages are available; for example Sunshine on Sale includes the third night free in winter, the fourth night free in summer. The Family Plan offers the second room at half price, year-round.

Dining: Feasting on the local specialties is practically a requirement of your visit. Soft-shell crab, Maryland blue crab, Blue Pointe oysters, and rockfish are popular menu items, creatively prepared and presented. At Water's Edge Grill, enjoy breakfast, lunch, and dinner while watching it happen at the display kitchen. Outdoor dining may be enjoyed seasonally on the screened porch overlooking the crescent pool. At the far end of the resort overlooking the marina, sunsets and seafood specialties are equally famous at Blue Pointe Provisions, a freestanding restaurant almost on the banks of the Choptank River. The Eagle's Nest Bar and Grille, also on River Marsh Marina, is by the Golf Club, with scenic views of the greens. Perfect for sandwiches, wraps, and salads as well as nineteenth-hole libations. Dock's poolside bar personally serves you refreshments at any of the four pools, the beach, or even the hot tub. Stock up on snacks and provisions at either the Bay Country Market or the Quarterdeck Marina Store. Mitchener's Library, in the lobby, would do the famous author of *Chesapeake* proud. Stone fireplaces border a two-story glass wall with spectacular views, and outside benches invite you to tarry amid fountains or warm yourself at the fire pit. Little nooks, named after people connected to Cambridge history, like Harriet Tubman, King Ababaco, and Annie Oakley, provide cozy spots for reading, billiards, or just curling up next to the fireplace.

Children's World: Camp Hyatt at Pirate's Cove offers fully supervised fun for kids ages four to twelve daily from Memorial Day to Labor Day and on holidays and weekends year-round. Kids have their own reception desk, activity room, a multimedia room, and even an enclosed outdoor playground adjacent to the center. A long list of activities includes crabbing (of course, this is Maryland!), building sand castles, treasure hunts, kite contests, tennis, golf, and nature hikes. Indoors, kids color, play board games, and participate in arts and crafts, shell art, and storytelling, just to mention a few activities. The split-level pool is always an attraction, and is partially indoors for inclement weather. A full day with lunch, from 9:00 A.M. to 4:00 P.M., is $52.00; half-day morning or afternoon is $28.00 per child and $5.00 for lunch. Evening sessions run from 6:00 to 9:00 P.M. for $35 per child, so parents are able to have their own "night out."

Recreation: The Golf Club at River Marsh, an eighteen-hole championship course designed by Keith Foster, has an elaborate driving range, chipping and putting greens, and a pro shop. Don't know where to park your boat? The 150-slip marina should solve that problem. Relax by any of the four pools, both indoors or outdoors and on several levels. The Wintergarden pool is glass-enclosed, providing year-round enjoyment and views of the river. The volleyball court on the beach is fenced, so you don't have to chase those missed balls too far. The Stillwater European Health Spa offers twelve treatment rooms with unique indigenous spa treatments, and you can get or stay in shape at the fitness and aerobics center. Four lighted tennis courts also give a good workout, and jogging and walking trails wend through the eighteen-acre Heron Point Wildlife Refuge, where you might see an American bald eagle or a blue heron. Nearby visit Taylor's Island Wildlife Refuge, Blackwater Wildlife Refuge, or the Harriet Tubman Museum for a bit of local history.

100 Heron Boulevard
Cambridge, Maryland 21613
(410) 901–1234, (800) 233–1234
www.chesapeakebay.hyatt.com

KIAWAH ISLAND GOLF RESORT
Kiawah Island, South Carolina

In climate and scenery, the islands off the coast of the Carolinas offer some of the finest resort living. Set amid 10,000 acres, at Kiawah Island Resorts the beauty of the natural setting has been carefully respected, while man-made amenities have been added to provide visitors with the best in comfort, relaxation, recreation, and fun. The name Kiawah (KEE-a-wah) comes from the Indians who lived, hunted, and fished here prior to the 1600s when Charles Town was settled. An island with 10 miles of beach on the Atlantic Ocean, Kiawah is actually two resort villages, each with its own lodging and recreational facilities; and a new luxury hotel opened in 2004, The Sanctuary, which declares itself the finest oceanfront hotel built on the East Coast in the past twenty years. A shuttle bus connects the areas, the only resort/developments on the island.

West Beach Village (which dates from 1976) consists of the Kiawah Island Inn, condominiums, restaurants, a racquet club, shops, pools, and a golf course. At East Beach Village (the younger by five years), there are condominiums, restaurants, shops, a golf course, a tennis club, and Night Heron Park, a twenty-one-acre recreation area that encompasses pools, a lake, playgrounds, and picnic sites.

All these conveniences and amenities, and yet you still have the opportunity to feel close to nature. The sound ecological planning at Kiawah has preserved the lagoons and marshes and ensured homes for deer, raccoon, egrets, and brown pelicans; you might even get to see a loggerhead sea turtle, alligators, dolphins, or an eagle. The drive from the Charleston Airport is about forty-five minutes. As you enter the main gates to Kiawah, you'll be given a car registration pass that reads "Please respect the wildlife that inhabits Kiawah Island. Alligators are potentially dangerous and extremely fast. They should never be fed or teased in any way." When you see alligators plying the lagoon waters, you'll understand this warning.

Accommodations: The Sanctuary (877–683–1234) is Kiawah's newest, a most luxurious oceanfront hotel, with 255 rooms and suites, two elegant restaurants, and a nature-based spa. In addition to the ocean, two mineral spas, an indoor pool, a family pool, children's wading pool, and the adults-only oceanfront pool provide all the water you want. Built to resemble a Southern mansion, the lobby boasts walnut floors and Italian crystal chandeliers; even live oaks dripping Spanish moss have been imported to frame the driveway. Rooms are spacious (520 to 560 square feet), with multiple amenities, such as balconies, marble baths, and custom bedding. Winter rates begin at $243 non-ocean, $288 ocean view, and $364 for oceanfront; these same rooms in summer begin at $430, $505, and $595. Club level accommodations invite guests to enjoy a private concierge, continental breakfast, midday snack, and evening cordials and chocolates

in the Club Lounge. Available in summer only, rates range from $535 to $765.

If high-rise is not your style, choose from a villa or private home. The condominium villas, cedar-shingled or natural-wood frame structures, are dispersed throughout the island in different settings appealing to all different interests. You may choose one with an ocean view or one next door to the tennis courts, one alongside the lush green fairways of a golf course, one on a lake, or one nestled among oaks and hickories and sweet gum trees. These one- to four-bedroom units have well-equipped kitchens, and most of them have sundecks or screened porches— terrific spots for having breakfast or just taking in the views. Villas have AAA Four Diamond ratings. One- to seven-bedroom luxury homes are also available.

Rates vary depending on the season and location; one-bedroom villas range from $99 to $169 in winter; $179 to $375 in high summer. Weekly rates for villas are $600 to $2,250. Be sure to ask about any special packages, especially golf, or family specials (800–654–2924) that include many discounts. Cribs are $20 per day or $100 per week in the villas.

Dining: Shrimper's, in West Beach, is a casual dining spot that caters to families; it's open for lunch and dinner and features seafood and sandwiches. Nearby is Scooper's, where the ice cream and pastries are hard to resist (who can pass up an ice-cream flavor called Mississippi Mud?). The Market at Town Center, a casual market, is located in East Beach, offering a variety of quick meals, grocery items, newspapers, apparel, wine, and even take-out pizza.

On Monday evenings, families head to Mingo Point on the Kiawah River for an outdoor barbecue and oyster roast, followed by the down-home music of a bluegrass band. Another favorite is the Thursday Safari Night at Night Heron Park.

The four clubhouses are home to excellent restaurants as well. The Ocean Course Grille, Osprey Point Grill, and Haulover Creek Bar and Grill at Oakpoint serve breakfast and lunch; Turtle Point Sports Bar and Grill is open for lunch and dinner. Salads, seafood, and sandwiches are to be found until 8:00 P.M. poolside at the Night Heron Grill.

The Sanctuary features signature dining in the Ocean Room, with spectacular views; open for dinner only and jackets are required. The Jasmine Porch gives you a Southern experience of fresh local ingredients and traditional Low-Country favorites; serving breakfast, lunch, and dinner in a casual atmosphere with terrace dining an option. The Loggerhead Grill, steps away from the beach, and Beaches and Cream keep you from starvation while playing in the ocean waves or pool. The Morning Room serves afternoon tea (go figure!) and the Lobby Bar invites you to relaxing drinks and live music in the evening.

Freshfields Village, outside the main gate of Kiawah at the crossroads of Kiawah, Seabrook, and Johns Islands, features a Main Street–like collection of more than twenty unique stores and services—from restaurants and a coffee shop to clothing boutiques, a gallery, a bookshop, a general store, a pharmacy, and more. Stop at Newton Farms, a full-service market, or try Hege's for cocktails and French-inspired cuisine made with local fresh ingredients.

Children's World: From early March through Labor Day and at Thanksgiving, Christmas, President's Day, and Easter, children and parents alike find Kiawah Island the perfect destination for a family vacation.

Energetic college students with training in sports and recreation supervise young visitors in activities designed to ensure happy, fun-filled days. In fact, there's much more to do than we have room to outline, so check the Web site for all the details and themed days such as circus, pirates, safari, icky sticky slimy, and more. Kamp Kiawah in the spring season runs Monday through Saturday in March, April, and May, and accepts ages three to eleven. Hours are 8:30 A.M. to 1:30 P.M. for $45, including lunch. Kids Night Out is offered on Monday and Friday from 5:00 to 8:00 P.M., and costs $40, including dinner. In summer Kamp Kiawah is in full swing from Memorial Day through Labor Day, Monday through Saturday; Kids Night Out is again on Monday and Friday, 5:30 to 8:30 P.M., and cost is the same as in spring. As the day lengthens, so does camp, going from 8:30 A.M. to 4:00 P.M.; a full day is $59 with lunch; mornings from 8:30 A.M. to 12:30 P.M. are $39, while afternoons from 1:00 to 4:00 P.M. are $34. Divided into three groups—three to four years, five to seven years, and eight to eleven years—kids enjoy swimming, treasure hunts, crabbing, storytime, and crafts.

Youth activities designed for ages nine to twelve are scheduled at various times; arts and crafts projects, capture the flag, bingo, three on three basketball, paint tag, scavenger hunts, and more occupy youngsters for an hour or two, and range from free to $10 in cost. Teen activities (ages thirteen to seventeen) are similar, but add kayaking adventures ($30), Survivor Night, pool parties, and blacklight volleyball; most are complimentary. Special nature programs with a staff naturalist allow children, teens, and even adults to have a hands-on, fun experience with nature. Ocean seining with a huge 40-foot net, canoe trips through the marshes, pond exploration, night walks on the beach, bird watching—with more than 10,000 acres of marshland and five staff naturalists, the possibilities go on and on. Costs range from $3.00 to $15.00. The Discovery Room at the Sanctuary is an interactive environment that encourages children and adults to explore. Daily themes are enhanced by books, crafts, computer tracks, and even tours; and an on-duty naturalist answers all your questions.

Discovery Series, a free weekly program, features speakers accompanied by live snakes or alligators, fascinating historical tidbits, storytellers, and more. Kiawah has found a successful blend of activities that includes teenagers' favorite things: sports, music, food, and loose structure. Volleyball and basketball tournaments, "teen splash" (pool time only for them), T-shirt graffiti, and a Friday-night dance with DJ are just a sample of the options.

Children also enjoy the playgrounds filled with wooden climbing equipment, swings, and slides; the largest one at Night Heron Park is built in and among the trees, hardly disturbing the natural vegetation. The Night Heron Park Center features video games, live animals, and nature wear and gear, as well as a recreation concierge.

When you want to be together and join other families, afternoon and evening hours are filled with bingo, games, nature films, family movies, and cookouts; most of these activities are free. Particularly fun is the "dive-in movie"—movies shown at the pool, with swimming allowed. Babysitters are available when you want to indulge in a strictly grown-up evening.

Recreation: With five excellent eighteen-hole championship golf courses and a twelve-month golfing season, golfers think they've discovered a little bit of paradise at Kiawah. Host site of the 1991 Ryder Cup, the 1997 World Cup of Golf, and the 2007 PGA Seniors' Tournament, the Ocean Course, designed by Pete Dye, is known worldwide. The Cougar Point Golf Course was designed by Gary Player, the Turtle Point Golf Course by Jack Nicklaus, the Osprey Point Golf Course by Tom Fazio, and Oak Point by Clyde Johnston; talent like this ensures challenge in a beautiful natural

setting. You can enroll in group or private lessons or in a clinic, then practice newly acquired skills on the driving ranges and putting greens. The pro shops are well stocked with equipment, apparel, and accessories to enhance your game.

For tennis enthusiasts, the West Beach Tennis Club offers sixteen courts; the East Beach Tennis Club has twelve courts and a ball machine. Combined, Kiawah boasts twenty-three clay courts and five hard courts. Add a practice alley, resident pros, clinics, and group and private lessons and you have every opportunity to improve your game. In 2004 and 2005 Kiawah was ranked number one on the "Greatest U.S. Tennis Resorts" list by *Tennis* magazine.

Swimmers take to the ocean from April through October or dip into one of the two pools located in Night Heron Park and East Beach Tennis Club. You can sign up for swimming lessons for yourself or your child (even an infant). Other water sports, such as sailing, canoeing, and sailboarding, are also popular.

Bicyclists have more than 10 miles of hard-packed beach and 30 miles of paved trails to explore (rentals, many with baby seats, are available). Joggers find a good workout on the 1.1-mile parcourse fitness trail with twenty exercise stations. Try your luck fishing in the lake or creek and surf casting in the ocean, or introduce your child to the fun of crabbing, where an old chicken neck can net beautiful blue-legged crabs. Adult exercise classes (aerobics and water exercise) are offered weekdays during the summer.

Nature lovers can participate in numerous expeditions into wilderness areas and river tours for a close look at the Low-Country wildlife and vegetation and an education on barrier islands. The Nature Excursion Programs are unique to a barrier island, and more extensive than most resorts. Naturalists conduct marsh creek canoe trips, sea kayaking, birding walks, night beach walks, loggerhead turtle crawls, and even bird tours on bikes.

For unstructured fun, the twenty-one-acre Night Heron Park features basketball courts, a soccer field, swimming pools, a pavilion area, and a bicycle rental shop. Night Heron Park also serves as a popular gathering spot for special events, such as symphony concerts, family park cookouts, and beach music parties.

Over fifteen family activities are scheduled; crafts involve a small fee, others like sand sculpting, poolside games, bingo, and basketball are free. If shopping entices you, the Shops at Kiawah Island and the Town Center at East Beach Village have stores offering clothing, books, stationery, games, toys, jewelry, and gifts. And nearby Charleston (only 21 miles away) can charm you with historic houses and antiques shopping. With all it places at your disposal, Kiawah may tempt you back for many return visits.

---

12 Kiawah Beach Drive
Kiawah Island, South Carolina 29455
(843) 768–2121, (800) 654–2924,
(800) 845–2471 (South Carolina)
www.kiawahresort.com

KINGSMILL RESORT
Williamsburg, Virginia

In 1736, Richard Kingsmill was granted land along the James River near the new town of Williamsburg, Virginia. Centuries later, much remains the same—deer and waterfowl still live in the unspoiled forest, some of the original plantation buildings still exist near prehistoric Native American sites, and nearby Colonial Williamsburg remains as a unique example of eighteenth-century America. Some things, however, have changed. Developed by Anheuser-Busch Companies, the Kingsmill of today shares its natural beauty and sense of history with both a modern-day resort and a separate thriving community of 5,000 people. The 3,900-acre site was originally selected for a new brewery, and part of the agreement was the construction of a theme park, Busch Gardens. Development has been well planned, and none of this impinges on the resort itself.

Environmental awareness is also a priority as 40% of the area remains green space, and future expansion of one area currently depends on a bald eagle nesting in the treetops of fifty-two prime acres near the river, which Kingsmill is preserving. No wonder it has the Audubon International Certification!

Accommodations: Kingsmill offers 435 accommodations, including hotel rooms and villa-style one- to four-bedroom suites. Organized into villa-style clusters around the Resort Center, all are within walking distance of resort facilities. Each suite contains a complete kitchen and living room; many feature fireplace and balcony. Guestroom rates begin at $159 in winter (December, January, February); $229 to $299 March through November. Weekend rates are slightly higher. One-bedroom suites range from $259 to $449; two-bedroom suites are $399 to $729. Special lower rates are available when you purchase certain services, such as tickets to Busch Gardens or Colonial Williamsburg, a round of golf, or spa services. Be sure to check, as these are things you'll probably be doing anyway. March through Labor Day, special rates begin at $699 for a family of four for two nights, three days, theme parks, greens fees, tennis, daily breakfast, and more. Children under eighteen stay free in the room; rollaways are not available. A shuttle operates throughout the property, as well as to the local attractions of Busch Gardens, Water World, and Colonial Williamsburg.

Dining: Six restaurants and lounges offer a variety of styles and menus. Eagles, an authentic steak- and-chophouse, features exclusive beechwood-smoked cooking and hearty meals for breakfast, lunch, and dinner, along with panoramic views of the beautifully landscaped grounds and the river. The Bray Bistro brings past and present together in modern American cuisine served with indigenous ingredients and generous views of the James River. The most casual venue is Regatta's Café and Market, with its open kitchen and fun foods; it also has a deli, to-go selections, and convenience items. The Deck at the Marina is right on the river, with outside dining and a fireplace for cool weather, a seafood bar, sandwiches, drinks, and live entertainment. Bray Landing is the spot to relax for coffee or a drink, while Moody's Tavern is the nighttime gathering place.

Children's World: Make your first stop the sports concierge desk for Junior Guest Registration and everything you need to know about kids at Kingsmill.

Kingsmill Kamp uses the entire resort as a playground for five- to twelve-year-olds. Beach fun, limbo, and tug of war at the Marina; sports of all kinds; tennis and golf (including one-half hour instruction); carnival games; picnics; hiking; and crabbing; even building a bird feeder are some of the activities kids enjoy. Operating Monday through Saturday from mid-June to Labor Day, all programs include lunch and snacks. A full day (9:00 A.M. to 3:30 P.M.) costs $45; a half day is $30. As a special treat, Spa Kamp is ninety minutes of magic manicures, terrific toes, and mini-facials; at $40, it's sure to attract the young females of the species. Kids Night Out is offered Thursday through Saturday in summer and on select Friday nights in spring. It starts with pizza, is filled with fun, games, and crafts, and ends on a tired but happy note at bedtime; for ages four to twelve, $40 per child.

Recreation: Golfers are happy with three eighteen-hole championship courses and a nine-hole par-3 course. Awards are numerous, including *Golf Magazine's* Silver Medal, *Condé Nast's* Top 50 Golf Resorts, and *Golf for Women's* Top 50 Fairways. Pete Dye designed the River Course to challenge professionals but be enjoyable to the average golfer as well; it's characterized by rolling hills, thick woods, and water everywhere. The Plantation Course by Arnold Palmer and Ed Seay is a little more forgiving, but no pushover. The Woods Course, by Curtis Strange and Tom Clark, is a parkland-style course stashed in its own private corner of the resort. The Golf Academy has an extensive program of instruction with a maximum 1:5 teacher-student ratio.

Voted one of the World's Top 75 Tennis Resorts by Tennis Resorts Online, Kingsmill Tennis Club offers instruction academies, events, and packages. Fifteen courts include two lighted stadium courts, two Deco-Turf all-weather courts, and six hydro courts; court time is $10 to $16 per adult for the day.

The fifteen-slip Marina boasts a store, the Deck for dining, a small beach area, and the possibility of meeting visiting boat owners. The Sports Club is where you'll find the indoor and outdoor swimming pools, exercise classes, and fully equipped fitness room, whirlpool, steamroom and sauna, and 4-mile jogging course. Arrange a personal training session, work out, or simply play in the Game Room with billiards, table tennis, and video games. Stop by the concierge desk for the self-guided walking tour that includes all the plants and flowers. The Spa at Kingsmill is a welcoming place for massage, body treatments and wraps, facials, and even a special golfer's manicure.

And, of course, you'll need time for Busch Gardens, Water Country USA, and Colonial Williamsburg. Kingsmill runs frequent shuttles to all of these destinations. All different and all fun for families, you'll find more information on their Web sites. And remember to search for packages that include these attractions, which may be a value for your particular family needs.

1010 Kingsmill Road
Williamsburg, Virginia 23185
(757) 253–1703, (800) 832–5665
www.kingsmill.com

SEABROOK ISLAND CLUB
Seabrook Island, South Carolina

Sunshine and sandy beaches; lazy strolls under moss-draped oaks, palmettos waving in the breeze; enough fresh crabs, shrimp, and oysters to make your mouth water; golf, tennis, horseback riding, marina, fitness center, and water sports—is this a little bit of paradise? Visitors to this unique, private island believe so. Seabrook has the feel of a country club—no neon, no high-rises, not even any hotels! Share nature in harmony with eagles, dolphins, and bobcats, in a place where the beach is private and nothing is higher than two stories. All this is only about thirty minutes from beautiful, historic Charleston; it almost seems as though you can have your cake and eat it too. Activities and events for every member of the family support Seabrook's "something for everyone" philosophy. The resort is open year-round.

Accommodations: The one- to three-bedroom villas—all with fully equipped kitchens, many with sundecks or balconies—are distributed throughout the 2,200 acres of Seabrook Island property. Some are ocean-side, with expansive views of the Atlantic and close to the Beach Club, some line the scenic fairways of the golf courses, and some overlook the racquet club, marshlands, and tidal creeks. Some villa clusters have their own swimming pools. Rates depend on size, location, and time of year. During low season, December to mid-February, one-bedroom villa rates are $143 to $160. The weeks around Easter and early June through early September are high season, $227 to $304. A two-bedroom villa in summer ranges from $277 to $359. Weekly rates are lower, and there is a three-night minimum stay required. Rates are for villa accommodations only; most recreational activities have separate charges. Weekly rates (for six to seven nights) provide a savings, as do tennis, golf, honeymoon, or getaway packages. A family recreation package during June, July, and August is a good value, with 20% discounts on most things, including golf.

Dining: Restaurants are seasonal at Seabrook, so be sure to check specifically during your stay. As a treat from dining in your villa, you'll find hot and cold breakfasts year-round at the Pro Shop Patio Breakfast Bar overlooking the golf courses, and the Seabrook Shoppe in the Beach Club. Spring weekends and summer, also at the Beach Club, you can grab a casual lunch at the Poolside Grill on the deck.

The Island House Restaurant is elegant and offers traditional Southern cuisine and tempting seafood specialties; jackets are preferred for men at dinner. Here you might choose a sweet-potato soufflé or prawns stuffed with crabmeat. Bohickets Lounge has equally good food in a more casual atmosphere overlooking the golf course— you can watch the greens and eat them at the same time! Island House is dinner only, while Bohickets serves lunch, light dinner, and full bar service. Both are open only in fall and winter. Try the famous Seabrook Sunday Brunch at the Island House, a lavish buffet with live entertainment. For steak and seafood and an ocean view, during summer head to the Seaview Restaurant, more informal than the Island House and more family oriented. The Friday seafood buffet is a real extravaganza. All restaurants have children's menus. A friendly atmosphere in which to sip a drink and discuss the day's events is provided at the outdoor Pelicans Nest Bar, Half Shell Lounge, and Bohickets Lounge.

Children's World: From Memorial Day to Labor Day, children ages four to twelve have their own Monday-to-Friday Kids Club recreation program. Meeting from 9:00 A.M. to 12:00 P.M. in the Kids Club, supervised activities include golf and tennis clinics, pony rides, crabbing adventures, swimming, treasure hunts, nature hikes, puppet shows, storytelling, and arts and crafts. The cost is $27 including lunch. A children's playground offers lots of equipment for the younger set.

Wednesday Night Owls features sunset beach walks, games, crafts, and alligator or turtle hunts for four- to twelve-year-olds. Program runs from 6:00 to 9:00 P.M.; cost is $27 and includes dinner. Older children from twelve to nineteen are invited to the Recreation Pavilion every night from 8:30 to 11:00 P.M. This is their own time for video games, pool, table tennis, foosball, air hockey, and socializing. Special theme parties, teen casino night, and even teen cruises are planned. Special nights are also planned for the entire family at a small cost.

The fun keeps on rolling at holiday times like Christmas, Thanksgiving, and Easter. Added to the regular activities may be Christmas caroling and a visit from Santa, The Little Pilgrims Program, or an Easter decorations crafts class and an Easter egg hunt. A day of adventures will give your child fond memories for years to come. With all of this, normal babysitters may seem a bit of a letdown, but they are available.

Recreation: With average midday temperatures of sixty degrees in January and eighty-nine degrees in August, golfing's fine in the Carolinas. Seabrook has two vastly different eighteen-hole courses; Crooked Oaks was designed by Robert Trent Jones Sr. and meanders through majestic oaks and dips along the sea marshes. Ocean Winds, designed by Willard Byrd, catches some of the tricky ocean breezes that make the play challenging and interesting. A fine teaching staff can help you smooth out the rough spots of your game, and the pro shop can fill in the gaps for clothing, equipment, and accessories. Seabrook is the first golf facility in South Carolina recognized as a certified member of the Audubon Cooperative Sanctuary Program for golf courses.

Enjoy one of fifteen clay tennis courts at the Raquet Club. The Raquet Club offers a pro shop and a staff of pros who can do wonders for your backhand in individual or group lessons, camps, and clinics.

With 3½ miles of glorious private ocean beach, you might suspect that water sports tempt many visitors here. There are sunbathing, swimming, ocean fishing, and shelling. Canter along the beach at the edge of the surf or take a leisurely ride through the forests—both are possible at Seabrook, one of the few resorts with an on-site Equestrian Center. The center offers trained instructors who can give you tips to improve your technique. Parent-led pony rides create lots of excitement in the under-eight crowd. A junior Olympic pool, a heated pool, and a wading pool for children more than accommodate both serious swimmers and sun lovers. There's fun for the whole family with Poolside Pandemonium every Monday, Wednesday, and Friday; as well as water basketball and volleyball. With their palm trees, gardens, and lovely surroundings, the pools also charm serious loungers in for just a quick splash. Perhaps you don't want to sing for your supper, but if you want to *catch* your supper, try fishing (in the ocean or the creeks) or crabbing and shrimping in the tidal marshes. Bicycle along the island's 10 miles of roads—many rental bikes come equipped with baby seats—or join the current craze for in-line skating.

The Recreation Pavilion, open year-round, takes care of a lot of your needs (rental beach chairs, in-line skates, bikes, and fishing and crabbing equipment) and is the focus of the Family Fun Program— activities that all the family members can enjoy together, like nature walks, family games, cookouts, bingo, and water volleyball. You may even challenge your child to an evening of video games.

Within 1 mile of Seabrook's gate, stroll the Bohicket Marina for chartered deep-sea fishing, creek fishing, and three family-style restaurants and shops. For the essentials and the fun of shopping, Seabrook has several stores: the Village Market for groceries; the Seabrook Shoppe for gifts, clothing, souvenirs, and sundries; and the golf and tennis shops for the latest fashions and equipment.

Freshfields Village, outside the main gate of Kiawah at the crossroads of Kiawah, Seabrook, and Johns Islands, features a Main Street–like collection of more than twenty unique stores and services—from restaurants and a coffee shop to clothing boutiques, a gallery, a bookshop, a general store, a pharmacy, and more. Stop at Newton Farms, a full-service market, or try Hege's for cocktails and French-inspired cuisine made with local fresh ingredients.

3772 Seabrook Island Road
Seabrook Island, South Carolina 29455
(843) 768–1000, (800) 341–4248
www.discoverseabrook.com

THE TIDES INN

Irvington, Virginia

In eastern Virginia, peninsulas of land reach out like fingers between the many rivers heading into the Chesapeake. It is a region steeped in history, from the early-seventeenth-century settlements of Jamestown and Yorktown to the family homestead of Robert E. Lee. Its people have always had close ties to the water, originally for commerce and travel and today for recreation.

The northernmost of these peninsulas, bounded by the Potomac River and the Rappahannock River, is known as the Northern Neck. On its southern shore, on a bluff overlooking Carter's Creek, sits the Tides Inn. The hotel is surrounded by water, and yachts literally dock in the front yard. A member of the Leading Small Hotels of the World, the Tides emphasizes uncrowded luxury and informal elegance in a leisurely atmosphere. Originally a stop for the steamboat lines between Baltimore and Norfolk in the late 1800s, the nearby small community of Irvington remains a quaint, picture-perfect town with friendly smiles for everyone.

Accommodations: All 106 rooms and suites are newly renovated; many have balconies or terraces and almost all have great views of Carter's Creek. Rooms are located in the Main Building, the Garden House, the Windsor House, and the Lancaster House. Choose from deluxe rooms or premium rooms ($295 to $325), or Vista Suites ($465 to $535). Four luxury suites are also available. Children are free in the room with parents if beds are adequate; cots are $25; cribs are complimentary. A meal plan (breakfast and dinner) is available for $99 per adult, $50 for children

ages ten through fifteen, and children under ten are free per one paying adult. Full American Plan, including lunch, is $120 per adult. The high season at the Tides is May to October; the inn is closed from January to April.

Dining: Breakfast and dinner are served in the Dining Room. Breakfast is from 6:30 to 10:30 A.M., with an "early bird" continental breakfast or a "sleepyhead" breakfast later in the morning. At dinner jackets are required after 5:30 P.M. Just off the main lobby, the Chesapeake Club is open from 11:00 A.M. until 11:00 P.M., serving lunch, dinner, lounge food, and cocktails. Sit inside or out and enjoy the casual setting with nightly entertainment. Creekside, Commodore's is a casual seasonal restaurant for enjoying lunch and sunset drinks overlooking the pool and beach; late dinners are served on weekends. Also seasonal, Cap'n B's on the Golden Eagle Golf Course is open from lunch to sunset. It's a popular spot even with nongolfers, as the 400 rolling acres with lovely lakes and unspoiled woodlands add an extra dimension of pleasure to the New Orleans-style dining. On Saturdays in summer, splurge on a dinner cruise on the Rappahannock River on the historic yacht *Miss Ann*. And finally, if it fits your schedule or your mood, room service or picnic lunches are always options.

Children's World: In addition to the beach and swimming pool, a grassy playground with slides, swings, climbing bars, and the Chesapeake Bay Lighthouse attract young guests. From Memorial Day to Labor Day, the Crab Net Kids children's program is in session daily from 9:30 A.M. to 3:30 P.M., with lunch at the pool and swimming twice a day. All activities are covered for $45 per child per day. Morning sessions with lunch and snack are $30; afternoon sessions with snack only are $25. Crafts and games, scavenger hunts, sand sculpting, tennis, pitch and putt golf, bicycling, boating, and of course, crabbing keep youngsters from four to twelve years old busy. On Friday and Saturday evenings from 5:00 to 9:00 P.M., children meet as a group for dinner and evening activities, such as a "coketails and pizza party," followed by a movie; cost is $40. Babysitting is available at $10.00 an hour for one child with a three-hour minimum; add $1.00 an hour for each additional child.

Recreation: With water on practically all sides of the inn, boating is a natural sport here. The Premier Sailing School offers classes for all ages and experience levels. You can take off in a small craft like a sailboat, canoe, or paddleboat, or check out the yacht program and cruise the creek, the river, and the bay. The weekly routine schedules varied yachts for luncheon cruises, cove cruises, and bay-shore picnics. No additional fees are charged for use of the paddleboats, canoes, kayaks, or some of the yacht programs. In fact, rates include almost all activities—tennis, nine-hole par-3 golf course, bicycles to explore scenic Irvington, evening music and dancing, and the fitness and health facility.

Golf is also available, with twenty-seven holes that skirt the waterways and dip back into the trees. A nine-hole executive course is on the inn's property. A challenging course with more hilly terrain is the championship Golden Eagle, 2½ miles from the inn.

Many of the ponds along the golf courses are well stocked for the fisherman, who may also, in search of a saltwater catch, line up a trip with the dockmaster. A saltwater pool overlooks a small sandy beach, and table tennis, a pool table, video arcade, croquet, basketball, and shuffleboard are available in the activities cottage. For your evening entertainment, enjoy dancing, movies, bingo, or a pleasant stroll. The Chesapeake Club features live entertainment nightly.

For history buffs, nearby sightseeing excursions lead to Stratford Hall Plantation (the birthplace of Robert E. Lee), Wakefield (George Washington's birthplace), Christ Church, and Epping Forest, where George Washington's mother lived. Colonial Williamsburg is just an hour and fifteen minutes away and makes a nice day excursion.

**480 King Carter Drive
Irvington, Virginia 22480
(804) 438–5000, (800) 843–3746
www.tidesinn.com**

WILD DUNES RESORT

Isle of Palms, South Carolina

Have you ever watched a three-year-old scamper across a sandy beach to the ocean? A biker pedal down paths through the marshes? A fishing boat return to harbor after a successful day's mission? A sailboat catch the sun and the wind in one skillful motion? An ace serve zing across the net? Or a golf ball soar over the fairway and over grand oaks on its way to a perfectly manicured green? Award-winning Wild Dunes can package all of these images into quite a family vacation for you.

Wild Dunes has garnered some of the best features of the Carolina coastal islands and wrapped them up into a fine year-round resort. It is recognized by *Better Homes and Gardens* as one of thirty "Favorite Family Resorts." This relaxed and gracious community occupies 1,600 acres of the northern tip of the Isle of Palms, just thirty minutes from historic Charleston. Bounded by the Atlantic Ocean on the east and the Intracoastal Waterway on the west, Wild Dunes delights in mild temperatures, soft ocean breezes, and fresh salt air. Relax and rejuvenate your spirits here in South Carolina's Low Country.

Accommodations: Wild Dunes offers Four Diamond accommodations with the new ninety-three-room Boardwalk Inn, located in the heart of the resort. These luxurious accommodations provide amenities of the finest full-service hotels and access to world-class recreational facilities. From early June until mid-August, daily rates are $190 to $380. Winter and spring nightly rates are $110 to $350. Rates are based on double occupancy. A Victorian-style boardwalk leads from the inn to the villas and the Grand Pavilion with its open-air gazebo, two

oceanfront pools, and 2 miles of sandy beach. The one-, two-, and three-bedroom villas are grouped in two- to five-story buildings. Many are arranged along the beach, some border the tennis center, others look out on the fairways of the golf course, and still more enjoy the seclusion of the woods and marshland scenery. Inside decor ranges from dramatic, bold interiors to soft pastel furnishings that reflect nature's seaside colors; a fully equipped kitchen is standard in every unit. Cribs can be provided for infants and toddlers.

Spring and winter rates for a one-bedroom villa range from $110 to $330; two-bedroom villas range from $165 to $395. Early June to mid-August is high season; rates are $190 to $385 for a one-bedroom and $275 to $525 for a two-bedroom. Ask about weekly rates and special packages.

Private homes are also available. Category and location of a rental property will also determine the price; an oceanfront location commands the highest rate. Included with all rentals are one hour of tennis court time per bedroom per day, guaranteed golf tee times, complimentary one-hour daily family program, access to the Fitness Center, Grand Pavilion, and the Sports Pavilion Swim Center, local phone calls, and on-property transportation. Golf, Town and Country, and Winter Extended Stay packages are available.

Dining: It is not surprising that seafood is highlighted on the menus of Wild Dunes's restaurants; gumbo and she-crab soup are favorite Low-Country dishes. But beef eaters can find tasty, tender selections here too. With the opening of the Boardwalk Inn, Wild Dunes gained a luxurious restaurant. The

Sea Island Grill, serving breakfast, lunch, and dinner, features the freshest seafood available, prepared in myriad ways. Guests may dine in the casually elegant dining room or alfresco on the piazza overlooking a lush tropical environment. Casual dining for breakfast, lunch, and dinner is found at Edgar's Italian Restaurant in the Links Clubhouse. Edgar's offers the flavors of Italy and welcomes families. Both restaurants have children's menus. Entertainment is offered in Edgar's Bar five nights a week, and summer Mondays are Family Nights, when kids are supervised on the patio for dinner, allowing parents to enjoy quiet dining inside. The Grand Pavilion, open only in summer, has early-twentieth-century architecture, an old-fashioned boardwalk, Coney Island-style food, and an airy gazebo. Duney's serves sandwiches, snacks, ice cream, and cocktails by the sea. If you have a hunger attack on either golf course, you're in luck. Hot dogs, sandwiches, and drinks are to be found at the Half-Way House, on the Links. The Dunes Deli & Pizzeria features light fare for breakfast and lunch, as well as limited grocery items, on the Harbor Course. Both are open year-round. At least twelve restaurants offer a variety of dining on nearby Sullivan's Island and the Isle of Palms.

Children's World: Ranked one of the top five by *Tennis* magazine for having the "Best Kids' Program," Wild Dunes knows just how to make your little ones' vacation special. Using college students majoring in recreation and child development, the scheduled activities are both impressive and nonstop. Fun begins in early April to mid-May with Friday night field trips from 6:00 to 9:00 P.M. Dinner and action (putt-putt and go-karts, or bowling and rock climbing) are on the menu; cost is $40 per child. Themed activities on Saturday from 10:00 A.M. to 3:00 P.M. might be sports, island adventures, or wacky water ($35.00

per child plus $5.00 lunch). Wild Dunes's summer program for kids runs from the end of May through Labor Day. Dunes Discovery Club for ages three to five provides structured sessions with two full-time staff members. Parents are welcome to drop in as kids enjoy tumbling, storytime, and arts and crafts. Operating from 10:00 A.M. to 3:00 P.M. Monday, Tuesday, Thursday, and Friday, the cost is $40.00 with lunch for $5.00 extra. Older children, from six to ten years, are part of the Wild Adventure Club, held Monday through Friday (again, no camp on Wednesday), from 10:00 A.M. to 3:00 P.M. Kids enjoy beach games, swimming, crabbing, scavenger hunts, putt-putt golf, and other "wild" adventures including field trips to local parks for water fun, go-karts, or bowling. Cost is $60 when off-resort trips are scheduled. The full-day session costs $40.00, plus $5.00 for lunch. Every Wednesday and Friday, Youth Adventures at the Dunes takes kids eleven and over off resort for exciting adventures. Wednesday from 5:00 to 9:00 P.M. is indoor rock climbing and bowling ($50) and Friday from 10:00 A.M. to 3:00 P.M. finds youngsters at the Whirlin' Waters, the biggest water park in town ($60).

Teens gather on the beach for volleyball or at the Grand Pavilion for live music. They are welcome on the Wednesday and Friday Youth Adventures. Video movies, special pool games, and black-light beach volleyball allow teens to socialize and hang out.

Li'l Dune Bug Club allows younger kids (ages three to ten) to leave their parents at home for a night out to play games, watch movies, and munch goodies. These sessions are held two days a week (Tuesday and Friday) from 6:00 to 10:00 P.M.; the cost is $50, and kids get a T-shirt to wear and keep. Space is limited, so reserve in advance.

Special programs incorporate the natural surroundings—e.g., the Barrier Island Marine Bio-Camp for ages five to twelve presented on Monday, Wednesday, and Friday from 9:00 A.M. to 1:00 P.M. ($40.00 plus $8.00 for lunch). Visit a barrier island; throw a cast net; crab, fish, and catch animals to make a touch-tank; use found items in arts and crafts. And bring your bathing suit! Kids and parents both can participate in at least twenty crafts and games for an hour or two—make scrapbooks, T-shirts, suncatchers, and birdhouses; check the schedule for your favorite. Some activities are complimentary; some have a small materials fee.

Recreation: A day of golf can begin on one of the two eighteen-hole golf courses designed by Tom Fazio. The older course, the Wild Dunes Links, is on the resort's ocean side and provides interesting play with its many water hazards. Two holes edge by the sand dunes of the beach and are dramatically beautiful as well as challenging. The newer Harbor Course is across the island, surrounding the marina and harbor, and has its own fair share of demanding water hazards. One example? Check out the photo of a twelve-foot alligator, surrounded by a dozen golf balls! We swear he's smiling. A practice range, professional instruction, and a pro shop can help you over the hurdles with improved style and equipment. Wild Dunes is ranked as "Best in the State" by *Golf Digest.*

In addition to golf, Wild Dunes offers tennis facilities, which have been ranked in the "Top 10 Greatest U.S. Tennis Resorts" by *Tennis* magazine. Guests receive one hour of free court time per day per bedroom. With a total of seventeen Har-Tru courts, including five lighted for night play and one stadium court, tennis players might not want to go home. Tennis instruction can take the form of private or group lessons, clinics, and camps for a week, a weekend,

or an intensive one-day session. Along with its well-stocked pro shop, this tennis facility leaves you very few excuses for not improving your game.

The Isle of Palms Marina has 200 boat slips. Here you can dock your own vessel or rent a boat for fishing in the Gulf Stream. Join a charter if you need an experienced captain's guidance in snagging the big ones, or finish off a day with a cruise in Charleston's harbor. Besides taking deep-sea excursions, fishermen can cast their lines in the ocean's surf, the creek, and the lagoons.

Swimmers have pools at most of the villa complexes, the main pool at the Swim Center, two oceanfront pools on the Grand Pavilion, the pool at the Boardwalk Inn, and, of course, the beautiful Atlantic Ocean. Joggers and bikers share the nature trails, where pine, oak, and magnolia trees grow; the hard-packed sand beach is also suitable for running and biking. Along the 2-mile stretch of beach, you'll find sunbathers, strollers, and seashell collectors, and just offshore, sailors and sailboarders. At the beachfront picnic area, the kids' playground consists of natural-wood climbing equipment under the trees. For a close look at the egrets, herons, and pelicans of Wild Dunes, take a canoe trip through the creeks and marshes.

Indulge in head-to-toe "therapies" at the spa and salon, or have a relaxing massage. Take a yoga or Pilates class, try a personal trainer, or get a physical fitness or sports training assessment.

Wild Dunes has one of the most extensive family programs we've seen, and is rated in the top five in the country. Check their Web site, and you can be busy probably more than twenty-four hours a day. Eco-sunset tours, sailing and dolphin viewing, creek fishing, kayak adventures, or watching the River Dogs, a minor-league baseball team, play are just a start and charges vary for these activities; complimentary fun encompasses putt-putt, sand soccer, cookouts, treasure hunts, and much, much more.

Nighttime comes alive at Wild Dunes with live music five nights a week at Edgar's Bar. The Grand Pavilion swings with live music, tennis exhibitions, a Low-Country luau, and more.

From mid-June to mid-August the resort features a Sunday welcome party, "Shaggin' at the Beach" on Tuesday and Friday (with Shag lessons!), karaoke on Wednesday, and steel calypso music Saturday and Sunday afternoons.

And when you decide to take a break from the fun and recreation, don't forget how close Charleston is. In a day of sightseeing, you can enjoy a historic Charleston tour of antebellum houses, fine restaurants, and shopping for antiques or at more modern boutiques.

5757 Palm Boulevard
Isle of Palms, South Carolina 29451
(843) 886–6000, (800) 845–8880,
(888) 845–8926
reservations@wilddunes.com
www.wilddunes.com

SOUTHEAST

Alabama
Florida
Georgia

AMELIA ISLAND PLANTATION

Amelia Island, Florida

Driving into Amelia Island Plantation, amidst the live oaks dripping Spanish moss, one immediately feels encircled and welcomed. With a sigh of relief, you can just sink into that lush vegetation and Southern hospitality. Like many of its counterparts along the coasts of the Carolinas and Georgia, Amelia Island Plantation is a well-planned and carefully executed development that combines resort living with an appreciation for natural beauty. Similarity to its sisters is no surprise, for this land was purchased in the late 1960s by Charles Fraser of Sea Pines in Hilton Head, one of the first resorts to blend nature's beauties with gracious amenities, setting the standard for resort communities that followed.

Amelia Island Plantation, which opened in 1974, occupies 1,350 acres of the southernmost island in the Golden Isle chain along the eastern seaboard of the United States. Open year-round, it is on the coast of northeast Florida, about a forty-five-minute drive from Jacksonville. Besides palmettos and oak trees, a 4-mile sandy beach, marshlands, and lagoons, this corner of paradise is blessed with mild temperatures year-round and balmy ocean breezes. Amelia Island Resort is a two-time winner of *Family Circle* magazine's "Best Family Beach Resort" award, AAA Four Diamonds, and *Southern Living's* Reader's Choice award for "Best Resort."

Accommodations: You can lodge in one of 249 oceanfront hotel rooms at the Amelia Inn and Beach Club—all with private balconies —or in a villa or hotel room overlooking the ocean or a lagoon, bordering the tennis complex, or one of the fairways of three golf courses. The one- to three-bedroom villas have complete kitchens; many have private patios, balconies, or screened porches. Architecturally, the multilevel accommodation buildings arranged throughout the property are of various contemporary styles, with stucco or natural-wood facades. Each villa complex has its own swimming pool.

Rates vary according to size, location, and category; for the villas, some rates are per person, others are per unit. Packages are plentiful and suit every need imaginable. Be sure to ask when you call for reservations, as Amelia Island practices yield control—if your dates fit a time when they have vacancies, the price will be even better. Some all-inclusive packages that feature family weeks or recreation and the children's program can be very cost-effective. Regular daily rates in the Amelia Inn range from $186 to $286 resort view and $256 to $356 ocean view, double occupancy. Children under age sixteen stay free in the room; cribs are available. Daily rates for a one-bedroom resort villa range from $236 to $336, while an ocean villa costs from $276 to $426.

Dining: When cooking in your villa seems just too strenuous after a day of sunbathing, gather the family at the Verandah in Racquet Park. Located in a building tucked among old oak trees, the dining room has large windows overlooking the tennis courts. Sample such fresh seafood from the Atlantic as sea bass, flounder, shrimp, and crab in the family-style atmosphere.

More elegant dining is available in the Ocean Grill. With expansive views of the ocean, this restaurant features seafood, quail, and roast duck and desserts like

Southern pecan pie. In addition to dinner, breakfast and a sumptuous brunch on Sundays are offered in the Sunrise Café. PLAE, People Laughing and Eating, showcases innovative cuisine at the spa and shops, plus an intimate lounge with fireplace and live entertainment.

Stop by the Marche Burette, an old-fashioned fresh-food market, for fruits, vegetables, meats, and fresh baked breads. You may be tempted by the delicious aroma to stay for a sandwich and coffee. Also appropriate for breakfast and lunch is the Golf Shop Restaurant at Amelia Links or the Longpoint Clubhouse, about a mile and a half south. At the Beach Club Grille, burgers, wings, and ribs are served; TVs add action to a meal or dine outside. Seaside Sweets, at poolside (seasonally), will satisfy your sweet tooth, while the Dunes Club Bar serves light lunches and tropical drinks poolside (seasonally) between Sea and Turtle Dunes. Roberto's will deliver pizza to your door, and Cooper's has scrumptious homemade ice cream. Falcon's Nest for happy hour and evening entertainment is the place to see and be seen on Amelia Island.

Children's World: Kids' Camp Amelia children's program entertains three- to ten-year-olds daily, year-round. Three- and four-year-olds attend the morning camp only. Activities include swimming, crabbing, sports, and arts and crafts, all with a daily theme. Take nature walks and enjoy many activities with the resident naturalist for a small fee. June through August, golf and tennis clinics and field trips are offered at special rates.

The cost for the full-day kids' program (8:30 A.M. to 4:00 P.M.) with lunch is $55, the morning session (8:30 A.M. to 1:00 P.M.) with lunch is $40, and the afternoon session (12:45 to 4:00 P.M.) is $30. The Kids' Camp is included in the recreation package.

Teen Explorers has just the kind of loosely structured activities that older children (eleven and up) prefer. Minigolf, basketball, scavenger hunts, bowling, barbecues, and bonfires provide a chance to socialize while participating in fun activities. Programs and costs vary (from free to $50), so check with the recreation department for details and to register.

Just for Kids presents themed dinner parties for ages three to ten. Hours are from 6:00 until 9:30 P.M. Wednesday through Saturday from March 1 to Labor Day, when a buffet dinner is served; it drops to Thursday through Saturday (room service menu) for the rest of the year. The cost is $30, but it's half price ($15) if parents are dining at the Ocean Grill or Verandah Restaurant.

At Aury Island, a tree house and a dock for fishing and crabbing are reserved just for the twelve-and-under set. At the Beach Club little ones have their own wading pool and a playground filled with wooden climbing equipment. To find a babysitter, you can pick up a list of names and numbers at the main registration desk; rates begin at $12.50 per hour, with a four-hour minimum.

Daily at 2:00 P.M. the whole family can join in poolside activities such as trivia, volleyball, games, and contests. At 3:00 P.M., try your hand at creative crafts—days, prices, and type of craft vary throughout the year, and again, the crafts program is covered in the all-inclusive recreation program.

Recreation: The Amelia Links, thirty-six holes of golf designed by Pete Dye and Bobby Weed, offer variety in play, as each course has its own personality. Oak Marsh weaves through groves of oak, palmetto trees, and marshlands, while Ocean Links skirts the Atlantic Ocean, with five holes along the sand dunes and sea oats of the beach. The eighteen-hole Long Point Golf Course was designed by Tom Fazio. Lessons can be arranged through the pro shop, where you will also find equipment and fashions.

Racquet Park is well situated among beautiful live oaks, a lovely setting for twenty-two Har-Tru courts. Some are lighted for evening play. The site of the Bausch and Lomb Women's Championships, this tennis complex offers adult and junior clinics, ball machines for solo practice, and a pro shop for equipment and apparel.

Also part of Racquet Park is the Health and Fitness Center. Complete with racquetball, indoor heated lap pool, exercise equipment, steam room, sauna and whirlpool facilities, and aerobics classes, it fits the bill for a good workout. For relaxing rejuvenation, visit the spa, with full services and delightful treats like a Watsu massage, performed in thermal mineral water.

Swimmers can choose the ocean or pools for their hours of fun in the sun. In addition to the Olympic-size pool at the Beach Club, each of the groups of villas (except the Lagoon Villas) has a swimming pool—twenty-three pools in all.

The Nature Center is open daily from 9:00 A.M. to 5:30 P.M. with several naturalists, resident critters, a fun retail shop, and a large classroom for presentations. Explore the natural beauty of the island on several different excursions, geared for all ages and interests. Beach bounty, edible plants and wildflowers, birds of Amelia, and nature photography are just the beginning.

Along the 4-mile beach, you can collect shells, sunbathe, play volleyball, ride horseback (the Seashore Stables are just 2 miles away), and fish in the surf for whiting, sea trout, and bluefish. Surrounding the island in bays and sounds and the Gulf Stream are tarpon, flounder, trout, redfish, red snapper, and king mackerel. The waters in this area give up some beautiful prizes, and for advice, insider's hints, tackle, and information on charters, head to the Amelia Angler.

Bicycle along 7 miles of trails (rental bikes with baby seats and children's bikes are available), jog along the wooded paths and down the beach, or maybe even challenge the kids to a half hour of video games at the Beach Club Game Room.

Always wanted to try one of these new Segway self-balancing, personal transportation devices designed to go anywhere people do? Here's your chance! Satisfy your curiosity or take a tour through the natural surroundings along the bike paths. Junior Segway Experience allows kids to participate with parents in this novel activity. If you really like it, you can buy it on the spot.

For an outing of a different sort, browse through the shops at Amelia Island Plantation, or discover the Victorian district of Fernandina Beach at the north end of the island. The Amelia Island Plantation Resort Guide is worth checking upon your arrival; here you'll learn of classes, movies, hayrides, and cookouts.

Venturing out, visit the Amelia Island Museum of History, Florida's only oral museum, for fascinating stories of the eight flags that have flown over Amelia Island; and Fort Clinch State Park, where on the first weekend of each month, rangers reenact the 1864 occupation. Jacksonville attractions are just a forty-five-minute drive; and farther south (1½ hours from the resort) history buffs will find St. Augustine, the oldest European settlement in the United States, founded in 1565 by the Spanish. Visit the restored Spanish Quarter, and of course, Ponce de Leon's Fountain of Youth.

6800 First Coast Highway
Amelia Island, Florida 32034
(904) 261–6161, (800) 874–6878,
(888) 261–6161
www.aipfl.com

THE BREAKERS

In the 1880s Henry Flagler, a railroad magnate and cofounder of Standard Oil, was advised to spend time in Florida for his health. From this happenstance evolved a world-class luxury resort. Flagler discovered the warm climate of the Atlantic Coast, was captivated by the scenery, expanded railroad lines down the eastern seaboard, and set into motion the development of Palm Beach as a winter playground of the wealthy.

The original Palm Beach Inn, built in 1896, was destroyed by fire in 1903. A second hotel, The Breakers, also succumbed to fire in 1925. Efforts to rebuild were begun immediately, and the new facility was opened at the end of 1926. The project was inspired by buildings of the Italian Renaissance; the era's artistic influence is evident in the loggias, courtyards, and hand-painted vaulted ceilings that adorn The Breakers. Open year-round, the hotel has completed a $100 million renovation and maintains its status as a Mobil five-star and AAA Five Diamond resort. Listed on the National Register of Historic Places, The Breakers is also a member of the Leading Hotels of the World. The grand beauty of this sparkling structure is perhaps met only by its natural setting on 140 acres of lush semitropical landscape bordering the blue-green waters of the Atlantic Ocean.

Accommodations: The 560 comfortably elegant and well-appointed guest rooms, including fifty-seven suites, have views of the ocean, the well-tended formal gardens, or the golf course. During the summer (low season), from mid-May to October 31, rates for a single/double room are $285 to $570 per day; there is no charge for children sixteen and under sharing a room with parents.

Cribs and rollaways are provided at no charge but must be requested prior to arrival. You may also request complimentary childproofing for children under three. During the high season, from November to early May, rates range from $395 to $795 per day. Holiday and vacation packages are also available. Suites range from $520 to $4,000.

For those who enjoy more privacy, choose the Flagler Club, The Breakers's concierge level located on the top two floors, with restricted access and additional guest services and amenities. Rates here are $485 to $960 (varies by season).

Room rates are European Plan, without meals; however, options for meal plans exist. Breakfast only is $23 per person; MAP (breakfast and dinner) is $87 per person; children two to twelve are $25. Tax is not included, and a $25 surcharge applies to L'Escalier, The Breakers's French restaurant.

Dining: Dining at The Breakers can be as formal or as casual as one desires, with eight restaurants to choose from. An array of hot and cold breakfast items, as well as an a la carte menu, is available in the Circle Dining Room, with splendid ocean views and an intricate handpainted ceiling. Lunch at The S.S. Reef Bar, Palm Beach's only bar on the beach, offering refreshing libations and light snacks; or at the new Beach Club Restaurant, the heart of The Breakers's new spa, featuring classic luncheon fare and selections of spa cuisine. Lunch and dinner are served in The Seafood Bar, an upscale oceanfront raw bar reminiscent of the plantation homes of old Florida; or The Flagler Steakhouse, featuring oversize steaks and chops. For dinner only, experience L'Escalier, with its French ambience; jackets are required and reservations are recommended. To say L'Escalier's wine list is exceptional is an understatement; it has consistently earned *Wine Spectator's* "Grand Award" every year since 1981. More than 500 vintages are represented in the display wine cellar. Five minutes from the hotel, in the heart of Palm Beach, Echo offers a culinary adventure with unique and sophisticated Asian cuisine. For cocktails, appetizers, and afternoon tea, the elegant Tapestry Bar is the place to be.

At The Breakers restaurants, the under-elevens have their own menus. Children under two eat free, and everyone gets a special coloring book. A family-friendly dining facility, located in the new Family Entertainment Center and called simply the Italian Restaurant, serves dinner daily.

Children's World: With its broad spectrum of amenities, creative recreational programs and activities, and family-friendly mind-set, The Breakers formed a Kids' Advisory Board, composed of young people ages five to twelve, to advise the resort on children's wants and needs. In response to this advice, there is now a year-round children's program called Coconut Crew Camp.

Children ages three through twelve enjoy Coconut Crew Camp's year-round supervised activities, including active sports, contests, pool and beach games, arts and crafts, indoor games, seashell hunts, nature walks, lawn games, swimming, croquet, and more. "Parrots" (ages three to five) and "Coconuts" (ages six to twelve) have flexible, age-appropriate programs. Offered daily from 9:00 A.M. to 3:00 P.M. as a full-day experience ($80, lunch included) or a half day ($50, morning or afternoon; lunch included).

The agenda for all programs is relaxed and flexible, so your child has the freedom to choose only specific events or to stay with the group for longer periods. Parents are encouraged to participate with their children, or monitored free play for ages five to seven is $10 per hour. Babysitting is available around the clock.

The new Family Entertainment Center houses an arcade, movie, huge TV, computers, crafts, playroom, and pizza available right next door at the Italian restaurant. Children ten years and older are welcome on their own; younger children may be accompanied by parents, or supervised by on-site staff for a $10 hourly fee.

From March through October, families have lots of options for activities. Every week on Friday, the complimentary Family Fun Pak orients families with activities and refreshments. On Saturday, Kids Rule! is another complimentary event where kids "compete" against their parents in a game, and January to March, Friday Beach Bonfires kick off the weekend. Holiday weekends, everyone can take part in Saturday's Family Night Out theme party (Harry Potter, Survivor, Palm Beach Rodeo); $50 per person includes dinner and a souvenir; children over six may attend alone. On other Saturdays, The Breakers Fun Zone ($20 per child, no dinner) provides an outdoor activity and unlimited tokens for the arcade—a child's dream. Families may also arrange A La Carte Time together; snorkeling, croquet, biking, or a kayaking trip are some ideas.

Recreation: Allow yourself to be pampered; a staff of 1,800 people is dedicated to making a stay here memorable. Stroll through the beautiful gardens or the half mile of private beach, linger under the palm trees, find the children's Secret Garden, relax on a patio surrounding a fountain, or indulge at the new Oceanfront Spa and Beach Club.

The award-winning Breakers Palm Beach features a vintage golf experience, resulting from the recent renovation of its historic eighteen-hole Ocean Course and the creation of a golf and tennis clubhouse designed in the grand "Old Florida" style.

Another eighteen-hole course, Breakers West, is located 10 miles away.

On par with the revitalized golf facilities are ten newly constructed tennis courts, all of which are surrounded by lush gardens, lighted at night. Tennis fans will enjoy the spaciousness of the easily accessible clubhouse.

The Mediterranean-style Beach Club offers four pools, including a lap pool and children's pool, a Jacuzzi, and ten cabanas overlooking one-half mile of private beach. The Spa at The Breakers features seventeen private treatment rooms, steam and sauna rooms, men's and ladies' lounges, a beauty salon, and an ocean-view fitness center.

Sunbathe beside the majestic Atlantic, or sip a tall, cool cocktail on the patio or at the Reef Bar. Bicycle or jog on the paths through the gardens, join a deep-sea fishing or fly-fishing excursion for an offshore adventure, go snorkeling, or sign up for scuba instruction. For periods when you are not feeling so energetic, play a game of shuffleboard, croquet, horseshoes, boccie ball, bridge, or backgammon. Other events throughout the week include exercise classes such as water aerobics, yoga, and Tai Chi; family movies; shopping at any of the resort's twelve boutiques; and historical tours. Add lectures, crafts, garden tours, concerts, shopping on the famous Worth Avenue, and cooking demonstrations and you'll have to stretch your vacation to fit it all in.

One South County Road
Palm Beach, Florida 33480
(561) 655–6611, (888) BREAKERS
www.thebreakers.com

CALLAWAY GARDENS
Pine Mountain, Georgia

Cason Callaway was a textile industrialist in Georgia. In the 1930s he became so enamored of the countryside around Pine Mountain that his life began to change. He turned from industry, first to farming and then to gardening. He learned that the plumleaf azalea was peculiar to this area of Georgia, and he was determined to nurture it and share its beauty with others. He established the Ida Cason Callaway Foundation, in honor of his mother, and opened his gardens to the public in 1952. While the gardens remain the focal point of the setting, the resort has grown to include gracious lodging, pleasant restaurants, and sports activities such as golf, tennis, swimming, and fishing. This naturally wooded and carefully cultivated land—14,000 acres of lakes, woodlands, and gardens—is located 70 miles south of Atlanta, in the Appalachian Mountain foothills of west Georgia. Callaway's stated purpose is to provide a wholesome family environment where all may find beauty, relaxation, inspiration, and a better understanding of the living world. A public, educational, horticultural, and charitable organization, it is owned and operated by the nonprofit Ida Cason Callaway Foundation. Its wholly owned subsidiary, Callaway Gardens Resort, Inc., a regular business corporation, operates the recreational, lodging, and retail facilities at Callaway. After-tax proceeds go to the foundation to support its efforts. And it shows. Highway 27 bisects

Callaway Gardens and makes it seem very spread out; having a car is helpful, if not essential, and it's easier to find your way once you get oriented to the layout.

Accommodations: The Mountain Creek Inn, near the entrance to the gardens, is a 325-room hotel, which also houses restaurants, lounges, and the Fitness Center. From mid-March through December a double room starts at $134 a night. During the winter months rates start at $103; suites are $150 to $309 a night.

Next door to the inn is the Tennis and Racquetball Club; next to that are the luxurious Mountain Creek Villas: one- to four-bedroom units with fireplace, screened porch or patio, and fully equipped kitchen. Nightly rates for a two-bedroom villa are $309 to $379, depending on the season.

Many families opt for one of the Southern Pine Cottages, which are arranged in small clusters amid tall trees near Robin Lake. All have well-equipped kitchens; some have fireplace, screened porch, deck, or outdoor grill. Daily rates for a two-bedroom cottage range from $275 to $329. Rates include admission to the gardens, use of the Callaway Fitness Center, in-room coffee and daily newspaper, and admission to Robin Lake Beach (open seasonally).

Summer Family Adventure, a tradition for forty-three years, has been expanded to include four-day packages beginning on Wednesday, as well as the weekly Saturday to Saturday packages. Monday through Friday, from 9:00 A.M. until 3:00 P.M., guests participate in "day camp." Mom and Dad can participate in planned activities for adults or have time to enjoy their own activities while the children are at camp. Evening events focus on the entire family. Four-day rates are $1,599 for cottages, $1,799 for villas. Seven-day rates are $2,331 (cottage) and $2,962 (villa); rates are for two-bedroom units. Many other packages are offered; inquire about weekend, recreation, or extended stays. Cribs are provided at no charge; rollaway beds are $15 per day in the inn only.

Dining: Located in the inn is the Plantation Room, known for its buffets—particularly the Friday-night seafood buffet and the Sunday brunch—open for breakfast, lunch, and dinner. The Piedmont Dining Room, in the Conference Center, is open daily for all three meals, and offers both a la carte and buffet service.

With red-checked tablecloths supporting the atmosphere that its name connotes, the Country Kitchen, located in the Country Store on Highway 27, serves breakfast, lunch, and dinner in a friendly, family-style setting. It's famous for its muscadine bread and country bacon. Sandwiches and snacks are available in the Champions Restaurant at the golf pro shop and the Flower Mill Deli, a soda-shop/diner near the cottages (open seasonally). At the Robin Lake Beach Pavilion, grab a snack and sit at one of the picnic tables overlooking Robin Lake. The Fine Cone is perfect for ice cream on a summer day. A welcome addition to Callaway dining is the Discovery Café, where the view is as enjoyable as the food. It offers indoor/outdoor eating overlooking mountain and lake. The Gardens' clubhouse has been transformed into the charming Gardens Restaurant, with a lovely porch overlooking lake and golf course that invites you to tarry.

At the end of the day, stop at the cozy Lobby Bar & Grill in the Mountain Creek Inn for a drink and a light meal, or stop by the Ironwood Lounge for billiards and a drink by the fireplace.

Children's World: For forty-five summers Florida State University's Flying High Circus has performed at Callaway Gardens. With the big top pitched at Robin Lake Beach, this area becomes the focus of the Summer

Family Adventure Program from June through mid-August and it's summer camp for everyone. If daily (except Wednesday) circus performances are not enough to charm youngsters, the performers also act as counselors, directing kids in games and sports and teaching them a few juggling tricks and circus acts too. In addition, kids go sailing, swimming, waterskiing, roller skating, and biking. They attend golf and tennis instruction and grow imaginative in crafts classes. Kids ages three to eighteen can participate. The Summer Discovery Program provides an informal look at the animals, plants, and ecology at Callaway Gardens. Family events, such as barbecues, square dances, and movies, are also planned.

If you cannot schedule the Summer Family Adventure and are staying a couple of days at the inn, you can enroll your child on a daily basis for $50 a day. Besides the program, there are children's playgrounds at the inn and at the cottage area.

Recreation: The Virginia Hand Discovery Center, nestled in the woods on the edge of Mountain Creek Lake, should be your first stop. It's several facilities in one, all devoted to enhancing the harmony between man and earth. A staffed information desk and interactive kiosks provide guests an overview of all there is to see and do in the Callaway's 14,000 acres. Inside an orientation theater, the film *Time & the Gardens* plays continuously, depicting the evolution of the Gardens at Callaway. The center also houses an education wing, lecture hall, museum/exhibit hall, the Discovery Gift Shop, and Discovery Café. Outside, a transportation court provides guests with alternate means of getting around.

The gardens are a continuous source of beauty, pleasure, peace, and serenity. This is a place to enjoy, to reflect, and to learn. The colorful, changing displays of begonias, snapdragons, geraniums, zinnias, pansies,

tulips, marigolds, chrysanthemums—the list seems endless—are presented in the outdoor garden of the John A. Sibley Horticultural Center. Depending on the season, visitors who explore the walking trails are treated to mountain laurel, hydrangeas, narcissus, magnolias, dogwoods, crabapples, hollies, wildflowers, and 700 varieties of azaleas (the famous plumleaf blooms during the summer). At Mr. Cason's Vegetable Garden, you can wander through row after row of more than 400 different types of fruits and vegetables. Workshops on topics like flower arranging and bonsai techniques are available year-round. The John A. Sibley Horticultural Center, a five-acre, innovative greenhouse design, is an architectural as well as a horticultural feat. The Cecil B. Day Butterfly Center houses up to 1,000 butterflies (representing more than fifty species) in a lush tropical setting. Learn about eagles, hawks, and owls as they swoop over your head in the Birds of Prey show.

In 1999 Callaway Gardens added the world's largest azalea garden. The Callaway Brothers Azalea Bowl features more than 5,000 specimens of both hybrid and native azaleas in a forty-acre landscape.

Besides its magnificent gardens, the resort also offers more traditional diversions. Two golf courses unroll past forests and lakes. The names of the courses are descriptive of their surroundings—Mountain View (the most challenging and home to the PGA tour's Buick Challenge for twelve years) and Lake View (the most picturesque). A driving range, two pro shops, and a year-round instructional program complete the golfing facilities.

The Pete Sampras in your party has ten lighted tennis courts from which to choose. Eight clay and two Plexipave courts are at the Tennis and Racquetball Club, which also houses two racquetball courts and the pro shop. The instructional program includes private or group lessons, or you can practice on your own with a ball-machine. *Tennis* magazine consistently awards the Tennis Club with a five-star ranking.

Robin Lake is the center of lots of summer fun, from paddleboat rides and circus performances to swimming and sunbathing along the mile-long sandy beach. Besides the lake, overnight guests can enjoy the pools at the inn, at the Mountain Creek Villas, and at the cottage area.

On the shores of Mountain Creek Lake is a boathouse where you can rent a motorboat and fishing tackle—the lake is stocked with bass and bream—or a Sunfish sailboat, paddleboat, or canoe. You can also discover the lakes from their shores as you bicycle along the trails and paths.

Sportsmen enjoy fly-fishing on thirteen lakes or shooting skeet, trap, and sporting clays at the Gun Club. You may want to spend an afternoon at an organ concert (daily during the summer) in the chapel on Falls Creek Lake. For indoor exercise the Fitness Center offers equipment for unwinding. For an afternoon of history, you can take the 15-mile trip to Warm Springs and Franklin Roosevelt's Little White House.

U.S. Highway 27, P.O. Box 2000
Pine Mountain, Georgia 31822
(706) 663–2281, (800) 225–5292
www.callawaygardens.com

CHEECA LODGE AND SPA
Islamorada, Florida

Stretching more than 150 miles south from Miami, the Florida Keys enjoy a subtropical climate and a friendly, laid-back philosophy. Just getting there is an adventure. As you travel along U.S. Highway 1, you get the feeling that you're the string connecting a necklace of islands. And sometimes there are no islands—just a narrow ribbon of concrete in the middle of a very wide ocean—or two! The Atlantic Ocean and the Gulf of Mexico both border this strip of islands. Islamorada is just 75 miles from Miami, but really it is another world.

Cheeca Lodge and Spa is a twenty-seven-acre luxury oceanfront resort (AAA Four Diamonds, a RockResort, and member of Small Luxury Hotels of the World), with more than 1,000 feet of palm-lined beach, not often found in the Keys. "Barefoot elegance" is Cheeca's trademark and it was

named one of *Travel + Leisure's* 500 Greatest Hotels in the World in 2005.

Accommodations: Set in the main lodge and low-rise villas spread throughout the landscaped grounds, 201 rooms await your pleasure. Generous in size, all guest rooms are air-conditioned and also have ceiling fans, and many have a private balcony. Sixty-four villa suites feature kitchen, screened-in porch, living room, and one or two bedrooms. Mid-December to April rates are the highest, when standard rooms range from $350 to $395; oceanfront rooms are $569 to $799; and one-bedroom suites are $529 to $1,000. In summer the rates drop to $179 to $465 for rooms, $350 to $825 for one-bedroom suites. Children under sixteen stay free in their parents' room. Specials and packages are offered year-round. A daily resort fee of $39 covers housekeeping gratuities and other amenities and is inclusive for tennis, golf, kayaks/paddleboats, spa exercise classes, beach cabanas, fitness studio, and more.

Dining: Savor fine dinners at the Atlantic's Edge, a plantation-style restaurant with lovely panoramic views of the ocean. Dine inside or outside next to the free-form swimming pool at the Ocean Terrace Grill, sampling the local specialty, stone-crab claws, or soups and sandwiches; there is a special children's menu. Another indoor/outdoor dining option is the Curt Gowdy Lounge, great for snacks, cocktails, and piano entertainment in the evenings. Nearby dining choices range from casual to fine dining, and night life options include sunsets, live music, cigar bar, and billiards or darts.

Children's World: Award-winning Camp Cheeca has a mission: learning about the environment while having fun. Children ages five to twelve are busy from 9:00 A.M. to 1:00 P.M. year-round. Camp Cheeca does not operate on Sunday in high season (mid-December to April), or on Sunday and Monday in summer. Cost is $35 per child for the morning session, including lunch.

Learning to snorkel and fish, creating nature art or sand sculpture, feeding the fish or exploring the beach—everything has an ecological approach that kids really respond to. There's a good mix of activities, with field trips, scavenger hunts, arts and crafts, and Saturday Sundae (everyone's favorite). "Kids Night Out," Friday and Saturday from 6:00 to 10:00 P.M., costs $30 and includes entertainment, pizza dinner, movies, crafts, and games. Families with three or more children receive a reduced rate. Babysitting rates vary according to season.

Recreation: You can be on the go from dawn to dusk, or make the most strenuous activity of the day deciding between a hammock, chaise longue, or tiki hut on the beach. Consider renting a catamaran or beach cruiser bicycle, or try parasailing. Paddleboats and kayaks are complimentary. Deckboats, sailboats, and windsurfers are available to rent, with instruction. Maybe just a pool float is more your speed. The three pools are all very different; a free-form swimming pool, a lap pool, and a saltwater lagoon keep boredom at bay. Play tennis on one of the six lighted courts, or try the Jack Nicklaus–designed nine-hole executive golf course. Take a self-guided walk along Cheeca's Nature Trail, or watch the sunrise from the pier—or maybe the sunset.

The Avanyu Spa is Cheeca's newest amenity. Avanyu is a mythical water serpent of the Tewa Indians; Cheeca integrates the life-giving power of water into spa therapies. This state-of-the-art health spa and fitness center offers the latest in massage therapy, facials, aromatherapy, body wraps, spacious fitness room, men's and women's steamrooms, and a spa boutique.

It's a fisherman's paradise here, with more than 600 species of marine life and a calendar of what's running each month that fills a page. No wonder Islamorada is known as the sportfishing capital of the world. A nice touch is that the chef will, on request, prepare your hard-won catch. Cheeca has its own dive center, with equipment and instruction. The *Cheeca View* doubles as a dive boat twice a day, then does sunset and moonlight cruises. The biggest problem is trying to fit in all the options.

Theater of the Sea, the world's second-oldest marine park, is a natural lagoon where humans and marine animals interact (kids love getting kissed by a sea lion!). They've gone beyond a glass-bottom boat—here they have a bottomless boat. Hmm, neat trick. If you want to range farther afield, the concierge can help arrange a swim with the dolphins, or a trip to either

Key West, the southernmost U.S. city, or Pennekamp State Park, the first underwater state park. Combine a visit to Miccosukee Indian Reservation with an airboat ride through the Everglades.

81801 Overseas Highway
Islamorada, Florida 33036
(305) 664–4651, (800) 327–2888
www.cheeca.com

THE CLOISTER
Sea Island, Georgia

Charming, gracious, and oh, so civilized— The Cloister is in the heart of the "Golden Isles," one of the most historic areas of the old Spanish Main. Family holidays at this fine old resort are fun-filled, and the elegance of a bygone era prevails. The Cloister boasts that here children learn manners as well as golf, tennis, and swimming. The dress-for-dinner standard and the children's weekly dances (seasonally) reinforce this philosophy.

Sea Island's rich history dates back to the antebellum days of the Old South, when a large cotton plantation was active on what is now the Sea Island Golf Club. The ruins of a slave hospital standing near the Clubhouse recall this period. In the early 1900s the property was acquired by Howard Coffin, an automobile engineer who had visions of creating a resort on this lovely 900-acre island, with its temperate climate and ocean breezes. His dreams were realized in the construction of The Cloister. Designed by Addison Mizner, who is known primarily for his work in Palm Beach, this "friendly little hotel" (as Coffin described it) opened its doors in October 1928. It successfully weathered the Depression and over the years has warmly greeted guests from the rich and famous to the mere plebeian with good taste. Ivy-covered walls, gently swaying palm trees, impeccable gardens, and wide verandahs

set the stage for a memorable vacation. The resort is open year-round.

A two-phase, five-year project to completely rebuild The Cloister and expand residential options began in late 2003. The company is committing $200 million to the project, and promises to retain the gracious hospitality and attributes that have made the hotel special for the past seventy-five years.

Accommodations: Choose from 207 rooms and suites, all on the beach side of the island; Guest Houses, also all on the beach; and Terrace Houses, located on neighborhood streets between the beach and tennis center. The original structure (currently being renovated) has a Mediterranean style with red-tile roofs and courtyards. The architecture of the newer buildings and the gardens complement this style and maintain the flavor of a gracious island retreat. Rooms range from traditional, tastefully decorated bedrooms and baths to deluxe rooms and oceanfront suites. Also available are privately owned "cottages" (two to eight bedrooms) ranging from modest to grand. View them at www.seaislandcottages.com.

Room rates (double occupancy, not including meals) range from $300 to $775 per night, depending on the type of room and time of year; suites are $350 to $1,500. Children fifteen and under stay free when sharing a room with parents.

Dining: Guests may dine either at The Cloister or at the Lodge at Sea Island, a premier destination on neighboring St. Simons Island where classic traditions and modern luxuries meet and golf's glorious past is not only revived, but revered. At the Lodge, The Terrace is like dining in a fine old Southern home; collared shirt required for breakfast and lunch; add long pants for dinner. Colt & Alison's is the finest dinner dining experience (closed Monday) and requires a jacket. Throughout the day, enjoy a tavern-style menu and drinks at the Oak Room Bar; casual and golf attire throughout the day.

While the main building is being renovated, dining at The Cloister itself is either beachside or overlooking the fairways. The Beach Club Dining Room goes from casual for breakfast and lunch to "elegant casual" for dinner (slacks and collared shirts for males over twelve). Select from a full dining menu or indulge in the abundant buffets. The Davis Love Grill at the Retreat Course specializes in Southern cuisine at lunch and dinner; enjoy casual al fresco dining or fireside evenings. The Loggia Bar at the Beach is ideal for a cold drink or light fare without missing anything going on at the beach. A lovely Sea Island tradition, the Plantation Supper on Rainbow Island is a Friday event. Bluegrass music, Southern gospel, pulled pork barbecue, and pecan pies—it's the best, and a vacation to Georgia is just not complete otherwise. Cost is $39.00 per adult, $18.50 for children ages four to twelve; plus $4.00 per person for the round-trip Jeep Train.

For light refreshments during spring and summer, there's a snack bar near the swimming pools at the Beach Club. High tea is served afternoons during cooler months in the Spanish Lounge, and afternoon juice and cookies in the Davis Love Grill are a favorite pastime. Special evenings are frequently scheduled, such as the supper at Rainbow Island.

Children's World: The Junior Staff of specially selected college students will charm your child with active days. From Memorial Day through Labor Day, and during Easter, Thanksgiving, and Christmas holidays, energetic, friendly counselors provide daily supervised play for youngsters ages three (no pull-ups or diapers, please) through eleven, from 9:30 A.M. to 1:00 P.M. for $35 per child. Program operates daily except Sunday. From mid-March to mid-April, and again in summer, the hours extend to 3:00 P.M. for ages five and up. Cost becomes $55 for the day. Fee includes lunch. Activities include swimming, fishing, crabbing, art sessions, games, boat rides, dunes discovery, and nature walks, just to mention a few. On Saturday, with a minimum of five children, kids can make and bake (and eat!) cookies for an hour; cost is $20 per child. The Children's Activity Center at the Beach Club invites kids to play table tennis and foosball from 9:00 A.M. to 5:00 P.M. daily (1:00 to 5:00 P.M. on Sunday). It's just like going to the office for adults.

During the summer months children ages three through eleven can even join their counselors for dinner from 6:30 to 9:00 P.M. (Sunday and Family Beach Supper nights excluded), allowing parents to dine at their leisure. Cost is $35 per child. For younger children, babysitters are available.

Juniors and teens (ages twelve to nineteen) also have access to excursions and activities, including shopping trips to the Village of St. Simons Island, "dive-in" movies in the pool, kayaking, and socials. Some excursions do require small fees, such as Friday night bowling ($15) or Saturday movies at the Island Cinema ($15). It's essential to check the weekly calendar for additional events, because the Junior Staff also plans various activities for different age groups. Teen dances and pool parties, table tennis tournaments, swimming and hamburger parties, and crabbing parties frequently appear on the agenda. A daily Family Activity Hour features fun for all ages.

Tennis clinics for ages four through twelve are offered by the professional tennis staff and regional tournaments and invitationals are on the schedule. Junior Sailing School (once a week) or Kayaking Clinic (twice a week) for ages ten to twenty-one years help youths hone their skills ($29 or $25 per hour, per person).

Recreation: Whether you choose a leisurely stroll along the 5 miles of private beach, a rigorous game of tennis, a round of golf, or a refreshing dip in the pool, your vacation stay can be as relaxing or active as you wish.

The Cloister offers twenty-five well-maintained Har-Tru clay courts, an automated practice court, and instruction by a professional teaching staff. Even a little criticism of your backhand is easy to take in a setting graced by oak trees and azaleas. At the pro shop you can pick up equipment and new tennis togs and sign up for a tournament or partner matching. Court fees are $15 per day for adults, $10 for children under twelve and seniors over seventy.

The Sea Island Golf Club, located on neighboring St. Simons Island, is just a short drive over the small bridge spanning the Black Banks River. Once you arrive you'll be charmed by the Avenue of Oaks—majestic moss-draped oak trees leading up to the Lodge at Sea Island Golf Club. There are thirty-six championship holes. The Seaside Course, redesigned in 1999 by Tom Fazio and listed on numerous top courses lists, is a par-70 links course. The Plantation Course, redesigned by Rees Jones in 1998, is a par-72 parkland-style course. A third course, Retreat, was redesigned by Davis Love III and reopened in August 2001. The Golf Learning Center, a joint

venture of Sea Island and *Golf Digest,* offers state-of-the-art practice and learning facilities with a video analysis system. There's a driving range at each club, and back on Sea Island you'll find a putting green and a chip 'n' putt area for some extra practice time. And if you're a real devotee, rest assured that golfing interests do not fade with the setting sun; join the discussions with the pros at golf seminars two evenings a week.

The Beach Club overlooks the Atlantic, so you can choose an ocean swim or a few laps in one of the two pools. Besides a dining room and a snack bar, the Beach Club offers table tennis, volleyball, shuffleboard, and a terrific soak-up-the-sun atmosphere. Other water sports include sailboarding and sailing in the ocean, snorkeling and scuba diving, and boating and fishing in the river. After excursions through the waterways, you might try exploring the grounds as you jog, bike, or ride horseback. Many folks enjoy a horseback ride along the beach or through the marshes, or you may contact the stables about moonlight supper rides. At the Shooting School you'll find instruction in sporting clays, trap, and skeet shooting as well as all the equipment necessary to learn these sports. And after golf, tennis, swimming, sailing, and skeet-shooting lessons, if you're still dying to try something new or to brush up on dusty skills, sign up for dance instruction. After a couple of sessions, you'll no doubt be a hit dancing nightly to the hotel's Sea Island Orchestra.

The Sea Island Spa offers a full range of services. You can join an exercise class, develop an individualized program, consult a nutritionist, have a massage, or relax with a facial.

Special programs are planned throughout the year; they may be just the thing to schedule a family vacation around. Food and wine seminars, bridge festivals, and a personal financial-planning seminar are standard events at The Cloister.

At any time of the year, be sure to check the weekly calendar. You might want to see a movie, play bingo, listen to a classical piano concert, head to an exercise workout, join a nature walk, or take in a lecture on the local wildlife. But don't crowd your schedule too much, for one of the nicest pleasures at The Cloister is simply strolling through the gardens and discovering the camellias, gardenias, wisteria, geraniums, petunias, and time.

---

100 First Street
Sea Island, Georgia 31561
(912) 638–3611, (800) SEA–ISLAND
www.seaisland.com

CLUB MED/SANDPIPER
Port St. Lucie, Florida

Club Med is practically synonymous with a carefree, fun-in-the-sun holiday, a tradition going back more than forty years. In fact, they opened the first Mini-Club for children in 1967. The only warm-weather village that Club Med operates in the United States is Sandpiper, and it has not only a Mini-Club but a Baby Club as well. Located in Port St. Lucie, Florida, about an hour's drive north of Palm Beach, the Club Med village covers more than 400 beautifully landscaped acres along the St. Lucie River. The verdant green landscape and the clear blue waters make an attractive setting for a fun-filled, sun-filled vacation.

Accommodations: Sandpiper is one of the most luxurious Club Med properties, termed the "finest." It seems more like a deluxe hotel, boasting brick-colored tile floors covered with kilim carpet, original artwork by local artists, and a separate dressing area, with large closets. Unlike most Club Med villages, the rooms here have telephone, TV, and minifridge. Each room has a private balcony or terrace and is located in one of several three-story buildings near the river. Renovated in 2000, it now features a Florida Country Club look.

Club Med now offers special accommodations: family marina suites, two connecting rooms with DVD player, turn-down service, and fully stocked refrigerator; and one family suite, two bedrooms with kitchen and Florida room.

Club Med pioneered the concept of all-inclusive vacations—rates here include everything except scuba, ATP tennis, and some golf. And that's everything! Accommodations, all meals, children's programs, sports and instruction—even all-day snacks, drinks, and an open bar. Rates are complex and changing—it's best to inquire for your specific dates. Club Med has three seasons: winter, summer, and holiday. Winter and summer weekly rates are similar, beginning at $965 per adult, $497 for children ages four to fifteen years, and $308 for toddlers two to three years. Infants under two are free, but infants and toddlers pay $30 per day for the programs. The family marina suites cost between $200 and $400 more per adult. Prices are based on availability and when you book—early reservations can result in substantial savings. During certain weeks in spring and fall, kids under twelve (one per adult) stay free. Club

Med rates often include air flights—ask for specifics. Three-night packages and day passes are also available. A Club Med annual membership is required; $55 per adult and $25 per child.

Dining: The main dining room is informal, serving breakfast, lunch, and dinner buffets. Dining at Club Med is a bountiful experience, with selections of American, French, and Continental delicacies. It's also a good chance to meet people and socialize. The Club has its own baker and pastry maker—yum. No fewer than twelve different fresh-baked breads are served at every meal. But not to worry, there are enough activities daily to work off any calories from over-indulging. A special kid-friendly menu is served to children early at lunch and dinner. Parents may join their children while they eat, and the G.O.s (*gentils organisateurs* —French for "gracious organizers") super-vise as well. High chairs and booster seats make life easier for the little ones. After their early dinner, kids return to the Mini-Club. Mom and Dad, meanwhile, savor a superb and blissfully quiet dinner, perhaps in the Riverside specialty restaurant— beautifully decorated, smaller, and more intimate, table service is the order of the day here. Complimentary wine is served with lunch and dinner, thanks to the French her-itage of the Club. In keeping with the times, four menus are offered: wellness, discovery (world cuisine), energy, and indulgence. A new policy at Club Med is a completely open bar, so that drinks and snacks are now avail-able all day long, whenever you desire. No more pop beads!

An all-day casual grill is available between meals to assuage any hunger attacks. Need juice or milk in the middle of the night? No problem; just go to the twenty-four-hour convenience room.

Children's World: Kids are thoroughly entertained at Club Med. In fact, you may almost have to make an appointment to see your little one. The Baby Club is available for infants ages four to twenty-three months from 9:00 A.M. to 5:30 P.M. Baby Club is a paid service with an additional charge of $30 per day. Strollers, baby monitors, bassinets—all the necessary equipment can be borrowed; and a pediatrician is either in the village or on call, plus one registered nurse. Each baby gets her own crib, and there's even a special Baby Chef, who pre-pares food using only natural ingredients. Lunch is handled by the G.O.s, but parents are on duty for dinner. Depending on their ages, babies are changed, fed, napped, and played with in the garden, with swings and toys. The more mobile go on walks or play on the beach.

Little ones may be brought to the Siesta Club in the evening, in their pajamas, and can sleep there while parents take in a show or stroll along the river. The Siesta Club is provided from 8:00 P.M. to 1:00 A.M. at a cost of $20 per child per night.

The Petit Club is for two- to three-year-olds, and is also a paid service charging $30 per day. Open six days a week, it runs from 9:00 A.M. to 5:30 P.M. and again from 7:30 to 9:00 P.M. Generally toddlers are divided into two age groups. The Mini-Club is for four- to ten-year-olds, and the Junior Club entertains eleven- to thirteen-year-olds at no additional cost. Each has its own area with clubhouse, its own G.O.s, and an unbelievable number of age-appropriate activities. During peak holi-days special programs are also available for fourteen- to seventeen-year-olds to meet and interact.

In addition to all the usual activities of children's programs, Club Med also offers circus workshops, with real trampolines, trapeze and low-wire work, juggling, trick bikes, and clowns. At the end of the week, the entire group puts on a show under the

Big Top for adoring parents. It's really ter-rific, and the kids are so proud of them-selves. There's intensive tennis for kids eight and older, and soccer, softball, in-line skating, sailing, waterskiing, and much more—all included in the one price. A pro-gram called Mini-Scientist makes science fun and engaging (and educational, although no one notices). Hip Hop Kids brings out musical talents, as does the Musical Discovery Adventure. Evening fun continues with "disco," pajama parties, and games.

Recreation: The sun is warm, the water inviting. You have five swimming pools (one exclusively for adults and one for Mini-Club) to choose from and a little sandy beach where you can splash in the river. A shuttle leaves hourly for the twenty-minute ride to the Atlantic for ocean swimming. In the calm water of the river, you can glide along on a sailboat and later have a go at waterskiing or wakeboarding (summer only). Tennis clinics are held daily on the nineteen courts; after intensive sessions, you will surely find improvement in your game. Nine courts are lit for evening play. A program with one-hour daily lessons at all levels is another option. Aerobics classes, calisthenics, and volleyball games always pop up on the agenda. Perhaps you prefer a routine in the fitness center or biking and jogging along the paths through the prop-erty. Group lessons are to be had in just about every sport; catamaran sailing and archery are only at beginning levels, but golf, tennis, waterskiing, wakeboarding, cir-cus school, in-line skating, and Crunch Fit-ness are taught at all levels. A note on Club Med Crunch Fitness: It's taught at various levels, and encompasses yoga, cardio tai box, BOSU Bootcamp (a cross between a core board and a stability ball), and finally, Revolution with Smart Bells, using smart bells instead of dumbbells, that blends

yoga and strength training. It's fitness with pizzazz! A real thrill is the flying trapeze—with the greatest of ease, of course. Free play with just about any kind of ball you can think of: volleyball, mini-soccer, table tennis, pitch 'n' putt mini-golf, water polo, basketball, softball, and boccie ball. Did we miss any?

Unique to Sandpiper is a concentrated golf program with free group lessons at all levels. On-site golf includes an eighteen-hole championship golf course, Sinners, designed by Mark Mahannah, a driving range, a free nine-hole par-3, two putting greens, a chipping green, and a practice sand trap. For serious golfers, the Golf Academy provides three-hour clinics on Tuesday, Wednesday, and Thursday with clubs and balls during the session for $170. You may want to bring your own golf balls (or purchase them there); clubs may be rented. Greens fees are quite reasonable ($42 for two days or $62 for three days) and include a golf cart.

The Mini-Clubs run from 9:00 A.M. to 9:00 P.M. Afterward the whole family can enjoy the evening entertainment, usually a show or participatory fun. After the kids finally fall into bed, the nightclub continues into the night.

If you have time, which we doubt, Club Med offers a mind-boggling array of excur-sions. You may not want to mention it to the kids, but Disney World is only two hours away. Also nearby are the Kennedy Space Center, hot-air ballooning, and deep-sea fishing. Palm Beach shopping is also within close striking distance.

3500 SE Morningside Boulevard
Port St. Lucie, Florida 34952
(772) 398–5100, (800) CLUB–MED
www.clubmed.com

HAWK'S CAY RESORT
Duck Key, Florida

Located in the heart of the Florida Keys is Hawk's Cay Resort, on a tropical sixty-acre island. The resort, built in the late 1950s, has hosted numerous presidents and film stars. The rambling Caribbean-style hotel sets the tone for the relaxed, elegant atmosphere that you'll find here. Ceiling fans, indoor plants, wicker furniture, and French doors in the lobbies and lounges echo the easygoing pace. The temperatures are mild, averaging in the low eighties in summer and the low seventies in winter, and the water stays warm and comfortable year-round. Water sports, from deep-sea fishing, fly-fishing, sailing, diving, and snorkeling to swimming, sunset sails, ecotours, and water-skiing, are, naturally, the main focus of this island resort. The only living coral reef in the continental United States is just offshore, and Hawk's Cay has seven resident dolphins.

Accommodations: This comfortable inn has the ambience and style of a Caribbean resort. Most of the 161 rooms and 16 suites are wrapped around a saltwater lagoon and several freshwater pools, with views of the Atlantic Ocean or the Gulf of Mexico. Each spacious room has a private balcony, separate dressing area, and a small refrigerator. During the high season, January through April, room rates range from $260 to $440; suite rates, including the presidential suite, range from $460 to $1,300. Low-season rates, May through mid-December, are $220 to $355 and $380 to $1,200, respectively. Children sixteen and under stay free with existing bedding. The resort also has 295 two- and three-bedroom villas, modeled after Key West conch houses, which offer water settings and a full kitchen. They are the perfect home away from home

for families and range from $390 to $1,300 in low season; $450 to $1,500 in high season. A daily resort activities fee of $10 per unit for the inn and $20 per villa covers unlimited tennis, daily access to Indies Club and fitness center, use of the boat ramp, chaise lounges, towels, and more.

Dining: If you like fresh seafood, you'll find dining here a treat. There are four tempting restaurants to choose from, each with its own distinctive style and menu selections.

Start the day with a fabulous breakfast buffet presented in the Palm Terrace. Breakfast hours begin as early as 7:00 A.M. and continue until 11:00 A.M. For casual lunches and dinners, the Cantina at poolside offers a variety of Mexican or Caribbean fare, as well as rum concoctions that recall the island's history as a stopover for Prohibition rumrunners. Also enjoy casual outdoor dining at the Indies Grille, featuring sandwiches, snacks, and a kids' menu.

The WatersEdge, dockside at the marina, is open for dinner, specializing in steak and fresh-off-the-boat seafood. Porto Cayo features a blend of Mediterranean and Floridian specialties in an elegant indoor setting or outdoor cafe ambiance. Truman's Bar brings back the nostalgia of when President Harry Truman vacationed here.

Children's World: Hawk's Cay is going all out to please the kids, and the program is growing and changing as their returning families change. Operating daily year-round, the schedules are flexible and geared to the needs of guests. The Indies Club is the new area dedicated to kids. Here you'll find two pools, one with pirate ship/water cannon playground in the center and a new tree house that presents the opportunity for hours of climbing fun with slides, a bridge, tire swings, and lots more. Dolphin Dayz is the area for kids eleven and under, while teens have the Cove, their own recreation room filled with all that's dear to teenage hearts: music, dance floor, Internet, karaoke, games, and beverages. Cover charge is $5.00. Open 4:00 to 7:00 P.M. for ages nine through twelve years; teens only (thirteen to seventeen) between 8:00 P.M. and midnight. There's a teen spa (ages eight to fifteen) with mini-treatments and a fitness center.

Hawk's Cay is experimenting with some new concepts. When the resort is filled, the more traditional program will be in effect. Daily full- and half-day Kids Club programs will keep children happily occupied with swimming, tiki-boat races, scavenger hunts, fishing, and ecology tours. Little Pirates is for children ages four to five years, while the Islands Adventure Club entertains ages six to eleven years with sports and nature-oriented games. Cost for either program is $55 for the full day (9:00 A.M. to 4:30 P.M.), including lunch; $28 for half days. Lunch is $7.00 for half-day sessions, and hours vary according to whether or not lunch is served.

A more flexible plan designates a supervised area where kids can come and go on a sign-in/sign-out basis, participating only in activities that interest them. Charges will vary. Additionally, every day there are at least two free planned activities—volleyball, limbo contest, face painting, and the like.

Kids Night Out, for ages four to eleven, includes dinner, a movie, and a make-and-take craft. It's available on Friday and Saturday evenings from 7:00 until 10:00 P.M. for $30 per child. Individual babysitting can also be arranged.

Recreation: Hawk's Cay guests have playing privileges at the eighteen-hole Sombrero Country Club championship course, approximately 10 miles away. For tennis buffs, two Har-Tru courts (lit for night play) and six Laykold courts beckon. Get instructions from on-site pros, participate in a variety of scheduled clinics, tournaments, and round-robins, or sharpen your skills with a ball machine.

But truly, the water tempts, entices, and captures the heart of visitors. It establishes the mood and is the setting for most of the recreation. Swim in one of the many pools or the saltwater lagoon, or stretch out beneath the tropical sun, but don't forget the sunscreen!

Discover the mysteries and wonder of undersea life. The coral reef offshore is home to a colorful array of tropical fish and is one of the best spots in the country for snorkeling and scuba diving. The Scuba Center has everything you need to immerse yourself in the scuba and snorkeling experience. Sailing clinics from two hours to ten days can make you an expert, while water-skiing, wakeboarding, kayaking, and para-sailing allow you a familiarity with the water from all angles. Wrap it all up with champagne and a sunset on a catamaran—does it get any better?

Fishing here puts you in the big league, and it's exciting. Just offshore you'll find red snapper and mackerel; farther out in Gulf Stream waters are marlin, dolphin, and tuna; and tarpon ply the waters in Florida Bay. Charter a vessel at the marina for an excursion. The Marina at Hawk's Cay offers eighty-five slips and can dock yachts more than 100 feet long.

Explore the island by bicycle—child-, teen-, and adult-sized bikes are available for $6.00 per hour, with helmet. Or take a self-guided walking tour to learn about the indigenous vegetation and tropical birds such as the brown pelican and the blue heron. Family, kids, and adult activities are scheduled just about every hour or two; some are complimentary, some have a nominal fee. After all that activity, a trip to the Indies Spa may be in order for massage, facials, a Vichy shower, and a complete fitness room to care for your entire body. Teens even have a special spa experience to revel in.

Unique to Hawk's Cay is the Dolphin Connection, a program designed to study, protect, and increase public interest in dolphin biology and ecosystems. Training sessions and interactive programs are offered daily. Sign up for a once-in-a-lifetime memory-making swim with the dolphins.

Mile Marker 61
Duck Key, Florida 33050
(305) 743–7000, (800) 432–2242,
(888) 443–6393
www.hawkscay.com

JEKYLL ISLAND CLUB HOTEL
Jekyll Island, Georgia

Jekyll Island, midway between Savannah, Georgia, and Jacksonville, Florida, and just 6 miles off the Georgia coast, is truly a gem. A barrier island, it's only 1½ miles wide and 9 miles long. Part of the state park system, a state law limits development on Jekyll to 35% of land above mean high water. Therefore, only one-third of the island can be developed, leaving wonderful beaches, ancient oaks, and dense maritime forests untouched and in their natural state. Of the approximately 5,000 acres, 65% will remain a nature preserve for future generations to enjoy.

Jekyll has an illustrious history that began in 1886 when it became a huge private club for some of America's wealthiest tycoons. The Rockefellers, Vanderbilts, and Morgans were the first families to vacation here, so you're keeping good company when you vacation on Jekyll Island. Their "cottages" (only 8,000 square feet or so, not the size of the Newport mansions) are now part of the Historic District, with museums, tram, and carriage tours.

The club has been restored to its original splendor, completely modernized, and is now enjoying a new life as the Jekyll Island Club Hotel. The hotel complex is the focal point of the historic district, and their goal is much the same as one hundred years ago—to provide relaxation and recreation in an exclusive setting. The four-diamond, four-star resort is part of the National Trust for Historic Preservation, and a registered National Historic Landmark. *Travel + Leisure* ranks the club one of the 500 best hotels in the world, and its elegant architecture, proud heritage, and excellent service explain why.

Accommodations: One hundred and fifty-seven guest rooms and suites tastefully blend century-old mahogany furnishings and Victorian fireplaces with marble bathrooms with whirlpools and telephones with data ports. Lodging prices listed are in the Clubhouse, the annex, or Sans Souci, originally built in 1896 as a six-unit apartment building—perhaps the first ever condominium? High season is early March to mid-August; rates range from $169 for a Clubhouse Double to $399 for the Presidential Suite; from December 1 to early March rates range from $129 to $359 for the same accommodations; children eighteen and under stay free in their parents' room. Another option is one of the beautifully restored historic "cottages": Crane Cottage, offering thirteen rooms and suites within a grand Italian-style villa, or Cherokee Cottage, a stately villa with ten rooms, named for the Cherokee roses growing at the entrance. Crane and Cherokee Cottages have comparable rates—talk with the resort for the best selection for your family. The Summer Family Getaway package offers a traditional room with two double beds, breakfast for the kids, and the children's program for $555 for three nights, or $745 for five nights. Meal plans, per person, are $82 for Full American Plan, and $64 for Modified American Plan (breakfast and dinner); children twelve and under pay half.

All rooms are subject to a $10 per night resort fee, which provides housekeeping gratuity, beach chairs and umbrellas, pool towels, phones, newspapers, bottled water, and coffee in the Boars Head lobby.

Dining: The Grand Dining Room is open daily for breakfast, lunch, and dinner, and boasts a scrumptious Sunday brunch. Emphasis is on seafood and gourmet Continental cuisine. The new Courtyard at Crane, open for lunch daily and dinner Sunday through Thursday, offers alfresco dining with Northern California cuisine. Café Solterra bakes their own yummy pastries and breads, along with New York deli offerings, and will pack a picnic lunch for you to take on your travels. Sit on the sunshine-filled porch and enjoy your food, but watch out for the crows—they are bold enough and big enough to steal half of your croissant while you read the paper! Grab a light snack at the Beach Pavilion or the Poolside Bar and Grill and never have to leave your lounge chair, or get "fancy" with the daily Victorian Tea. At the end of the day, Vincent's Pub encourages conversation and cocktails.

Children's World: Memorial Day to mid-August, Club Juniors is available for ages five to twelve years, Monday through Friday from 9:00 A.M. to 4:00 P.M. Cost is only $18 per day per child, with lunch included. Half days are $10. There may be additional fees for some activities. Days are filled with bicycle safaris, sand casting, treasure hunts, a dolphin cruise, tennis, canoeing, crafts, and crabbing at Clam Creek. And, of course, swimming, including trips to the nearby water park, is high on the favorites list. Kids will be delighted, and should certainly sleep well after all of this activity! That's Entertainment! livens up Friday mornings in summer with a series of performances and workshops showcasing Jekyll Island. Kids learn pizza baking, how to be a clown, all about sea turtles, how to make shadow puppets, archeology, and storytelling.

Recreation: Choose between the outdoor swimming pool or the Beach Pavilion, 1 mile away on the Atlantic Ocean. Of course, the club has a regulation size croquet lawn, so do bring the proper white clothing—you know, long flowing dresses for women, white duck for the men, short pants for boys, and hair ribbons for the girls. Rent a bicycle or try the putting green and in August enjoy hands-on cooking school at Crane Cottage. Just strolling around the grounds is a trip back in time to another century, as the hotel is the centerpiece of the island's Historic District. Visit the shops for unique souvenirs, stop by the museum to see the telephone from which the first transcontinental phone call was made, see where the Federal Reserve Banking System originated, or enjoy the sights from the motor-tram or horse-drawn carriage. Art galleries, sculpture at Mistletoe Cottage, and restaurants will beckon.

Don't miss the Faith Chapel with its fabulous Tiffany stained glass window, one of only two remaining.

Complimentary transportation is provided for guests to points throughout the island.

Jekyll Island Recreation: Families have the entire island as their playground. The island is actually a state park, so much of the recreation is leased or run by the state. When entering the island, there is a $3.00 entry fee per car. In fact, Jekyll Island has Georgia's largest public golf resort. Sixty-three holes (three eighteen-hole and one nine-hole course), with professional instruction and a clubhouse with pro shop, rental clubs, restaurant, and lounge, meet your every golfing need. Picturesque but demanding, Dick Wilson's Oleander is consistently ranked among the best courses in the state. A driving range, putting greens, and practice bunker complete the golf scene. And for the budding Tiger Woods in your family, start at the two miniature golf courses or try some junior instruction. A first-class tennis center with thirteen courts (one indoors); Summer Waves Water Park; and boating, from paddleboats on the lake to sea kayaking, are all here. Fishermen can choose from surf fishing, off the pier, or two freshwater lakes. Crabbing and seining for shrimp are options, but be aware that wading birds and porpoises may follow you.

There's a wonderful new playground for children, with areas for both toddlers and older children. A relaxed sunset horseback ride along the beach promotes mind and body relaxation. And the beach stretches the length of the island, calling for nice long walks, jogging, or collecting shells. Twenty miles of bicycle trails and jogging paths provide the perfect way to enjoy this island. Treat all your senses as you watch for deer, marsh hares, and beautiful shorebirds; smell the wonderful pinewoods and salt air; listen to the sound of the ocean and feel the wind on your skin. The Tidelands Nature Center educates and explains about barrier islands, and encourages kids to "please touch" the flora and fauna. Loggerhead sea turtles have found a safe haven on Jekyll Island and nightly turtle walks on the starlit beach allow guests to share that magic. The hotel is adding a special research/educational exhibit about these fascinating creatures. Jekyll Island is also part of Georgia's Coastal Birding Trail, with three sites and an October festival. Many restaurants and shops will beckon. For a change of view, take a water taxi to nearby St. Simons Island. It's definitely easy to adjust to this lifestyle.

---

371 Riverview Drive
Jekyll Island, Georgia 31527
(912) 635–2600, (800) 535–9547
www.jekyllclub.com

MARCO ISLAND MARRIOTT RESORT

Marco Island, Florida

Close to 2,000 years ago, native peoples discovered the beauty of Southwest Florida's Gulf Coast and Marco Island, and people have been coming there ever since. The Calusa tribe lived off the abundant shellfish and used the discarded shells to raise their dwellings above water level. Many of these ancient mounds remain today. Perched on the northernmost point of the Ten Thousand Islands of the Everglades and just south of Naples, the island is graced with miles of white sand beaches and is noted for its gorgeous sunsets. The resort's guests get lost in the intriguing contrasts: Waves of sun-drenched beaches, always-warm Gulf waters, and passionate sunsets present a tame, pampered complement to the tangled wildness and sweeping sawgrass prairies of Florida's famous nearby Everglades.

Not just your typical high-rise-on-a-Florida-beach, the three-star, four-diamond Marco Island Marriott completed a $90-million renovation and expansion in 2004. All deluxe guest rooms have been redesigned and renovated, plus there are new restaurants, a Fantasy Tiki pool with water slides and cool features, and the Balinese Health Spa.

Accommodations: All of Marco Island Marriott Resort's 727 guest rooms and 54 suites have private balconies. Poolside or beachfront lanais—each with a private balcony entrance—and a secluded cluster of seaside villas complete the resort's accommodations. Daily rates, depending on size, are $150 to $330 in the low season (May through September) and $320 to $530 in the high season (December through April);

weekends are more expensive, and packages are available.

Dining: Shimmering turquoise-flecked waters, sweeping white sands, and lush gardens create a tropical backdrop for four distinct restaurants at the resort. Tropiks provides great family dining for breakfast and lunch, and Kurrents has an upscale and trendy ambience for fine seafood and steak dinners. Quinn's on the Beach cooks up a treasure trove of savory sandwiches and Caribbean appetizers from almost dawn until after dusk, while the Calypso Grill at Quinn's serves unique seafood dinners. For a change of pace, just 7 miles away in Naples, you may have breakfast or lunch at the Rookery Clubhouse on the golf course. Check out Scoozie's for pizza and sandwiches, or have a light lunch and drinks at the Tiki Bar and Grill. For coffee and pastries, try Fidalgo Bay.

Children's World: The Tiki Tribe at Marco Island Marriott Resort—the first resort in North America to be awarded the National Parenting Center Seal of Approval—is a lot of pint-size fun, occupying youngsters ages five to twelve with sand-castle creations, coconut bowling, arts and crafts, and zany relay races. The program operates daily year-round, from 10:00 A.M. to 3:00 P.M. The cost is $30 for a full day, including lunch and an ice-cream snack. A second child is $25. A unique Rainy Day program offers hours of indoor entertainment for the whole family on those rare days without sunshine.

Recreation: Choreographed by a team of fun-in-the-sun experts, daily activities are scheduled hourly from 9:00 A.M. to 3:00 P.M.

and include aquaslimnastics, tennis aerobics, island bike and trolley tours, beach volleyball, table tennis, and step aerobics. Usually at least one activity per day is complimentary. Sun worshippers and soul searchers relax under thatch-topped tiki huts, play beach volleyball, or scour the shore for seashells. Endless Gulf activities include sailing, kayaking, windsurfing, waterskiing, bumper tubing, Wave Runners, and parasailing. Two swimming pools offer refreshing plunges; the Tiki Pool begins at zero depth, good for splashing with toddlers. Older kids and even adults enjoy the water slide and other special water features found here.

Golfers can enjoy the off-site, Robert Cupp Jr.–designed eighteen-hole championship golf course called the Rookery. The clubhouse facility includes an elaborate pro shop, complete locker room facilities, the Clubhouse Grill for breakfast or lunch, and Nick Faldo's School of Golf. For tennis enthusiasts, there are eight red clay courts (four lighted for night play), a tennis shop, daily clinics, private lessons, and round-

robins. Fabulous fishing is accessible, or you can work out with Florida-style aerobics and fitness programs.

Treat yourself to a session at the Balinese Spa for a massage and perhaps a milk-and-honey or lavender-and-rose-petal Bali Bath. Be sure, though, to save time for eco-tour adventures. Briggs Nature Center is only 8 miles away, or you can visit Everglades National Park (30 miles). Unlike many tropical places, Marco Island and the surrounding area have an abundance of art galleries, museums, concerts, cultural heritage centers, and even a film festival. The Big Cypress Gallery, located in the heart of the Everglades, showcases Clyde Butcher's nature photography, described by some as the Ansel Adams of the new millennium.

---

400 South Collier Boulevard
Marco Island, Florida 34145
(239) 394–2511, (800) 438–4373
www.marcoislandmarriott.com

MARRIOTT'S GRAND HOTEL RESORT, GOLF CLUB & SPA
Point Clear, Alabama

The charm and graciousness of the Old South has not faded in southern Alabama. Marriott's Grand Hotel has preserved its rich tradition of elegant service as a premier resort for more than 150 years. Known as the Queen of Southern Resorts, the four-diamond hotel is set on 550 acres in Point Clear, on a peninsula in Mobile Bay and 23 miles from downtown Mobile. In this secluded location, the quiet lagoons, majestic oak trees draped in Spanish moss, and beautiful gardens can

make you forget the worries and concerns of the workaday world. Leave your troubles and anxieties on the doorstep and enter this vacation retreat, where your biggest dilemma will be how to best enjoy yourself.

The fascinating legacy of the Grand Hotel captures the heart of many a history buff. First discovered as an ideal location for a resort retreat in 1847, the hotel was the site of lively antebellum social events in its early years. Then, during the days of the

Civil War (or as some folks down here still call it, the War of Northern Aggression), it served as a hospital for Confederate soldiers. After the war the hotel resumed its original function and once again became the center for leisure activities. A fire in 1869 and a hurricane in 1893 destroyed some of the old facilities, but rebuilding efforts and expansion were frequently undertaken in order to maintain accommodations for guests. Today's main hotel building was constructed in 1941. In 1967 the Bay House was added, and 1983 brought the addition of two buildings—the North Bay House and the Marina House. The most recent renovation and addition of a European-style spa was completed in 2003.

Accommodations: The main building has been described as rustic, but don't be deceived; this is rustic in a grand old manner. The lobby here is a charming octagonal structure that focuses on a massive fireplace. From its wide planks of pine flooring to its cypress-beamed ceiling, visitors immediately sense a warm, hospitable atmosphere. There are a total of 405 guest rooms in the different buildings and the cottages. Many rooms are decorated with white cypress paneling and ceiling fans (maintained primarily for ambience, but also to capture the bay breezes; air-conditioning relieves the sultriness of summer days). All rooms were refurbished in 2004 and most offer private balconies with bay/marina or pool/garden views. Open year-round, the hotel has two rate structures. In the winter season (November through February), daily room-only rates range from $184 to $244 midweek. Special rates that include breakfast for two are just $10 more, and children under five can dine from the special children's buffet. Summer rates (March through October) are higher: $199 to $259 weekdays or $299 to $359 weekends. There is no charge for cribs and rollaways.

Inquire about the many specials and packages available.

Dining: The Grand Dining Room offers an elegant but casual atmosphere for breakfast, lunch, and dinner. An orchestra performs Tuesday through Saturday nights during dinner and afterward for dancing. Since the hotel is located on Mobile Bay and so close to the gulf, many of the house specialties rely on the fresh local seafood. Oysters, red snapper stuffed with crabmeat, and seafood gumbo are a few of the selections. The hearty-meat-and-potatoes fan will find excellent prime rib of beef. The gourmet will be enticed by the elegant Bayview Restaurant where New Orleans–trained chefs prepare Cajun and Creole favorites for intimate and scenic dining.

For a sumptuous buffet breakfast, try the Grand Buffet in the Grand Dining Room, where you may sit in a gazebo area with beautiful bay views. Lunch is served not only in the Grand Dining Room but also at the Lakewood Golf Club and Grill Room, set in a wooded landscape. While soaking up the sunshine, you may choose snacks, sandwiches, and grilled favorites poolside at either the Pelican's Nest or the Blue Marlin Bar. Bucky's Birdcage Lounge also serves light snacks and delightful cocktails with spectacular views, and live entertainment nightly.

Children's World: The Grand Fun Camp is in operation daily year-round. Every day a group of friendly counselors coordinates fun-filled activities. Four- to twelve-year-olds frolic from 10:00 A.M. to 2:00 P.M. and from 6:00 until 10:00 P.M. The cost is $40 per session including lunch or dinner. The second sibling is $20, and the third is only $10. Shuffleboard, putt-putt golf, arts and crafts, video games, fishing, and sand-castle building entertain children, who will no doubt entertain their parents as they recount a day's adventures. Special events include movies and puppet shows. A new swimming pool on Mobile Bay with waterfalls and slides also has a children's area with playground and tree house that kids love. Individual babysitters are also available on an hourly basis.

Recreation: In the old days of the resort, two favorite spots were the wharves—one for men and one for women, because sunbathing and swimming in mixed company were unacceptable. Having come a long way since then, the Grand now offers innumerable popular activities for its guests. Given this prime location and mild climate, water sports attract many visitors. After a little warm-up fishing in the bay, you might take on the challenges of deep-sea fishing. Your catch may be your evening's dinner, prepared especially for you by the hotel chefs. Reserve a sailboat or paddleboat for an afternoon's outing, or bring your own boat to the thirty-seven-slip marina. Splash in the waters of the bay along the sandy beach, or take a dip in the beautiful pool, the largest on the Gulf Coast, with waterfall and slide. There's also a family pool, a child-entry pool, as well as a new indoor pool and two whirlpools.

If you're more of a landlubber, the championship thirty-six holes of golf are a suitable diversion. Regardless of their level of play, all golfers appreciate the rolling, wooded setting of the Golf Trail Courses designed by Robert Trent Jones. The facilities of the club include instructors, carts, putting greens, and locker room. The eight rubico tennis courts (four lighted) lure many ace players, and novices can enroll for lessons with one of the pros. Head to the stables at Ocala Farms for horseback riding around the picturesque lakes and lagoons, or jog or bicycle (rentals available) through the gardens and along the boardwalk.

Slower-paced activities include croquet, putting green, and video games. You may want to wind up the day in the hot tub or with a treat from the full-service spa, where treatments are luxuriously relaxing in a serenely beautiful setting. In the 1930s the Grand Hotel advertised itself as the place of "Every Creature Comfort." Many visitors today feel that reputation has withstood the test of time.

One Grand Boulevard
Point Clear, Alabama 36564
(251) 928–9201, (800) 544–9933
www.marriottgrand.com

THE RESORT AT LONGBOAT KEY CLUB

Longboat Key, Florida

An island retreat, the Resort at Longboat Key Club specializes in relaxation and recreation for golfers and tennis players. Located on a barrier island in the Gulf of Mexico just west of Sarasota, it doesn't shortchange swimmers and sun worshippers either. One of *Travel + Leisure* magazine's "Top 500 Resorts in the World," consider it your private oceanfront country club. The resort enjoys a lush, tropical setting between the Gulf and Sarasota Bay that seems worlds away from regular routine, yet is only fifteen minutes away from the Sarasota Airport.

Accommodations: Seven modern buildings, four to ten stories high, are arranged throughout the property to afford guests magnificent views of the Gulf, the bay, and the golf course fairways. Of the 232 accommodations, each with its own balcony, the majority (220) are suites, each with a king-size bed, a sleeper sofa, and a fully equipped kitchen. Summer (June through September) is the low season, when guest rooms range from $215 to $255 a night and club suites start at $250 a night; the deluxe two-bedroom suites command $550 to $580 a night. During the high season (October through May), a guest room is $245 to $295 a night, while suites cost $315 to $600 a night. During the rest of the year, prices fall between these parameters; holidays are more expensive. Up to two children (seventeen and younger) can stay in a suite with their parents at no additional charge. A Family Stay and Play package for two adults and two children includes four nights' suite accommodation, daily breakfast, two days at the Kids Klub, daily Fitness Centre, tennis, bicycles, and one beach lounger. Summer rates begin at $1,160, with a resort fee of $15 per room, $25 per suite.

Dining: Dining can be as elegant or as casual as you choose. On the sophisticated side is Sands Pointe, the signature restaurant. Tempting fresh seafood dishes are frequently featured on its menus; open for breakfast, lunch, and dinner. Next to the restaurant, try Sands Pointe Lounge for a light menu, specialty drinks, homemade desserts such as raspberry-key-lime pie, and live entertainment in the evenings. For more casual dining, drop by Spike 'n' Tees for breakfast or lunch overlooking the fairways; and for truly relaxed mealtimes, saunter over to Barefoots, at poolside; no shoes required, with live music. Enjoy lunch and dinner at the nearby Grille at Harborside, 11:30 A.M. to 4:30 P.M. on weekends,

set among gigantic oak trees. Traditional country club lunches and steak and seafood dinners are a welcome option. The Dining Room, with its view of the marina waterways lined with mangrove trees, serves seasonal evening buffets and Sunday Brunch as well. Or simply enjoy room service served on your own private balcony.

Children's World: The Kids Klub operates year-round, Tuesday through Saturday. Experienced counselors direct youngsters ages five to twelve in a full 9:30 A.M. to 3:00 P.M. program. Swimming, beach fun, volleyball, basketball, field trips, and arts and crafts are all part of the schedule. The program is $25 per child per day, and includes lunch and admission to attractions. Regularly visited attractions and things to do include the Mote Marine Laboratory, Sarasota Jungle Gardens, Gulf Coast World of Science, Planet Fun, movies, bowling, skating, and miniature golf at Pirate's Cove. The average cost of individual babysitting is $15 an hour, with a three-hour minimum.

Recreation: The Islandside Golf Course has eighteen holes, and the Harborside Course has twenty-seven holes. Recipient of *Golf Magazine's* Silver Medal, with palm trees and quiet lagoons throughout these courses, who can have a bad game? Two complete pro shops, a golf school, and professionals to guide players in private lessons and tournaments round out the picture for golfers.

Thirty-eight Har-Tru tennis courts await your ace serves and graceful lobs. Six of these are lighted for night play. Two tennis shops, ball machines, a videotaped game analysis, and a professional staff will urge you on to better play. Recognized as a "Top 50 Tennis Resort" by *Tennis* magazine, tennis play is complimentary here.

Swimming in the outdoor pool or the gentle waters of the Gulf may top off your day. Bicycle along the nature trails, stroll on the snow-white beach, or spend an afternoon snorkeling or sailing. You can even organize a deep-sea fishing expedition through the concierge.

The resort's newest recreational amenity is a 4,000-square-foot fitness center, which features weight-training and cardiovascular equipment as well as instructor-led aerobics classes. Fitness-center equipment is available to guests on a complimentary basis. For soothing life's daily stress and the ultimate in personal pampering, neuromuscular, sports, and Swedish massage are also available.

301 Gulf of Mexico Drive
Longboat Key, Florida 34228
(941) 383–8821, (800) 237–8821
www.longboatkeyclub.com

SOUTH SEAS RESORT
Captiva Island, Florida

Located at the northern tip of Captiva Island on the Gulf of Mexico, 3 miles off Florida's southwest coast, Captiva Island is connected to the mainland via Sanibel Island and the Sanibel Causeway. It has a fascinating history going back at least 5,000 years and involving Calusa Indians, pirates, homesteaders, and a prosperous key-lime plantation. South Seas Resort is approximately 30 miles from the Southwest Florida International Airport in Fort Myers.

Dubbed "Florida's Tahiti" for its subtropical climate and lush foliage indigenous to the Southern Hemisphere, Captiva Island— famous for its shell-covered beaches—has been rated one of America's most romantic beaches. South Seas Resort is a 330-acre island resort with 2½ miles of beach, a full-service yacht harbor and marina, recreational options from golf and tennis to island excursion cruises and water sports, fine restaurants, shopping, children's programs, and a complimentary open-air trolley transportation system.

NOTE: South Seas Resort suffered extensive damage in 2004 from Hurricane Charlie. They have spent two years and $140 million to restore and improve all aspects of the resort. South Seas will celebrate a full reopening on President's Weekend in 2006, better than ever. This entry is as accurate as it can be under the circumstances, but we encourage you to check directly with the resort to ensure up-to-the-minute information.

Accommodations: The South Seas Resort boasts more than 600 luxurious units, ranging from deluxe hotel rooms and villa suites to three-bedroom beach homes and cottages. Rate ranges from May to mid-December are $249 to $689 and January through April are $389 to $1,249, reflecting accommodation type, location, and view. Children sixteen and under stay free, and four-day Family Fun packages can provide good value. The resort has promised to always offer the best rate available—you don't even need to ask.

Dining: The resort's legendary King's Crown Restaurant features exquisite architecture and an award-winning culinary team. Discover fine dining in an elegant waterfront setting where New American cuisine is graciously served, traditions of yesterday are preserved, and new traditions are created. Florida Living magazine readers have honored King's Crown with the distinction of "Best Restaurant with a View." Chadwick's Restaurant features casual dining in a tropical setting. It is open for breakfast seasonally, and menus feature daily breakfast and lunch buffets, a Sunday champagne brunch, and evening theme buffets, including Caribbean Celebration Buffet, Bourbon Street Bash, Key West Clambake, and Seafood Extravaganza. The mahogany and leather Porter House is the place for steaks and wine.

Dine indoors or in the open air at Cap'n Al's Dockside Grille overlooking the yacht harbor. Cap'n Al's serves breakfast, lunch, and dinner daily with a children's menu. Enjoy Mama Rosa's Pizzeria, offering eat-in or take-out dining; the convenience of delivery is provided after 5:00 P.M. Choose from mouthwatering pizza, garden-fresh salads, and delicious subs. Fresh dough is made daily on the premises. Uncle Bob's Ice Cream Emporium serves delicious, old-fashioned soda fountain and ice-cream treats and tempting candies, and sells educational toys and kites. Pelican Pete's Pool Bar and Grill is a full-service bar specializing in tropical libations; poolside dining at the north end features grilled sandwiches, snacks, and more. C.W.'s Deli has an online grocery list with prices to stock your refrigerator before your arrival.

For dining entertainment, the King's Crown Lounge, located in the King's Crown Restaurant, offers cocktails and live, easy-listening entertainment. Chadwick's Lounge has a full bar and live entertainment nightly. A steel-drum band is featured Tuesday evening and a jazz quartet during dinner on Thursday evening.

Children's World: Activities for all ages are available year-round. A professional staff organizes daily itineraries of recreational and educational activities, where kids dress up like pirates or mail coconuts to their friends. Fun Factory™, for children ages four to eleven, includes activities such as Nature Camp, Pirate Mania, Circus at South Seas, and Dinner Theatre. Fun Factory is a program offered by Meri-star resorts at eleven properties, with supervision by "funologists" and innovative educational programs, sports, activities, and creative projects. While there's a somewhat standard formula for success, each resort customizes the program, and kids become members, with newsletter and Web site fun available after returning home. Two age groups, four- to six-year-olds and seven- to twelve-year-olds, may combine if groups are small. Each day is centered on a theme unique to the individual resort—for Captiva, it's often pirates and shells. Nursery Rhyme Day for the younger set and Cartoon Craze for ages seven to twelve are always popular, where kids get to become their favorite characters. The program runs year-round, Monday through Saturday from 9:00 A.M. to 1:00 P.M. Evening sessions from 5:00 to 8:00 P.M. on Thursday and Saturday give Mom and Dad an opportunity for a quiet dinner or a solitary seaside stroll under the stars. Each session costs $35.

Teens are well looked after, in the style they like. Sunday kayak excursions ($12) or a Monday Fishing Tourney ($10) get them acquainted with each other, easily. Monday Pool Party evenings ($10.00), Hangout ($5.00), and a wild game of Ultimate Capture the Flag ($10.00) on Saturday night round out the offerings.

Supervised social events for teens, such as parasailing, waterskiing, volleyball tournaments, pool parties, canoeing, kayaking, and golf are sure to provide hours of enjoyment.

Recreation: Dozens of recreational activities are available to guests of South Seas Plantation, including a par-36, regulation nine-hole seaside golf course; tennis on eighteen courts; biking; and water sports, including game fishing, sailboarding, snorkeling, sailing, and excursion cruises to nearby islands. Paddle a kayak into a mangrove forest, zoom around on a WaveRunner, or just watch the manatees play around the marina.

Workshops feature yoga, professional fitness training, aerobic exercise classes, canoe excursions, sailing clinics, guided shelling excursions, family fishing, shell art, and more. Family activities include log rolling contests, bingo, alligator races, or hydrocycles. A variety of nature activities for the whole family include Dolphin and Manatee Awareness, Shells of Captiva, Wildlife Refuge Trips, and Birds of Captiva. The Nature Center celebrates the bio-diversity of these barrier islands with a "please touch" approach. *The Explorer Bulletin,* a current schedule of activities, is given to guests upon check-in. Preregistration is required for all activities.

Shopping at South Seas includes quality boutiques, gift shops, pro shops, grocery store and gourmet deli, ship's store, and full-service beauty salon.

P.O. Box 194
5400 Plantation Road
Captiva Island, Florida 33924
(239) 472–5111, (800) 965–7772
www.south-seas-resort.com

SUNDIAL BEACH RESORT
Sanibel Island, Florida

Sanibel is a barrier island off the southwest coast of Florida that has some of the best shelling in the world. Two-thirds of the island remains a nature preserve—it also preserves a taste of Florida as it once was. No neon and high-rises here; in fact, locals call it Nature's Theme Park. The Sundial is the island's only full-service resort, set on thirty-three lush, tropical acres along the Gulf of Mexico. Completely renovated in 2005 as an aftermath of Hurricane Charlie, it's back and in fine shape.

Accommodations: Two hundred seventy condominium units provide a home-away-from-home atmosphere; choose a one- or two-bedroom and revel in full kitchens, comfortable and roomy bedrooms, and living areas, most with screened balconies. Select a garden view, partial gulf view, or gulf-front unit; rates vary according to season and location. A one-bedroom unit is $189 to $299 May to mid-December; $395 to $549 between February and late April. Children sixteen and under stay free with existing bedding. A three-night/four-day all-inclusive Family Getaway package treats your family to champagne, all meals including snacks and drinks, beach chairs, nonmotorized water sports, bicycles, tennis equipment and courts, and the Explorer Kid's Club Camp program including crafts. What a deal! Cost for two adults and two children is $1,530 for a one-bedroom and $1,689 for two bedrooms.

Dining: Hunger is easily satisfied at Sundial. Windows on the Water boasts unique gulf-shore cuisine garnished with spectacular beach views. Open for breakfast, lunch, and dinner, it's noted for the Sunday champagne brunch. Teppanyaki tables at Noopie's put you in the midst of the cooking action—performance cuisine at its best.

Open nightly from 5:30 P.M.; check the times for one of the seven shows. Crocodial's Poolside Bar & Grill has sandwiches, salads, cold drinks, sunset happy hour, and afternoon entertainment on weekends. Beaches Bar & Grill serves up views, happy-hour specials, and nightly "island style" entertainment Tuesday through Sunday until 11:00 P.M.

A five-minute drive brings you to Rassa, at the Dunes Golf and Tennis Club. Creative seafood and traditional steakhouse favorites are served up in this intimate setting. Named after Punta Rassa, the old port used to ship cattle to Cuba, meats are positively works of art here. Dine indoors or on the patio. Lunches of salad, homemade soups, and sandwiches are offered Monday through Saturday; open for dinner Wednesday through Saturday with Mexican or Italian themes. You've an entire island of dining choices as well. In fact, two islands, as a bridge connects Sanibel to nearby Captiva Island and its associated property, South Seas Resort. Stock your larder or buy goodies to take home at local grocery stores and shopping centers.

Children's World: The concept behind Explorer Kid's Club is that if kids don't have a good time on vacation, you won't either. They're dedicated to helping you achieve that goal. Year-round programs for children ages four to eleven are extensive and flexible. Part of the Fun Factory program, it's by no means an assembly-line production, as each resort puts its own personal touch on activities and themes. Aquacize, hermit crab races, and shell crafts are on the agenda. The program blends games, sports, and learning, and all with equal parts of fun and action. The morning session is from 9:00 A.M. to 1:00 P.M., and costs $25. In addition, activities are planned daily between 10:00 A.M. and 4:00 P.M.; some are age specific (four and up or seven and

up) and some are for all ages; kids may participate as they like. Fees range from complimentary to $9.00 for materials or excursions. Wacky Sunglasses, Coconut Painting, Dolphin Discovery, Oceans Alive, and even a worm-eating contest are just some samples. When you check in at the front desk, make sure you're a member of Explorers so you'll receive a discount. Kid's Night Out from 5:30 to 8:30 P.M. on Friday and Saturday ($25) has a weekly theme, such as Luau, and gives parents a chance to kick up their heels.

Sun-Dial-a-Story line provides a two-minute bedtime story or nursery rhyme for your child. Different every day, it may become a habit.

Recreation: A professional recreation staff plans myriad daily activities for all ages. In addition to the Explorer Kid's Club Camp, teens and 'tweens are enticed into participation with beach volleyball, bicycles, or boogie boards. Family activities bring everyone together for squirt gun painting, shell symposiums and crafts, crazy sand bottles, or candy bar bingo. Some activities are complimentary; others may have a small fee for supplies.

Close by, the Dunes Golf and Tennis Club offers a championship course, an aqua driving range, and two practice greens. Better practice your swing before hitting the course, as the back nine is part of a wildlife preserve and plenty of critters are watching. It's equal parts sports and nature experience. Are you a tennis family? Sundial's got something for everyone: $5.00 clinics for the Tiny Tots (ages four to seven) and junior (ages eight to fourteen), and adult clinics for $15.00. Between the club and the resort there are nineteen courts for practice and play. Courts are complimentary for guests and two of the hard courts are lighted for night play. Golf and tennis pro shops have all the latest gear and game advice.

Fish from beach, pier, bridge, or boat— gulf waters have more than 1,000 species of marine life. Or stay on top of the water with kayaks, windsurfers, and catamarans. Swim in one of the five heated pools—kids love to slide down the huge Nautilus Shell—or work out in the fitness room.

Sanibel has an exciting selection of cruises: Cruise the bay with a marine biologist to watch dolphins and visit a deserted island; take an out-island luncheon cruise to Cabbage Key and Useppa, a shelling cruise, a sail, or a beautiful sunset cruise. Environmental Discovery Programs schedule both lectures and hands-on experiences. The ECO (Environmental Coastal Observatory) Center was the first to be situated in a resort. Spend fascinating hours with a simulated mangrove forest, the aquarium, the touch tank, and a hermit crab petting zoo learning about all that surrounds you on this beautiful island. May to October is sea turtle nesting season.

Sanibel is an active place, with theater groups, Tanger outlet shopping center, shops, and art galleries. Since Sanibel is one of the three best shelling areas in the world, it's only natural to have a Shell Museum. Nearby attractions include the "Ding" Darling National Wildlife Refuge, Corkscrew Swamp Sanctuary, Calusa Nature Center and Planetarium, and the Edison-Ford Estates.

1451 Middle Gulf Drive
Sanibel Island, Florida 33957
(800) 965–7772, (239) 472–4151
www.sundialresort.com

TRADEWINDS ISLAND RESORTS/ISLAND GRAND
St. Pete Beach, Florida

Hugging the sugary white sands of the Gulf of Mexico, two stellar beach resorts, the Island Grand and Sandpiper, comprise TradeWinds Island Resorts. These properties occupy twenty-three of the most desirable acres on St. Pete Beach. With limitless beachfront recreation, sumptuous dining, and exclusive golf privileges at the area's private country clubs, the TradeWinds Island Resorts offer guests access to two resorts in one.

The Island Grand resort is a classic four-diamond, family-friendly beach resort. Canals with white swans meander through the property, awaiting your visit via gondola or paddleboat. The Grand Palm Colonnade, a garden atrium lined with two-story palm trees, provides a shady welcome. The children's program is headquartered here, so it's most convenient for families. An eighteen-acre island hideaway, TradeWinds Island Grand offers endless diversions, award-winning service, and classic Florida charm.

Accommodations: The 378 guest rooms and 207 suites are all newly renovated (2002/2003) with bright, colorful tropical furnishings and clean white accents. Every room features a microwave, refrigerator, toaster, and dishware. Suites have separate bedrooms, kitchenette, and living area, most with balconies. February, March, and April are high season, when hotel rooms range from $229 to $369 and one-bedroom suites are $325 to $459. May through mid-December rates are lower; $197 to $295 for rooms and $255 to $377 for one-bedroom suites. No charge for children twelve and under sharing the room. A daily Explorer Value Pass ($12 per room; $17 per suite) is required; this covers parking, telephone, tennis courts, fitness center, beach cabanas, and other services. Summer family packages are well priced and offer many extras; inquire about "Beach Blanket Bingo," with a 1950s theme, or "Swashbuckling by the Sea," with pirates and a yo-heave-ho! Contact the resort for information on the many packages offered with a price range that is sure to fit your family quite nicely.

Dining: Feast on the specialties of the house: island medleys of Gulf Coast cuisine, tall tropical coolers, and barefoot beach bars. Enjoy breakfast buffets, poolside lunches, and sunset dinners. Savor aged steaks and fresh native seafood, or experience the intimate elegance and excellent fare at Palm Court. Indulge in room service, deli specialties, an ice-cream shop, and even a Pizza Hut. Unwind at the waterside piano bar or enjoy evening entertainment at the lounge. At TradeWinds Island Resorts, multiple dining and entertainment venues, with options to charge them to your room account, await your pleasure.

At the Island Grand Resort, choose from the Palm Court, an elegant bistro where you may dine indoors or on the patio under the stars; Bermudas, open for breakfast (try the buffet) and dinner, offers seafood, regional specialties, and steaks, with a children's menu; or the Flying Bridge, an authentic floating Florida "cracker cottage" docked over the main canal—probably one of the only restaurants you can boat under! Fare and dress are casual; appetizers, salads, and sandwiches are served. Step back into the 1940s in the Old Florida Shrimp Shack

for shrimp and cold beer, or catch the big game at B.R.Cuda's Sports Bar. Enjoy seasonal live entertainment at B.R.Cuda's, the Flying Bridge, the Shrimp Shack, or Salty's Beach Bar. Capt. Redbeard's Sharktooth Tavern is host to food and drink and seasonal live entertainment. A variety of activities let you meet the captain, celebrate a Pirate Island Party, try Buccaneer Breadmaking, race crabs, make shark's-tooth necklaces, and view fishermen's exhibitions.

Children's World: Tuesday through Saturday, the enthusiastic recreation counselors (known as T.A.Z. Team members) of TradeWinds Action Zone offer activities from A to Z, with recreational options for every member of the family. T.A.Z. Team members supervise tons of planned fun stuff from aerobics to zany, wacky wordies, family swim meets, suncatcher creations, or a hunt for treasures.

The KONK Club, short for "Kids Only, No Kidding!" is specially designed for children four to eleven years old. Each day's program is themed a little differently, lasts from 9:00 A.M. to 1:00 P.M., and includes a meal ($30). KONK kids even have their own special nighttime programs from 6:00 to 9:00 P.M. (Tuesday through Saturday; cost is $35 with dinner), providing a great way to make friends with other kids, and giving Mom and Dad a little time alone. Monday evening is reserved for the family "dive-in" movie. On Wednesday and Saturday, when Captain Redbeard comes to Pirate Island, all the kids get dressed up and tall tales and swashbuckling songs break out. After a search for shark's teeth, everyone heads for the pool for a "dive-in" pirate movie—great fun for all.

Be sure to look for Beaker, the TradeWinds huggable purple toucan mascot. You're likely to spot Beaker at KONK Club activities or making rounds at each of the resorts. Or call Activities to schedule a bedtime tuck-in: Beaker will come to your room to make sure all kids are tucked in toucan-style.

Teens will enjoy the variety of activities and attractions at the three resorts and in the surrounding area. With tennis, golf, swimming, snorkeling, WaveRunners, Shell Island and Dolphin Watch Cruises, minigolf, parasailing, and numerous other activities, teens can be as active as they choose. If there's enough interest, the T.A.Z. Team will schedule excursions or special events. What a great opportunity to meet young people from all three resorts. Preregistration is required for off-site trips.

Recreation: Escape to the magic of the TradeWinds Island Resorts and discover a place where you can do "everything under the sun"—or absolutely nothing at all. The Golf Concierge Desk will arrange tee times at any of the public courses in the Tampa Bay area; guests also enjoy privileges at the private Pasadena Yacht and Country Club, just ten minutes away. Four Har-Tru clay courts serve all resort guests, so reserve early. The Action Zone Activities Center coordinates all the recreation activity for every member of the family—and it's extensive. Whether aqua aerobics, tie-dye towels, glow-in-the-dark

volleyball, or Hunt for Redbeard's Buried Treasure, the T.A.Z. staff has you covered. Minigolf, life-size chess, or sunset yoga may tempt you; the water beckons with parasailing, snorkeling, WaveRunners, waterskiing, boat rental, and fishing charters; take a dolphin or manatee encounter cruise; walk along eighteen acres of soft, white-sand beaches; or try your hand at beach volleyball.

The swirl of whirlpools, the heat of sauna, the refreshing depths of five pools entice. Dip into the shimmering surface of the sea. Comb the sandy beach for shells. Curl up with a book in a tropical courtyard or a beach cabana. Toast the sunset. Explore the resorts' meandering waterway, complete with swans, ducks, and egrets. Pamper yourself at Body Works salon with massage, aromatherapy, and body wraps. Relax. You're a million miles away . . . from everything. You're now on island time.

5500 Gulf Boulevard
St. Pete Beach, Florida 33706
(727) 367–6461, (800) 360–4016
www.tradewindsresort.com

MIDWEST

Illinois
Michigan
Minnesota
Missouri
Wisconsin

EAGLE RIDGE INN AND RESORT

Galena, Illinois

With 6,800 acres of rolling, wooded terrain and sixty-three challenging holes of golf, Eagle Ridge is a major Midwest golf resort, awarded *Golf Magazine*'s "Silver Medal" for excellence eight times. When you're not on the links, you'll find that 220-acre Lake Galena is a focus of resort activity. Located in northwest Illinois, just minutes from historic Galena with its well-preserved nineteenth-century architecture, Eagle Ridge is only 150 miles from Chicago, great for weekend escapes.

Accommodations: The Eagle Ridge Inn, with its eighty rooms, sits in the center of the resort, on a bluff overlooking the lake. Enjoy relaxing and share good conversations around the fireplace in the spacious common room. In addition, resort homes and villas are scattered throughout the hills and consist of one- to eight-bedroom accommodations; choose from views of the fairway, the lake, or secluded woods. During peak season, from late May to late October, inn rooms are $199 to $309 a night (children under eighteen sharing a room with parents are free); a one- to three-bedroom villa is $249 to $429; the resort homes are $399 to $1,129 a night. January to mid-May and late October to mid-December, inn rooms are $149 to $309; villas run $169 to $329 and homes are $309 to $989. The resort homes are also available for weekly rental, and many different packages are offered.

Dining: An elegant dining spot in the inn is the Woodlands Restaurant, where you'll enjoy steaks, pastas, and seafood along with beautiful views of the lake. Next door is the Woodlands Lounge, for cocktails and more casual dining. Each golf course has its own snack bar and nineteenth hole. Spike's Bar and Grill offers great views of Eagle Ridge's newest golf course, the General, and a casual lunch menu of appetizers, soups, salads, sandwiches, and barbecue favorites. At dinner, only the finest-cut steaks are the specialty. Children's menus are available. Paisano's, offering a casual cafe and take-out, satisfies your (or your child's) passion for pizza and pasta, and offers Italian desserts and coffees as well; and they deliver. When stocking up on provisions, stop by the General Store for deli selections, fresh produce, and freshly baked pastries.

Children's World: The Camp Eagle Youth Program is in operation from Memorial Day through Labor Day as well as Saturday and holiday times throughout the year; it is designed for four- to twelve-year-olds. Monday through Saturday the 9:00 A.M. to 4:00 P.M. day is filled with swimming, hiking, boating, games, and arts and crafts; the fee of $50 a day includes lunch. A half day with lunch is $35 (9:00 A.M. to 1:00 P.M.); from 12:00 to 4:00 P.M. without lunch is the same cost. An all-ages playground adjacent to the tennis courts requires parental supervision, and can entertain children for hours with the tot tree for toddlers and more challenging slides and climbing for older kids. On Friday and Saturday nights, dinner, movies, and games entertain children from 7:00 to 10:00 P.M. ($35 an evening). June through August and major holidays, teens are able to meet their peers around canoe trips, paddleboat races, volleyball, and other games. If enough interest exists (sometimes unpredictable with teens), the resort will arrange a Saturday-evening excursion ($25) that might include cosmic bowling, a movie outing, or Alpine slide—all with dinner at a local pizza parlor. Individual babysitting is available at $10 an hour.

Recreation: The North and South Courses each provide eighteen holes of championship golf set in rolling hills and wooded countryside. The nine-hole East Course, characterized by elevated tees, is an excellent test of accuracy. The latest addition, the General (1997), is a challenging layout and rated best in the state and twenty-sixth in the Top 50 Courses in America in 2004 by *Zagat Survey*. For serious instruction, the professionals of the Troon Golf Institute at Eagle Ridge can guide you in everything from the basics to business golf. One-, two-, and three-day programs are offered.

On Lake Galena, fishermen go in search of bass, walleye, and crappie, and fly-fishing school improves their catches. Boaters head out in paddleboats, canoes, and pontoons. Swimmers can take a dip at the indoor pool adjacent to the fitness center in the inn; or pamper yourself at the Stonedrift Spa. Horseback riding along 40 miles of trails begins at the Shenandoah Riding Center. Rent a mountain bike or hike the trails to seek out native plants and wildlife. For a solitary excursion, the fitness trail has twenty-one exercise stations, or round up the whole family for a volleyball game (two courts) or a tennis match (four courts). Family Time activities feature Movies in Tubies in the pool, junk-food bingo, and Pictionary. Special events happen all the time at Eagle Ridge. In June the Great Galena Balloon Race fills the sky with over twenty hot-air balloons. All season you can discover the thrill of ballooning with a daily dawn or dusk flight ($150 per person). Fourth of July brings a rodeo and carnival; and in August the Civil War returns with battle reenactments, Lincoln's Gettysburg Address, and a Victory Ball. In October the annual Galena Country Fair, in nearby Galena, of course, showcases artists and their work, with games, raffles, and prizes. From the end of July to mid-August, you can combine an Eagle Ridge holiday with watching the Chicago Bears in summer practice at nearby Platteville. You'll keep busy with Ghost tours, Tea and Tarts with the General's Lady, night sky viewing, scads of demonstrations—cooking, stained glass, beads, pottery—history lessons, and costumed presentations; check the Web site or the concierge for all the happenings during your visit.

In the winter, sports lovers turn to tobogganing, sledding, and ice-skating. Forty miles of cross-country ski trails are carefully groomed. Nearby Chestnut Mountain offers downhill skiing on seventeen runs.

Other area attractions centering around Galena are art galleries and shops; a vineyard; The Belvedere, an Italianate mansion dating from 1857; the museum of Architecture and Design; and the home of Ulysses S. Grant. The Celebration Belle is a deluxe riverboat plying the waters of the upper Mississippi River on a day-long cruise. And cross the state line into Dubuque, Iowa, to find casinos, botanical gardens, Crystal Lake Cave, and the National Mississippi River Museum. A little farther afield, you can visit the Field of Dreams movie site and sit in the bleachers with dreams of your own.

444 Eagle Ridge Drive
Box 777
Galena, Illinois 61036
(815) 777–2444, (800) 892–2269
www.eagleridge.com

GRAND GENEVA RESORT

Lake Geneva, Wisconsin

Tucked into the southeastern corner of Wisconsin, between Milwaukee and Chicago, are Lake Geneva and the four-diamond Grand Geneva Resort and Spa. Less than a day's drive from nine states and sixty million people, the resort sits in the midst of 1,300 acres of pristine Wisconsin countryside and has as its stated goal "to be a destination for relaxation and pleasure." Built in the 1960s as a Playboy Club, it has undergone extensive renovations, overcome its past, reopened in 1994 with a brand-new image, and currently enjoys AAA Four-Diamond status. The town of Lake Geneva has been called "the Newport of the Midwest," and that flavor is cultivated here.

Accommodations: A total of 355 elegant guest rooms, including forty-one suites, overlook the rolling green hills and private clear blue lake (some also overlook a courtyard parking area, so specify view desired when you book). Decor is that of an elegant and comfortable vacation home. In summer, rooms are $249 to $319 and in winter $149 to $239. Junior suites range from $229 to $249 in winter and from $359 to $389 in summer. Timber Ridge Lodge provides 225 one- and two-bedroom all-suite accommodations. Located near the water park, it's spacious and convenient for families. Rates begin at $129 to $299 and include admission to the water park. Children stay free in the room with parents; a daily resort fee of $12 per day covers transportation within the resort, telephone, Spa and Sports Center, newspaper, and in-room coffee. Rollaways are $15. A one-night water park package offers accommodations, four admissions to the water park,

and resort fees; cost is $179 weekdays, $239 weekends.

Dining: Almost everyone likes Italian food, so the bistro-style Ristorante Brissago is sure to please. Open for dinner only, the restaurant features wood-roasted pizza and homemade pastas; the atmosphere is special without being stuffy. Another restaurant choice, the Geneva Chophouse, puts the kitchen right on display, so you get the full effect of sight and aroma as well as the taste of typical Midwestern dishes such as grilled steak, chops, and fresh seafood. The Chophouse is open for dinner only but serves a bountiful Sunday brunch. The Grand Cafe offers American cuisine and buffets; it's open for breakfast, lunch, dinner, and a special Sunday brunch. From 6:00 A.M. till dusk, snacks and sandwiches are available in the Links Bar and Grill at the golf pro shop. At Timber Ridge Lodge, Smokey's Barbecue House serves dinner (and lunches in summer season), or grab a bite at the Hungry Moose Food Court throughout the day. All of these restaurants have a children's menu. For evening cocktails or live entertainment, stop by Evolve or the Lobby Lounge.

Children's World: Located in the Spa and Sports Center, Kids Are Grand provides children ages four to twelve years with fun, age-appropriate activities. Scheduled year-round on Friday and Saturday, it becomes daily during the summer, from mid-May through Labor Day. Morning sessions from 10:00 A.M. to 1:00 P.M. and afternoon sessions from 1:00 to 4:00 P.M. are $40 per child per session. Evening sessions from 6:00 to 10:00 P.M.

are $50 per child and are also daily in the summer. In-room babysitting services are available for children under four years of age; cost is $18 per hour and can include up to two children.

Each week is themed, and activities are central to that theme: Carnival; Wild, Wild West; Art of Culinary; the Great Outdoors; Turn Back the Clock (to the '50s); and more. Swimming, pony rides, paddleboating, and hiking are regular activities.

Recreation: All the amenities for a resort vacation are here. Two championship golf courses lure golfers. The Highlands, one of the first Scottish-design courses in the United States, was designed by Jack Nicklaus and Pete Dye. The other course, the Brute, designed by Robert Bruce Harris, is one of the longest courses in the Midwest, measuring over 7,000 yards. Putting greens, driving ranges, and scrupulous attention to grooming keep golfers coming back. *Golf for Women* recently placed Grand Geneva on its list of "Top 100 Women-Friendly Fairways." So much for "the Brute"! Other awards include *Golf Magazine*'s Silver Medal for seven consecutive years, and its reader survey for being one of the top three courses in value and in the top four for speed of play. Pick up a tennis game on one of the two indoor or five outdoor courts, or work out at the Sport Center, which features a variety of cardio and weight-resistance equipment and indoor volleyball, basketball, and a climbing wall. The Spa and Sport Center is an adult facility, and an adult must accompany children and teens at all times. Age restrictions also apply; ages sixteen and up may use the basketball court; ages ten and up may use the climbing wall by appointment ($20 for three climbs); and ages vary for spa treatments. Facials, massages, and herbal body wraps are guaranteed to make you feel like

a new person. A private lake provides paddleboating or hydrobiking opportunities. Exercise your arms with a rowboat or your legs with a paddleboat, or just relax and cruise beautiful Lake Geneva on one of the excursion boats, like the *Lady of the Lake*, a modern reproduction of a Mississippi paddle-wheel steamer. More water opportunities present themselves at the indoor and outdoor 50,000-square-foot water park, Moose Mountain Falls, at Timber Ridge Lodge. Slides, pools, a lazy river, and two activity pools make this a very popular spot. Admission is $21 per person per day; admission is included if you are staying at Timber Ridge Lodge. For serious swimming, try the lap pool. Jogging, biking, and fitness trails wind through the property, taking advantage of the natural beauty. Finish the day with a quiet carriage ride under the stars.

In the wintertime Grand Geneva has its own skiing. Even if there is no snow elsewhere in Wisconsin, with snowmaking there will be snow at the resort. Fifteen slopes descend from the top elevation of 1,086 feet, with a 211-foot vertical drop. Night skiing, 10 kilometers of cross-country skiing, and a special area for snowboards ensure winter fun for everyone. The Ski School uses Station Teaching to allow individuals to progress at their own rate, mastering each "station," then moving on. Enjoy sleigh rides, hot chocolate, and ice-skating when the pond freezes over.

Lake Geneva is the city, while the body of water is Geneva Lake and of course, the resort is Grand Geneva! However you say it, there are lots of activities and events nearby. We always talk about what to do *on* lakes; in this case, the interesting fun facts are *under* the lake—an elephant was buried in Delavan Lake when the city was a winter home for circus troops; and at the bottom of Geneva Lake you can find, among other things, a Nash, a Volkswagen, and a cabin cruiser from the 1950s. Go to www.lake genevawi.com for a complete listing of mansions, mazes, festivals, cruises, hot air balloon and parasailing rides, museums, parks—more than we can list.

Highway 50 East at Route 12
7036 Grand Geneva Way
Lake Geneva, Wisconsin 53147
(262) 248–8811, (800) 558–3417
www.grandgeneva.com

GRAND TRAVERSE RESORT AND SPA
Acme, Michigan

Long known as the Cherry Capital, this area of northwest lower Michigan has a lot more to offer visitors than just its beautiful orchards and fine fruit. Besides providing memories of Ernest Hemingway, who spent many summers here and used this area as the setting for several short stories, Grand Traverse Resort and Spa offers guests golf, swimming, sailing, cross-country skiing, and a complete sports complex and spa. Set on 950 acres of forests and orchards with ½ mile of shoreline on East Grand Traverse Bay, the year-round resort boasts fine golf courses designed by Jack Nicklaus and Gary Player.

Now owned by the Grand Traverse Band of the Ottawa-Chippewa Nation, the resort was extensively renovated in 2004–2005.

Accommodations: The six-story resort hotel and even taller Tower, which together house 424 rooms, are adjacent to the Plaza, the site of summertime barbecues and wintertime ice-skating. With four distinct seasons, hotel room rates range from $115 in winter to $235 in summer, mid-week; weekends are slightly more expensive. The deluxe Tower encompasses 186 suites, 2 lounges, a restaurant, and boutiques. Rates range from $145 to $285 for luxury with a view and your own private whirlpool. The 236 condominium units are spread throughout eight clusters of buildings. Some overlook the bay, and some skirt the golf courses; many have a fireplace. A shuttle service connects the condominiums with the other resort facilities. Rates for a one-bedroom unit range from $125 to $295; about $30 more with valley view. Studios, two-, and three-bedrooms are also available. Children under eighteen sleep free when sharing a room with their parents. Be sure to inquire about the many package plans. Cribs are available at no charge; rollaway beds are provided at a daily charge of $15.

Dining: Sweetwater Cafe features an open kitchen in the center of the restaurant and offers casual family dining with a children's menu and local in-season specialties such as cedar-planked whitefish and cherry cobbler. It is open seven days a week for breakfast, lunch, and dinner. The Trillium Restaurant, located on the sixteenth and seventeenth floors of the Tower, serves panoramic views of the bay and golf greens along with a fine dining experience of northern Michigan regional specialties. Open for dinner daily, and an a la carte Sunday brunch; reservations are recommended. A children's menu is available in most restaurants. The Grille, in the resort's Clubhouse, also provides an informal setting for dining and cocktails. Marketplace is where you'll find sandwiches, pizza, ice cream—even the daily newspaper. Other choices include Jack's Lounge, the Trillium Lounge, and the Shores Beach Club, on the bay.

Children's World: Grand Traverse provides grand care for children ages three months to eight years, Monday through Saturday, year-round at a state-licensed 2,000-square-foot day-care facility called the Cub House. Rates are hourly; $7.50 per hour for children under two and a half, and $6.50 for older children. The ratio is one caregiver for up to four infants and toddlers. Hours are Monday through Thursday from 7:00 A.M. until 8:00 P.M.; until 10:00 P.M. on Friday and Saturday. Diapers and snacks are provided for a small fee, or you may bring your own. Each event through the day is geared to a specific age group; you must register in advance.

Camp Traverse operates mid-June through August for ages six to twelve, and offers a full- or half-day program with a weekly theme and field trip, plus sports, crafts, cookouts, swimming, and hiking. Generally the camp is divided into two groups for more age-appropriate activities. Full-day (9:00 A.M. to 4:00 P.M.) cost is $40; 9:00 A.M. to noon is $25; and noon to 4:00 P.M. is $30. Lunch is $3.00 extra. A full-week camp is $145 plus lunches. Kids may arrive early (7:00 to 9:00 A.M.) or stay late (4:00 to 6:00 P.M.), having a pre- or post-camp adventure, for $8.00 per child. In addition, Friday night is Junior Night Out, when kids gather for pizza, tennis, and a swim from 7:00 to 10:00 P.M. for $25. On Saturday, Kid's Club offers dinner, crafts, and games and maybe a bonfire, for $28 from 6:00 to 10:00 P.M. or $33 from 7:00 until 11:00 P.M.

An adventure playground near the Spa Complex also keeps youngsters well entertained, and the electronic-game room may mesmerize them. Also somewhat mesmerizing is Bogey Bear, an amiable 6-foot-tall teddy bear, who makes an appearance at 11:00 A.M. on weekends. Usually dressed as a golfer or a surfer, he shares cookies and milk with the youngsters, and parents get a complimentary photo. Individual nannies can be scheduled with the assistance of the spa staff.

Recreation: The pride of Grand Traverse Resort and Spa is the Bear. Designed by Jack Nicklaus, this golf course meanders through cherry and apple orchards, with plenty of hardwood forest areas for contrast; it is quite scenic as well as challenging. The older course, Spruce Run, also offers championship play. The resort's third course is the Wolverine, a championship course designed by Gary Player in 1999, complete with a state-of-the-art clubhouse. Located within walking distance of the main resort, the clubhouse serves all three courses. The Jim McLean Golf School program provides sessions from May through September. For your comfort and refreshment, beverage carts tour the greens and there's a halfway house, the After Nine, on the Bear.

Year-round, tennis plays a major role here. Instruction, leagues, tournaments, and junior clinics keep the staff of six busy and guests happy. Chris "Mick" Michalowski, the director of the program, was selected USPTA (U.S. Professional Tennis Association) Michigan tennis pro for 2004. Four outdoor and five indoor courts are available for play. The Spa Complex is a championship setup too. With indoor and outdoor swimming pools and an exercise/weight room, you'll get quite a workout. Afterward you'll probably head straight to the saunas. A full-service spa provides all the pampering you need with signature services such as hydrotherapy, body wraps, massage, and exfoliation featuring the area's famous cherries.

If water sports capture your interest, Grand Traverse has just about every type of boat imaginable: power boats, ski boats, sailboats, sailboards, jet skis, parasailing, catamarans with special breakfast cruises for children, sunset cruises, canoes, kayaks, fishing boats, and even tall ships. River floating is an adventure for the whole family, from knee-deep streams to more challenging rivers. Swim or sun at the private Beach Club, with its own pool and poolside bar, where lazing away the afternoon is a worthwhile activity in itself. Fishermen seek out the many lakes and streams for trout and salmon; farm fishing or a charter trip on the bay are also options. Hike or jog through the hills and past the orchards; the scenery is so good for the soul that you may not notice you're also helping your body. Or rent horses from a nearby stable and let them do the work! Croquet and volleyball are complimentary, so challenge the kids, if you dare. Picking fruit at one of the nearby orchards allows you to truly savor the results of your work—cherries, apricots, peaches, apples, or blueberries, depending on the season. And speaking of savoring something, at Moomer's you can sit on the porch eating homemade cherry ice cream while watching the cows in the pasture. Yum.

But don't be deceived; Grand Traverse is not just a summertime resort. In the fall trees burst into autumn colors and make a beautiful backdrop for horse-drawn hayrides and trips to nearby wineries for sampling and festivals. In the winter cross-country skiing takes over; on-site, the golf course transforms into a ski trail (up to 2 kilometers) with woods and gently rolling hills, covered only with natural snow. More dedicated skiers can do cross-country at the Vasa Pathway, less than 1 mile away; and three downhill ski/snowboard areas are less than an hour away. Take a sleigh ride through the woods; or try the complimentary sleds, tubing, or ice-skating in the Plaza. And remember, while working out at the Spa Complex, you'll never know how low the temperature dips outside.

In the spring, when the weather is warm enough for you to want to pick up a golf club, the cherry orchards come to life. The white blossoms of the trees blanket the hillsides for more than half the month of May.

---

100 Grand Traverse Village Boulevard
Acme, Michigan 49610
(231) 938–2100, (800) 748–0303,
(800) 236–1577
www.grandtraverseresort.com

GRAND VIEW LODGE
Nisswa, Minnesota

Nestled among the Norway pines on the north shore of Gull Lake is Grand View Lodge, the focal point of this 900-acre resort. Built in 1918 of native cedar logs and now a National Historic Site, the lodge welcomes guests year-round. If charm and friendly service, style, and attention to

detail are important to you, this is your place. Awards are common to the Grand View, but well deserved. *Midwest Living* rates them one of the "Top 40 Best of the Midwest"; *Golf Digest* gives it a five-star rating, one of only twelve such courses in the United States, as well as ranking it the only "Silver Medal Resort" in Minnesota in 2002. Located 142 miles northwest of Minneapolis, the lodge is within a fifteen-minute drive of seven golf courses, Paul Bunyan Center, and animal parks.

Accommodations: In addition to the lodge, sixty-five cabins border the lake. Deluxe suites and townhomes are also nearby. The twelve rooms in the lodge are comfortable for couples, while a cabin is the right choice for a family. Since these range in size from one to eight bedrooms, owner Fred Boos explains that they "try to fit the cabin to the family." Some cabins feature a kitchenette and living room; all have decks as well as large picture windows and views of the lake. Suites and town houses overlooking the Pines golf course also are available. Daily maid service is provided for both the lodge and the cabins. Reservations are accepted on a daily as well as weekly basis. Based on two adults and two children, rates are $375 to $425 per day and include two meals a day; golf at the Garden Course; discounted golf rates at the Pines, the Preserve, and Deacon's Lodge championship courses; unlimited tennis with clinics; nonmotorized boats; and the children's program. For additional children, the charge is $45 in spring and fall, $60 in summer. Winter Getaways, including two nights' accommodation and daily breakfast, begin at $238.

Dining: There are several restaurants: the Grand Dining Room in the historic lodge, Freddy's Tavern in the Pines Clubhouse, the Preserve Steak House in the Preserve Clubhouse, Palmer's Grill, Sherwood Forest (also a historic building, nestled in the woods), and the Italian Garden, a magical little cottage really in a garden. Dress is casual. From Memorial Day to Labor Day, enjoy a burger or a cold drink from the Beach Pavilion while sunning yourself, and sample yummy cappuccino, cookies, and pastries at Julia's, a charming French country cottage/

gift shop. Barbecues on the beach are often planned. Children may dine with their parents or their counselors when on the kids' program. A special menu for children features fresh fish, steaks, chicken, and ribs. Cocktails are served on the large, three-level redwood deck or in the North Woods Lounge, where you'll hear live music nightly. The smorgasbord is a traditional Sunday event—great fun and all you can eat.

Children's World: From Memorial Day weekend to Labor Day weekend, Grand View has two well-organized programs, for children ages three to six and seven to twelve. There is a wonderful wooden playhouse in the woods with slides and climbing equipment, a well-stocked play area, the beach along Gull Lake, and a swimming pool that your kids probably won't want to leave—ever. This pool has jets, geysers, waves, and slides, oh, my! The programs run from 9:00 A.M. to 3:00 P.M. and from 6:00 to 8:00 P.M., Monday through Saturday. The schedule includes arts, games, storytime, movement activities, exercise, and swimming.

The staff is college age and generally has past experience with children. The program is included in many of the packages; otherwise the cost is $25.00 for a full day, $12.50 for half-day sessions, and $18.00 for the evening program, which includes dinner. For those under age three, the front desk can arrange babysitting with either an off-duty staff member or selected local persons.

Recreation: The lake attracts swimmers, fishermen, sailors, and sunbathers. Here you can also venture out in a pontoon or kayak or practice some waterskiing. A twenty-seven-hole championship golf course is aptly named, given its setting: The Pines. The nine-hole Garden Course is perfect for the entire family. The Preserve, an eighteen-hole championship course, is located just 10 miles north of Grand View Lodge. Arnold Palmer's Deacon's Lodge, rated one of the

"Top ten new public courses in the nation" by *Golf Magazine,* is the newest addition to Grand View's golf family.

A tennis complex with seven Laykold courts is set among tall trees. Court time is free. The tennis pro teaches private lessons, organizes tournaments, and conducts free group lessons for children eight to nineteen years old. Two hitting walls and an automatic ball machine allow for extra practice before a good match. For a change of pace, take a yoga or cooking class, visit the fitness center and hot tubs, or enjoy the new indoor pool. Rent a bike, or go for a horseback ride through the wooded trails. Celebrate the new Glacial Waters Spa, an Aveda Concept Resort Spa with full services. In winter the north woods become a wonderland of snow. Enjoy ice-skating, build a snowman or snow-woman (or snowchild!), or go for walks in the snow. Then jump in the Jacuzzi, cozy up to the fireplace, and just enjoy.

23521 Nokomis Avenue
Nisswa, Minnesota 56468
(218) 963–2234, (800) 432–3788
www.grandviewlodge.com

THE HOMESTEAD
Glen Arbor, Michigan

The Great Lakes are truly great—and not just in size. While Lake Michigan's 22,400-square-mile area is indeed impressive, imagine the possibilities it affords in recreation and relaxation: swimming, boating, and fishing in the water, and on land, hiking and biking the wooded trails beyond the lake's sandy beach. At The Homestead all this great potential is realized, and that may be why it's called America's "freshwater resort."

Voted "The #1 Nature Escape in the Midwest" by readers of *FamilyFun* magazine, The Homestead is a waterfront resort community located on the northwest shore of lower Lake Michigan. Its 500 acres embrace gently rolling land covered with pine trees, aspens, and oaks; 1 mile of sandy beach on Lake Michigan; and 6 miles of shoreline along the banks of Crystal River. Surrounding the resort is the Sleeping Bear Dunes National Lakeshore; besides ensuring The Homestead's secluded position, this national preserve opens up additional opportunities for nature explorers. The resort is closed in April and November.

Accommodations: The Village is the center of most activities; accommodations, restaurants, shops, and a heated swimming pool are located here. Fiddler's Pond and Little Belle in the Village offer guest rooms and suites overlooking the pond. Fiddler's Pond underwent a $1.2-million upgrade and renovation in 2002, harking back to the traditional decor of decades of wooded lakeshore summer cottages—the kind one remembers from childhood. One- to four-bedroom condominiums, each with a full kitchen, are located on the beach, along Crystal River, on a ridge overlooking the shoreline, and in the Village. Crystal River cuts through the hills and runs more or less parallel to the lakeshore a short way before emptying into the lake. Where the river and the lake merge is another center of activity, the Beach Club.

Fiddler's Pond rooms are $84 to $239 a night; Little Belle's rates are $123 to $287 a night. In Stony Brook Lodge a one-bedroom condominium unit ranges between $175 and $403 a night depending on the location you choose; lakefront and lake-view units are the most expensive. The rates for larger units graduate to $720 a night for a four-bedroom home/condominium. Rates vary with season, location, and view; from May through October, a "Family Fun" package offers a family of four two nights' accommodation, and is all-inclusive for meals and activities at the resort and at the National Seashore. Priced at $87 per person per night, you even get to take your picnic basket home with you! Ask about other weekend packages. Cribs are provided at no charge; children are free when staying in their parents' room. An on-property shuttle service is available to guests.

Dining: At the Beach Club the Cafe Manitou draws diners to its ideal location on the beach; open daily in the summer only, its setting and attire are casual, and you can dine indoors or out.

Around the bend in the Village, Nonna's boasts a bountiful breakfast and northern Italian dinners, and Whiskers attracts pizza and burger fans. Also in the Village, at Cavanaugh's you can pick up groceries, deli sandwiches, a ready-to-serve meal, or snacks all day long. In the winter skiers gather in CQ's Cabin for its cozy atmosphere and friendly conversation.

Children's World: Camp Tam-A-Rack was built especially for children and is the center of the summer program. Indoors, there's space for art, cooking, music, stories, film, and napping. Extensive outside play areas include a tepee, a multilevel fort, water cannons, woods, creeks, lawns, and two gyms. Care is available for ages eighteen months to three years; cost is $12 per hour

with a three-hour minimum. Scouts is geared toward three- to ten-year-olds. Sessions are from 9:00 A.M. to noon, 1:00 to 4:00 P.M., and 5:00 to 8:00 P.M.; cost is $27 for half-day or evening sessions and $50 for the full day. It's available from June through late August and on select weekends throughout the year.

Teenagers enjoy meeting other teens at the game room or during canoe races, volleyball games, tennis matches, and pizza parties. Like the events for the younger group, some are free, while others require a fee. Private swimming lessons can be arranged; junior tennis and golf clinics are offered for young adults ages twelve to seventeen and juniors ages six to eleven.

In the winter the children's program teaches five- to twelve-year-olds fun-in-the-snow activities with ski lessons. It is offered for 2½ hours twice a day, Friday through Sunday, and on holidays from late December through March. Costs are comparable to the summer program.

Any time of year, individual babysitters can be hired, at approximately $7.00 per hour. The resort staff assists in making the arrangements.

Recreation: The clear waters of Lake Michigan are fine for sailing, boating (rentals available), fishing, and swimming. Maybe still a little nippy in June, the lake's temperature averages 65–70 degrees by July and August, and its sandy bottom is particularly attractive to young swimmers. The Crystal River waters tend to be warmer, and both the Beach Club and the Village have a heated pool and a hot tub, so guests have their pick of swimming conditions. Fishing is good sport in the river as well as in the lake, and canoeing up the river allows you to investigate the local wildlife. Sailing and windsurfing in the river can be a challenge, but tubing, kayaking, and canoeing are very manageable. And Lake Michigan is always an option. The 1 mile of beach along the shore is a real luxury.

Hike, jog, and bicycle (children's bikes and bikes with children's seats are available for rent) on the 24 miles of wooded trails; a self-guided nature tour can introduce you to the area's flora and fauna.

For tennis players, the Beach Club, with its five clay courts, is the site of many exciting matches. Here you can join a clinic, take private lessons, and watch real talent during professional exhibitions. If you're still looking for things to do, drop by the aerobics exercise class; work out on the fitness trail, with twenty exercise stations; head to the playground at River Park; or throw your hat into a volleyball tournament. Now here's ingenuity in utilizing space: A nine-hole par-3 golf course is built in part on the downhill ski slopes! Four nearby golf courses will suit your mood on any given day.

Many fun family activities are scheduled; most involve a small fee. Participate in family-friendly golf, Mishe-Mokwa's cookout, songs and s'mores, a bonfire, a tubing flotilla downstream, a fishing derby, and a great white water duck race just for a sampling.

Being surrounded by the Sleeping Bear Dunes National Park is a real treat. The largest freshwater sand dunes in the world, some reach up to 450 feet and 40 degrees of steepness. The Dune Climb is a thrill for everyone; you may climb and play on the land-side of the dune or sit at the picnic tables and laugh at others. It's a memorable experience either way. Take a ferryboat ride to the islands in Lake Michigan, sample the wines of local vineyards, or just take a relaxing stroll along the beach at sunset.

When the weather cools, the swimmers give way to skiers and snowboarders, who discover nature's wintertime beauty. Take a brisk hike on the beach or boardwalks. Try cross-country skiing or snowshoe the wooded hills. The frozen ponds are ideal for ice-skating. Downhill skiing is modest, with fifteen runs and 350 vertical feet, but the view down a snowy slope to whitecaps on the lake is an uncommon juxtaposition you'll long remember. All runs benefit from artificial snowmaking, and those lighted for nighttime skiing add another dimension to a winter holiday.

Wood Ridge Road
Glen Arbor, Michigan 49636
(231) 334–5100
www.thehomesteadresort.com

THE LODGE OF FOUR SEASONS
Lake Ozark, Missouri

Lake of the Ozarks, a man-made lake developed in the 1930s, has provided scenic and recreational diversions for the residents of central Missouri for more than sixty years. Overlooking the lake, in the wooded gentle hills of the Ozarks, is the Lodge of Four Seasons. Opened in 1964, the family-owned lodge has grown over the years into a major year-round resort. Today it is a convenient escape from city cares for St. Louis and Kansas City residents and is a vacation spot for visitors from farther afield as well. Native limestone decorates the entrance, and the warmth of a Midwest welcome is balanced by the beauty and serenity of the Japanese gardens.

Accommodations: Guests select from 350 spacious guest rooms or two- and three-bedroom condominiums—lodging is spread throughout the 3,500-acre resort community. Connecting rooms are available and most feature balconies. Choose from standard, deluxe, or premier rooms or VIP suites in the main lodge, Lanai, or Atrium. Lodge Condos (starting at $245) are located in a landscaped, semi-secluded community; Charleston Condos starting at $275, the newest, are set on a cove overlooking the Lake of the Ozarks. Room rates for fall, winter, and spring range from $89 to $169 weekdays; summer rates are $159 to $219; weekends are $20 to $40 more year-round. Children under eighteen share their parents' room at no extra charge; complimentary cribs are available.

Dining: HK's is back, now in the lodge, with atrium windows that encompass views of the lake and the Japanese garden. Order Angus beef from a custom grill or try the signature favorite, turkey steak. Have breakfast or lunch inside or outdoors at Breezes; and be sure to be there Friday evenings for the Pasta Bar. Breakfast with warm, freshly baked bread and pastries or light lunches may be consumed while enjoying the "sidewalk waterfall" at Soleil. It only feels like it's outside. Seasons Ridge Sports Bar & Grill is found on the nineteenth hole; in summer, the poolside Parrot Bar is great for a sandwich and drink and sunning. Start the evening with cocktails and friends at the Lobby Bar, and wrap it up with dancing and easy listening music at the Blue Moon Jazz Club and Martini Bar. The Blue Moon also has the requisite large-screen TV to catch your favorite game.

Children's World: The Adventure Club provides a fun-filled day of activities for children ages four to twelve with Gabby the Gopher. The Adventure Club is open every day Memorial Day to Labor Day, from 10:00

A.M. to 6:00 P.M. The cost is $7.00 per hour for the first child, $5.00 per hour for each additional sibling. And everyone gets a free Club T-shirt. Kids enjoy swimming, nature walks, fishing, games, movies, arts and crafts, theme days, and cookouts. Kids Night Out operates from 7:00 to 10:00 P.M. on Friday and Saturday during the summer and includes dinner, games, movies, and time well spent with peers. The cost is the same: $7.00 per hour, $5.00 each subsequent sibling. Many resort activities encourage quality time for families to enjoy together, such as ice-cream socials, crafts, and demonstrations. The Adventure Club's staff is certified in Red Cross first aid and water safety training.

Recreation: The sports enthusiast will be well satisfied at the Lodge of Four Seasons, named one of the "Top 50 Golf Resorts" by *Condé Nast Traveler.* Witch's Cove, a championship eighteen-hole golf course designed by Robert Trent Jones Sr., interests players with its narrow, undulating fairways and glimpses of the lake's blue waters. A second eighteen-hole championship golf course, Seasons Ridge, is carved into the rolling Ozark terrain, where multiple tee boxes accommodate golfers of all skill levels. Golf instruction is offered at both of these courses. In addition, golfers can turn to the nine-hole executive course to sharpen their skills. Equipment and attire can be purchased at the pro shop, if you've forgotten anything. If water sports are your life's love, you certainly won't feel slighted with both indoor and outdoor pools to enjoy. Swimmers can also venture out into the lake or sunbathe on the private beach. The lake is a favorite of boaters; the full-service marina can handle more than 200 boats and is the base for lake activities, from boat rentals, WaveRunners, and waterskiing to fishing guide services and parasailing. The Lodge of Four Seasons also offers a scenic excursion boat that takes guests on a smooth journey around the lake.

Guests can truly unwind at Spa Shiki. Try a full body massage or other services at the full-service spa. Browse through on-site shops, catch a movie in the lodge's cinema, or simply take a stroll through beautifully landscaped Japanese gardens. If you have any energy left, hike along wooded paths or try your hand at trapshooting. Volleyball, basketball, and tennis are even more options to fit into a busy schedule. At the end of a very full day, you may choose to stop and have a drink at the Lobby Bar, dance at Blue Moon, or retire early for a well-deserved repose.

Horseshoe Bend Parkway
Lake Ozark, Missouri 65049
(573) 365–3000, (800) THE–LAKE
www.4seasonsresort.com

LUDLOW'S ISLAND RESORT
Cook, Minnesota

Minnesota has a reputation as the land of 10,000 lakes (ever wonder who counted them all?), and Ludlow's Island Resort is well situated on one of these—picturesque Lake Vermilion. The resort facilities are located on Ludlow's Island and on the north and south shores of the lake. And there's nothing on the island except the resort—talk about private! A boat shuttle connects the three areas. Water-related activities are the primary recreation at this three-star, three-diamond wooded resort "where luxury and wilderness meet." Fishing, swimming, sailing, and exploring any of the 365 islands provide wonderful experiences. The seclusion among the pines and birches, with the lake practically at your front door, makes this retreat a real back-to-nature experience. The resort is open May through September, and is a member of the "Distinctive Lodges." The resort is run by the Ludlow family—for families—and has been for sixty-five years.

Accommodations: Twenty cabins with enchanting names like Stardust, Evergreen, and Twilite are located on the island and the shores; Dream Catcher was featured on the Travel Channel in February 2004. Designed with knotty pine or cedar interiors, all have a fireplace and outdoor deck; most have a screened porch. They range from one to five bedrooms, with a fully equipped kitchen (yes, even a dishwasher and microwave). Spring (May) and fall (September), daily rates start at $250 for two adults and $30 for each child under seventeen. Early June through September, the most common rentals are weekly. Rates for two adults range from $2,000 to $3,150 for a four-story "tree-house"; ages eighteen and over are $175 per week; ages six to seventeen are $100; and ages five and under are $40. Daily summer rates are calculated at one-sixth the weekly rate. And packages are available—some out of the ordinary, such as "Breakfast with the Bears," "Visit the Wolves," or Family Fishing Camps. Ludlow's rates include just about everything—the newspaper delivered to your cabin, daily towel exchange, firewood at your door, all the facilities of the lodge, tennis, boating, camping (with gear!), recreation, and blissfully, television is limited to three cabins on the island and in the lounge. Maid service is available daily; cost is $200 to $230 per week.

Dining: You may dine in your cabin, and do your own cooking. The Gourmet Pantry is open twenty-four hours—here you can find groceries, tackle, or personal toiletries, and woks, waffle irons, and ice cream makers can be borrowed at no charge. More grocery stores can be found 8 miles away, in Cook. Or you may dine in your cabin and have meals delivered by The Harvest Moon Cooking Co., owned by the Ludlow's son and daughter-in-law. Full menu choices are posted in the cabins; burgers and pizzas are also available. Place your order by 5:00 P.M. and dine by 7:00 P.M. Or, if you're getting cabin fever, try one of the several local restaurants, where dining is casual and family-oriented and someone else does the dishes!

Children's World: At least one planned activity (from one to three hours) just for children is scheduled every day Monday through Friday. Boat rides, nature hikes, and fishing derbies introduce kids to the surrounding woods and waters. Pontoon tours give an opportunity for viewing beaver lodges and eagles' nests; and planting a white pine with your name on it is a great introduction to ecology. Waterskiing, tubing, basketball, and picnics keep kids active, and seaplane and Friday afternoon amphibious car rides in the lake are exciting for the whole family. Unique is the only word for a 1954 Chris-Craft Constellation converted to a "playhouse," and kids love it for picnics and fantasy voyages to faraway places.

The island is not open to the public and no cars or traffic are allowed, so children have the security and freedom to roam—with an entire island to explore, Ludlow's keeps structured activity to a minimum. Movies are shown in the afternoons, and one lodge has a goodly supply of books and games. Teens like to gather at the video-game room or in the evening for more "grown-up" movies. The two-story tree house and a small camping island for overnight trips are among the biggest attractions for the younger set, but the swings, the lake (with a section roped off for children's safety), and the sandy beach are good play areas, too. Kids also enjoy exploring the trails in the forest, just like Paul Bunyan of Minnesota lore. The recreation complex on the south shore has a children's play area. The management will arrange babysitters; cost is $6.00 per hour.

Recreation: Fishing buffs relish this bit of paradise on the south shores of Lake Vermilion. Walleye, bass, and crappie lure fishermen to these waters. There's no excuse for not landing the big one; a fishing clinic is held every week, and a guide is available for private excursions. The staff at the lodge will fillet and freeze your catch. Besides fishing boats, the lodge has canoes, kayaks, paddleboats, old-fashioned rowboats, and a sailboat for guests' use. Waterskiing and hydrobikes add a new dimension of fun to water sports.

The South Shore Sports Complex houses an indoor racquetball court, two Tru-Flex tennis courts, and a fitness center. After a good workout there, you may enjoy a leisurely swim or a relaxing sauna. Along the north shore you can take a stroll down the 1½-mile hiking trail. There are many additional miles of hiking and biking trails in the area. Half a dozen or more golf courses are within an hour of Ludlow's, including the Legends, *Golf Digest's* pick for the number-one public golf course in the country.

P.O. Box 1146
Cook, Minnesota 55723
**(218) 666-5407, (877) LUDLOWS
(583-5697)**
www.ludlowsresort.com

GRAND HOTEL

Mackinac Island, Michigan

The world's largest summer hotel since 1887 is also the grande dame of Mackinac Island. Afternoon tea, croquet on the green lawn, seemingly endless white columns stretching to the blue sky, and flowers everywhere reflect the best of the Gilded Age. Relax on the front porch, the longest in the world, and visible even from Lake Michigan. Offering gracious hospitality, the serenity of age and privilege permeates the Grand Hotel, open from May through October.

Regarding a visit, the Grand lists 129 "Reasons Grand and Small": #11, it's listed by *Travel + Leisure* magazine as one of the top-ten kid-friendly hotels in the United States and Canada; #112, Mark Twain lectured here; #12, room keys are actually keys; #1, no tipping please; #21, a self-serve snow-cone machine by the pool; #20, a giant caterpillar in the pool; #53, having fun in a tie; #28, dancing with your six-year-old to Big Band sounds at dinner; #41, the barbecued salmon with peppermint ratatouille; #55, the way the waiters pour milk; #42, the stuffed animal in every baby's crib; and #56, taxis with four hooves. Still need convincing? Check out the other 117 reasons on the Web site.

Accommodations: Past the red-carpeted entry and beyond the impressive Victorian Parlor and public rooms lie almost 300 guest rooms and suites, no two of which are alike. Each has its own unique character, and the suites are filled with antiques and furnishings from around the world. They are also named: after presidents, first ladies, and famous people and places. Take some time choosing, as a wide variety of room sizes, locations, and rates are available. When the hotel opened in 1887, the rates were $3.00 to $5.00. Today's rates in the peak Social Season (mid-June to late August) are per person, MAP (breakfast and dinner), and range from $205 for a small inside room to $325 for a named suite. Shoulder season rates are approximately $20 lower. Children to age eleven are complimentary, twelve to seventeen are $49, and eighteen and older are $99. A $6.50 per person baggage transfer fee is automatic.

Dining: In all public areas of the hotel, the dress code is casual resort wear during the day and formal attire after 6:00 P.M.; jackets and ties for men, ladies in their finest. Start the day with breakfast in the Main Dining Room with a wide selection of choices. Dinner at the Grand is everything you'd expect, right up to demitasse in the Parlor and nightly orchestra music. Lunch choices include the Jockey Club at the Grand Stand, Pool Grill, Carleton's Tea Store, Fort Mackinac Tea Room, and Woods. The Main Dining Room tables groan under the weight of the Grand Luncheon Buffet, a tradition here. Full breakfast and five-course dinner are included; children under eleven eat free.

Children's World: From Memorial Day to Labor Day, children ages five years and up are welcome to join the complimentary daily activities from 11:30 A.M. to 2:30 P.M. and again from 6:00 to 9:00 P.M. Different things are planned each day; for example, a hike, picnic lunch, and duck-pin bowling; a trip to Fort Mackinac; or dinner and a movie. Older children (twelve to teens) are welcome if the program interests them; they often come with friends or younger siblings. Babysitting is available at $15 per hour.

Recreation: The Jewel is the Grand's golf course, comprised of Grand nine and Woods nine. Although you arrive at the course by horse-drawn carriage, there are gas-powered carts on the course. The tennis pro will help you with your game on the clay courts, and you can stay in shape on the jogging trail, or the ½-mile Vita exercise course. Exercise machines and masseuse are in the cedar grove by the swimming pool, and bicycles are available to rent. Riding stables are near the hotel, with more than 40 miles of bridle paths. The serpentine-shaped Esther Williams swimming pool is a popular gathering spot—*The Time for Keeps* with Esther Williams and Jimmy Durante was filmed here in 1949. Another movie involving time was filmed here in 1980: *Somewhere in Time,* with Jane Seymour and Christopher Reeve. If you wish, sit on that famous porch in one of the hundred rocking chairs, and watch the gardens, the ferries, and activity on the ever-changing lake, largest body of fresh water in the world; play croquet or boccie ball in the tea garden; enjoy the art and antiques that surround you; tour the butterfly conservatory; or visit Rebecca's or Carleton's Tea Store for delightful treats. Delight-filled days are what it's all about. The hotel is happy to arrange any off-site excursions you desire, such as a carriage tour of the island.

Mackinac Island, Michigan 49757
(906) 847–3331, (800) 33–GRAND
www.grandhotel.com

MISSION POINT RESORT
Mackinac Island, Michigan

Northern Michigan is known for its glorious outdoors; add to this the quaintness of a historical island, subtract automobiles, and you have the perfect equation for a family resort. Mission Point nestles gracefully on its eighteen acres overlooking Lake Huron, just minutes from the village. It's summer Victorian, but substantial, and quite pleasing to the eye.

Taking advantage of existing architecture, Mission Point has renovated the Observation Tower, offering island visitors extraordinary views of Lake Huron and the Straits of Mackinac. This all-glass structure on the resort's property serves as the perfect spot to watch sailboats approach the southeast coast during the island's annual yacht races.

Accommodations: In the recently renovated 242 guest rooms (including ninety-two suites), casual and comfortable elegance is reflected in three styles: Nautical, Lodge, and Northern Michigan. Views of the island are superb, some rooms offer fireplaces and Jacuzzis, and all have goose-down comforters and feather beds. Shoulder season rates range from $119 (Carriage room) to $309 (Lodge Suite); weekends cost more. Peak season (June through August) rates are $194 to $374, respectively. Rates are based on double occupancy, and children eighteen and under stay free with parents. Family packages are available from $336 to $466 per night (peak weekend) and include lodging, some meals, ferry transportation, and activities. Teens (thirteen to eighteen) pay $107; under twelve are free. Regular season is May through October. Check with the hotel in October for winter dates (generally Christmas to March if they're open). A $4.00 per adult luggage transfer fee gets your bags from ferry to room.

Dining: Here's the great thing about dining at Mission Point: Not only is it delicious, it's free for ages twelve and under when ordering from the children's menu and accompanied by parents. Well, a $1.50 service charge is added for each child, but really! Who could complain? And all the restaurants have children's menus. At the Epicurean, Chef Phil adds his flair to a culinary palette of fresh fish and steaks. For the casual side of island dining, try the Round Island Bar and Grill, where guests can watch passing freighters while enjoying appetizers, sandwiches, and spirits in an alfresco setting. It's also the place for "late nighters" and live entertainment. Lakeside Marketplace offers sandwiches and salads for guests on the go as well as indoor and outdoor dining with spectacular views of Lake Huron and the Straits of Mackinac. The Euro Garden Cafe, an open-air dining experience, serves a tempting array of European dishes from the chef's own personal recipes. It's worth noting that the resort has gourmet picnic baskets to go, a great addition to a day of island exploration. The Straits Lodge opens mid-December to mid-March for hearty winter fare.

Children's World: The Kids Club is Mission Point's answer to that age-old question, "What can I do now, Mom?" Near the Activity Center, the Kids Club offers 3,000 square feet of indoor space plus activities throughout the resort and field trips for older children. Little Ones, ages two to four years, have circle time, balloons, and bubbles, or a teddy bear picnic. Ages four to ten enjoy themed days, such as Wild Kingdom or Space Day, with outdoor games, arts and crafts, storytelling, and nature hikes. 'Tweeners, from eleven to fifteen, are not too cool to enjoy pool and pizza parties and back-to-the-'60s tie-dye sessions. Kids Club sessions run from 9:00 A.M. to 10:00 P.M. throughout the week from Memorial Day to Labor Day, and on weekends only to the end of the season. The program is flexible and activities vary depending on the average age of the group. Each counselor accepts only six children, so it's a good idea to sign up early. The cost is $10 per half-day session, *but*—a half-day session is either 9:00 A.M. to 4:00 P.M. or 4:00 to 10:00 P.M.! And it's $16 for a full day (both sessions). Meals are extra.

With a 3,000-square-foot area in which kids spark their imagination with a variety of interesting activities, Kids Club includes a Parent and Toddler Room, Gross Motor Skills Rooms, and a Kreative Korner Room, as well as some of the kids' traditional favorites like the 12-foot tepee. The active atmosphere of the resort is complemented by Mackinac Island itself, a natural adventure park offering outdoor explorations and historic sites.

At Kids Club kids enjoy a variety of supervised opportunities including arts and crafts, learning ancient Indian lore, plus field trips to the island's Butterfly House, the 150-year-old British Fort, or along the island's bluff for bald-eagle spotting. Parents are encouraged to sign children up one day in advance, allowing the counselors to plan appropriate activities and guarantee its one-to-six counselor/child ratio. As an added convenience, pagers are available for parents of young guests.

Activities for the entire family embrace poolside bingo, build your own sundae, lawn games, video arcade and billiards room, and old-fashioned picnic games. Think the magic has gone? Not at Mission Point. Tuesday through Sunday in summer, Matthew J serves up magic, illusion, and excitement—the audience may even participate!

Recreation: The Greens, an executive eighteen-hole putting green, is identified as "a short course in relaxation." With picturesque views and restaurants within walking distance, it's a fun course. Several championship courses are nearby; guests receive a discount. If you're a tennis buff, register early for the one court. The Activity Center is the heart of the resort's recreation, sheltering the Health Club and Spa, with Kids Club adjacent. Tennis, mountain cruisers and tandem bikes, in-line skate rentals, and the indoor game room are here, along with exercise equipment and massages—marvelous at the end of an active day. Relax by the outdoor heated pool or hot tub with a cool drink or take a leisurely stroll drinking in the view. Enjoy a hay ride, lawn bowling, or croquet. Step back in time at the early-twentieth-century theater that presents the latest movie releases Monday evenings in summer. The waterfront gazebo, with glorious views, is a great place to relax—as long as a wedding isn't happening.

One Lakeshore Drive
Mackinac Island, Michigan 49757
(906) 847–3312, (800) 833–7711
www.missionpoint.com

RUTTGER'S BAY LAKE LODGE
Deerwood, Minnesota

If you have ever entertained thoughts of owning your own lakefront cottage in the land of 10,000 lakes, Ruttger's Bay Lake Lodge may satisfy your yearning. Set on 400 acres directly on Bay Lake, in north-central Minnesota, the Lodge emphasizes relaxed outdoor recreation in surroundings of clear lake waters, tall trees, and pine-scented air. Open May through September, it is family run and family oriented. With its old-fashioned hospitality, a family tradition since 1898, the lodge allows you a well-deserved escape to the peace and serenity of the North Woods.

Accommodations: Five dollars for bed, board, and boat. Prices may have changed over the last hundred years, but the ambience hasn't. For years the lakefront cottages and the lodge rooms have been favorites among vacationers. To these have been added condominiums and villas. Many have kitchens, porches, and views of the lake, and all include a refrigerator, cable television, and air-conditioning. Ruttger's has both EP and MAP rates. The Modified American Plan includes not only breakfast and dinner daily, but complimentary golf on Alec's Nine and Kids Kamp, plus many other resort activities; the same rate applies to a variety of accommodations, and is mandatory for the Lakeside Cottages. Children under three years old stay at no charge; ages four to eight are $60; ages nine to fifteen are $80 in high season; rates drop to $40 to $50 per child over three at other times. On the European Plan, rates vary according to season, weekends, and size and location of accommodations; children under the age of eighteen are free. Early July to mid-August is the high season and weekend rates are the most expensive. As an example, the Lakeside Cottage MAP plan ranges from $90 to $185 per adult; on the EP plan (lodging only, use of pools, tennis, and beach) per room rates vary from $87 to $202 in the lodge or villas; $105 to $235 in a one-bedroom, and $140 to $385 in a two-bedroom golf course condo. Located 1 mile from the main lodge and secluded in the woods overlooking the lake, the newly renovated Battle Point condominiums offer studio to three-bedroom units. Rates range from $85 (low season, studio) to $420 (high summer, three-bedroom) per night. On all lodging, MAP is always an option; rates vary. One week in July is designated Family Value Days, when kids stay and eat free (one per adult through age fifteen), adults pay only $150 per person per night (MAP), and daily special family events are planned. Cribs and rollaways are $10 each.

Dining: The Modified American Plan is mandatory for cottage guests, and the homemade pastries are practically a requirement. Ruby's Dining Room, built in the 1920s, is an inviting setting, with natural logs, an open-beamed ceiling, and a stone fireplace. Service is a la carte or buffet, and for more than twenty years, Chef Dot has maintained Ruttger's tradition of excellent food. For casual dining and drinks, lunch and dinner are also served at Zig's, which overlooks Bass Lake and the eighteenth hole of the Lakes golf course. Auntie M's Kaffeehaus offers specialty coffees, panini sandwiches, pastry, and ice cream. The main lodge and Zig's both have picture windows that are great for viewing the North Woods while sipping a cool drink. Enjoy casual dining at Zig's between 11:00 A.M. and 9:00 P.M. The Bear Pine Bar is a full-service bar with appetizers and sandwiches, which can be enjoyed on the deck or around the pool with a spectacular view of Bay Lake.

Children's World: Kid's Kamp is a supervised program for ages four to twelve that runs Monday through Friday, from mid-June to Labor Day. Planned by a certified teacher and kept in motion by energetic young counselors, from 9:00 A.M. to 3:00 P.M. (9:00 A.M. to 1:00 P.M. on Wednesday) kids are occupied with swimming, boating, fishing, and nature hikes. Indoors the fun continues with music, crafts, and games; or time at the playground near the cottage. Teens are neither ignored nor over-structured; golf mixers, or waterskiing and wave-boarding clinics suit them just fine. Kids Kamp is complimentary on the MAP program; for EP guests, the charge is $22 for the day session, $18 on Wednesday. Babysitting can be arranged by the staff.

Recreation: With such a beautiful lake, you might find yourself drawn to the water almost continuously through the day—for sunning, swimming, waterskiing, water tubing, teen wakeboarding, fishing, and boating, and for building sand castles along the beach. Take a morning coffee cruise or an evening pontoon cruise and relax on the lake. Swimmers also enjoy the indoor and outdoor pools, and tennis fans turn to the two Omni-turf and three Laykold courts. Round up a game of volleyball, basketball, or horseshoes; play table tennis and shuffleboard; or go walking through the woods. Practice on the putting green, and plan a round of golf on the Lakes, the eighteen-hole championship course, or Alec's Nine. Ruttger's was *Golf Minnesota* magazine's "Golf Resort of the Year" in 2004. And treat yourself to pure relaxation in the lounge or TV lobby, the whirlpool or sauna, or just pull up a lawn chair and kick back.

The new Day Spa follows Ruttger's tradition of using existing buildings, renovating and updating while keeping the original flavor. Set in a house in the woods, guests can take pleasure in massage, body wraps, facials, and all the beautifying rituals. Other old places to explore are the Country Store, now upscale clothing and home furnishings, but set in a building that over the years has been a general store, a feed store, the post office, and an antiques shop. Next door is The Garage—just that, it's an old filling station from the 1920s, now rejuvenated with toys, books, and casual clothing.

The staff naturalist directs programs introducing visitors to the loon, osprey, and bald eagle, along with garden tours and nature trails. Waterskiing, sailboats, motorboats, pontoon boats, and fishing boats are available. Families can partake of bonfires and cookouts, pontoon cruises, stargazing, talent shows, and family movie nights. Evenings come alive with adult pleasures such as wine tasting, bridge socials, or karaoke.

Box 400
Deerwood, Minnesota 56444
(218) 678–2885, (800) 450–4545
www.ruttgers.com

SHANTY CREEK
Bellaire, Michigan

Shanty Creek, a four-season resort located in northern Michigan, is actually three resorts in one, which translates into a bit of variety for guests. Summit Village is elegant and contemporary, with stunning 360-degree views encompassing Lake Bellaire; Schuss Village has the European charm of an Alpine village; and Cedar River Village sits amidst the gentle hills and hardwoods and is home to the Lodge, a collection of eighty-five modern luxury suite condominiums. Together they encompass 4,500 acres of rolling woodlands on the shores of Lake Bellaire. In the summertime golfing is the favorite activity; in winter skiing is the preferred sport.

Accommodations: Lodging choices are innumerable: guest rooms, studios, condominiums, and chalets. Some are equipped with a fireplace or whirlpool; others have a deck. You might have a view of the lake, the forests, a fairway, or the Alpine village. Rates start at $95 to $110 a night for a guest room and rise to $275 to $330 a night for a deluxe two-bedroom condominium. Children ages seventeen and under stay free when occupying a room with their parents. Cribs can be added to your accommodation for a fee of $10 a day. The many package plans available offer good savings.

Dining: The Lakeview Dining Room is an elegant restaurant at Summit Village. Open for breakfast, lunch, and dinner, it's hard to decide which is better, the food or the view. Lakeview draws its menu from the fields, forest, orchards, and lakes of northern Michigan and has a children's menu. La Vigna Italian Bistro at Cedar Ridge Village is a delightful addition to the dining scene and serves dinner nightly overlooking the eighteenth green at Cedar River Village. Other dining choices are Arnie's, in the Clubhouse at the Summit, serving sandwiches and soups at lunch and dinner; and light fare and hearty breakfasts at the Weiskopf Grill in the Lodge at Cedar River, or the Schuss Golf Deck at the Schuss Mountain Golf Club on weekends. On weekends, choose your preferred style of evening entertainment: dueling pianos at Arnie's, cool jazz at Cedar River, or American favorites at the Lakeview.

Children's World: We may have become accustomed to purple dinosaurs, but a purple goose? That would be Gandy, Shanty Creek's mascot, with his own Web site fun page so kids can meet him before they actually meet him! Shanty Creek programs serve children from two months to twelve years old during most of the year. The programs are planned and supervised by a recreation specialist and an experienced childhood educator, so there's expertise combined with enthusiasm, which in this case equals innovation.

Shanty Creek is justly proud of their new Family Activity Center. They've made a real effort to make things more efficient and easier for parents by consolidating kids' camps and family activities in one area of Schuss Village. The camps have their own dedicated wing, and there's easy access to the outdoor pool, a large play area, and deck. In summer, the Children's Center with day care will also be in the village, at Cortina Lodge. Drop-off and pick-up will be in the same vicinity and parents can then stay for family hayrides or campfires.

The Shanty Creek Children's Center is open every day from 9:00 A.M. to 5:00 P.M. for children two months through age five, mid-June through Labor Day, and late November to mid-March. It's a nurturing, playful, and safe environment, with a separate area for naps. Full-day rates are $35 with snacks; lunch is $6.00. If you prefer, hourly rates are $7.00.

Camp Gandy, operating daily from mid-June to Labor Day, has hiking, swimming, fishing, disc golf, music, and arts and crafts and is specially designed to meet the needs of younger children, ages four to eight years. Camp is open from 9:00 A.M. to 5:00 P.M. at the Family Activity Center in Schuss Village. Full-day sessions are $31; half-day sessions from 9:00 A.M. to 1:00 P.M. or 1:00 to 5:00 P.M. are $21. Lunch is $6.00, and again, if your child chooses, hourly rates are $7.00 per hour. Reserva-

tions by 4:00 P.M. the day prior are critical—if no children are registered, camp will not operate.

Adventure Camp for ages eight to twelve has the same hours, rates, and location, but the activities are more challenging and age-appropriate and include sports, disc golf, field trips, and longer hikes.

When the ski season starts, the daily Children's Center program accepts infants to six-year-olds. In addition to stories and indoor play, the older children discover the excitement of outdoor play in a winter wonderland. The same fees as above are charged for this program.

Young skiers-to-be, ages three to five, combine indoor play with sledding and ski instruction in their 10:00 A.M. to 4:00 P.M. schedule. Snow Stars, for ages three to five years, helps kids learn to ski and have fun doing it. Cost is $50 for a full day, $40 for a half-day session, and includes lunch, lift tickets, and snacks; equipment rentals are $10 to $14 additional. Snow Angels is a similar program for the same age group, but is more individualized, with smaller groups. It's the "fast track" and is generally available on weekends. Cost is $90 for the full day and covers everything, even a pager for parents.

Kid's Academy, for older children (ages six to eleven), runs from 10:00 A.M. to 4:00 P.M. daily. This is more serious instruction but still doesn't lose sight of the fun of skiing. The fee is $50 full day, $40 half day with lunch. Ski rentals are not included in these fees. Smart Riders, for budding snowboarders, is available most weekends and holidays for ages six to twelve years. Sessions are at 10:00 A.M. and 1:30 P.M. and the cost is $40.

Just for You is another child-care service that matches caregivers with your child's age and needs. Cost is $8.00 per hour, with a two-hour minimum. A second sibling is $1.00 per hour. With parents' permission, children may use the resort facilities under this individual supervision. Shanty Creek also will do their best to accommodate children with special needs—call them. In February, the resort hosts the Special Olympics.

Recreation: Golfers experience a bit of a dream come true here. The resort's original course is the eighteen-hole Summit Golf Course. Another championship eighteen holes make up the beautiful Schuss Mountain Course. And the crowning gem is the Legend, an exciting eighteen-hole course designed by Arnold Palmer. With the carefully maintained courses complemented by an experienced teaching staff, all golfers will surely improve their games here. The new Cedar River Golf Club, designed by Tom Weiskopf, is another winner. Awards are numerous: *Golf Magazine* rates Cedar River among the "Top Ten in the U.S. You Can Play"; the Legend as one of the top four courses; and Shanty Creek in the "Top 5 in Quality of Main Course." *Golf for Women* calls Shanty Creek "one of the most women-friendly." PGA professionals at the Golf Academy can give you all you need to really enjoy the game.

Other summertime activities include tennis, with eight courts; biking on the mountain trails; and boating. At the Fitness Center work out on the Nautilus equipment, hit the steam room or sauna, and wind up the day with a massage. Schedule time at the Wellness Spa for a real treat. Water urges may be satisfied at one of the five swimming pools or sandy beaches at Torch Lake, Lake Bellaire, or Elk Lake. With indoor swimming pools and a heated pool outdoors, swimmers are satisfied whatever the season.

On-site diversions are too numerous to list, but start with basketball, croquet, disc golf, volleyball, board games, and shopping. The state's only solar-lighted disc golf is here at Shanty Creek, and evening family clinics are fun for all. Add evening entertainment and nightly family activities such as bardic storytelling at the campfire, and you may not have time for a sunset sail aboard a tall ship, or a visit to the Turtle Creek Casino or nearby Traverse City.

The ski season starts in November and continues through late March or early April, depending on how generous Mother Nature has been. There are forty-six runs for downhill skiers, almost 20 miles of groomed trails for cross-country skiers, and two terrain parks for snowboarders. When you're not on skis, pile the whole family into a horse-drawn sleigh for an old-fashioned ride in the woods. Or if you're brave enough, take a dip in the heated outdoor pool. Après-ski at any of the three villages is easy with the free resort shuttle service that operates year-round.

One Shanty Creek Road
Bellaire, Michigan 49615
(231) 533–8621, (800) 678–4111
www.shantycreek.com

TAN-TAR-A RESORT

Osage Beach, Missouri

Located in central Missouri, the Tan-Tar-A Resort rests comfortably in the foothills of the Ozark Mountains. The resort complex covers 420 lush acres and stretches along the shores of the scenic Lake of the Ozarks. Once the largest man-made lake in the world, it was created in 1931 with the construction of Bagnell Dam, a project of the Union Electric Company. This 54,000-acre lake with 1,150 miles of shoreline (more than the state of California, they boast) is now the centerpiece of Missouri recreation. As their publicity says, "Lake of the Ozarks offers visitors gallons (about 617 billion) of fun and adventure." The hilly terrain and lakeside exposure provide a lovely backdrop for many recreational activities. Tan-Tar-A is a AAA Three Diamond resort and was rated by *Midwestern Living* magazine as one of the top three resorts "families would love most." Tan-Tar-A is only a three-hour drive from either St. Louis or Kansas City.

Accommodations: The 989 guest rooms and suites are in the main resort buildings and in smaller two-story accommodations bordering the lake. Some have a fireplace and a deck or patio. This is the resort complex, within walking distance of dining and most activities. A variety of room plans exist, from two-double-bed rooms and one-bedroom units with kitchenettes, and two bedrooms with full kitchen. High season is mid-May to mid-August, when rates range from $139 to $184 for rooms and $159 to $234 for suites. In nonpeak periods, these rates drop to $80 to $154 and $100 to $194 for suites. The estate's complex surrounds the nine-hole golf course, and is a seven- to ten-minute drive from the restaurants and activities. With the ambience of a neighborhood, units of two to four guest rooms appear to be houses from the outside; floor plans are different and contain rooms or suites, each with its own private entrance. Rates here in high season are $149 to $199 for rooms; $194 to $244 for suites. Nonpeak times rates drop to $90 to $169 for rooms and $130 to $204 for suites.

Dining: If you like to start your day with a latte, Java Lakes is the spot for you. For casual family meals, the Black Bear Lounge serves breakfast, lunch, and dinner in a rustic hunting lodge setting and has a deck for summer dining. Children three years and younger have complimentary breakfast and Sunday brunch. For a fancier evening, try Windrose on the Water, where you'll enjoy luscious steaks and fresh seafood. If all you want is a quick bite, the Food Court has Burger King, Sbarro, and Eskimo Pie ice-cream shop. At the golf course, the Oaks serves lunch overlooking the course or watching a game on the big-screen TV. For liquid refreshment and snacks the Jetty Bar is adjacent to the Arrowhead Pool (seasonal). Mr. D's Lounge serves cocktails at days' end.

Children's World: Camp Tan-Tar-A, for children ages four to ten years, is in session Monday through Saturday, from early June through mid-August. The fee for the 10:00 A.M. to 4:00 P.M. schedule is $25 for the first day and $20 for each additional day and includes lunch and a T-shirt. Half-day sessions are $15. Activities include swimming, beach games, races, treasure hunts, and crafts. Kids ages seven to thirteen can join a guided fishing tour for two hours ($40 per child).

A less structured routine is found at the Kids Cabin—filled with games, toys, dress-up, Legos, and more. In summer the Cabin is open in the evenings only, Monday through Saturday, from 6:00 to 10:00 P.M.; cost is $9.00 per hour for one child; $1.00 per hour each additional child. For $17 during summer season only, kids may attend from 5:00 to 10:00 P.M., with "dinner out" at Burger King, a movie, and games. Fall, winter, and spring, the program operates on Saturday only, from 6:00 to 9:00 P.M. The cost is the same as summertime. Children under age four are welcome to the Cabin on Friday and Saturday evenings, but must be supervised by a parent. These rates also apply to in-room babysitting, available on a limited basis, with a three-hour minimum.

Recreation: The lake is the venue for boating fun for everyone. You can rent ski boats (waterskiing instruction available), sailboats, paddleboats, kayaks, fishing boats, and Wave Runners. You can even try parasailing. Though there's a small sandy beach that's nice for sunbathing, the lake is primarily the domain of boaters and fishermen. Swimmers usually opt for time at one of the three pools (two outdoor, one indoor). The Arrowhead Pool complex beckons with waterfalls, the Jetty Bar, a 125-foot water slide, and a toddler splash pool.

You may lose the children forever in the new Timber Falls Indoor Waterpark. Set in a three-story wilderness tree house topped with a 6-foot-wide wooden bucket, it's filled with interactive fun, water blasters, suspension bridges, and web crawls; plus four water slides, an activity pool, and a lazy river area for tubing. And what about that bucket, you may ask? Oh, it tips over every two minutes or so, drenching everyone below with 700 gallons of water! Open daily in summer, on weekends year-round; passes are $15 per person per day.

Golfers can take on the challenges of the Oaks (an eighteen-hole course) or Hidden Lakes (nine holes). Liquid refreshments from the on-course "jigger joggers" may or may not improve your game. The Racquet Club houses indoor tennis and racquetball courts as well as billiards. Outdoors and adjacent to the club are basketball and volleyball courts. Tennis buffs can also try the complimentary outdoor tennis courts near the Racquet Club.

At the fitness center you can use the exercise room and whirlpool, or indulge in the many programs at the Windjammer Spa. Facials, massages, aromatherapy, and detoxification treatments are just some of the pleasures from which to choose.

If it's to do with video or electronics, the Bear's Den Arcade probably has it. Fun for all ages and tickets won can be exchanged for prizes.

Back in the great outdoors, find a good horse at the stables for a nice trail ride, jog along the paths around the property, or challenge the kids to a round of miniature golf. If you still have time and energy, try bowling, billiards, shuffleboard, or table tennis. Even the shoppers in your family will have plenty of fun in the dozen shops, featuring jewelry, toys, fashions, and country crafts. Be sure to take an afternoon cruise on the lake; the *Ozark Princess* sails four times a week during the summer season.

Lots of activities and attractions in the area may pique your interest. Budding spelunkers take note: Over 5,000 recognized caves exist in Missouri and 300 of them surround the lake. "Show" caves have been tamed with paved walkways and lights—four of the twenty-two are within 30 miles of one another. For shoppers in your party, Factory Outlet Village may satisfy; if you want to rummage through history rather than read about it, several antiques shops will oblige. Country Western music shows are great for family entertainment, and more outdoors can be celebrated at two nearby state parks. Ha Ha Tonka is the newest park in Missouri with lots of wildlife, natural bridges, and spectacular scenery. Lake of the Ozarks State Park is the largest park, and has not only foot trails, but the unique Aquatic Trail, designed for boaters to explore the lakeshore.

State Road KK
Osage Beach, Missouri 65065
(573) 348–3131, (800) 826–8272
www.tan-tar-a.com

SOUTHWEST

Arizona
New Mexico
Texas

ANGEL FIRE RESORT

Angel Fire, New Mexico

Impressed by the pink glow on the mountains, Indians named this area "the land of Angel Fire." This year-round resort in the ancient Sangre de Cristo Mountain range of northern New Mexico allows for escape, renewal, and rejuvenation. Angel Fire encompasses 20,000 acres of scenic mountain beauty and seems to sit at the top of the world. The air is clear, and the vistas stretch for miles in all directions. The Village of Angel Fire, actually a small incorporated township, is spread out over about 3 miles; so when we refer to "the village," think driving or taking the Magic Bus ($1.00) that goes just about everywhere.

Accommodations: Angel Fire can accommodate approximately 4,000 guests in a variety of lodges and condominiums scattered through the village area. At first glance, this number of guests conjures up images of crowds, but remember that this still leaves approximately five acres of land per person! The Angel Fire Resort Hotel offers 129 rooms located at the base of the ski mountain. Prices range from $80 to $209 for a room. Mountain condominiums, within walking distance of lifts, restaurants, and shops, include studio to three-bedroom units; price range for a two-bedroom is $125 to $364 (holidays). Cribs are provided at $15 per night.

Dining: Hungry? Choose from a variety of foods including Italian, Mexican, and steak house specialties. Dress is casual, and many restaurants have special menus for children. At the resort have breakfast or dinner at the Branding Iron; Jasper's Bar serves drinks and a bar menu; while the Lazy Lizard is a favorite with kids and adults alike. In the village have your favorite pizza at the Pizza Stop, try the barbecue at Smoke House Willie's, or enjoy good old-fashioned family fare at Zebbediah's. For a splurge, with older kids or even without kids, sample the Roasted Clove. The Angel Fire Country Club matches up spectacular mountain views with tasty lunches and dinners in summer only. In winter, live entertainment enlivens weekends at Angel Fire Village House.

Children's World: During winter, from Thanksgiving to the end of March, the focus is on snow sports, skiing, and snowboarding. Young skiers ages four to twelve can join the Children's Ski and Snowboard Center, which runs from 9:00 A.M. to 3:30 P.M.; a $65 to $78 daily fee covers lessons, lift tickets, rentals, and lunch.

Very young or nonskiing children can participate in daily activities at the newly built (2003) and state-licensed Angel Fire Resort Day Care. Children six weeks to six years old can join the fun from 8:00 A.M. to 5:00 P.M. daily in winter; Monday through Friday in summer. These sessions are a combination of indoor play—such as games, treasure hunts, and crafts—and outdoor play that emphasizes winter fun in the snow, such as "snowercise" and snow sculpture. The fee for a full day is $65 for ages six weeks to twenty-four months; half day is $45. Ages twenty-five months to six years pay $55 and $40 respectively. Parents must provide diapers, bottles, formula, lunch, and immunization records.

In summertime the Angel Fire community sponsors children's supervised activities in June and July. Monday through Friday, from 8:00 A.M. to 5:00 P.M., ages six to twelve can join local children in mountain summer activities such as paddleboats on Monte Verde Lake, fishing, hiking, and the usual summertime "camp" diversions. Weekly camps for basketball, arts and crafts, and cross-country running are open to ages six to fourteen years. Call (505) 377–1544 for details and cost.

Recreation: While the primary diversion in winter is skiing or snowboarding, Angel Fire considers itself a "snow sports" resort. Sample 22 kilometers of cross-country skiing at the summit of the mountain, plus snowmobiles, snowshoes, snow biking, snow skating, snow blades, and snow tubing. If it has to do with snow, you can do it here! One weekend every February Angel Fire hosts the annual World Championship Shovel Races. Yup, two categories (for all ages): sitting on the shovel, or building a race car on the shovel. You've got to see it to believe it! For more ordinary ways of getting down the mountain, first-time skiers over sixteen get a free ski/board lesson with purchase of lift tickets, and children six and under ski free. More than two-thirds of the trails are for beginners and intermediates. The vertical drop is 2,077 feet, and the longest trail is a cruising 3½ miles long. Seven chairlifts cover 30 miles of trails, two ski shops are ready to rent or sell equipment and accessories, and lessons are available.

Once the snow melts, these same trails offer fantastic opportunities for mountain biking, hiking, backpacking, ATV tours, and horseback riding. Catching a trout from the annually stocked lake can be an exhilarating experience, but if fishing is not your sport, you can canoe or paddle in these waters. Have a swim in the pool, play tennis, or bicycle on the paths around the resort. At an elevation of 8,600 feet, the eighteen-hole golf course weaves through a wooded terrain of aspen, spruce, and ponderosa pine. Practice on the driving range and putting green, or enlist the expert advice of the golf pro. For a unique tour, go in search of elk; photographic shots only! A good summer option for the entire family (if parents have the stamina!) is the High Adventure Passport. A two-night stay garners two coupons for any activity; upgrade the passport with extra activities for $4.00 per coupon and indulge in fishing, the human maze, mini or disc golf, paddle- or rowboats, mountain biking, chairlift rides, tennis or golf range, or game room tokens.

Nearby, raft on the Rio Grande or visit Eagle Nest, a little town where Old West–style gunfights may erupt on the street at high noon. In August enjoy Music from Angel Fire, a twenty-year tradition of classical music concerts performed by professional musicians from across the country. Angel Fire Village has something going on just about every weekend in summer: a home and garden show, quilt exhibitions, arts fest, sportsman show, and more. Whatever your activity, the crisp mountain air and clear azure sky enhance it.

P.O. Drawer B
Angel Fire, New Mexico 87710
(505) 377–6401, (800) 633–7463
reserve@angelfireresort.com
www.angelfireresort.com

THE ARIZONA BILTMORE

Phoenix, Arizona

A classic hotel, the Arizona Biltmore is often referred to as the "jewel of the desert." At the entrance to the grounds, Main Drive is lined with lovely private homes and landscaped with citrus trees and flowering oleander, petunias, and pansies. The main structure at the end of this drive is an architectural masterpiece. Inspired by Frank Lloyd Wright and constructed of Biltmore blocktile, the buildings reflect the gracious charm and innovative spirit of the 1920s. Exploring the thirty-nine acres of this fine establishment is an adventure in architectural history and a delightful experience in imaginative landscaping. Stroll along the beautifully manicured lawns and gardens for visual delights in carefully tended beds of yellow pansies, pink petunias, or multicolored snapdragons. In dining, shopping, and recreational activities, the Biltmore has consistently maintained its reputation as a world-class resort and is open year-round.

As at many urban resorts now, the Biltmore's primary clientele during the week is business groups or conventions, with families visiting more often on weekends. One result of this pattern is that activities for children and families tend to cluster around weekends and holidays only, although they are presented year-round.

Accommodations: Of the 738 well-appointed rooms and suites, approximately one hundred are located in the main building; others are arrayed in several buildings and cottages bordering flower beds. Many rooms have mountain or garden views, and all rooms have been recently remodeled. Rooms rates range from $195 to $650 for a villa suite, mid-May through September, when temperatures of over 100 degrees Fahrenheit are not uncommon; $325 to $1,100 October through December; and $425 to $1,325 in the more temperate winter months, January to mid-May. Summer specials with such features as the third night free may be offered, so do inquire about packages and specials. Children under eighteen can stay free in the same room with their parents. Cribs are provided at no extra charge.

Dining: Enjoy regional and American cuisine for breakfast, lunch, and dinner in the casual atmosphere of the Biltmore Grill, featuring an exhibition kitchen and outdoor patio overlooking the gardens. The Café, with its outdoor terrace and terrific views of the Squaw Peak Mountain, is open daily for "deli-style" breakfast and lunch. Both have menus for children and teens. Have dinner at Wright's, the award-winning signature restaurant, where the striking architecture enhances the enjoyment of the food. As if Maine lobster with truffles and fennel or filet mignon Roquefort with caramelized shallots and pomegranate syrup needed enhancing! Private wine tastings can be arranged—the Biltmore has one of the most extensive wine lists in the region. If you're near the water slide and new pool, try the Cabana Club Restaurant and Bar for sandwiches and cool drinks during the day and cocktails and entertainment in the evening. The only thing watery about the drinks is the setting, at the swim-up bar. Being right next to the water slide makes it a good place for lunch with the kids, and they have their own menu favorites such as macaroni and cheese and hot dogs. The grand atmosphere of the lobby also provides several grand options for the tummy. Traditional tea is served from 2:30 to 5:30 P.M. The Squaw Peak Lounge allows you to sit either indoors or outdoors, listen to music, and savor the view of the mountain along with your drinks and hors d'oeuvres. At the Biltmore you also have room service with a twist; guest room dining allows you to order multicourse meals and have them delivered separately, so your entree doesn't get cold while you savor the appetizer. And, if you have a patio grill, a chef will come and do the cooking. Sweet.

Children's World: Kids Korral offers a structured program only on weekends, for ages five to twelve years; however, it is presented year-round. During summer and holidays, the program is on Friday, Saturday, and Sunday, from 9:00 A.M. to 5:00 P.M. Swimming, hikes, cooking classes, yoga, golf, and tennis are on the menu. Water Balloon Launch is one of the most popular "sports"—as fifty-plus kids line up around the swimming pool with slingshots and water balloons—best observed from a safe distance. Full-day ($65 with lunch) and half-day ($35) sessions are an option; also, there is an hourly rate of $15.

Kids Korral is also a canopy-draped area with rubberized floor to provide shade and fun things to keep kids happy and out of the sun. Playground equipment is extensive and includes a track ride, snake pole, triple slide, chain net climber, arched bridge, a bowed ladder—the list goes on and on. Picnic tables and chairs give a place in the shade for parents to sit and supervise. While there's no evening supervised program for children, families can enjoy dive-in movies, s'mores and bonfires, pottery painting, the putting course, and the game room with table tennis, pool, air hockey, and music.

Recreation: The setting of the Biltmore alone could charm you for days on end, but once the inner spirit is renewed, try your hand at some of the many recreational activities. Seven lighted tennis courts

attract tennis enthusiasts; schedule yourself for a tennis clinic or private lessons.

The avid golfer can take on one of the two eighteen-hole PGA courses or refine a technique on the putting greens and driving ranges. At the pro shop you can seek out the guidance of the teaching staff, pick up some vital accessories, or rent equipment.

The eight swimming pools can mean either invigorating laps or a relaxing dip. One of the fifteen cabanas will protect you from the desert sun, and the 92-foot water slide is guaranteed to get a "wow!" To check out the scenery and still test your athletic abilities, rent a bicycle or jog along the trails flanking the Salt River Canal. Indulge at the Biltmore Spa, which offers more than eighty European body and skin treatments, fitness center, steam room, saunas, and whirlpool. Or perhaps you will alternate rigorous athletics with less demanding games of croquet or lawn chess.

If shopping is your interest, discover a varied and extensive line of merchandise in the hotel shops: jewelry, silver, and regionally crafted products of both Southwest and Native American artists; and tennis, golf, and swimming clothes and accessories. Adjacent to the grounds is the Biltmore Fashion Park, filled with more shops and restaurants and reached by a shuttle bus.

Venturing farther afield, take an excursion to the Grand Canyon, visit the spectacular red rocks of Sedona, or float aloft in a hot-air balloon. Horseback riding or Jeep tours give an up-close view of the desert. And, of course, the delights of metropolitan Phoenix are at your doorstep.

**2400 East Missouri
Phoenix, Arizona 85016
(602) 955–6600, (800) 950–0086
www.arizonabiltmore.com**

THE BISHOP'S LODGE RESORT AND SPA

Santa Fe, New Mexico

Just a ten-minute drive north of Old Santa Fe, 1,000 acres of the foothills of the Sangre de Cristo Mountains comprise the range of the Bishop's Lodge. At an elevation of 7,200 feet, this area of north-central New Mexico shares its warm sunny days with cool crisp nights. The clean mountain air, the setting, and the atmosphere of the lodge combine to enhance the flavor and traditions of the old Southwest. The adobe architecture, a reminder of the area's Spanish and Native American heritage, and the friendly spirit of the staff give the Bishop's Lodge its true Western flair.

In the nineteenth century the ranch was the home of Archbishop Jean Baptiste Lamy, a pioneering French cleric who became the Southwest's first Catholic bishop. His life was the inspiration for Willa Cather's novel *Death Comes for the Archbishop* (good background reading for an introduction to the history and topography of the region). The private chapel built by the archbishop still stands, a sentinel to the lodge's history. The property was purchased by the newspaper publisher Joseph Pulitzer and then acquired in 1918 by James Thorpe. A National Historic Hotel, the lodge is currently managed by Lendlease. The facilities have undergone expansion and renovation, with a strong emphasis placed on customer service and satisfaction. The lodge is open year-round, and many families return year after year; three generations of family visitors are not uncommon.

Accommodations: The lodge's one hundred–plus rooms and suites are grouped in several adobe buildings nestled among fruit trees and flower beds. The North and South lodges are the oldest, both having been grand summer homes before World War I. All of the rooms are decorated in warm earth colors with a Southwestern flair; deluxe rooms include fireplaces and many have outdoor sitting areas. The beds are simply delicious, firm mattresses with soft, feathery inserts. Rates are based on double occupancy; children under age four stay at no charge, others pay $15 per day. Cribs and rollaways are available on request. January through May, historic rooms range from $189 to $259; summer rates are $259 to $369. September through November, rates are $189 to $369. Deluxe rooms are generally $50 to $75 more. Holidays and weekends are more expensive, as are suites.

A resort fee of $14.50 per day per person (thirteen and older) allows use of the facilities (pool, tennis, fitness center); activities such as yoga, Tai Chi, aerobics, and hiking; fishing, with all the equipment; and shuttles to Santa Fe and the nearby ski area in winter. Also included is the daily gratuity for housekeeping, in-room coffee and tea, daily newspaper, parking, and local and long-distance telephone access.

Dining: Las Fuentes (The Fountains) reflects a new concept in cuisine, Nuevo Latino, bringing together the color, taste, and music of Puerto Rico, Cuba, Argentina, Salvador, Colombia, the Caribbean, and other Central and South American countries, for your dining pleasure. It's open for breakfast, lunch, and dinner, with a children's menu in summer.

The decor is classic Santa Fe: beamed ceilings, Navajo rugs, Spanish chandeliers, and four life-size murals done in the 1920s by W. E. Rollins. For cocktails and lighter fare, stop by El Rincon, a cozy corner bar opening onto the Terrace, with al fresco dining for all meals. Sunsets, stars, and soft summer breezes accompany the nightly entertainment. Santa Fe, with its myriad dining possibilities, is ten minutes away.

Children's World: During the summer months, Memorial Day to Labor Day, kids four to twelve years old gather down by the corral, at Camp Apaloosa. Children under four are welcome when accompanied by an adult. Different activities every day and a ratio of one counselor to seven children keep it interesting and interactive. Full-day programs (8:00 A.M. to 4:00 P.M. and 6:00 to 9:00 P.M.) include a daily afternoon swim and a mix of activities: nature hikes, pony rides, archery, tennis, a "Kid's Rodeo," and Frisbee golf on the active side; sand art, plaster sculpture, murals, and animal masks for artistic expression. In addition a pond stocked with trout and an outdoor play area with swings, a slide, jungle gym, and a sandbox translate into active fun for kids.

Evening sessions feature Native American stories and crafts, movies, pajama parties, and skits. The day program includes breakfast and lunch for $52; the evening program is $39, including dinner. Children may have meals with their counselors in their own dining room or at picnics, pool parties, and cookouts.

While Bishop's Lodge doesn't have a winter program for kids, Chipmunk Corner Children's Center at Ski Santa Fe, fifteen minutes from the lodge, offers day care from 8:30 A.M. to 4:30 P.M. for ages three months to three years. Rates are $58 for a full day, $42 for a half day, or select hourly care at $12 per hour. Only full-day packages are available during holidays. Snacks and lunch are provided, and children are divided by age. Snowplay, which has the same hours, is a fun introduction to the skiing environment for ages three and four, with indoor and outdoor play, games, and activities. Full-day rates are $64; half day is $48.

The Little Chips Ski Program for four-year-olds provides a full day ($64) that includes a two-hour lesson in the morning with lunch and snacks provided. The afternoon continues with Snowplay (outdoor and indoor ski play), activities, and games. The half-day session ($48) is a two-hour lesson only, with snacks and lunch included. Children may be transferred to Snowplay at their instructor's discretion. Chipmunk Corner, for ages five to nine, places children into classes according to their age (five to six and seven to nine) and abilities. All children are tested to determine accurate levels. The same rates apply: $64 for a full day, 8:30 A.M. to 4:30 P.M.; and $48 for a half day, 8:30 A.M. to 1:00 P.M. or noon to 4:30 P.M. Equipment rental is $12 for either program.

Recreation: Except on Tuesday, the horses' day of rest, recreation at the Bishop's Lodge begins with horseback riding on scenic mountain trails. Experienced wranglers match you and your ability with the appropriate steed from a stable of thirty horses. Children must be over eight years old and four feet tall (free pony rides are offered for the little ones), and the maximum weight is 225 pounds. Choose from a group ride (more sedate) or schedule private rides if you want to canter and gallop through the mesa. A memorable experience is a sunrise or sunset ride through the canyons and foothills of the Sangre de Cristo Mountains; once a week in summer you can enjoy a hearty "cooked on the range" breakfast or an evening barbecue.

The Santa Fe National Forest is adjacent to the grounds of the lodge and provides more opportunities to explore the gorgeous scenery on horseback. If you're a little skittish about mounting a horse, there are many hiking trails both on the resort grounds and nearby, ranging from moderate to strenuous, with the same great views.

Lots of other recreational fun can easily fill your days. Fish the mountain streams for trout, swim in the pool, or just bask in the glorious New Mexico sunshine. The nearby country clubs of Santa Fe, Cochiti Lake, and Towa Golf Resort grant lodge guests golfing privileges on their eighteen-hole courses. At the Tennis Center, you can play on one of the two courts, have a lesson with the resident pro, and purchase some new accessories at the pro shop. At 7,000 feet, you'll need stamina, lots of water, and perhaps special tennis balls. On the skeet and trap-shooting ranges, experts offer instruction, and rental equipment is provided. Play a game of table tennis or treat your sore muscles to a relaxing hour in the whirlpool.

ShaNah is a native word meaning vitality and wisdom, and the highly acclaimed ShaNah Spa & Wellness Center is more than a place to be pampered; it's also about healing, nurturing, and ancient native wisdom. You can experience a facial, massage, body polish, native hot stone massage, or Ayurvedic treatment. All sessions begin with an optional (but highly recommended) Native American Blessing Ceremony to open the heart and set the intention—it may change your whole outlook on life. A real treat is having an outdoor massage under that very special New Mexico sky.

Be sure to reserve at least a day to discover the narrow streets, interesting adobe architecture, quaint shops, and art galleries of Old Santa Fe. Open-air performances of the Santa Fe Summer Opera Festival are a special attraction, and dance and music performances abound. Pueblo Indians show their jewelry and pottery on blankets around the Palace of the Governors or at the famous Tesuque Indian Market, and visitors are often welcome to attend the colorful ceremonies at nearby pueblos.

Fall brings crisp days with dazzling colors. The horses are energized and the ski lift opens for spectacular views from the top of the mountains. In winter, Santa Fe's cultural events are still in full swing, entertainers are showcased at the reservation casinos, and the big fireplace at the lodge is a welcome gathering spot. The lodge offers a "Ski and Spa" package in winter: Monday through Thursday two adults ski free at the nearby Ski Santa Fe slopes, then return to enjoy a rejuvenating spa visit. The 12,053-foot summit at Ski Santa Fe boasts 1,703 vertical feet of skiing and forty-four runs winding through stunning terrain with the perfect powder typical of New Mexico.

P.O. Box 2367
Bishop's Lodge Road
Santa Fe, New Mexico 87501
(505) 983–6377, (800) 732–2240
www.bishopslodge.com

ENCHANTMENT RESORT

Sedona, Arizona

Nature was about 350 million years creating the incredible landscape surrounding this area, but it was well worth the wait. Reputed to have special magnetic energies, Sedona has become a focal point for metaphysical healing and "New Age" spirituality, as well as an international art scene. Whatever it is, there is indeed something magical in the air, in spite of encroaching commercialism. Enchantment Resort is very well named. Nestled within the walls of Boynton Canyon, 5 miles northwest of town, it is surrounded by the Coconino National Forest, and is a welcome escape from touring and town. The land surrounding the resort is sacred to the Yavapai-Apache as the birthplace of their tribe; in fact, the resort has a Native American ambassador on staff to explain the land and share tribal stories and tradition. This four-star, four-diamond resort has awards too numerous to list that include being one of the Top 10 Family Resorts in America according to *Parents* magazine; one of the Top Five Family Resorts in Arizona by *FamilyTravel;* one of *Conde Nast's* Top 30 North American Resorts; one of *Travel + Leisure's* Top 100 Hotels of the United States and Canada; and one of the Top Ten Hotels & Resorts in the United States in the 2003 *ZagatSurvey.*

Accommodations: Pueblo-style architecture blends in with the landscape, and the 220 rooms can be arranged in various combinations of guest rooms, studios, and junior suites; when connected, these create one- or two-bedroom casitas or haciendas. This also creates many rates. Basically rates begin at $295 for a casa bedroom or studio; $395 to $495 for a casita junior suite; one-bedroom casita suites are $555 to $755;

hacienda one-bedrooms are approximately $75 more. Two-bedroom suites range from $875 to $1,075. Suites feature Southwestern decor with beehive fireplaces, high ceilings, native crafts, and patios with dramatic views. High season is mid-February to mid-June, and the end of August through December. A daily $18 per room resort fee covers use of the spa, mountain bikes, courts, and most activities, with the exception of tennis lessons, Camp Coyote, and spa treatments.

Dining: People drive up from Phoenix and down from Flagstaff just to experience the Yavapai Restaurant. With menu items such as cold smoked buffalo tenderloin; Anaheim chile relleno, stuffed with duck and rolled in blue corn; and Southwest spiced salmon with lobster potato cake, it's no wonder! Huge windows reveal a 180-degree vista of the stunning red rocks of Boynton Canyon; dinner, lunch, and a breakfast brunch are served daily, while a Sunday Jazz Brunch is very popular. Tii Gavo, a more casual restaurant serving lunch and dinner, has a children's menu and entertainment on weekends. Mii amo Cafe is part of the self-contained spa, offering eclectic and healthy cuisine. In summer, guests may dine on their terraces or poolside as well.

Children's World: Daily year-round, trained counselors at Camp Coyote keep children ages four to twelve active and engaged at the colorful Camp Center. Kids enjoy treasure hunts, swimming, tennis and golf, outdoor crafts, and games, all with a daily theme: Desert Dweller, Canyon Fun, Wild West, Southwestern, or Native American days. Often, a park ranger or a Native

American storyteller will drop in for a surprise visit. A full day, including lunch, is from 9:00 A.M. to 3:30 P.M. and costs $70; half-day morning ($35) or afternoon with lunch ($40) is another option. On Friday and Saturday, the dinner and evening program operates from 5:00 to 9:00 P.M. ($45). The Resort Concierge can arrange babysitting for $15 per hour, with a three-hour minimum, for one child. Additional children in the same family are $2.00 extra per hour per child. Payment in cash is requested directly to the party providing the sitting services; there is no charge from the resort.

Recreation: If you can tear yourself away from just staring at the landscape, lots of activities await. At the resort, activities are nonstop from 7:00 A.M. to evening: Tai Chi, cooking demonstrations, yoga, basket making, power Pilates, aqua aerobics, Quigong, a vortex walk, tennis drills, photography—the list goes on and on. Walk leisurely along the trails with your sketchbook or take a more strenuous hike. Mountain bikes are here for the adventurous, or championship croquet, boccie ball, and table tennis for a slower pace; swimming, of course, under an unimaginably blue sky; or combine the two with a rousing water volleyball game. A Cayman-style pitch-and-putt golf course and a putting green will whet the golfer's appetite for the two championship courses nearby in Sedona. Tennis players are well served by a variety of clinics and mixers on the seven courts. U.S. Park Rangers are stationed at the resort, and give lectures and guided walks three times weekly. Enchantment Resort and the U.S. Forest Service have jointly established the Boynton Canyon Preservation Fund, a privately funded effort to create programs to improve and preserve the tranquil beauty of the canyon. It's a stellar spot for stargazing through the resort's telescope, especially with an expert to explain what you're seeing. Curious about what a vortex really is? Come to the lobby on Tuesday at 5:00 P.M. and understand the mystery. Enchantment Marketplace is not the usual resort retail shop; here you'll find local art, photography, music, and jewelry.

Mii amo is a full-service destination spa located within the resort—the name is a Yuman word for "journey, or moving forward; a passage." Actually a boutique hotel within the resort, it offers seventeen rooms and suites, with three- to seven-day packages. It has its own fitness room, indoor and outdoor pools, and a restaurant, along with twenty-four treatment areas where magic is created with blue corn body polish or Sedona-clay wraps. Mii amo blends spa services with Native American healing and spirituality, and takes full advantage of an exquisite natural setting. Enchantment guests over age sixteen have access to spa facilities and treatments.

In other venues, music and nature blend at the 5,000-seat amphitheater in the Sedona Culture Park, Oak Creek Canyon beckons you with gorgeous winding drives and picnic areas along the creek, and Slide Rock is a natural combination of smooth rocks and splashing water that kids love. The Grand Canyon is only two hours away. You can even get there by steam locomotive. Tour this spectacular Sedona area by four-wheel-vehicle, helicopter, or horseback. It's awesome any way you approach it.

---

525 Boynton Canyon Road
Sedona, Arizona 86336
(928) 282–2900, (800) 826–4180
www.enchantmentresort.com

FLYING L GUEST RANCH

Bandera, Texas

Bandera, 40 miles northwest of San Antonio, claims to have invented dude ranching during the Depression when an enterprising rancher decided to take in "dudes" for extra money. So now, in true Texan style, they have laid claim to being the "Cowboy Capital of the World." Seven rodeo world champions have hailed from here, however, so there may be something to it. Set in the midst of the beautiful Texas Hill Country, this is not the dry, barren Texas of the movies. Here there are verdant hills, oak and maple trees, wildflowers and flowing rivers, not sagebrush and sand.

The Flying L Ranch was first settled in 1874. It became a dude ranch in 1946 when Jack Lapham, a retired Air Corps colonel, started to realize his dream of a place where "a modern person can go and find himself in the midst of yesterday." (OK, who can figure out the name of the ranch based on this story? You already did? Good!) The ranch became a favorite "watering hole" for celebrities, including John Wayne, Tex Ritter, Buck Owens, Chill Wills, Slim Pickens, and Willie Nelson; the television program *The Cisco Kid* was filmed here. Recognitions include *Family Vacation Magazine*'s "Top 100 Family Vacations"; one of the best spring break family vacations from *Southern Living* magazine; *Golf for Women* rated it one of the top 100 places for women; and *Smart Money* magazine put it in the top 5 vacation spots in the country. The motto of this award-winning ranch is "Whoever says you can't have it all has never been to the Flying L."

Accommodations: You can bunk in style here—all forty-four suites offer real Texas-style lodging with room to spread out. The villas are geared toward comfort; all include a refrigerator, microwave, coffeepot, cable TV,

daily maid service, and a real wood-burning fireplace. Daily rates in low season are $80 to $99 per adult; high season (summer and holidays) rates are $98 to $118 per adult. Children twelve to seventeen are two-thirds of the adult rate, and ages three to eleven are half the adult rate. Children under three stay free. Family packages include villa accommodations, breakfast and dinner buffets daily, horseback riding and use of the ranch amenities, nightly Western entertainment, and the supervised children's program. Discount rates are given for five nights or more.

Dining: Breakfast and dinner are included in the rate and are hearty examples of fine Texas Hill Country cuisine. Seven days a week, from 7:30 to 9:30 A.M., start your day with a delicious breakfast buffet in the Main House dining room. Breakfast here was rated "#1 in Texas" by the tourism council. Lunch is on your own, with burgers and fries at the pro shop or an afternoon picnic from your refrigerator. Dinner is from 5:30 to 7:30 P.M., either in the Main House dining room or creekside. During summer and holidays, the buffet menu is loaded with favorites that "kids hanker for." Always popular are the cookouts by the creek, under the open sky and old live oaks. Especially when you arrive by hay wagon and horseback.

At 5:00 P.M. the Branding Iron Saloon opens, and there's family entertainment every night—cowboy music, dancing, gun slinging, or a rodeo, usually topped off with a marshmallow roast and making s'mores. Do the kids love that!

Children's World: Children are divided into two groups, ages three to six and seven to twelve. Programs run from 8:30 A.M. to noon, when children lunch with their parents, and from 1:00 to 3:00 P.M. Activities include feeding animals, nature walks, scavenger hunts, sports, fishing, and crafts, such as making leather bracelets and vests. Golf and tennis clinics are included for the older children along with trail rides with the grown-ups (children must be at least six), while the little ones can take pony rides at the Kids Korral every day. Afternoons usually feature an activity for the entire family, such as roping lessons or a family greased-pig chase. The program runs Monday through Saturday during summer, spring break (March through April), and major holidays. The supervised children's activities program is included in the rates.

Recreation: Since this is a ranch, and it is Texas, of course horseback riding is a major focus. The winding San Julian Creek and huge old oaks amid the rolling hills are great for riding, and you're likely to encounter all types of critters like rabbits and even deer. With approximately forty horses to choose from, you'll soon have a new best friend.

The only activity not included in your price is golf. Drive, chip, and putt on the popular par-72, fully irrigated course. A driving range lets you perfect your skills if you don't get distracted by the beautiful view; private lessons are also available from two PGA professionals. Try the outdoor heated swimming pool or venture off the ranch to the Medina River for a little inner tubing or canoeing. Tennis, bikes, sand volleyball, horseshoes, hayrides, rodeo events, a playground, and a seasonal petting corral add to the fun. And after all that exercise, a good soak in the outdoor Jacuzzi may be just what the old bones need.

In the Bandera area, fish in the crystal waters of Medina Lake, tour a working longhorn ranch, visit the Cowboy Artists Museum in Kerrville, tour the World War II Nimitz Museum, or enjoy antiquing in the German town of Fredericksburg. On Bandera's Main Street there's a working blacksmith shop. Nearby excursions include San Antonio (the Alamo, Market Square, and the River Walk) and various theme parks such as SeaWorld, Fiesta Texas, and Splashtown. Visit natural wonders such as the caverns. All in all, the ranch promises "a rootin', tootin' time."

566 Flying L Drive
Bandera, Texas 78003
(830) 460–3001, (800) 292–5134
www.flyingl.com

HYATT REGENCY HILL COUNTRY RESORT
San Antonio, Texas

The Texas Hill Country is as much a state of mind as it is a region. It certainly doesn't look like Texas—its green rolling hills, abundance of water, wildflowers, and variety of trees surprise the first-time visitor. San Antonio calls itself "a big city with small-town charm," and, as the number one tourist destination in Texas, has a multitude of attractions for families to enjoy—including the famous Alamo, centerpiece of Texas history, and the River Walk, lined with shops and restaurants along the tree-shaded banks of the San Antonio River.

Twenty minutes from downtown, a scenic drive meanders through the landscape, culminating at the Hill Country Hyatt lobby entrance, reminiscent of a Texas ranch house and complete with fireplaces, antler chandeliers, and overstuffed furniture—even a shady back porch. In fact, the resort's 200 acres are a part of the Rogers–Wiseman Ranch, honored for being in continuous agricultural production at the hands of one family for one hundred years or more. Hyatt has successfully adapted a full-scale destination resort into this casual, laid-back lifestyle; the results are downright pleasurable. Especially the Ramblin' River—the centerpiece of the property and the greatest place to get into an inner tube, kick back, and just relax. Accolades include being one of *Travel + Leisure*'s Top 25 Family-Friendly Resorts, and on *Condé Nast*'s 2004 Gold List of the world's best places to stay.

Accommodations: Of traditional German-style Hill Country architecture with native limestone and decorative wood exterior, the two- and four-story hotel has nine guest-room wings, housing 500 rooms. A stand-alone two-story luxurious guest house styled after a ranch house is in the courtyard—there's even an authentic windmill! As usual with Hyatt, the rooms are large and well decorated, ranging from standard to Regency Club level, with no-smoking rooms and suites available. Room rates are from $210 to $315; suites from $695 to $2,250. Children under eighteen are free in the same room as parents. Packages are a good value and may include golf, the children's program, or other family excursions; Sunshine on Sale, for example, gives you the fourth night free. At most Hyatt Resorts, Family Plans allow an opportunity to reserve a second room for children at half price, based on availability—be sure to ask.

Dining: The flavor is definitely Tex-Mex, so expect tortillas even for breakfast, but you have lots of options here. The Springhouse Cafe features regional specialties, a large buffet and salad bar, and Sunday brunch. A wood-burning oven makes great pizzas. In the clubhouse, the Antlers Lodge has the ambience of a country lodge and puts the accent on regional Southwestern cuisine of steak, chicken, and seafood. Many entrees are mesquite-grilled and accompanied by a spicy Tex-Mex sauce. Golfers will find sandwiches and light snacks in the Cactus Oak Tavern at the halfway point on the golf course. It's a strange phenomenon that in this part of Texas, cacti that normally like sand have decided to grow in oak trees, hence the name. The General Store offers hamburgers, deli sandwiches, and home-baked cookies as well as licorice sticks, wine, sodas, fresh coffee, and muffins. Papa Ed's Pool House serves up sandwiches and grilled food by the pool. In the evening relax at Aunt Mary's Porch, an open-air bar just off the lobby, or kick up your heels at Charlie's Long Bar, an old-fashioned Texas saloon complete with tin ceiling and a 56-foot copper-top bar. Yes, they have the tequila with the worm. Pool, shuffleboard, backgammon, and chess enhance the bar area.

Children's World: Camp Hyatt, only at select Hyatt resorts, offers not only supervised programs but also children's menus and an opportunity to buy a second room for the kids at half price. Custom tailored for ages three to twelve, Rowdy's Camp Hyatt operates year-round during holidays and weekends, and daily throughout the summer. The program runs from 8:00 A.M. to 5:00 P.M. and keeps the kids busy with games and activities. Activities have a decidedly Western flavor, with a cowboys-and-Indians theme predominating: searching for arrowheads, watching for coyotes on the golf course at sunset (yes, they are sometimes there), totem poles, Wild West collages, and rodeo round-up games join the nature hikes and sandcastle building. A special Camp Hyatt room serves as a meeting place and for indoor activities; a different schedule is posted for every day of the week. Full- and half-day sessions may be arranged; cost for half-day sessions is $35, lunch is $10 extra. If you want to have an evening for grown-up pursuits, the evening session runs from 6:00 to 10:00 P.M. daily in summer, on Friday and Saturday year-round, and costs $40 with dinner.

The perfect "spot" for youth may be the new *SPAhhht,* a first-class spa experience for today's youth—bright and colorful, with the accent on vibrant energy, not serene calm. Air-brushed nail art, hair weaving and up-do's, henna tattoos, and massage are what's happening here.

Recreation: Golfers enjoy the Arthur Hills–designed course with its 170 acres of rolling, scenic terrain. It truly blends into the countryside and has been recognized as one of the premier courses in the United States. Tennis is available on three courts, with a pro on hand. Walking, jogging, and biking paths crisscross the property, and the health club features aerobics classes and all the latest equipment—and, of course, a massage to help you recover from your workout. Windflower, the Hill Country Spa, has twenty-one treatment rooms to pamper you. Using all-natural, mostly local

ingredients in the services, try a peach pecan body scrub and what else? Yellow rose facials, of course.

By far the most popular spot, though, is the Ramblin' River, modeled after all those Hill Country river experiences. Pick up an inner tube, drop your cares, and let the lazy current carry you away. The journey varies from brisk to slow and allows riders to swim, walk, float, or take detours into two swimming pools, a cascading waterfall, or even a little sand beach.

Day excursions to SeaWorld, Six Flags, Fiesta Texas, Splashtown water park, or many of the nearby Hill towns, each with its own personality and charm, can pleasurably fill your days or evenings. Visit the Natural Bridge Caverns, with active formations more than 140 million years old, or stroll through Bandera, the self-proclaimed "cowboy capital." The Alamo is a must, and missions, museums, and Market Square, which feels like shopping in Mexico, are all nearby.

9800 Resort Drive
San Antonio, Texas 78251
(210) 647–1234, (800) 233–1234
www.hillcountry.hyatt.com

HYATT REGENCY SCOTTSDALE
RESORT AT GAINEY RANCH
Scottsdale, Arizona

Entering the private road that leads to this resort does not prepare you for the beauty of this lush and luxurious oasis in the midst of the Arizona desert. Water surrounds, cascades, falls, bubbles, flows, even sprays from the air; water and flowers are everywhere. You

feel as though you are part of the landscape, not separated from it. Twenty-eight fountains, forty-seven waterfalls, and hundreds of palms, fir trees, and flowers create a twenty-seven-acre garden, part of the 560-acre Gainey Ranch, a planned residential complex that includes golf, parks and lakes, private homes, and businesses. Ecologically, this is a fragile area; fortunately the Hyatt has an admirable environmental program that focuses on reducing energy consumption and landfill; a waste-water reclamation plant irrigates the golf course.

Accommodations: The double "H" shape of the four-story resort provides five court-yards and four glass-enclosed atriums, with a movable 820-square-foot glass wall at the center of the lobby that allows a panoramic view of the McDowell Mountains and Sono-ran Desert. The main building, inspired by the desert work of Frank Lloyd Wright, houses 493 rooms and suites; on either side are seven two- and four-bedroom freestanding casitas with fireplaces and terraced balconies overlooking the lake. The decor blends with the desert setting, using natural textures and artifacts. Children under eighteen stay free in existing bed space of parents' rooms, and every room has the Disney channel. Rates vary according to season and range from $180 to $530. Rates are higher in the Regency Club, which offers VIP service, complimentary breakfast, beverages, and evening hors d'oeuvres. Casitas are adjacent to the lake, with a residential feel; rates range from $690 to $3,000 per night. Subject to availability, parents receive 50% off a second room.

Dining: Vu, the innovative and award-winning new restaurant open for dinner only, has a new two-story design as well. Sophisticated is the key word, with 10-foot floor-to-ceiling windows to showcase the lagoon and resort gardens, and outdoor dining in the gazebo. On the second level, Pre-Vu invites you into the comfort of Southwest colors amid suede and velvet to enjoy designer martinis and "pre-apps." The Squash Blossom restaurant is open for breakfast, lunch, and dinner, with a warm Southwestern ambience and regional specialties (try the Arizona toast

or a wide variety of salads and sandwiches or fajitas). Ristorante Sandolo is a casual Italian bistro, overlooking the pool, where the servers serenade you. After you dine, enjoy a Venice-style gondola ride on the resort's waterways. Again, a *sandolier* will sing to you. (You can enjoy the gondola ride for $8.00 even if you don't eat.) Both restaurants have a children's menu and indoor/outdoor seating with very clever "air-conditioning." A very fine, invisible mist cools and moisturizes the air above you, making it comfortable year-round. Poolside, the Waterfall Juice Bar and the Water Garden Grill serve snacks, lunch, yogurt, and fruit drinks. The Coffee Bar features gourmet blends complemented by homemade Italian biscotti. In the evening watch the cascading fountains and listen to classical flamenco guitar or perhaps a marimba band as you relax in the Lobby Bar.

Children's World: Camp Hyatt Kachina, designed in 1989, is the prototype children's program for all Hyatt resorts. It operates daily year-round and offers three- to twelve-year-olds a well-balanced program of activities focusing on the flora, fauna, culture, and geography of the area. A specially appointed Camp room has all the crafts and games children like best. And don't forget the ten swimming pools, one complete with a white-sand beach and a three-story water slide. Each day has a different theme, related to the geographic area. Making tribal clay beads or arrowhead necklaces, designing sand pictures in the Salt River, listening to a Hopi storyteller, or planting a cactus garden put children firmly in their environment while having fun. Campers enjoy a desert scavenger hunt, puppet theater, close encounters with desert critters, Mexican bark painting, Native American dancing, and much more.

Age groups are three to five and six to twelve. The morning session, from 9:00 A.M. to noon, is $30, and the afternoon session, from 1:00 to 5:00 P.M., is $40.

Lunch, from noon to 1:00 P.M., can be added to either session for $10. The full day costs $80, including lunch. Friday and Saturday only Camp Kachina continues with an evening session from 5:00 to 9:00 P.M. The cost is $50, including dinner. During holidays the resort offers activities designed for the entire family, from cowboy roping, cowboy guitarists, and Native American dancing to family fun sing-alongs round the campfire and "dive-in" movies. Another pursuit that families enjoy is the Lost Dutchman Mine, a hands-on "dig" for jewels. A poster helps identify your find, and you get to take your treasures home.

Recreation: Where do we start? With the twenty-seven-hole championship golf course at Gainey Ranch Golf Club? Actually, it's composed of three separate, individually designed courses—the Dunes; the Lakes, with five lakes and lots of water hazards; and the Arroyo, the most difficult. Or with the eight tennis courts or 3 miles of jogging and cycling trails? Or the Sonwai Spa, with facials, massage, and body treatments incorporating ancient Hopi and Sonoran Desert traditions?

Let's start with the two-and-a-half-acre water playground—most impressive in this dry, desert area. The design is a combination of Roman, Greek, and Art Deco and is truly spectacular. Zip down the three-story water slide, stroll over an aqueduct connecting six of the ten pools, swim around (or through!) the "Big Gun," a 5-foot-wide waterfall, or "thunderfall" as the hotel terms it, at the end of the aqueduct. Relax in the Grecian temple with 16-foot hot tub and four "cold plunges" in each corner. Water comes from all directions—from fountains, trailing down tall glass columns, and from waterspouts along the roof. Build sand castles on the beach at one end or play volleyball at the other. Kids may never want to leave this watery fantasyland.

Hyatt at Gainey Ranch's goal is to combine luxury with learning and light adventure. Toward this end, guests may enjoy presentations on Hopi Silver overlay, Native American and Gypsy dancing, a docent-led tour of the hotel's extensive art collection, or Southwest flora and fauna. During holiday periods, lots of complimentary activities introduce the entire family to history, reptiles, birds of prey, the Anasazi, singing cowboy songs, sampling Native American food, and the tale of El Conquistador, a first-person narrative.

As part of the Native American and Environmental Learning Center, the Native American Sculpture Garden features the bronze and marble works of Apache artist Craig Dan Goseyun. The award-winning Native Heritage Seed Garden, with over thirty indigenous plants, has been carefully researched and developed and represents early agricultural practices of the natives of the area. And it's practical as well—plans are to eventually use the produce in the resort's signature cuisines.

Phoenix attractions include a zoo, a desert botanical garden, and stately old homes; in Scottsdale, find an IMAX theater, the world's highest fountain, and shopping on Fifth Avenue. View large cats in the wild at Out of Africa; experience a re-creation of the Old West at WestWorld or Rawhide, Arizona's largest Western–themed attraction. Pick up a copy of *GUEST* for lots more ideas. If you have time to venture farther, the concierge will help you plan excursions to the Grand Canyon (five hours away) or Montezuma Castle, a 600-year-old Pueblo Indian cliff dwelling only ninety minutes away. Who knew the desert could be like this?

**7500 East Doubletree Ranch Road
Scottsdale, Arizona 85258
(480) 444–1234, (800) 233–1234
www.scottsdale.hyatt.com**

HYATT REGENCY TAMAYA RESORT AND SPA

Santa Ana Pueblo, New Mexico

Not many families can boast a vacation on a Native American reservation. Set on over 500 acres of protected land along the Rio Grande between Albuquerque and Santa Fe, in an area steeped in history that goes back over 1,000 years, the Hyatt Tamaya is unique. Owned by the Santa Ana Pueblo tribe, it is actually on the reservation. The architecture is reminiscent of a Southwestern pueblo, and artwork and cultural treasures are displayed throughout. Every effort has been made to honor the culture, history, and people of the area, and the natural beauty of the Sandia Mountains and the Bosque surrounds you with tranquillity. You're invited to experience this very special place and step into the traditions and sanctity of another culture.

Accommodations: Open-air courtyards and patios or balconies overlooking the scenic mountains abound throughout the resort's 350 pueblo-style guest rooms and suites. Traditional designs used in Santa Ana pottery and blankets decorate the rooms, along with textures of natural stone, wood, and adobe and the colors of maize, pumpkin, and turquoise. Coffeemakers and refrigerators add convenience, and suites offer a small separate parlor. Rates during the low season (November through April) are $275 to $350; $300 to $400 during the May to October high season. Children seventeen and under stay for free in the room with parents, or a second room for children may be reserved at a 50% discount. There is also a $12 per room daily resort fee. The resort amenities program includes tennis; fitness room; trail bikes; cultural events such as tribal dances, storytellers, and nature walks;

shuttles to the golf courses and casino; and organized recreation.

Dining: The Corn Maiden, the signature restaurant, serves dinner only, Tuesday through Saturday. Tapas, grilled specialties, an exhibition kitchen, and perfect sunsets are the order of the day. The Santa Ana Café has unusual regional cuisine, such as wild-mushroom and duck enchiladas, in an indoor or outdoor setting for breakfast, lunch, and dinner casual dining, with a children's menu. Expect red and green chilies—they're found in most dishes, even breakfast eggs, but are generally mild. The atush bar and grill on the Twin Warriors Golf Course attracts nongolfers as well as golfers for lunch and cocktails, while the Plaza Pool Bar and Grill satisfies your hunger without having to leave the pool. The Trading Post Deli and General Store can supply morning coffee and pastries along with sandwiches and snacks—and the requisite jars of salsa and chilies to take home. Turquoise margaritas and live entertainment are enjoyed from the porch of the Rio Grande Lounge—the sunset and view of the Bosque are on the house.

Children's World: Camp Hyatt activities are steeped in the history and lore of the Santa Ana people, the Tamaya; but it's so much fun the kids barely realize they're learning. Tribal storytellers and traditional dances both entertain and educate; learning about the Rio Grande, the local vegetation, and native wildlife, such as reptiles and coyotes, occupy the nature hikes; and learning to weave or baking bread in traditional ovens gives a tangible reward for effort. Camp Hyatt operates year-round, daily from 9:00

A.M. to 9:00 P.M. with an option for lunch ($10 extra) with the morning or afternoon sessions ($45). Evening sessions (5:00 to 9:00 P.M.) include dinner; cost is $55.

Recreation: Golf fans will like the eighteen-hole, 72-par Twin Warriors Golf Course designed by Gary Panks, with cascading waterfalls, arroyos, and juniper and piñon trees. The nearby stables are reached by wagon ride, and you'll find horses to suit every taste. Hay-wagon rides and complimentary pony rides are available for the younger set, and guests from eight to eighty can enjoy a calm trail ride through the back country of the Santa Ana reservation's cottonwood forests, ancient ruins, and 1,200-year-old Indian petroglyphs. The three-hour Chuckwagon Experience promises to work up an appetite for the ribs, baked beans, and apple pie that wait for you at trail's end. A wonderful (and comfortable) way to enjoy the sunset is on a carriage ride.

A huge circular swimming pool dominates the courtyard, looking very much like a *kiva* (the sacred place in the pueblo, generally underground). Two other pools and a two-story water slide provide plenty of water time. Two tennis courts, bike riding, and nature trails along the Rio Grande, plus a fitness center, keep you active. More sedate pleasures might include a tour of the art collection or a visit to the on-site Tamaya Cultural Museum and Learning Center. Ashtanga yoga and meditation areas contribute to a feeling of relaxed yet energized well-being. The Tamaya Mist Spa, a full-service luxury spa, uses distinctive treatments with native herbs and natural ingredients of the earth to soothe your inner self. Shop at the Galleria Tamaya, take a hot-air balloon flight—the sky's the limit here. Branching out from the resort, you'll find Harley-Davidson rentals, mountain biking and hiking, rafting, and fly-fishing. In the wintertime, enjoy downhill and cross-country skiing. And of course, the pleasures of Albuquerque and Santa Fe are quite close by.

Srai-Wi is the new family program with unique and unforgettable shared experiences—in fact, the word means "to gather children together and share with them" in the Tamayan language. Cooking, baking bread in traditional huruno ovens, stargazing, nature hikes, storytelling, adobe-making lessons, lassos and horse care, and much, much, more—all with the distinctive Native American perspective and tradition. Program operates April through October.

1300 Tuyuna Trail
Santa Ana Pueblo, New Mexico 87004
(505) 867–1234, (800) 233–1234
www.tamaya.hyatt.com

LOS ABRIGADOS RESORT AND SPA
Sedona, Arizona

Close to the Grand Canyon and just two hours from Phoenix, Sedona is noted for its spectacular red rock formations and scenic canyons. For centuries it has been a sacred place to the People, the earliest inhabitants, and legend holds that the Grandmother Spirit of the World still lives here. There is a magic quality in the air that many attribute to the energy points that converge here. At the least, the light, color, and awe-inspiring red rocks combine with the many artisans living here to create something special.

Accommodations: Los Abrigados, Portuguese for "the shelters," is in the heart of the small town of Sedona but stands in the midst of twenty-two acres of private ranchland/park and feels more secluded. The resort has recently become a time-share property, part of ILX Resorts. All 175 guest suites have oversize living rooms and separate bedrooms plus a balcony or private patio. Many feature a private whirlpool and fireplace. Plazas, walkways, and bridges connect the suites and main hotel area. Suites range from $225 to $285 (one bedroom); $240 reserves one with spectacular views of the red rocks. Two-bedroom suites range from $395 to $425, but can be confirmed only ten days prior to arrival. Children fifteen and under stay free in the same room with parents. Cribs are available at no charge. The Los Abrigados Lodge, a sister property located a short mile away, provides optional lodging. A two-story motel-like structure in the heart of "uptowne," it's literally in the middle of the action. Steps away are restaurants, galleries, shops, and tours; the rooms are pleasant, with balconies, gas fireplaces, and limited views. A concierge in the well-appointed lobby is helpful in planning your stay, and guests here enjoy privileges at the Los Abrigados Resort. Joey Pizza, adjacent to the lobby, is a branch of the main lodge restaurant known for inventive Italian cuisine—kids love the breakfast pizza with bacon and eggs. Rates range from $119 to $169 nightly.

Dining: Steaks and Sticks, for casual dining with a Southwestern flavor, also provides diversion in the billiards room (hence the "sticks"). An open copper and brass kitchen and library-style lounge with fireplace add to the coziness. More intimate dining is found in the Celebrity Room, lined with caricatures of famous guests. Serving breakfast, lunch, and dinner, imaginative dishes with an accent on indigenous ingredients make dining an adventure. The restaurant offers a children's menu and also features a "spa cuisine menu," lighter versions of many favorites. On the Rocks Bar & Grill serves lunch, snacks, and dinner in a casual atmosphere. You'll always know the score, as the television with the area's largest screen is here. Frequently kids eat free when accompanied by an adult diner—be sure to ask. Forty "Joes" from literature, sports, and entertainment line the walls of Joey Bistro. Think you know Italian food? The imaginative dishes here may challenge you. Imagine marsala sauce mozzarella, roasted eggplant pesto, or Gorgonzola and mascarpone cheeses in crisp pasta shells—it's not just spaghetti and meatballs! A variety of restaurants can be found right next door at Tlaquepaque Village, a re-created Mexican village/plaza with tiled courtyards, fountains, and many craft shops.

Children's World: Leapin' Lizards! No, you won't find Little Orphan Annie here, for kids are far too well looked-after. But that is the name of the children's program at Los Abrigados. Children entering kindergarten through age twelve can spend the day (9:00 A.M. to 4:00 P.M.) or pick and choose from a different list of a la carte activities each day. Monday through Saturday, from early June until mid-August, kids are entertained by such things as wacky water relays; sand castles and sculptures; tie-dye shirts; Creature Feature Play in the mushroom waterfall, where kids get a "beach ball creature"; and games galore. There are plenty of things to do: tennis, miniature golf, volleyball, giant beach ball, and other ball games; swimming, playing at the creek, or a water rodeo Wet Wild West. Kids can even bead their own leapin' lizard. Tuesday and Friday, from 5:00 to 8:00 P.M.: Kids' Kamp Out features campfires, flashlight tag, burgers, hot dogs, s'mores; and a pow-wow, with dinner at the firepit and tepee making ($18). A la carte activities last from one to three hours, and prices range from $6.00 to $16.00 when purchased individually. Cost for the full day with lunch is $32; supervised free play occupies the time between organized activities. Preregistration is not required. Babysitting can be arranged.

The Teens Program is just what this age group wants. A happy hour at the pool with soda and pizza and movies at a local theater are offered twice a week; selected activities enable them to socialize with their peers, but casually, with a lot of space, and in a cool way, dude.

Recreation: Roll over Beethoven, Tchaikovsky is playing through! Next to Oak Creek, among tall sycamore trees and colorful flowers, the new eighteen-hole family miniature golf course not only offers fun for golfers of all ages and skills, but it's done to classical music!

After a game of tennis, basketball, or volleyball, relax at the heated outdoor pool and chat with other guests. Enjoy the jogging and walking trails or just sit by the creek or in the sculpture garden and dream. It may be difficult to choose between the family pool with water features and the adult pool with Jacuzzi, but you can do both. The Sedona Spa—10,000 square feet of state-of-the-art equipment and professional services—provides a combination of fitness and relaxation. Hot stone massage, full body treatments and masks, facials, and fitness classes/personal training contribute to physical and mental well-being. Weekly classes in watercolor painting, Native American medicine wheel, cooking, or astronomy are both educative and fun.

Golf on-site is rather unique. Stop by the ILX Premiere Country Club and try a full-swing golf simulator, allowing you to tee off at any of thirty-three internationally known courses. For the real thing, nearby are two championship golf courses, designed by Robert Trent Jones and Gary Panks. Hiking, fishing streams, horseback riding, and four-wheel-drive tours can also be arranged. The Grand Canyon is a two-hour drive away; and closer is Oak Creek Canyon, with Slide Rock State Park, aptly named for the stretch of slippery creek bottom that forms a natural slide. For Southwestern art at its best, Tlaquepaque Village, next door to the resort, demands a visit.

Red Rock Fantasy is the West's largest holiday light display, with more than one million lights. From late November until mid-January it transforms Los Abrigados into a spectacular holiday light show.

160 Portal Lane
Sedona, Arizona 86336
(928) 282–1777, (800) 521–3131
www.ilxresorts.com

TANQUE VERDE RANCH
Tucson, Arizona

In the Arizona desert, 2,800 feet high in the foothills of three mountain ranges, Tanque Verde Ranch has been serving travelers for more than one hundred years.

Once merely a stagecoach stop, today it is a year-round resort, voted one of the top ten Family Fun Resorts of North America by the Travel Channel. The owners live on the property, adding to the feeling of a "family place." The area is rich in the history of Native Americans and Spanish settlers who dubbed the area Tanque Verde—immortalizing the deep pools of artesian water found here. Located 12 miles outside Tucson, it borders Saguaro National Park. The saguaro cacti are immediately recognizable to anyone who has seen a Western movie or a picture of the desert. They stand quite tall, with "arms" curving up toward the sky.

Accommodations: The seventy-four guest rooms and suites are scattered throughout the grounds in individual cottages called "casitas"; most of the casitas have patios, corner fireplaces, and a feeling of privacy. The decorative motif is Native American, and antiques and original art are carefully arranged to lend warmth. Cribs are available, and there are refrigerators in the rooms. Room rates range from $290 to $375 based on double occupancy, from May through September. October to mid-December rates are $310 to $400. Suites are slightly more. Children three and under are $15 per day; pricing for children four and older is based on number of people in the room. Three people pay $405 to $505; four people pay $500 to $580. Based on a Full American Plan, room, three meals a day, and all ranch activities, including the fully supervised children's program for ages four through eleven, are included in the rate.

Dining: Most meals are served in the Main Dining Room, with beautiful views of the pool and the Rincon Mountains. A variety of tables, seating from two to ten people, make shared dining easy and encourage an informal, friendly atmosphere. Dress is casual and appetites are generally big due to the desert air and the exercise. American and Continental dishes are standard fare and, as expected, Spanish and Mexican specialties also appear on the menu. A separate children's dining room is reserved for

youngsters and their counselors, who can take all meals together. Children are also welcome to dine with their parents. The food is delicious and plentiful. Breakfast combines a buffet and a la carte ordering; lunch is a lavish buffet with the famous "sweet talk" table. Early morning rides with a cowboy breakfast on the trail and a twice-weekly outdoor barbecue around the campfire in the cottonwood grove with foot-tapping live Western entertainment are popular meal options.

Children's World: The ranch offers a year-round, seven-day-per-week, fully supervised program for four- to eleven-year-olds; twelve-year-olds may participate if they like. This is an active program that provides a fantastic ranch experience. Horseback riding forms the core of the program and is adjusted to fit the abilities and interests of the youngsters. Buckaroos (ages four to six) generally ride in the corral, starting at 7:00 A.M. in the summer (8:00 A.M. in winter). Riding lessons, swimming, hikes, tennis, nature lessons, playtime, and Western crafts are nonstop until 3:00 P.M. If that's too strenuous for your child, pick up a weekly schedule at the front desk and pick and choose. Kids are excited with the new playground featuring slides and a fort. The Wrangler Kids (ages six to twelve) have the same hours, but a more active, individualized riding program geared to their skills. Again, it's go, go, go all day, but the kids love it. Parents may ride with their children if they wish. In the winter months the fun continues with an evening program from 6:00 to 8:00 P.M. The children's programs are included in the rate. Babysitting can be arranged for infants and toddlers at an additional cost.

During the summer, Tanque Verde also runs a totally separate Kids Camp—ten-day sessions for children ages nine to fourteen years. Kids get their own horse, they bunk in a separate building riverside, and all activities are separate from daily guests at the ranch. In 2005, the ranch added a teen camp for girls ages fourteen to sixteen. This camp involves more advanced riding and a few days' excursion to Bellota Ranch, another smaller ranch on the east side of Tucson in the valley between the Rincon and Santa Catalina Mountains. Cost is approximately $1,500—call the ranch for details.

Recreation: Active relaxation is the byword at Tanque Verde. The clear desert air and low humidity, coupled with abundant sunshine, make all the activities pleasant. Horseback riding is the major part of the program. Whether you're interested in a slow-moving trail ride or a spirited sprint, the right mount can be found from a string of 150 horses, the largest in Arizona.

Early morning and late afternoon are perfect times for strenuous outdoor activities such as tennis on one of the five courts. In the middle of the day, seek out one of the two swimming pools or the children's wading pool for a cool dip. Numerous guided nature walks introducing visitors to the Sonoran Desert ecology are conducted along trails throughout the 25,000 acres. Some 200 species of birds have been identified in the area, making the ranch very popular with avid birdwatchers. It's not uncommon to see wildlife such as rabbits, coyotes, and snakes on trail rides. Catch-and-release fishing is also a popular pastime. If you prefer wheels to hooves, take a mountain bike for a spin. The final touch to the active relaxation concept is the El Sonora Spa, well equipped with its swimming pool, sauna, whirlpool, exercise room (although who would really need it?!), and lounge. The Nature Center allows a fascinating close-up view of desert life. Weekly classes encourage you to capture the essence of the desert in watercolors, charcoal, pottery, and mixed media. In nearby Tucson, six championship golf courses grant playing privileges to ranch guests. From here visitors can take side trips to Tucson, to old Spanish missions, and to Mexico, which is about a ninety-minute drive away.

14301 East Speedway Boulevard
Tucson, Arizona 85748
(520) 296–6275, (800) 234–3833
www.tanqueverderanch.com

TAOS SKI VALLEY
Taos Ski Valley, New Mexico

In the early 1950s, Ernie Blake searched carefully for just the right spot for a ski resort and rediscovered this bit of northern New Mexico. Since then, skiers have been coming to Taos Ski Valley for the incredible powder snow and the glorious sunshine. Several ski magazines are calling Taos one of the hottest places to ski, citing the steep, challenging terrain and trails for all abilities so all levels may ski together. Once again, Taos has the number one ski school in North America, featuring the Ski-Better-Week. Grouped according to ability, each group remains with the same instructor, developing new, close friendships and improving skills.

Two hours from Santa Fe, or a three-hour drive from Albuquerque, Taos Ski Valley combines lodging, restaurants, shops, and a beautiful mountain. The town of Taos is only 18 miles away and, with its Native American and Spanish heritage, is an interesting alternative for dining, shopping, and entertainment (see end of listing). The Taos Valley operates during the ski season only, which generally runs from Thanksgiving through mid-April, and provides good value for families. Although a few properties may open in summer, the lift operations and facilities are limited.

Accommodations: Every skier's dream is to be on the mountain. The Taos Valley Resort Association (800–776–1111) represents more than 95% of all lodging in and around Taos. Taos Valley has an amazing variety of lodging: bed-and-breakfasts, hotels, ski lodges, condominiums, and private houses/cabins snuggled in the trees—it's all here.

For lodges right near the slopes—such as Hotel St. Bernard and the Thunderbird Lodge—rates for a one-week package run $1,690 to $1,865 per adult double occupancy; besides the room, this package includes meals, lifts, and morning lessons. Children between three and twelve are $980. As an example of rates, a one-bedroom condominium at the slopes averages $1,550 per week; about a mile away, the cost drops to $1,400. A cabin with two bedrooms, off the slopes, is $175 to $225 per night. The Inn at Snakedance, 10 yards from the lift, has nightly rates of $175 to $250. Opened in 2005, the Edelweiss Lodge and Spa is a ski-in ski-out, hand your skis to a valet, and hit the riverside hot tubs kind of place. Upgraded from an existing property, there's now a spa and fitness rooms, game room, a heated outdoor plaza, entertainment, and a Kids Club. Another favorite property is the Bavarian, an alpine-style ski-in ski-out lodge on the back side of the mountain.

Dining: On the mountain there are quick and easy stops like the Phoenix Grill at Kachina Bowl, where you can sit on the outdoor deck and watch others ski, or the Whistlestop Cafe, serving soup, sandwiches, and pizza. Tenderfoot Katie's Cafeteria, with big windows facing the slope, is the breakfast spot, and serves a quick, economical lunch of burgers, tacos, and pasta, with a fresh salad bar. Upstairs at the Martini Tree Bar is the après-ski action. Meet your friends, play pool, eat, drink, and watch Monday Night Football. Rhoda's Restaurant, slopeside in the Resort Center, is open from 11:00 A.M. until 9:00 P.M. Savor an over-stuffed sandwich or some dish with those famous New Mexico chilis; be prepared, as the most frequent question you'll be asked is "Red or green?" If you don't know, say "Christmas," and you'll get both! Dinner offers steaks, chicken, and seafood at affordable prices, and a kids' menu. The outside deck is the place to watch what's happening at the base of Al's Run. Tim's Stray Dog Cantina is a bar and restaurant with a wide variety of satisfying food. On the way to Taos, you'll find the Old Blinking Light, a fun Mexican restaurant; or try the Steak Out, on the mountainside with beautiful views overlooking the Rio Grande Gorge. In the town of Taos, a wide selection of restaurants awaits you. And, of course, there's always your own fine cooking in your condominium!

Children's World: The Kinderkäfig is Taos Ski Valley's children's center and site of the ski school and day-care facility. It's the hub of activities for children ages six weeks to twelve years; a safe and creative learning environment with its own pint-sized lifts, terrain, and qualified instructors. It's totally for the kids and there are areas where the NO PARENTS ALLOWED sign is up. You'll find kids-only bathrooms, snacks, and shops. BebeKare is for infants six weeks to one year old. Operating from late November until the end of March, the nursery staff keeps your "bebe" comfortable and happy. Full day is

$70, half day is $50, or $20 per hour. Early and late season prices are $35 per day.

The Kinderkare (one to three years old) full-day program includes two snacks, lunch, creative activities, and nap time. The half-day program includes snack and either snow play or nap time. Reservations are required. Walk-ins are accepted on a space-available basis only; the cost for this program is the same as for BebeKare. The Junior Elite program for three- to twelve-year-olds is also divided by age groups and includes all-day lesson, lift ticket, lunch, and rentals. Junior Elite I is for children ages three through first grade, while Junior Elite II covers second grade up to twelve years, with further breakdown of ages. Junior Elite I kids learn the basics of skiing and have fun with indoor and outdoor play. The programs run from 8:00 A.M. to 4:00 P.M.; older children are on the slopes from 9:45 A.M. to 2:30 P.M. Full-day cost is $95. Five- and six-day packages are $450 and $540. The Junior Elite programs are all-inclusive: lift tickets, rental equipment including helmets, morning and afternoon lessons, and lunch. The last lesson finishes at 2:30 P.M., so you may ski with your children or they are welcome to remain in the center until 4:00 P.M. Children should be checked in between 8:15 and 9:00 A.M.

Also for kids, there's tubing on the bunny hill on Wednesday, Friday, and Saturday between 4:00 and 7:00 P.M. The cost is $7.00 and parents need to supervise (or participate!). There is no snowboarding at Taos Ski Valley. When not on the program, kids under six years old ski free with a ticketed adult.

The new Teen Center has comfortable couches, TV, games, pizza, and the latest extreme skiing movies to inspire them. Snacks and drinks, and open from 11:00 A.M. to 8:00 P.M., what more could teens ask? Activities at the Out-to-Launch Terrain Park are for all ages, but teens find a lot to do with their friends there.

Recreation: Partially located in the Carson National Forest, the Taos ski area is in the Sangre de Cristo Mountains, the southernmost part of the Rockies. The base village sits at 9,207 feet, and the peak towers above at 12,481 feet, affording skiers more than 2,600 feet of vertical drop. This is a challenging mountain with over 1,200 acres of skiable terrain down 110 different runs; just over 50% of its runs are classified as expert; however, even the novice can feel that classic mountaintop high, since some beginners' runs descend directly from the highest lift at 11,819 feet. In a ski season that lasts from about Thanksgiving to Easter, there are 300-plus days of sunshine, and the average annual snowfall is over 305 inches, plus there's snowmaking on more than 98% of beginner and intermediate terrain.

When you can pull yourself away from the open bowls, dramatic chutes, and lazy meandering-down trails lined with spruce and aspen, you might consider an evening skier's seminar on such topics as avalanches and adjusting to the altitude. Take a snowmobile tour with Big Al to the peaks above the valley for some spectacular views. Taos is too steep for cross-country skiing, but if you're a real fan, it's available about forty-five minutes away. This is a family-owned and family-enjoyed resort and alpine skiing is really the focus. One of the best-kept secrets? Taos seldom has a lift line.

Skiers in January experience the added pleasures of Taos's jazz festival. Also in January is the two-week Winter Wine Festival, when the grape takes over the Ski Valley. Scores of vintners come from faraway places bringing their wares; seminars and wine tastings warm the winter cold. Several restaurants in Taos build special menus around a particular vineyard, and your dinner is accompanied by a lesson in wines and food.

Taos Pueblo has been inhabited for over 1,000 years, and offers a view into the past and traditions of the Tiwa tribe. Check www.taospueblo.com to see when they are open to the public. Another adventure is a hot-air balloon over the Rio Grande Gorge; sunrise is incredible, but if that's too early, other times are also beautiful.

P.O. Box 90
Taos Ski Valley, New Mexico 87525
(505) 776–2291, (800) 776–1111,
(800) 347–7414
www.visitnewmexico.com
www.skitaos.org

EL MONTE SAGRADO

Taos, New Mexico

Winter's not all there is in the valley, as the pleasures of the town of Taos are to be had throughout the year. Late spring and summer bring great white-water rafting, trout fishing, mountain bikes and hikes, horseback riding, and golf. Add museums, art galleries, and music festivals and it's a whirl of activity in a gorgeous setting. Special events include a Kite Festival in June, the Taos Pueblo Pow-Wow in July, a storytelling festival in September, and the Hot Air Balloon Rally in the fall, when the trees are gloriously adorned in color.

El Monte Sagrado means the sacred mountain; it is an exciting and unusual new resort (2003) right in the heart of Taos, ½ mile from the Plaza. The concept and underlying philosophy of the resort is based on sound environmental development and water conservation, geared to demonstrate that you needn't give up comfort or even luxury to protect our natural resources. At the core of the resort is the Living Machine®, the resort's effective system for treating and recycling water. Guests, as well as the public, may take an ecotour to see environmental responsibility in action; the resort utilizes the most current concepts in ecopreservation and sustainability. Spend relaxing time in the Biolarium®, where out-

doors comes indoors, for the pleasure of plants and people alike. El Monte Sagrado is where nature and nurture meet. In 2005, *Spa* magazine named the resort one of the "Top Ten Best Mind/Body Retreats" and *Travel + Leisure* called it "One of the Top 15 Resorts to Watch Out For."

Accommodations: On site, find eighteen casita-style rooms, each with a Native American cultural theme; and twenty suites, each with a global theme—Japanese, Egyptian, Balinese, Mayan, and Moroccan are examples. The months of April and November are off season, when rates range from $255 (standard) to $575 (grande exclusive). Two-bedroom global suites cost between $895 and $1,095, depending on the number of people. On-season rates are $395 to $650; global suites are $1,095 to $1,295. Room rates are based on double occupancy; children twelve and under are complimentary; additional per-person rate is $100. Rates include valet parking, two daily maid services, aqua and fitness center, and a turndown gift.

An interesting option, especially for families, is the El Monte Casitas. Eleven off-site private homes in and around Taos Plaza provide historical adobe-style lodging with kitchens, fireplaces, and patios, even yards (that you don't have to mow!). The resort will gladly stock the pantry with your favorite foods. Guests have open access to resort facilities; weekly rates begin at $2,500.

Dining: *De la Tierra* means "of the earth," and that's precisely the focus of the resort's main restaurant. New Mexico flavors and foods and artistic presentation are highlighted. De la Tierra has been named one of the world's best new restaurants by *Condé Nast* (2004). One of the specialties, and quite unique, is yak chili or carpaccio of yak tenderloin. Open for breakfast, lunch, and dinner. The Anaconda Bar opens at noon, closes at midnight, and is a lively gathering spot. You can't miss the namesake—a huge sculpture that snakes across the ceiling—or the 1,100-gallon saltwater aquarium that mesmerizes you along with the martinis. Next door, seek out The Gardens, with an imaginative menu in a casual, exotic indoor garden setting, complete with water. Open for breakfast, lunch, and dinner. And we don't even need to mention that you are in the heart of Taos, with over fifty fine choices for dining and entertainment.

Children's World: While there is no organized program, children are welcome and there is a definite interest in family activities. The resort owners, Dharma Living, also own the adjacent Yaxche School, an alternative learning experience for children in kindergarten through eighth grade. Outdoor family activities include horseback riding, river rafting, carriage rides, and even a llama trek into the mountains. Hiking trips integrate natural movement and meditation, or watch the full moon rise from the mountainside. Babysitting is available on request.

Recreation: An all-natural swimming pool without chlorine is a wonderful experience. You can also swim in the outdoor pond that's part of the water reclamation project—the resort will explain how it all works. Visit Detlevs, the full-service spa showcasing soaring glass ceilings, waterfalls, and tropical plants, or lounge in the Jacuzzi under the stars. For true relaxation, sit in the large grassy "sacred circle," where food and drink are not allowed and a peaceful atmosphere prevails. So sit back, relax, and savor the experience of Taos.

Guests may also visit Latir Mountain Ranch, a sister property chock full of wonderful experiences. Try llama trekking, horseback riding, fly-fishing, and hiking. On the mountaintop find an upscale wilderness camp with deluxe tepees, bathrooms, and showers. Savor gourmet meals in a log cabin. Here you'll discover the third largest yak farm in the United States and the only certified organic one; two yaks have even been blessed by the Dalai Lama!

---

125 La Posta Road
Taos, New Mexico 87571
(505) 758–3502, (800) 828–TAOS
www.elmontesagrado.com

ROCKIES

Colorado
Montana
Utah

ASPEN/SNOWMASS VILLAGE
Aspen, Colorado

Say "a small mountain town in Colorado with a very cosmopolitan feel" to anyone, and the response likely will be "Aspen." Aspen is synonymous with chic, the playground of the rich and famous; Snowmass is devoted to its motto "A Mountain of Family Fun." Each has its niche, and who splits hairs when the best of both worlds is all within a 10-mile radius in one resort area? When talking Aspen skiing, you've actually got four mountains to consider: Aspen Mountain (sometimes called Ajax), Snowmass, and Aspen Highlands and Buttermilk in between. A combined skiable terrain that totals more than 4,000 acres provides more runs and variety than you could possibly test in a two-week ski vacation. Lift passes are valid for all four mountains. Though best known for skiing, both resort areas are open year-round.

Aspen's origins are rooted in the silver boom of the early 1880s. Many of the charming Victorian structures have been preserved and renovated; today they house boutiques, art galleries, hotels, and restaurants. Aspen is just waiting to tempt you. Folks here boast that 75% of their visitors return every year and more than 90% come back sooner or later. So if you give it a shot, you may just have to plan on being hooked.

Accommodations: Whatever your preference in lodging, you should have no problem finding the perfect place to hang your hat in the Aspen and Snowmass area. From moderate to expensive, from quaint to modern, all the possibilities seem to be here. For the most part, lodgings in Aspen are in the village; at Snowmass they're slopeside with immediate access to trails. This is not, however, a hard-and-fast rule, and because shuttle buses always cruise the roads, there's no problem getting to the lifts and from one mountain to another.

With close to one hundred hotels, lodges, inns, and condominiums in the Aspen area, it is indeed fortunate that the resort associations publish descriptive lists to help you sort through the possibilities. You'll discover everything from a cozy cabin to a five-star deluxe hotel. Just have your priorities straight and decide what's important to you—space, location, a hot tub, spa shower, or fireplace and bear rug? And contrary to the image, costs range from $79 for a room up to $5,000 for a presidential suite. If you're adventurous and a last-minute type, you may find great deals at the Virtual Hostel, which features last-minute specials on lodging and lifts within the upcoming two-week period, winter and summer. Central Reservations (www.stayaspensnowmass.com or 888–649–5982) has all the details and can help you plan what's exactly right for your family, as far in advance as you want.

Dining: As with lodging arrangements, the dining possibilities seem almost limitless. Whether you've got a hankering for pizza, quiche, fresh veggies and salads, a juicy steak, spicy Szechuan, or northern Italian cuisine, you'll find the right spot among the more than one hundred restaurants in and around Aspen. Seventy-five are listed under "family oriented atmosphere." Particularly family-friendly restaurants are Boogie's Diner, Brothers' Grill, Little Annie's Eating House, and S'no Beach Café and Bar. And, of course, restaurants and refreshment stops are at the mountain bases and on the mountains. For sweets, stop by the Paradise Bakery or Cafe Ink.

Children's World: For the 2006–2007 season, Snowmass has plans for a brand new, state-of-the-art children's center, to be located at the base of Fanny Hill for easy snow access from slopeside lodging. Children two months to eighteen years will have 25,000 square feet of fun with an interactive design that incorporates reading caves, sound systems, climbing structures, mobiles, and aquariums just for starters. A private on-snow learning area and nighttime offerings for both kids and teens will provide excitement for all ages.

At Snowmass, even the youngest traveling companion will not keep you from days on the slopes. From 8:30 A.M. to 4:00 P.M., Snow Cubs caters to infants and toddlers, eight weeks to three and a half years old, in a play program filled with puppet shows, stories, arts and crafts, snowman building, and sledding.

Children are grouped by age, with dedicated rooms for each group; lunch is included. Three-year-old Cubs can learn to ski on a contoured slope with magic carpet. The Bear Den is the indoor center for Big Burn Bears, kids three and a half to four years old; preschoolers learn to ski in their own area; ski time varies by individual child. Grizzlies, for ages five to six, spend their day on the mountain with their own beginner area and direct lift; classes range from beginners to accomplished. A full day is $98; half day is $65 for all programs; equipment is not included. Powder Pandas is Buttermilk Mountain's ski school for three- to six-year-olds, with the same hours and rates; it's convenient for parents skiing Aspen Mountain. For Aspen Highlands, Bighorns provides ages five and six, levels five and up the ski experience at the same times and rates. The $98/$65 rates are for pre-booking; "at the window" is more expensive.

Bears and Pandas on Boards are the popular snowboard programs for ages five to seven. Groups of three children learn safety and skills; the full-day cost of $169 includes equipment, five-hour lesson, and lunch. Bears are at Snowmass, Pandas gather at Buttermilk. Night Hawks is a winter evening camp program on Monday, Wednesday, and Friday for ages three to ten available from 4:00 to 11:00 P.M. at $13 per hour; late-afternoon and evening babysitters are also available through Snowmass Ski School.

Older kids and teens are also well treated at Aspen/Snowmass. Kids First Turn introduces seven- to twelve-year-olds to skiing and snowboarding; Kid's Group Lessons divides into small groups by ability. From 9:30 A.M. to 3:15 P.M. with instruction, lift tickets, equipment, and lunch is $95; both programs are offered at Buttermilk and Snowmass. The teens "Too Cool for School" skiing and snowboarding program operates every day of the season at Snowmass ($75 for instruction only, 9:30 A.M. to 3:15 P.M.). First Turn Teen Group lessons and Extreme Camps are organized by age (thirteen to seventeen) and skill, and taught by the most experienced instructors. Hours are 9:30 A.M. to 3:15 P.M. and cost is $95, lift ticket, equipment, lunch, and instruction included. Optional evening activities with other teens include ice-skating and pizza parties.

Operating a summer program (June through August), Camp Snowmass emphasizes a healthy, active outdoor schedule of fishing, hiking, swimming, nature walks, visits to the nature preserve, and picnics. Camp Snowmass is located slopeside at the end of the Snowmass Mall and is divided into Junior Base Camp for ages three to five, and Base Camp for ages six to ten. Three-year-olds join nature play groups, while four- and five-year-olds take short field trips to Hallom Lake and the gondola as well as walk-around horseback rides. Base Camp adds paintball, mountainboarding, rafting, horseback riding, and minigolf. For a day's events from 8:00 A.M. to 4:00 P.M. Monday through Friday, the cost is $80; multiple days cost less. Kids can bring their own lunch or it's provided for $6.00. Adventure Series, for eight- to fourteen-year-olds, allows children to create their own adventures. That way they can't complain at the end of the day! They may choose from all the excitement of everything already mentioned for $130 per day. Special camps and sessions for mountainboarding and skateboarding are available for ages six and older—inquire for details. In addition to daily activities, other special activities are regularly planned; a camp ticket plus an extra charge will apply. Friday is generally special-activities day, with such events as rafting, go-karts, climbing wall, miniature golf, swimming, and the fairy caves. Rocket Days, where budding scientists build their own rockets, and Nights on the Mountain (overnight camping) are also planned at special times.

Fun for Kids, on Aspen Mountain, has free activities and entertainment for kids of all ages and families from mid-June to Labor Day. A different two- to three-hour activity every day might include arts and crafts, cooking classes, yoga for kids, adventure hikes, or carnival games. ARC, the Aspen Recreation Center, is 83,000 square feet of fun, with an NHL-size ice rink, climbing wall, and Aquatic Center with pools, beach, river currents—the works. And Aspen boasts one of the top five skateboard parks in the country. Whew, almost too much fun!

Recreation: From the end of November to mid-April, skiing is on everyone's mind, and regardless of your skiing ability, you'll have plenty of runs to schuss down. Aspen's reputation as a mecca for advanced skiers is well earned, with 26% of the runs down Ajax ranked as expert, 26% most difficult, and the remaining 48% more difficult. But beginners and intermediates should not grow faint in the face of overwhelming ventures, for the other mountains accommodate those not quite so adept. Aspen Highlands is 30% intermediate and 18% each in advanced and beginner categories; the total vertical drop is 3,635 feet. The vertical rise at Snowmass is almost 4,400 feet, and 55% of the runs are intermediate. Buttermilk with 2,000 vertical feet is known as the best place to learn, with almost half of its runs designated for beginners. A teaching staff that totals more than 1,000 ski professionals can introduce a beginner to the slopes (except at Aspen Mountain) as well as help an expert perfect techniques in mogul skiing, snowboarding, and telemarking. At Buttermilk and Snowmass, look for special three-day, first-time-on-skis or -snowboard packages. But each mountain has its secrets: Parks and pipes are popping up at Buttermilk, and it was home to the 2003 X Games, the world's largest alternative sports championships; although Aspen Highlands is famous for black and double black runs, there's actually more green and blue; Snowmass is a haven for snowboarders, and offers everyone easy, uncrowded access to the mountains; and who knew that Aspen Mountain has groomed, intermediate cruising runs?

On-mountain family adventures are waiting everywhere. The Family Zone at Snowmass has adventurous kids' trails, a children's race arena, Trenchtown terrain park, and interactive tree trails. On Buttermilk, Max the Moose hosts Fort Frog, an adventure center with Western fort and Native American village. Twilight snowcat rides to dine in a rustic cabin, magic shows in Snowmass, sledding, tubing—no wonder *Child Magazine* calls this the number one family resort.

Wintertime fun continues with ice-skating at the Aspen Ice Gardens and the Silver

Circle, dogsled rides at Krabloonik Kennels, snowshoe tours, cross-country skiing, sleigh rides at Snowmass Stables and T Lazy 7 Ranch, snowmobiling, and hot-air ballooning (yes, even in winter!). A real treat is to ride with the trail groomers in the big rigs. It's free but limited space, so call early (970–925–5756). Many of the lodging complexes have swimming pools and exercise equipment. The tennis and athletic clubs also provide opportunities for indoor workouts. Evening entertainment includes films, concerts, plays at the Wheeler Opera House, and classical music at Harris Hall.

Though skiing is practically synonymous with Aspen, this place does not turn into a ghost town when the snow melts. During the summer, the hills are alive with cultural events. The Aspen Music Festival, nearly fifty years old, runs from the end of June to the end of August and is complemented by the Aspen Community Theater and the Jazz Aspen Snowmass Music Festivals. The Anderson Ranch Arts Center in Snowmass has a summer program of classes in photography, ceramics, painting, and printmaking.

You can just about have your pick of outdoor activities: horseback riding, hiking, jogging, rafting, kayaking, fishing, and four-wheel-drive tours. Snowmass Mountain Outfitters offers all sorts of adventures: hot-air balloon rides, run and gun paintball, bungee trampoline, and especially for the children, trout fishing and panning for gold. There is also lift-served mountain biking at Snowmass Ski Area, and it's free! At the top, test your agility on the climbing wall ($5.00). All ages are welcome. An eighteen-hole golf course is located on the west perimeter of Aspen; another is in Snowmass. Tennis courts at condominiums and racquet clubs dot the valley. Once a week the whole family can enjoy storytelling and a sing-along under the stars, and Friday night free movies. Bring your own blanket and popcorn. Even in summer you have to take at least one gondola ride—to the top of Aspen Mountain for a spectacular view of this bit of the Rockies.

---

425 Rio Grande Plaza
Aspen, Colorado 81611
(800) 598–2004, (888) 649–5985
www.aspensnowmass.com

BIG SKY OF MONTANA
Big Sky, Montana

The sky isn't really bigger in Montana—not by scientific measurements, that is. But don't tell the folks around here that. These die-hard Westerners believe they've got the market cornered on the best, biggest, bluest sky ever; and if you don't watch out, by the end of a visit here, you'll be a believer too.

In the wintertime, skiing Lone Mountain (summit elevation 11,166 feet) can make you feel that it's almost possible to touch that beautiful, clear sky. Lone Mountain and adjacent Andesite and Flat Iron Mountains are carved with more than 150 named runs covering 85 miles on three mountains; a terrain park and a half pipe add up to fine skiing at Big Sky.

During the summer, these mountains and their evergreens, the sunshine, and clean mountain air make the perfect setting for hiking, horseback riding, mountain biking, scenic gondola rides, white-water rafting, and fishing, as well as golf and tennis.

Open late November through mid-April and early June through early October, Big Sky is located in southwestern Montana just north of Yellowstone and is surrounded by rivers and national forests.

Accommodations: Two tall structures, the Shoshone/Huntley/Yellowstone Center and the luxurious new Summit at Big Sky, mark the Mountain Village at the foot of Lone Peak. Combined, they total nearly 500 hotel rooms, suites, and condominiums. Many more accommodations are in the vicinity, with different sizes and access to lifts. The Meadow Village, near the golf course, and the Canyon area along the highway complete the area's lodging choices. Big Sky Resort was the vision of the late NBC newscaster, Chet Huntley, who built it in 1973 and owned it until 1976. In 2001, Boyne USA announced a ten-year plan to include $400 million in improvements at Big Sky.

Recently remodeled, the Huntley Lodge is at the base of Lone Mountain; the Explorer chairlift is right out the back door. The lodge has 200 rooms, some with views straight up the mountain, and an outdoor heated swimming pool, sauna, and Jacuzzi. In the complex you'll find a dining room, lounge, shops, and ski storage.

Attached to the Huntley is the Shoshone Condominium Hotel, with ninety-five suites; it's also ski-in, ski-out. The newest property, the ten-story Summit, combines the best of a hotel and condominium stay. Ski-in, ski-out convenience, dining, lounge, and fitness center, and flexible lock-offs allow a variety of accommodations.

Children ten years and under stay free with existing bedding; $15 for cribs and rollaways. Hotel rates are based on season and number of people in the room; winter has four seasons. At the Huntley, based on

three people, rates range from $163 to $308 nightly. The Summit begins at $174 and goes to a high of $386 during the prime season; holidays are higher.

At the area's condominiums, the studios and one- to four-bedroom units have kitchens and fireplaces. While all the complexes (Stillwater, Skycrest, Lake Big Horn, Powder Ridge Cabins, Saddle Ridge Town Homes, Arrowhead, Beaverhead, Shoshone, Snowcrest Lodge) are in close proximity to the slopes, Snowcrest is closest to the lifts. Some complexes feature heated swimming pools, saunas, and Jacuzzis. Winter condominium rates have a wide range; from $153 for a one-bedroom in budget season to $1,248 at the Summit for a three-bedroom sleeping ten in holiday season.

Summer rates begin at $155 for a deluxe room at the Huntley Lodge and go up to $451 for a three-bedroom unit at the Summit. With dozens of choices for accommodations and several seasons from which to choose, you are sure to find amenities that meet both your expectations and your budget.

Dining: If you are staying in the Huntley Lodge or just cannot face cooking after a busy day, you can dine at the Huntley Dining Room. A breakfast buffet is included in room rates at the Huntley Lodge. Chet's Bar and Grill is popular for its warm atmosphere, nightly entertainment, and regular poker games. The Summit features the Peaks Restaurant and the Carabiner Lounge. In winter take the sleigh ride up into the mountains for dinner, and in summer join an outdoor Western barbecue. Next door to the Huntley Lodge is a collection of shops, restaurants, and bars in the Mountain Mall. Here you'll find casual spots for pizzas, deli sandwiches, and burgers; in winter, the Lone Peak Café offers hearty meals at breakfast, lunch, and dinner. On-mountain dining during ski season offers delis and coffee carts at the Mountain Village, the Dug Out, MR Hummers, Dante's Inferno, Sun Dog Café, and the Timbers restaurant. In summer the Bunker Bar and Grill is a good stop for lunch or dinner after a round of golf. Expanding out to the Big Sky area, restaurants and nightspots offer live music, dancing, and family fun nights.

Children's World: During the ski season, Handprints Daycare Center is open daily from 8:30 A.M. to 4:30 P.M. for children six months to eight years old. Located at the Snowcrest Lodge, across from the ski school, the facility is a state-licensed day-care center with experienced teachers. Lunch and two snacks are served daily, and two nap rooms provide a spot to rest. Little ones enjoy a combination of indoor and outdoor play: sledding, snow play, stories, songs, and arts and crafts. Open daily from Thanksgiving to mid-April; reservations and immunization records are required. Rates vary by age and activities and do not include ski equipment and lessons. Infants six months to two years are $85 for a full day, $65 for a half day; two to eight years are $75 full day, $50 half day (lunch included in morning session). Primarily for younger children, the center does offer skiing options (additional cost) for those children four and over who may not wish to ski all day. Lessons last two hours for ages four to eight. Ski equipment is not included. Day-care rates, including skiing, are $100 for a full day, $75 for half-day sessions.

The Snowsports School programs are for children ages three to seventeen. The Small Fry Try for ages three and four is forty-five minutes and the perfect introduction to skiing—of course, it takes almost that long to get them ready! The cost is $60, not including day care and equipment. Mini Camp, for ages four to six and Ski Camp, for ages six to twelve, have flexible schedules that allow for early drop-offs, afternoon activities, and morning or afternoon ski lessons with or without lunch. The complete package, 8:30 A.M. to 4:00 P.M., is $113 for Mini Camp and $110 for Ski Camp; a la carte prices are in place for various options. Prices do not include equipment and lift tickets for children eleven and over. Kids ten and under always ski free.

The Teen Mountain Experience is in operation during Christmas week and Presidents' week in February. Teens explore the mountain with a similar-age-and-skill group while refining techniques. Full day is $87; half-day cost is $48.

Snowboard School is divided not only into age groups, but also levels, beginning with level 1 grasshoppers (never tried it) to level 5 grizzly bears (bring on the greens and easy blues). Ages six to nine are $55 half day, $120 for a full day; ages ten to fourteen are $48 and $106; ages fifteen and up are $48 for each half-day session.

Monday through Friday in winter, the Kids Only Clubhouse in the Huntley Lodge lobby hosts fun after-hours sessions, free to guests of Big Sky Central Reservations. Original artwork, short hikes combined with crafts, face-painting, tie-dye bandanas, rescue dog demonstrations, and indoor/outdoor games keep kids happy and busy. Kids Only pizza parties ($25) and free family movies twice a week round out the fun. The game room in the Huntley Lodge, open from 10:00 A.M. to 10:00 P.M., is the gathering spot for video games and television. In summer, the Kids Only Clubhouse offers supervised activities from 3:00 to 5:00 P.M. for ages four and up; the program is free for guests.

Babysitting arrangements can be made any time of the year through the activities desk at the lodge. The average rate is $8.00 per hour.

Recreation: The 4,350-foot vertical drop takes you through open bowls and tree-lined trails. The average annual snowfall is an amazing 400-plus inches. Skiing starts mid-November (an opening guaranteed by snowmaking if Mother Nature is skimpy with her supply) and continues into April. Whatever your level of skiing, you can join lessons at the ski school. Cross-country skiers enjoy treks over broad meadows and through stands of pine trees. Just 5 miles from the resort, the Lone Mountain Guest Ranch maintains 65 kilometers of cross-country trails. When you're not on skis, swim in one of the heated pools or take a trip to Yellowstone for snowmobiling, snow-shoeing, and sightseeing with free ranger-guided wildlife tours. Dog sledding is fun and Cat skiing gives you access to over 1,000 acres of terrain that averages up to 10,000 vertical feet of skiing and snow-boarding. For the hardy, backcountry skiing gets updated avalanche forecasts with maps and rental equipment. Or take a sleigh ride combined with hearty food, live entertainment, and songs and stories. On Saturday night fireworks over the village thrill young and old.

When the weather warms up, the mountains are terrific for hiking and backpacking. For horseback riding, you can link up with Big Sky Stables through the resort concierge. You may prefer adventures in white-water rafting or the quiet solitude of fishing for prize-winning trout in the mountain streams.

The eighteen-hole golf course was designed by Arnold Palmer and is well situated in the mountain meadows. A la Tiger Woods (his father used the same system) Big Sky has the "Junior has a Nike Fit Guarantee." Using shorter shaft lengths and other design elements, it allows kids to purchase correct size clubs, trading them in the next year for 100% credit, as they grow. Play tennis (six courts, two of which are at the resort) and volleyball, or relax with a Swedish massage at the Solace Spa. Take a leisurely guided nature walk, learning about the wildflowers, animals, and birds of Big Sky. Spend the day at Yellowstone National Park—it's in your backyard.

P.O. Box 160001
1 Lone Mountain Trail
Big Sky, Montana 59716
(406) 995–5000, (800) 548–4486
www.bigskyresort.com

BRECKENRIDGE SKI RESORT

Breckenridge, Colorado

The town of Breckenridge likes to say it was born in the rowdy gold rush of the 1860s, spent its childhood in Prohibition, its teen years in the 1960s, and reached maturity at the turn of this last century. It's a town that doesn't stand still, a town where there's action-plus, all the time. An old gold and silver mining camp proud of its history, Breckenridge is a charming town with carefully restored buildings that attest to its Victorian–era heyday. And the years of skiing have resulted in the development of 2,208 acres of skiing territory on four beautiful mountain peaks. All this skiing in a historic setting is a one-and-a-half-hour drive west of Denver—not so close that it is inundated by Denverites, yet close enough that once you land at Denver International

Airport, your ski holiday begins immediately with a scenic tour through the Arapahoe National Forest on your way to Breckenridge.

Like every other Western mining town turned ski resort, Breckenridge has numerous hotels, vacation homes, and condominiums that can be explored through Breckenridge Central Reservations (800–221–1091). Best known as a winter recreation area, Breckenridge is in fact open year-round. Beaver Run Resort (800–525–2253, www.beaverrun.com) and the Village at Breckenridge (877–428–7829, www.breckresort.com) warrant special attention because of their locations and amenities. With lifts just steps away from either one, these self-contained resorts make life just a little bit easier for families. Besides their own restaurants and shops, the resorts both have independently operated child-care centers.

Accommodations: Beaver Run is an attractive complex of granite and wood buildings just skirted by the Country Boy trail and home to the Beaver Run Superchair. The 500 hotel rooms are spacious, and condominiums vary from suites with in-room spas to four-bedroom units. Fireplaces and private balconies are features of the condominium units; they also have fully equipped kitchens. Children stay for free when staying with their parents, and cribs for infants and toddlers are provided without charge.

During the high ski season, February 1 through March, a double hotel room is $180 to $305 and a one-bedroom/one-bath condominium that sleeps four is $235 to $545 a night. During the rest of the ski season, rates are lower, with the exception of the holiday period at the end of December and Presidents' Week in February. Summer rates are $145 for a hotel room and $180 for a one-bedroom suite. Two-, three-, and even four-bedroom suites are available. Packages and special offers include third night free, 30% discount for early booking, and ski, golf, and spa packages.

The Village at Breckenridge is a Western-style resort with 357 bedrooms in 270 guest accommodations, ranging from hotel rooms to condos; the Liftside Inn building features studio apartments; and Plazas I, II, and III house one- to three-bedroom condominium units. Most of the condo accommodations have kitchens, fireplaces, and balconies with views of the mountains or Maggie Pond, the ice-skating center. Children twelve and younger sharing a room with their parents stay for free; crib rental is available on request.

The Village defines the ski season as early November through late April; during this time a double hotel room is $125 to $195, studios are $150 to $220, and a one-bedroom/one-bath condominium is $190 to $290. Rates are lower during early and late weeks of the season and higher at holiday time. During the summer a double room is $89 to $150 a night, and a one-bedroom/one-bath condominium is $129 to $179 a night.

Dining: Elegant dining at Beaver Run takes place at Spencer's Restaurant in a warm setting enhanced by oak and cane furnishings. Menu offerings include inexpensive family dining as well as fine dining. Serves breakfast, lunch, and dinner. The Copper Top Cafe and Lounge is open winters only for skiers, but G.B. Watson's Deli is good for snacks year-round, and Downstairs at Eric's provides evening and nighttime amusement along with big-screen TV.

The Village at Breckenridge has limited on-site dining, but is in the heart of the village itself, with lots of dining options. Breck's, in the Great Divide Lodge, serves breakfast, lunch, and dinner featuring American cuisine. The Maggie, open winter only for breakfast, lunch, and après-ski, has a ski-in, ski-out location at the bottom of the Quicksilver Super6 chairlift. A deck and outdoor grill for sunny days and the largest big-screen TV in Breckenridge make this a popular place. The Bistro, again open winter only and steps from the ski slope, starts your day with a hearty breakfast, and continues with lunch and dinner. Relax and unwind at the Park Avenue Pub, with its own separate smoking lounge. Drinks, late-night snacks, and a varied menu have something for everyone.

In town more than five dozen restaurants and saloons (out West bars are called saloons—don't forget that!) offer atmospheres from quiet to lively and cuisines that run all over the globe—Mexican, Italian, Greek, and German. A popular spot for steak and seafood is the Whale's Tail on Main Street. The ice-cream shop, also on Main Street, makes for a nice break during an evening walk.

Children's World: Children of all ages have a plethora of riches in Breckenridge. Kinderhut, located at Beaver Run, provides for the wee ones; Beaver Run has their own nonskiing program for ages five to twelve (also in the summer); and Breckenridge's Ski and Ride School, in the Village, offers lessons for ages three to twelve. If you want to be near your infant, toddler, or first-time young skier, it's probably best to stay at Beaver Run and use Kinderhut.

Breckenridge's Ski & Ride School helps skiers and boarders of all ages improve their skills while having fun. The Children's Centers and slopeside nurseries at Peak 8 (Kid's Castle) and Peak 9 (The Village) provide individualized care for infants, toddlers, and preschoolers. Rates are $95 for a full day; $80 for half-day care. The school recommends the use of helmets for children fourteen and younger; helmets are available to rent or purchase. Ages three to six go from 8:30 A.M. to 3:30 P.M. for a full-day

session, including lunch and snacks. Prices are $91 to $101, without ski rental, depending on the season. Half days are based on available space, run $76 to $86, and do not include lunch. Ages seven to fourteen must have a lift ticket and go from 9:45 A.M. to 3:45 P.M. Lift and lesson are $101 to $111; snowboarding is the same ages and costs. Half-day classes again are based on availability, do not include lunch, and are offered in the afternoon only. A fast-track Learn to Ride (LTR) program for ages seven to fourteen includes trampoline training, snowboard lesson, and a low student/instructor ratio. Classes are from 9:00 A.M. to 3:00 P.M., limited to six people, or even preferably four, grouped by age, and include lunch with the instructors. The cost is $190 to $205 for everything.

The Kids Day Off program at Beaver Run Resort is loaded with activities for kids ages five to twelve. From 9:00 A.M. to 5:00 P.M. youngsters can swim, enjoy the Alpine Super Slide, visit museums, and go on hikes, treasure hunts, and gold-mine tours. Cost is $80 for a full day with lunch; $40 each sibling. Daily in the summer if needed; it operates on a demand basis. Kids Night Out, from 6:00 to 9:00 P.M., offers dinner, indoor miniature golf, arts and crafts, and more fun activities for $40; $20 each sibling. The program is flexible, generally on Saturday in the summer and three times weekly in the winter, and will run for three or more children. Mid-June through Labor Day, you can drop off your children, ages two months to five years, at the Peak 8 Children's Center for fun activities, snacks, and lunch. Open Monday through Friday from 8:00 A.M. to 4:30 P.M.; call (970) 453-3258.

Kinderhut (800–541–8779, www.khut .net) is a Colorado State–licensed day-care center and a Professional Ski Instructors of America–affiliated ski school located at

Beaver Run Resort, on Peak 9. The Infant Nursery for children six weeks to one year old has a ratio of 1:3, with a maximum of seven children. Care is highly individualized.

Toddler Nursery, for ages one to two and a half years, has a caregiver ratio of 1:5, with a maximum of thirteen children daily. Activities such as snow play, puppets, story time, and crafts keep children happy and busy. Nursery hours are 8:15 A.M. to 4:15 P.M.; a full day is $85, while a half day is $70. Kinderhut's Ski School provides beginner ski instruction for ages two and a half to six years, with progressive instruction in balancing, stopping, and turning. Mountain lessons on the Quicksilver Chairlift are for those children who have mastered basic skills, and teacher-to-child ratios will not exceed 1:5. A full day costs $120, a half day is $70; all Ski School prices include boots, skis, lunch, and a pager for parents. Kinderhut also helps with babysitting ($15 per hour with a four-hour minimum) and stages a New Year's Eve party for children.

Summertime is just as busy. Kinderhut offers child care for ages one (and walking) to three years; $55 for the full day (8:15 A.M. to 5:00 P.M.) and $40 for a half-day morning. Adventure camp is for ages three to nine, Monday through Friday from 8:15 A.M. to 5:00 P.M. ($55). Mornings only are also an option ($40). The camp's goal is to provide children with the opportunity to explore new activities in a safe, nurturing environment; to build confidence through successful interactions with the world. Horseback riding, yoga, swimming, rock climbing, ice-skating (yes, even in the summer), story time at the library, or a trip to the fire station are just a taste of the fun in store. Wow! How much can one kid do?

Recreation: If you said to some skiers that you'd found 146 trails, an average annual snowfall of 300 inches, a ski season from late October to early May, and a vertical drop of more than 3,398 feet, they might think you'd died and gone to heaven. Breckenridge gives you all this on its four interconnected mountains—Peak 7 is the latest addition in skiable terrain, while Peak 10 boasts the highest elevation, at nearly 13,000 feet. It also gives outstanding views over Summit County, with 55% expert runs, 32% intermediate runs, 13% beginner runs, bowl skiing, above-the-timberline skiing, and lots of famous Rocky Mountain powder. You can line up a free guided tour of the mountains or plunge right away into group or private instruction.

Cross-country enthusiasts head to the Breckenridge Nordic Center for more than 40 kilometers of groomed trails. Try snowmobiling or dog sledding; ice-skating on Maggie Pond, or the indoor, year-round ice rink; and a horse-drawn sleigh ride to a steak-and-baked-potato supper on the mountain.

At both the Village at Breckenridge and Beaver Run, you can jump into the indoor/outdoor pools, relax in one of the many outdoor hot tubs, or, if your muscles weren't tested enough on the slopes, finish up in the exercise rooms. An additional Beaver Run attraction is an indoor miniature golf course, where you can count on a fun family evening in a huge indoor area for video games and active play.

During warm-weather months venture out from the resorts and go biking through town, hiking in the woods, fishing in mountain streams, sailing on Lake Dillon, horseback riding on trails bordered by wildflowers, and white-water rafting on the Arkansas and Blue Rivers. Play a round on Breckenridge's twenty-seven holes of championship golf, a course designed by Jack Nicklaus; four other courses are nearby, two of them at Keystone. During July and August the mountains ring with classical and jazz music from the Breckenridge Music Institute. You can even tour a gold mine.

The Riverwalk Center, an award-winning performing-arts facility, is the focal point for summer cultural activities, including a kids concert series.

The Breckenridge Recreation Center is a state-of-the-art facility with both indoor and outdoor pursuits. Inside you'll find tennis, racquetball, and wallyball courts, a gym with running track, two pools (lap and leisure), dance/aerobics, and rock climbing. Outdoors there are more tennis courts, a basketball court and two softball fields, rugby and soccer fields, a skateboard park, a sundeck, and a playground.

Peak 8 Fun Park has a little bit of everything: a mountain bike park with 35 miles of trails, SuperChair rides for easy access to hiking trails; a SuperPutt miniature golf course; and a climbing wall. Six zip lines enable you to fly across the mountains. And check out the Bounce House and Spin Cycle. Most popular is the SuperSlide, which gives downhill thrills while sitting down. It's a ½-mile, three-track slalom course on a small sled. Add to this a Power Jump (a modified trampoline where you go so high you have to wear a harness) and Colorado's largest human maze, two levels of labyrinth twists and turns; the price tag for all this unlimited fun is $48.00 for a half day and $60.00 for a full day; tickets for each attraction range from $4.00 to $10.00. You just may need a longer vacation.

Box 1058
Breckenridge, Colorado 80424
(970) 453–5000, (800) 789–SNOW
www.breckenridge.snow.com

THE BROADMOOR
Colorado Springs, Colorado

As majestic as the neighboring Rocky Mountains, The Broadmoor reigns over Cheyenne Lake and 3,000 surrounding acres. The original hotel, known today as Broadmoor Main, was built in 1918 by Spencer Penrose, an enterprising man who made his fortune in gold mining in Cripple Creek (less than 20 miles from Colorado Springs) and copper mining in Utah. He dreamed of fashioning a Colorado resort along the lines of the grand European hotels that he had seen. The Mediterranean-style structure, with its pink-stucco facade, almost glimmers in the sunshine. Inside, the Italian Renaissance trappings include wood-beamed ceilings, crystal chandeliers, gilt-framed mirrors, and hand-painted wall and ceiling decoration. Penrose's dream was realized—The Broadmoor fared well indeed when compared with its European counterparts. And the guests who followed were as impressive as the hotel, from royalty and presidents to movie stars and millionaires.

Over the years, facilities and buildings were added to the original complex. Broadmoor South stands next to Broadmoor Main and is architecturally compatible with the original, because its design utilizes light-colored stucco for the exterior walls. Across the lake is Broadmoor West. A modern structure, it nonetheless blends well within the context of the resort as a whole. In

1995 an additional 150 guest rooms were completed, and Lakeside Suites was completed in 2001. This newer twenty-one-room building hosts the most luxurious accommodations on the property. The architecture of this wing is reminiscent of Broadmoor Main. The newer structures reveal precise attention to architectural design, aesthetic decoration, and fine art. In 2003 The Broadmoor completed a $75-million refurbishing, bringing new grandeur and elegance. The resort is open year-round and is the longest-running consecutive winner of both the Mobile five-star and the AAA Five Diamond awards.

Accommodations: Some 700 rooms and suites are divided among the five main buildings of The Broadmoor. All are handsomely decorated and look out at either the clear blue Cheyenne Lake, the gardens, or the dramatic Colorado mountains; it's a tough task to find a view that's less than terrific. Broadmoor West features rooms with private balconies. During the high season, from the first of May through October, superior rooms are $260 to $385 per night. Suites begin at $540. Winter room rates are $230 to $350; suites begin at $400. Rates are for one to four people. An "incidental services" fee of $14.00 per room and $2.50 per person (more than two guests) is added daily. Holiday family packages include extras such as complimentary meals for twelve and under, bikes and paddleboats, movies, and passes to the Cheyenne Mountain Zoo. Cribs are provided at no additional charge. For an extra $15 a night, a rollaway bed can be added to your room.

Dining: In the eighty-four-year history of the hotel, there have only been four executive chefs, so it's clear The Broadmoor's eleven restaurants have a tradition of excellence. On the top floor of Broadmoor South, the four-star, four-diamond Penrose Room is an elegantly formal restaurant, with traditional French menu, superb views, dinner music, dancing, and an Edwardian decor, with emphasis on elaborate styling. Jackets are required for men. Charles Court, another award-winning restaurant, in the West building, offers fine dining without the formalities, yet still with wonderful lake views. One of the world's most extensive wine lists (more than 600 choices and 3,000 bottles, with prices ranging from $12 to $1,300 a bottle!) complement such entrees as Colorado rack of lamb and Copper River salmon.

Also at Broadmoor Main are the Tavern, exquisitely adorned with Toulouse-Lautrec lithographs, and the Lake Terrace Dining Room, opening onto the Sun Lounge, with palms, ficus trees, and a tiered Italian fountain. Sunday brunches here are an extravaganza featuring more than seventy items. Café Julie, a sidewalk cafe in Broadmoor West, offers a relaxed shirtsleeves-and-shorts atmosphere for sandwiches, salads, and burgers. Espresso is a favorite stopping place for cappuccino, pastries, quiche, sandwiches, and eclairs in Broadmoor Main. One of the merriest dining spots is the Golden Bee, an authentic nineteenth-century English pub located behind and below the International Center; it is open for lunch and dinner and until the wee hours, with live ragtime and sing-alongs. Stratta's Italian Restaurant, at the Golf Club, is open for breakfast, lunch, and dinner with traditional American fare during the day and classic Italian favorites at night. The Grille at the Golf Club has all-day dining with a big-screen television, as well as take-out for sports enthusiasts. The Pool Café has two locations: seasonally outdoors with salads and grilled meats and fish plus summer drinks, and year-round at the spa with light snacks and smoothies.

Relax in the West Lobby Bar, with dark oak and overstuffed chairs, or on the outside terrace overlooking Cheyenne Lake; for the atmosphere of a fine English library, sip port in the Penrose Lounge. For evening entertainment, stop by Star's Lounge, a lively nightclub with dancing.

Children's World: Memorial Day to Labor Day, daily from 9:00 A.M. to 4:00 P.M., things are buzzing with the Bee Bunch. Scheduled for ages three to twelve years, activities vary daily and include trips to the Cheyenne Mountain Zoo, bowling at Bear Creek Lanes, arts and crafts, paddleboating on Cheyenne Lake, picnics in the park, and scavenger hunts. Pony rides are also available for younger children, while older kids can enjoy golf clinics, tennis lessons, and horseback riding at the Triple B Ranch. Separate day and evening programs are also offered to give parents maximum scheduling flexibility. However, a one-week advance reservation is requested, and a $25, twenty-four-hour cancellation policy applies.

The Bee Bunch Room in the West Building is the gathering center, and the staffing ratio is one counselor to five campers. Groups are divided into Explorer Bees (three to six years old) and Adventure Bees (seven to twelve years). Morning sessions meet from 9:00 A.M. to noon; afternoons from 1:00 to 4:00 P.M.; cost is $25 per session. Lunch can be added to either session for $15 and is served from noon to 1:00 P.M. The full-day program includes lunch and is priced at $65; family rates are available for the second child on the full-day program and evening camp. The youngsters meet again for dinner and games or a movie from 6:00 to 10:00 P.M., granting their parents opportunities to sample the gourmet creations of the Broadmoor chefs. The children's meals are planned to ensure cleaned-up plates; the pizza, fried chicken, and hamburger dinners are favorites among the younger set and are included in the program cost of $45. Babysitting is available ($12 per hour), again with one-week advance registration.

Contact the Children's Concierge (ext. 5160), who also has information on family activities at the hotel and nearby.

Recreation: Golfing at The Broadmoor began when the original hotel opened in 1918. Donald Ross designed that first course and was followed by Robert Trent Jones and Ed Seay/Arnold Palmer. Two of the courses are designated Audubon Sanctuaries. Once golfers discover the challenging variety of these forty-five holes, the incredibly scenic setting, the top-quality equipment and accessories of the golf shops, and instruction with the resident pro, they may never explore the rest of The Broadmoor—and that would be a pity.

Tennis magazine named The Broadmoor the fourth greatest tennis resort in America (2002) and has ranked the year-round tennis program under Dennis Ralston number one for three years. Seven landscaped Plexi-cushioned courts, all with Rocky Mountain views, are located at the Tennis Club. The club includes one stadium court, and two courts are covered with a heated, illuminated bubble for play during winter months. Play a set or sign up for classes and clinics.

An afternoon can be spent swimming at one of two heated swimming pools at Broadmoor Main and the Golf Club. Part of the renovation was the creation of a spectacular new infinity edge pool at the north end of Cheyenne Lake, complete with two water slides built into Slide Mountain, a connecting swim-under bridge, a children's wading pool, two fourteen-person hot tubs, thirteen cabanas, and the Main Pool Cafe. Rent a paddleboat for a spin on the lake or a bicycle for a tour around the lake. Twenty minutes away, the Stables at Broadmoor give you a chance to experience wilderness beauty close-up; along your trail ride, you may glimpse elk or buffalo. The many biking, walking, and running trails are another way to spend rewarding time in the great outdoors. Or stroll along One Lake Avenue to enjoy a variety of specialty shops and an art gallery.

The Broadmoor Spa, Golf and Tennis Club is more than 90,000 square feet of luxury: state-of-the-art fitness facility, full-service spa, full-service salon, and private locker rooms with all amenities, including fireplaces!

A nonstop itinerary of off-property activities includes white-water rafting, hot-air ballooning, fly-fishing, mountain biking, and hunting expeditions. Or perhaps you'll opt to take the famous cogwheel up to Pikes Peak. The quaint town of Cripple Creek, Garden of the Gods, the new Olympic Training Center, the Cheyenne Mountain Zoo, Manitou, and Seven Falls all make wonderful family excursions.

---

1 Lake Avenue
Colorado Springs, Colorado 80906
(719) 577–5775, (800) 634–7711
www.broadmoor.com

C LAZY U RANCH
Granby, Colorado

Ride 'em, cowboy! With a little time at C Lazy U Ranch, you could live up to this label. Experienced wranglers match you with just the right horse to call your own during a vacation stay, and guide you on trail rides through the gorgeous Colorado high country. Beautiful vistas stretch in every direction, with mountains everywhere. Expect to meet some locals on the trail rides—moose, coyotes, owls, and even mountain lions share the area. Situated two hours west of Denver, at an elevation of 8,300 feet, the ranch sprawls across more than 8,000 acres of Peaceful Valley. A lot of territory to roam combines with warm sunny days that give way to cool nights—a spectacular setting for learning Western ways. Since 1946, C Lazy U has operated as a guest ranch. That adds up to a lot of experience, not only in riding and roping, but also in welcoming and entertaining visitors. For thirty consecutive years, C Lazy U earned the Mobile five-star and AAA five-diamond ratings. Open from early June through mid-October, September is reserved for adults only. The ranch opens again from mid-December to mid-February for the winter holidays. The owners' philosophy is that C Lazy U is not just a hotel, nor is it a resort. Rather, it is a unique vacation spot, your home for the duration of your stay.

Accommodations: Forty comfortable rooms and suites are in the main lodge and the guest cottages that surround it. About 75% of these have a fireplace, stocked with wood and ready to take the chill off the evening. With no televisions or telephones in the rooms, it's a real vacation. But don't be nervous, at the Executive Corral you'll find two data ports, telephones, and a fax machine; and two public areas have televisions. Enjoy the little touches of luxury here—a plush bathrobe, fresh fruit basket, snacks, and nightly turndown.

Minimum stays vary by season: Summer requires a seven-night stay (Sunday to Sunday); holiday season (December 20 to January 3) has a five-night minimum; Winter Playtime has a two-night requirement; and

September, which is reserved for adults only, requires a three-night stay. Rates are per person and vary based on season, number of people, and size of accommodation. Rates per adult, based on double occupancy, average $2,150 per week in early June; mid-June to end of August averages $2,700. Daily rates during winter and holiday season are $245 to $285 per person per day. Children from three to five years old receive a $200 discount. During the winter season, children seventeen and under receive a 20% discount. These rates cover virtually everything you'll want or need during your visit: upscale lodging, three meals a day, afternoon and bedtime ice cream, all-day tea and lemonade, your own horse with five hours of daily trail rides or instruction, use of the recreational facilities, and the supervised children's program. The only extras are trap and skeet shooting, bar drinks, and a massage, if you choose.

Dining: At C Lazy U you'll get the hearty meals that you need to maintain an energy level consistent with the fresh air and outdoor fun. And note that hearty does not mean plain. The warm, rustic dining room is located in the lodge, the main building of the ranch. Here guests sit at tables set for ten, a good way to make friends and enjoy relaxed dining. But don't expect baked beans and coffee in a tin pot. C Lazy U's outstanding menus include Black Angus prime rib, rack of lamb, and jalapeno-stuffed mountain trout. Breakfast is the family meal, with just about anything you want to order; or try the special of the day—breakfast burritos, raspberry pancakes, or chocolate chip waffles for starters. Lunch is generally buffet-style, by the pool at the Patio House. Children and teens eat lunch and dinner with their counselors; families regroup at about 4:30 P.M. for ice cream and cool drinks and again after dinner for the evening activities. Evening cookouts are planned frequently.

The lodge also houses a comfortable living room, well-stocked with books, and a cozy bar, where drinks and hors d'oeuvres are served nightly at 6:30 P.M. Another bar is located in the Patio House, adjacent to the swimming pool, with both a television and fireplace; enjoy an evening cocktail and swap tall tales with other guests about the day's adventures. Then cap the day off at 9:00 P.M. at the Ice Cream Bar with something special for your sweet tooth.

Children's World: With C Lazy U's special attention to youngsters, the kids may turn into wranglers before you do. Starting at age three (the ranch does not provide care for younger children), kids get a good introduction to life out West. Three-year-olds are instructed in how to ride, and a little of how to feed and care for their horse, and they get the thrill of pony rides in the corral; at age six they can go out on trail rides. Everyone is assigned a horse for the entire week, based on individual ability, and children are divided into three groups: three- to five-year-olds, six- to twelve-year-olds, and teenagers. Some boots are available if children (or even adults) do not have their own, and helmets are recommended but not required.

The day begins at 9:00 A.M. with horseback lessons or a ride, and maybe lunch on the trail or a swim in the reservoir along the way. Lunch with the counselors, then "cabin time" during the heat of the day, or a nap and movie in the Children's Center, a comfortable indoor place for reading, art projects, and resting. Afternoon brings another trail ride or swimming, tennis, or games— the program is very individualized. Ice cream at 4:00 P.M., with a little "parent time," and then kids gather at 5:45 P.M. for dinner and evening activities until about 8:30 P.M., when families regroup for a hayride, games, or dancing. Teens, as they much prefer, have their own separate program of riding, hayrides, and cookouts. C Lazy U is well-arranged and safe for children to roam a bit; there's little or no traffic and everything is within easy walking distance.

The ranch opens again in mid-December, and remains open through Presidents' Week. During this time, the children's program is in full swing.

Recreation: The main attraction of a ranch is horseback riding, and this is one of the most comprehensive programs we've seen. From a string of more than 160 horses, you'll be assigned a mount that suits your ability. Guided by experienced wranglers, you'll ride the high country across mountain meadows or sage-covered hills, and through tall evergreens along Willow Creek. For three hours in the morning and another two in the afternoon, the focus is on horses. The programs are flexible, and participants may decide which they wish to join—it might be instruction (basic or advanced) in the outdoor or indoor arenas, or a choice of trail rides (slow and scenic, medium, or fast). On Friday mornings, family rides are scheduled. Everyone looks forward to the "shodeo" at the end of each week; especially kids as they "show off" what they've learned.

But there's more to this ranch than just horses. Enjoy a group walk before breakfast. Between trail rides, sneak in a little fishing in the pond near the lodge or at a secluded spot along Willow Creek, then have the trout for breakfast! Ranch hands are glad to instruct you in the art of fly-fishing. Adults have a catch and release policy, while kids can catch up to two fish. Take a pedal boat on the lake, go hiking, spend an afternoon on the skeet range (trap and skeet shooting are the only activities not covered in the package rates), play tennis on one of the two Laykold courts, or swim in the heated pool. Try volleyball, basketball, shuffleboard, or horseshoes, or take the ranch's name to heart, and simply laze about in the sunshine or the shade of a tree with a cool drink.

For more activities, seek out the Patio House, the principal recreation center, with a well-equipped fitness room, locker rooms, and showers. When you fear that saddle sores or tennis elbow may set in, retire to the whirlpool or sauna. A game room features foosball, table tennis, and billiards; a television room and a large all-purpose activity room with fireplace invite relaxing or socializing, as you desire. Complimentary laundry facilities are also found in this complex.

In the evenings the entire family joins in on campfire sing-alongs, hay rides, square dancing, and rodeos—just so you don't forget you're "out West." Nearby excursions might include Rocky Mountain National Park, with stunning scenic vistas, or the glacial snow fields and the Alpine terrain and tundra of the Continental Divide. Or visit the little town of Hot Sulfur Springs with over twenty naturally heated therapeutic pools. Off-site, white water rafting and golf can be arranged.

During the winter season guests take to skiing—cross-country on the 25 kilometers of trails maintained by the ranch and downhill at Winter Park (25 miles) and Sol Vista (10 miles) ski resorts, accessible via the ranch's complimentary shuttle service. Enjoy horseback riding in the snow or in the indoor 12,000-square-foot heated riding arena, or take a sleigh ride on an old-fashioned cutter. Ride an inner tube down the tubing hill or across a meadow behind a snowmobile, and ice skate or play hockey or broomball on the groomed skating pond. Then snuggle in for hot drinks, the fireplace, Western dancing, and cowboy songs. Yippee-yi-ay!

3640 Colorado Highway 125
P.O. Box 379
Granby, Colorado 80446
(970) 887–3344
www.clazyu.com

CLUB MED/CRESTED BUTTE

Crested Butte, Colorado

Crested Butte is Club Med's new ski hotel-village for families, replacing Copper Mountain. Open from mid-December to early April only, it makes the most of the short season—you'll find every imaginable snow sport here, along with all of Club Med's conveniences for families and totally all-inclusive policies. Set in southwestern Colorado, at an altitude of 9,375 feet within the Gunnison National Forest and the Elk Mountain Range, Crested Butte bills itself as "the last great ski town." From its beginning in the 1880s as a mining supply camp, now the town of Crested Butte has one of Colorado's largest National Historic Districts, with a permanent population of 1,600–plus hearty souls. The Gunnison Country is one of Colorado's most beautiful mountain regions of alpine valleys and 14,000-foot-high peaks.

Accommodations: This is Club Med's only U.S. ski village, opened in 2003 after a $6-million renovation of a former Marriott hotel. Sitting at the base of the Crested Butte chairlift, it's designed with lodging, dining, skiing, and entertainment all right there at your ski-tip. Two hundred fifty-six rooms and suites accommodate from one to eight people; amenities include TV, telephone, and minirefrigerators. Three-, four-, and seven-night stays are options. Club Med pioneered the concept of all-inclusive vacations; currently there are more than one hundred villages in more than forty countries all over the world, and definitely an international mix of guests. Three-night land-only packages are $540 to $810 for adults and $120 to $375 for children ages three to fifteen. Seven-night packages range from $1,400 to $1,750 for adults and $700 to $875 for children ages two to fifteen years. Packages include lodging, all meals and drinks, full-day ski and snowboard lessons, ski passes, complete children's programs, and all hotel amenities.

Dining: Mirabel, the main restaurant, has the traditional Club Med "bountiful buffet" and community seating, which creates a convivial atmosphere. Kids can eat lunch and dinner early in a special section of the dining room with the counselors. Junior Club Med (ages eleven to seventeen) also have their own section of the dining room. Wilderness, the second restaurant, requires reservations and is smaller and more intimate, with a la carte service and an upscale French cuisine.

Three bars serve guests: the Main Bar, near the big restaurant; the huge Sports Bar, with pool tables, games, and the ski-in, ski-out entrance to the slopes; and the fireplace skier's bar for gathering for warmth after fun times in the snow. Club Med's new policy of including all drinks and snacks in the package means that now everything you eat and drink is free!

For an adventure on your own, you might try dinner at 10,000 feet—an unusual dining experience where you ride up the mountain in an open sleigh pulled by a snowcat, then enjoy a four-course dinner at Andiamo Italian Restaurant.

Children's World: Club Med is famous for their nonstop activities, even for kids, who are accepted here from age four. Skiing lessons begin at age four, and snowboarding lessons start at age six. Certified Club Med instructors provide full-day lessons and clinics. Eight levels, from beginner to competition, are offered based on the skier's ability. Children must wear safety helmets during downhill ski lessons, which use more than eighty trails and all ski lifts, plus the Kids Corral for younger children. The Children's Club has its own facility, and the Kids Corral provides a gentle slope and tow ropes for the littlest family members.

In addition to skiing, Mini Club (ages four to ten) activities include puppet shows, video games, and snow-sculpting contests. All children participate in the Mini Club Show, performed weekly for delighted parents. Hours are 8:00 A.M. to 5:00 P.M., and again from 6:30 to 9:00 P.M.—you may see your children for a quick hug and clothing change; otherwise, they're far too busy. Mascots Clubber and Medy delight youngsters throughout the week by joining in their activities, even skiing with them. Once a week they lead a costume parade through the village where kids enjoy showing off the costumes they've made themselves. Mini Scientist programs engage children in educational explorations that just seem like fun. And finally, Siesta Club, nighttime supervision for the little ones, is available daily for $20 per child between the hours of 9:00 P.M. and 1:00 A.M. During certain holidays, informal programs are set up for teens to meet and socialize easily with their peers.

Recreation: The mountain is the centerpiece of recreation, and is quite impressive with a summit elevation of 12,162 feet and vertical drop of 2,775 feet. Eighty-five trails, served by fourteen lifts, break down into 15% beginner; 44% intermediate; 10% advanced; and 31% expert (that's the double black diamonds, you know). Extreme sports have a good hold here. There's also a Terrain Park and a new Snowdeck Park; a mini-terrain park, at the base of Keystone Lift, is open to snowdecks, skis, and snowboards until 8:00 P.M.

Included in the Club Med package is full-day ski and snowboard instruction at all levels, beginner to expert, for all ages, including adults; ski passes and all the amenities of the hotel. Equipment rental is not included in the price, but is available. There's a fitness room if you just can't miss your daily routine, a heated pool and sauna, whirlpool, and massage (extra charge) if you overdo.

Other off-site activities that are not included in the package are snowmobiles, snowshoeing, cross-country skiing, dogsled tours, snowcat rides, and ice-skating. If all of that sounds cold, warm up with a hot après-ski drink at the fireplace, a new movie at the cinema, or jump in the sauna or Jacuzzi. Evening entertainment is geared toward the entire family.

The little town of Crested Butte offers old-fashioned charm but up-to-date entertainment with its quaint shops and wide variety of pubs and restaurants. The village operates a free shuttle into town for exploring or dining out. Club Med Excursions (extra cost) include dogsled tours, the Black Canyon of Gunnison National Monument, and horse-drawn sleigh rides. Special events may be ski clinics by Kim Reichelm, Wayne Wong, and J.P. Auclair or other notable skiers, or special ski movies.

500 Gothic Road
Crested Butte, Colorado 81225
(970) 349–8700, (800) CLUB–MED
www.clubmed.com

FLATHEAD LAKE LODGE

Bigfork, Montana

Mix some city slickers with a few expert wranglers out in Montana horse country, toss in beautiful scenery and clear blue skies, and come up with quite a different vacation experience at Flathead Lake Lodge. On 2,000 acres in northwest Montana, just forty-five minutes south of Glacier National Park, this dude ranch specializes in water sports and just about anything that has to do with horses, from riding them to shoeing them. The lodge is situated in a private bay on Flathead Lake; at 15 miles wide by 30 miles long, it's the largest freshwater lake in the West. The surrounding timberland stretches up into the Rocky Mountains. The ranch is open from May to October, and one- or two-week visits are standard. July and August are popular with families.

Flathead Lake Lodge has been a working dude ranch in the Averill family since 1945; son Doug took over in 1971, and he and his family now live at the ranch. Hospitality is a way of life here, and families return again and again for a memorable vacation. The lodge has been rated in the top 2% of best vacation spots, and acclaimed by *Better Homes and Gardens, Bon Appetit, Sunset Magazine, Travel + Leisure,* and *Good Morning America.*

Accommodations: The main lodge is the focus of activities and dining; in a warm and rustic setting, the old stone fireplace lures many guests to gather for cozy chats. There are guest rooms here and in the south lodge; the historic log cottages accommodate four people with a small sitting area. Many families find the two- and three-bedroom log cottages particularly attractive; some of the lodge rooms and the guest cottages have views of the lake. The weekly

rate for an adult is $2,653; for a teenager, $1,981; for six- to twelve-year-olds, $1,785; for three- to five-year-olds, $1,099; and for infants and toddlers, $112. A one-week stay runs Sunday to Sunday; rates include lodging, three meals a day, and all recreation, including horseback riding, tennis, use of the boats and sports equipment, and the Kids Camp. Cribs are available at no additional charge.

Dining: Dining is a family affair, with good home cooking, and breads and desserts made fresh every day. Guests gather at the long tables in the lodge dining room or at the picnic tables out on the patio overlooking the lake. Children eat together before their parents, allowing grown-ups time to get acquainted and plan the next day's events. Kids eat at 8:00 A.M., noon, and 6:00 P.M.; adults eat half an hour later. A daily happy hour in the Saddle Sore Saloon allows tall tales to be swapped as you wet your whistle. With three hearty meals a day, you better work and play hard, although appetites are always good. An evening barbecue ride gives everyone a chance to sample buffalo, grown on the ranch.

Children's World: The children's program is for any child old enough to participate in organized group activities, and divides roughly at age six. The friendly staff—mostly energetic college students who can keep up with excited youngsters—guide children through the day's activities. They can swim, lend a hand with the daily chores, and learn to ride horses. Children six years and older join cowboys on the horseback-riding trails in the mountains. After the trail riders depart, children under six are given special attention and supervised pony rides. All kids become "junior wranglers" and learn about grooming, barn duties, and caring for the horses. On Saturday mornings, kids show off at the Children's Rodeo, much to the delight of parents. Arts and crafts are scheduled in the morning and afternoon and projects get pretty creative. All the other pursuits dear to kids' hearts are here as well—swimming, boating, tennis, volleyball—all the ranch activities are available to them. Youngsters ages six to twelve get to spend an overnight in authentic tepees, telling ghost stories around the campfire, and a fire truck ride to the ice-cream store is a real treat. Teens are encouraged to participate in all the ranch activities; some activities such as trail rides, team penning, games, and boat cruises are planned just for them. Child care for children too young for the camp is available but not included in the weekly rates.

Recreation: The great outdoors awaits you. Horses are a way of life here; ride 'em, rope 'em, or test your nerve and verve in competition. Take an early-morning breakfast ride to work up a good appetite, then enjoy a breakfast cookout amid the tall pines. Old-fashioned Western rodeos are part of the evening activities.

Take a dip in the large swimming pool or the crystal clear waters of the lake. Sailing, canoe races, and waterskiing may fill your afternoons. Cruises on the lake are organized several times a week. The sailing staff can take you on one of the two 51-foot Q-class racing sloops, prototypes for the America's Cup built in 1928 and 1929—it's quite a treat to sail on these beauties. Fish in the lake or the nearby streams, and add a trout to a cookout dinner or spin a good story about the one that got away.

It's easy to find partners for a game of tennis (four courts) and to organize table tennis, basketball, or volleyball. Eagle Bend Golf Course (twenty-seven holes) is just minutes away. Pick up a game of, what else? Horseshoes! You might take a stroll along the wooded trails and pick berries.

The whole family can enjoy an evening block fire with roasted marshmallows and sing-along country music. You can schedule full- or half-day excursions for white-water rafting, river tubing, and wilderness fishing. The National Bison Range, only an hour away, attracts many visitors; seeing real live buffalo is a highlight for kids and parents. Courtesy cars are available for trips to Glacier National Park and Kalispell, "The Best Mountain Town in Montana."

Box 248
Bigfork, Montana 59911
(406) 837–4391
www.averills.com

KEYSTONE RESORT
Keystone, Colorado

Like many fine Western ski resorts, Keystone first attracted settlers in search of the rich minerals in its mountains. Today visitors flock here seeking light powdery snow and the mountain high for which the Rock-ies are known. At the base of Loveland Pass, 70 miles west of Denver, Keystone has 116 runs on three interconnecting ski mountains and a vertical drop of 3,128 feet. The resort remains open year-round, so when summer rolls around, many folks hang up their skis and head for Keystone's golf course (designed by Robert Trent Jones Jr.), the Keystone Tennis Center, and the Keystone Music Festival.

Winter and summer there are more activities for families than you could possibly do in one vacation. There's even a special line, (800) 354-4–FUN, to help you plan it all. And at Keystone, you get more than a room. Summer and winter the Adventure Passport gives you access to lots of free activities, such as sleigh rides; hockey, ski, and Nordic lessons; Kids' Night Out; tennis clinics; bike rentals; wine tasting; yoga; and more.

Accommodations: Keystone stretches out 7 miles along the Snake River, with over 1,500 lodging units in seven neighborhoods; the Web site has an excellent interactive map with all the details of each area's lodging. If you want to walk or short shuttle to the slopes, Mountain House base area and River Run Village are within 200 yards of the lifts. Both areas have Children's Centers. Skier Services and the Ski and Ride School are located at Mountain House, along with mountainside dining and après-ski activities; this is the original base area of Keystone. The Inn at Keystone Hotel is an economical choice with a cozy lobby, restaurant, and nightlife—and the hot tubs are on the roof, with great views! Rates begin at $115 in winter, $99 in summer. A variety of condominiums offer more space, many only steps from the slopes or golf courses. Winter rates begin at $189; summer rates start at $130.

River Run Village is the heart of Keystone. Lone Eagle and the Timbers are ski-in, ski-out, upscale condos on the eastern slopes of Keystone Mountain, and are the closest lodging to the slopes; for a two-bedroom condo, rates range from $435 to $599 in winter; $309 to $395 in summer.

Cross over the Snake River to the pedestrian-style River Run Village for shopping, dining, and nightlife. River Run Village is the largest ski area development project in North America; eventually over 4,500 residential units are planned. In East Keystone, deluxe and premium condos are on the outskirts of River Run Village, in the White National Forest along the Snake River, and appeal to those who want to be close to nature and get away from it all. North Keystone, on Tenderfoot Mountain Ridge close to the conference center and Lakeside Village, offers good value condominiums and town houses, and is a shuttle ride to lifts and River Run Village. West Keystone and Keystone Ranch shelter a variety of lodgings, the golf courses, and Keystone's best restaurant, the Keystone Ranch. And last, but certainly not least, is Keystone Lakeside Village, center of the conference area. The Keystone Lodge Hotel, a rustic yet elegant four-diamond property, is in the heart of Lakeside Village, a festive place of shops, galleries, and restaurants spread along the lakeside. It's the center of the action, with a playground, ice rink, and the lake. Free shuttles run throughout Keystone and connect the mountain bases.

Dining: From romantic gourmet dinners in a mountaintop restaurant more than 2 miles high to family picnic lunches, unique and award-winning dining choices delight guests. The resort features dining options that range from gourmet six-course meals to sandwiches or a Western family-style cookout and include Summit County's only AAA Four-Diamond-rated restaurants—the Alpenglow Stube and Keystone Ranch. The Ski Tip Lodge is where it all began at Keystone. A stagecoach stop in the 1800s, today it is a charmingly rustic bed-and-breakfast with what is claimed to be the best comfort food on the Divide.

At the Keystone Lodge, Champeaux features fine cuisine and a Sunday brunch; the Edgewater is a casual restaurant open for breakfast and lunch. At Lakeside Village, you'll find Pizza on the Plaza and Bighorn Steakhouse. At River Run, Kickapoo Tavern, Paisano's, Great Northern Tavern, Pizza on the Run, and Fritz's Alpine Bistro all satisfy families. Several restaurants will provide take-out if you prefer eating in your condo. Two markets, a deli in Lakeside Village, SubFusion (subway sandwiches with a twist, in three areas), and four food courts on the mountain provide quick eating when you've other things to do. In the summertime you can hop a hayride to Soda Creek Homestead—in winter a sleigh ride takes you there—for a multicourse dinner. Take the gondola to Der Fondue Cheese for a fun evening of dipping and Bavarian music.

Children's World: Keystone has not one but two children's centers, one located at Mountain House base area and a new facility at River Run. Cost is seasonal, the "value" season costing slightly less than the regular season, which also includes Thanksgiving, Christmas, and March spring break. For ages two months to six years, both operate daily from mid-November to late April. River Run is modeled after a children's museum with bright colors, a central play area surrounded by breakout areas for different ages, and lots of hands-on, interactive play. A full day (8:00 A.M. to 4:00 P.M.) including lunch is $85 value season, $95 regular season; a half day in the morning is $75/$80. In winter, snowplay programs are designed to introduce kids to the snow. The Children's Camps at "Keystone University" have been rated a "Best Bet" by *Ski* magazine. Learn-to-ski programs begin at age three with Mini-Penguins group lessons and snow play. A full day includes an art project in the morn-

ing, skiing from 10:00 A.M. to 2:00 P.M. (1:4 ratio) and winding down with a movie from 2:00 to 4:00 P.M. Cost is $90/$100.

At Mountain House and River Run, Penguin Ski Camps for ages four to six, and Penguin Ride Camps for ages five and six use children's on-mountain adventure areas and trails. Children are grouped according to ability, and scheduled at the end of the day is a parent–teacher conference, progress report, and a level pin for each child. All packages include lesson, lift ticket, and lunch. One-day package is $101 to $111; multiple-day packages are also available. Ski and Ride Camps for seven- to twelve-year-olds are divided by age into beginner, intermediate, and advanced sessions so that kids have fun and learn as well. They also receive a progress report, and the cost is the same, $101 and $111. For all camps, you should register online two days in advance, or by 9:30 A.M. in the Ski and Ride School. Registration is from 8:00 to 9:30 A.M. and pickup is between 3:00 and 3:30 P.M. Equipment rental is $15. Helmets are recommended and may be rented for $12. Mom, Dad, and Me is a one-hour private lesson for two adults and one child every day at 3:30 P.M.; cost is $100, and it's a great way to spend family time on the slopes.

Keystone's summer program for ages two months to twelve years is set at River Run and runs from mid-June to late August, Thursday through Monday, from 9:00 A.M. to 4:00. The cost is $77, and reservations are required. For the wee ones, beginning at two months, the state-of-the-art day-care center is their kingdom. Keystone Mountain Rangers entertains children from three to six years old with a full calendar of events, with a different theme each day: pony riding, games, relay races, paddleboats, swimming, gold panning, hikes, and scavenger hunts. Some activities may have an age requirement. Summer X-Camps for ages seven to fourteen follow the same format but with more challenging fun: a resort field trip, hiking to back ranch for fishing, scavenger hunts, Frisbee golf, and silly human challenges. Afternoons are generally devoted to something wet—swimming or a wet-and-wild gauntlet. Keystone schedules family activities almost daily. Babysitting is available for $13.00 to $15.00; second child is only $1.00.

Recreation: With three interconnected mountains—Dercum Mountain, North Peak, and the Outback—Keystone offers terrain for skiers and snowboarders of all levels. Dercum Mountain offers mainly beginner and intermediate terrain, with night-skiing operations that keep the mountain open until 9:00 P.M. North Peak challenges guests with more intermediate slopes and runs that plunge down mogul-filled terrain. The Outback features only intermediate and expert runs. Some of Summit County's best tree skiing is found on the Outback. Skiers can find deep powder in open bowls adjacent to the Outback. The A51 Terrain Park sports rails, more rails, wall rides, pipes and super pipes, funboxes, and lots more in this exciting area. The park has tripled in size, has a new location, and a quarter of a million dollars of improvements were added in the 2004–2005 season. Add tubing at Adventure Point, Snow Hawgs snowbiking, and night skiing and you'll see why Keystone is proud of its mountains. Nighttime lighting makes Keystone's terrain garden and ski slopes the largest night-park operation in Colorado.

The ski season opens at Keystone in mid-October (Colorado's earliest opening date) and continues into late April. Whether you're trying to figure out what a snowplow is or you're looking for perfection in powder skiing, the more than 350 ski and snowboarding instructors can guide you through the 2,870 acres of terrain.

Other outdoor winter sports at Keystone include ice-skating at the Skating Center in Lakeside Village, cross-country skiing from the Keystone Cross-Country Center into Arapahoe National Forest (cross-country and telemark lessons are offered), snowmobile tours into the backcountry, sleigh rides, winter fly-fishing, and snowshoeing. Indoors, enjoy tennis, yoga, wellness clinics, and twice-weekly wine tastings. Some of these activities are included in your Adventure Passport.

Summertime at Keystone means golfing on the masterfully designed Robert Trent Jones Jr. course; eighteen holes with a Scottish flair respect the woodlands, meadows, and a nine-acre lake. The River Course, designed by Hurdzan-Fry, follows the path of the Snake River for the front nine. The back nine threads through a pine forest, bringing beauty and stunning views to the game. Courses are open from June to mid-October; golf pros offer private lessons and clinics.

Keystone is a haven, or perhaps heaven, for mountain-bike enthusiasts. The resort offers a special program for ages fifteen and older called Dirt Camp, a two-day series of instructional mountain bike camps that provides intense riding retreats for "mud studs" and "wannabes." Even if you're a beginner and conquering single-track, Dirt Camp helps you hone your mountain-biking skills. One-hour beginning clinics are free with the Adventure Passport. In addition, Keystone is the center of literally hundreds of miles of world-class single track. These tracks combined with branches from the Colorado Trail make it as good as it gets for mountain bikers. Ditto for downhill biking—aficionados probably recognize terms like burly trail, berms, table tops, and teeter totters, but Keystone's got a trail for you even if you're still riding the hard tail or beginning the sport. Mountain Bike Headquarters has everything you need. And for those of us who think biking means maybe shifting gears now and then along a smooth easy path—we're covered as well. Miles of paths run along the Snake River and hundreds of miles of road wait.

Another important summertime attraction here is the Music Festival. Ranging from classical to pop, the National Repertory Orchestra and the Summit Brass carry the season from June through Labor Day.

At the Keystone Tennis Center, two indoor courts permit year-round play, and an additional twelve outdoor courts expand summertime possibilities. Ball machines, video analysis, and group and private lessons aid players in their game.

Fishermen take to the local haunts for rainbow trout; boaters sail on Lake Dillon (5 miles west of Keystone) or skim across Keystone Lake in a paddleboat or kayak, while hikers walk along the trails through wildflowers and aspens into the national forest. Horseback ride from the Keystone Stables through the Snake River Valley (breakfast rides are specialties), tour the high country of the Arapahoe National Forest by four-wheel drive, go white-water rafting down the Colorado and Arkansas Rivers, be treated to a lunch of rattlesnake meat and buffalo, or enjoy the great outdoors and mountain scenery on a gondola ride to Dercum Mountain's summit.

Learn the basics of rock climbing and mountaineering, go white-water rafting, play mini-golf, try fly-fishing, or take a tour. Didn't we say there was a lot to do here? Summer and winter, Energy Alley in River Run Village encourages extreme games and challenging activities such as a quad bungee,

life-size Playstation 2, inflatables, and a dance revolution game—just for starters.

Weekly activities (usually for two to three hours) for kids and families happen almost daily, many are free: Tuesday is Kid's Discovery Day, a celebration of imagination; Wednesday brings evening S'more Stories at the firepit; Thursday's fare is hilarious comedy ($15.00); on Friday, sample children's theater ($3.00) or the National Repertory Orchestra ($18.00); and close the week on Saturday with a Frontier Fair and elegant Open-Air Market, culminating in spectacular fireworks over Keystone Lake. This is the current schedule; of course it changes, so check when you go. Past activities have included mural painting, stargazing, kite flying, and gold panning. Whatever is planned, it's all fun.

Pony rides, guided hikes, and free mountain bike clinics augment the playground in Lakeside Village and the family fun park in River Run. Miniature golf, strolling around the lake, and feeding the ducks—families don't lack for activities here.

Reservations and more information on these activities (including dining at Keystone's award-winning restaurants) can be arranged by the Keystone Activities and Dining Center well before a guest arrives, so that everything is already in place at vacation's start. The number to call is (800) 354–4-FUN.

P.O. Box 38
Keystone, Colorado 80435
(970) 496–2316, (877) 625–1556
www.keystoneresort.com

MOUNTAIN SKY GUEST RANCH

Emigrant, Montana

"Just turn me loose, let me straddle my own saddle underneath the Western sky." At Mountain Sky all guests (age six and older) are assigned their own special horse. Careful matching of horse and rider according to the latter's age and skills ensures a compatible duo during a vacation stay. Under the guidance of experienced wranglers, you'll be swaggering like a Montana cowboy before the week is out.

Mountain Sky Guest Ranch has a rich history dating back to the mid-nineteenth century. This is no modern mock-up of Old West ranching. It was an active operation during the days of cattle empires and witnessed the excitement of the gold-mining era. With its genuine Western flavor, Mountain Sky offers visitors a combination of "wide open spaces" and upscale comforts. Located just 30 miles north of Yellowstone National Park, Mountain Sky sits in Paradise Valley, in southwestern Montana. Surrounded by national forest and wilderness areas, the wooded mountainous landscape of Montana's high country is a beautiful vacation setting.

Accommodations: Guests are lodged in thirty rustic but modern cabins; each one has a refrigerator and fresh fruit delivered daily. Some cabins date back to 1929, when guests first began arriving; others have porches or picture windows to catch the spectacular mountain views.

All rates include lodging, meals, a horse for each guest over six years old, all ranch facilities, participation in all activities, and gratuities. Spring and fall have no minimum-stay requirements and are for adults only; rates are $310 per person, per night. June, July, and August are for

families, and weekly rates are $2,720 to $3,290 for adults; children seven to twelve years old are $2,240 to $2,685; and children six and under are $1,765 to $2,025. Children eighteen months and younger are $600 per week. Care is $10 per hour; or bring your own nanny and pay half of the adult rate.

During the summer the vacation week runs from Sunday to Sunday; within a couple of days, you'll make friends not only with your horse but also with the other guests. If you really have a hankerin' to get away from it all, stay in one of Mountain Sky's two remote cabins, hidden in the wilderness. Your cabin will be stocked with snacks and meals to prepare, and if you miss civilization you can hike or ride into the guest ranch. Vehicle transportation is also available, but that defeats the purpose, doesn't it? If this appeals to you, you might also make reservations for a day or two in the middle of your week. Call the ranch for details and rates.

Dining: Meals are served in the dining room of the main lodge and at barbecue cookouts. Understanding that the atmosphere of the great outdoors can generate healthy appetites, the chefs prepare hearty as well as gourmet meals. Buffet-style breakfasts with made-to-order omelets and huckleberry pancakes start the day off right. Lunches are generally served outdoors, in a casual buffet style, with homemade soups, salads, fruit and cheese, and "world cuisine" of Mexican enchiladas, Chinese stir-fry, or Italian pizza and pasta. And evening brings hors d'oeuvres at the Mountain View Lodge and a choice of poolside barbecue hot off the grill or gourmet dinners with wine. Desserts are famous here; chocolate decadence with an Irish cream anglaise or warm Valrhona cake with huckleberry ice cream and fresh huckleberries are just the beginning. Yum. Rugged attire (jeans, boots) is standard most of the time; Tuesday- and Saturday-night dinners are a bit more formal, with clean jeans and a denim skirt. For good conversation and evening cocktails, drop by the Mountain View Lounge.

Children's World: In summer trained counselors guide children of all ages in a program of activities. The youth schedule includes arts and crafts, nature walks, and swimming. There's even a small fishing pond reserved for children. Children ages seven and older learn horseback-riding skills with the Children's Wrangler. Six years and under have an hour of arena instruction and spend time getting comfortable around horses. Three program sessions each day allow breakfast and lunch together. From 8:45 to 11:30 a.m and 1:45 to 4:30 P.M. everyone is engaged in what interests them most. Evening session begins at 5:45 P.M. with dinner, and ends at about 8:30 P.M. Preteens have their own eating spot and counselors. With the exception of family cookouts twice a week, children can stay with their friends and counselors for evening meals. The game room for teens features table tennis, a jukebox, and a pool table. There is no additional charge for these activities; the supervised children's program is part of the weekly rate.

Mountain Sky's well-trained counselors promise everything from "cuddling your infant to amusing your teenager," so parents are free to enjoy some time on their own. The younger children, even infants and toddlers, are included in those activities that are appropriate, always with close supervision and care. Teens meet on Sunday evening to plan their week, so they can choose their own excursions; perhaps a teen day in Yellowstone, or a scavenger hunt in Gardiner.

Recreation: Horseback riding is the primary sport at the ranch. Mounting your own horse and exploring hundreds of miles of trails can be as invigorating or relaxing as you want to make it. Besides morning and afternoon excursions, guests enjoy evening dinner rides, morning rides with breakfast and cowboy coffee, and all-day treks through Paradise Valley with scrumptious picnics.

In between take a dip in the heated swimming pool, play a game of tennis, or hike in the woods. Go on your own, or join one of the twice-daily hikes or adventures to historic sites, flower-filled meadows, or the wonders of Yellowstone. You might glimpse moose, elk, or even a bear. Big Creek, right in front of your cabin door, beckons anglers; a fly-fishing instructor is ready to teach you the basics and the trout are waiting. Table tennis, volleyball, softball, and horseshoes are popular games at the ranch. After active adventures, unwind in the hot tub or sauna, often under a clear, starlit sky. Capping off a fun-filled day, evening Western dances, hayrides, and campfire sing-alongs are frequently planned.

P.O. Box 1219
Emigrant, Montana 59027
(406) 333–1491, (800) 548–3392
www.mtnsky.com

DEER VALLEY RESORT

Park City, Utah

Skiing for most folks means a little bit of the rugged outdoors—windburned cheeks, the raw natural beauty of mountain vistas, fresh tracks through pristine powder. Deer Valley has redefined skiing somewhat. It's all of the above but with an added twist. Instead of the Western flair you'd expect in Utah, there's a more sophisticated atmosphere at Deer Valley. This is warm hospitality with a heavy dose of pampering—from the guest-service attendants who help you unload your skis to the quite comfortable chairlifts to the signature food items in Snow Park Lodge.

Deer Valley, less than 40 miles east of Salt Lake City, is actually four mountains: Bald Eagle Mountain, whose summit is 8,500 feet; Bald Mountain, which rises to 9,400 feet; Flagstaff Mountain, with the summit at 9,100 feet; and Empire Canyon, with a summit of 9,570 feet. The hubs of activity are Snow Park Lodge at the base of Bald Eagle Mountain and Silver Lake Lodge at midmountain. Silver Lake Village is in effect the midmountain point, for it is from here that lifts ascend to Bald Mountain's summit. With the feel of a European village, the area has three restaurants and a small ski shop. Snow Park Lodge houses a restaurant and lounge, the ski school, the ski rental shop, the children's center, and a well-stocked ski shop. Free buses connect all areas with Park City (1–3 miles away).

Both lodges are very tastefully designed; inside the columns are natural tree trunks at least 2 feet in diameter, and wood accoutrements abound—from the handrails to the ceiling beams, from the facial tissue dispensers to the trash cans. You'll find no plastic chairs or Formica-topped tables in the dining areas here—no indeed! Understated elegance and tasteful attention to detail are hallmarks of Deer Valley, home of the first country club for skiers.

Accommodations: At 8,200 feet amid the aspens and pines, the midmountain Stein Eriksen Lodge (www.steinlodge.com) is a Norwegian-style hotel built of stone and wood. Stein Eriksen's name has been synonymous with elegant skiing since his gold-medal victory in the 1952 Olympics. It's fitting that the 2002 Winter Olympics were on his home mountain. Today, Eriksen serves both as host of the lodge and director of skiing for Deer Valley Resort. The lodge consistently garners awards and is a four-star, five-diamond property. Daily rates for the fifty-nine rooms range from $350 to $500 in winter value season; $750 to $1,060 at winter's peak. It is ski-in, ski-out. The 111 suites are $645 to $830 (value) and $1,390 to $1,810 at peak times. Summer season (June to mid-October) rooms range from $205 to $260 and suites are $285 to $415. Shops, two restaurants, a swimming pool, a health club, and a full-service spa complement the lodge.

In addition, there are more than 500 units at the base of the mountain, along the trails, and near Silver Lake Lodge. The condominiums range from one- to five-bedroom units with fully equipped kitchens and living areas with fireplaces. Most have private Jacuzzis and individual decks or balconies; some include saunas and some feature ski-in, ski-out access. Daily maid service is available. One-bedrooms start at $250; two-bedrooms at $350. There are substantial savings during value seasons, typically early December and April, while rates increase during holiday periods.

During the summer months rates begin at $104 per night for a one-bedroom unit to

$159 per night for a two-bedroom unit, with a minimum two-night stay. All summer bookings receive two chairlift ride vouchers. Contact Deer Valley Central Reservations (800–558–DEER) for complete customized vacation planning.

Dining: Dining at Deer Valley is a gourmet experience. The award-winning Glitretind at the Stein Eriksen Lodge heads the list in elegance. Also here, the Troll Hallen Lounge serves lighter fare and libations. Wintertime on the mountain equals good eating. The Snow Park Restaurant and the Silver Lake Restaurant in the lodges are "cafeterias." What misnomers! Though they're self-service, the lavish breakfast and lunchtime displays (homemade breads and pastries, salads, quiches, deli sandwiches) are hardly typical of the standard quick bite between ski runs. The newest day lodge in Empire Canyon offers deck dining with scenic views of the Daly Bowl and Chutes. Start with morning espresso, have lunch from the gourmet grill, and snacks are available until 3:30 P.M. For evening dining in the winter season the seafood buffet at the Snow Park Lodge is known for fresh seafood and lots of it; *Zagat Guide* even lists it in "America's Top Restaurants." The Mariposa at Silver Lake Lodge offers classic and current cuisine and candle-lit dinners. Every Wednesday and Thursday evening in winter try the unique fireside dining at Empire Canyon Lodge, featuring three courses served from the grand fireplaces. Each one is different; they are all mouth-watering. Want to take a little break between courses? Just step outside for a moonlit ride on a horse-drawn sleigh. The Royal Street Café, at Silver Lake Lodge, is open daily in winter for lunch, après-ski, and dinner; it's the only midmountain restaurant open in summer, for lunch only. Want to grab a quick bite and just keep skiing? Stop by Snowshoe Tommy's atop Bald Mountain or Cushing's Cabin on Flagstaff Mountain, winter days

only. If desserts are your favorite part of the meal, the Snow Park Bakery is the place for you—fortunately, it's also year-round! Another summer dining treat is to order a Deer Valley Gourmet Picnic Basket; $60 for two. Stelvio at the Goldener Hirsch Inn serves Italian/Austrian cuisine; and the Olive Barrel is always popular for northern Italian hearty dishes from the brick oven.

Children's World: Deer Valley's Children's Center is a state-licensed facility providing indoor supervision and activities for nonskiing children. Located on the main level of the Snow Park Lodge, the center is open daily from 8:30 A.M. to 4:30 P.M. during the ski season and can accommodate infants as young as two months of age up to twelve years. The cost for all children is $88 for a full day with lunch; reservations are essential, especially in peak winter months. Children are divided by age into groups for two to eight months, nine to twenty-four months, and two to twelve years old. Activities include storytelling, art, singing, toys, and lots of play time, and quiet time for the littlest ones.

The Ski School instructors are trained specifically in techniques that teach children not only how to ski, but to love skiing. A safe, fun, nurturing environment prevails; programs end at 3:45 P.M. so you may take a run with your child, and you'll get daily progress reports. Children may be dropped off early at the Children's Center. Fawns (three to three and a half years) meet from 9:00 A.M. to 4:30 P.M. and alternate Children's Center activities with snow play and a one-hour private ski lesson. Children must be four to participate in Bambi Club, and will have morning and afternoon lessons, along with indoor activities. Children must be willing to ski and the daily program cost is $135; ski rental is $17. Reindeer Club meets from 10:15 A.M. to 3:45 P.M. for ages five to six years and costs $135 for lesson, lift ticket, and lunch. Average class size is four to six students; Children's Center activities are available when needed. Adventure Club ($135), for the seven- to twelve-year-olds, has an average size of seven to ten students, and all levels will have the opportunity to improve their skiing. Classes begin at 10:00 A.M. Adventure and Reindeer programs feature theme-oriented activities with coloring books, fun races, special mountain scavenger hunts, and friendly animals who share secrets of safety and fun. And finally, the Teen Escape (ages thirteen to eighteen, $135) lets teens enjoy a mountain experience with their peers while being coached on the dynamics of skiing. They'll need pocket money for lunch, and the program is only offered during holiday and peak periods.

Deer Valley's Summer Adventure Camp is one of Park City's longest-running summer camps. Beginning mid-June, it operates from 9:30 A.M. to 4:00 P.M. Monday through Friday until mid-August. Drop-in hours are 8:00 A.M. to 5:30 P.M. at the Children's Center. Campers bring their own sack lunch and water. Programs are split into three groups, with excellent counselor-to-camper ratios: Adventure Camp Mountaineers for first graders through twelve years (1:8, $47); Adventure Camp Explorers for ages four through kindergarten (1:5, $47); Trekkers for ages three to four (1:4, $52); and Jamboree for the wee ones, ages one through three years (1:4, $52). Half days at Trekkers and Jamboree are $32, and based on availability; reservations are required. Jamboree activities include little-red-wagon rides, a walk to the duck pond, wading pool water games, and art, music, and movement.

All ages get to enjoy usual summer camp activities plus leisurely time to simply enjoy and appreciate the great outdoors and play with friends. Each week's activities revolve around a different theme and include nature studies, swimming, mountain biking and hiking, team sports, along with mini–film festivals (kids produce their own videos), karaoke, and talent shows. Weekly field trips incur an extra cost ($15 to $20).

Recreation: There are eighty-eight downhill runs, nineteen lifts, and a vertical drop of 3,000 feet. Combine these with well-groomed trails and a restricted number of skiers on a daily basis—what more could a skier ask for? Beginners are able to ski each of the four mountains. The mountains are beautiful, and the attention to them and to the skiers is high quality. Full- and half-day private and group lessons are available. Cross-country ski lessons are also offered nearby; trails roll over broad, open expanses and through aspens and evergreens. No snowboards are allowed at Deer Valley. Other winter pleasures include snowmobiling, snowshoeing, sleigh-ride dinners, heli-skiing, and even hot-air ballooning. Park City is alive with shopping, art galleries, theater, bars, and clubs. And of course, the Utah Olympic Park provides ski jumping, bobsledding, and luge rides.

If you don't have a sufficient workout on the slopes, maybe the exercise rooms will test your limits. Then relax your weary muscles in one of the saunas or Jacuzzis.

Though primarily a winter wonderland, Deer Valley operates year-round. In warmer weather, June to Labor Day, guests enjoy 50 miles of lift-served mountain biking/hiking and scenic chairlift rides. The Utah Symphony stages outdoor concerts, and all the summer mountain pleasures are here: golf, tennis, swimming, horseback riding, fishing, boating, rafting and kayaking, and hot-air ballooning. Stroll along Park City's Historic Main Street, which offers shops and dining options.

P.O. Box 1525
Park City, Utah 84060
(435) 645–6528, (800) 558–3337
www.deervalley.com

PARK CITY MOUNTAIN RESORT

Park City, Utah

Park City Mountain Resort has been consistently ranked in the top ten of *Ski Magazine's* reader's poll for the last seventeen years, and is one of Utah's most sophisticated resort communities. Three separate ski areas; a wide variety of lodgings from budget to luxury; a historic Victorian Main Street lined with shops, galleries, and restaurants; a superb setting in the gorgeous Wasatch Mountain Range of the Rockies; and all of this within a 7-mile radius and only 36 miles from the Salt Lake City airport. No wonder the 2002 Winter Olympic Games were held here. It's also very family friendly, and has garnered accolades from *Snowboard Magazine, Snowboarding, Money* magazine, *Fine Living, Freeskier,* and more.

Accommodations: Park City offers hotels, bed-and-breakfasts, lodges, and condominiums, with over 3,000 units available at the mountain base, a couple of blocks from the runs, and throughout town. Prices vary depending on the proximity to the slopes and the amenities offered. Value season is usually early December, April, fall, and sometimes summer; regular ski season and holiday season (Christmas, Presidents' Week) fill in the blanks. A free bus connects all three areas. Park City Visitor's Bureau brings together complete listings of accommodations, plus lots of other information about the area at www.parkcity .com. As an example, a two-night package at a preferred property with a $50 voucher for dinner can be $199 in nonpeak season and $249 in peak ski season.

The Town Lift condominiums, with spacious two-bedroom units in the heart of the historic district, are next door to the Town Chair Lift and Ski Bridge (with access to the mountain) and only five minutes from Deer Valley's Snow Park Base Lodge (888–976–2732). Per-night rates during value season range from $415 to $435; regular is $530 to $665; and summer rates are $155 to $175.

The Park City Marriott is a four-star hotel just 1 mile from downtown by complimentary shuttle. An atrium-style pool, hot tub, fitness facility, on-site restaurant, and covered parking make life easy, and the beautiful views are just icing on the cake. Winter rates for two adults (children under twelve are free in the room) range from $99 to $159 and include breakfast for everyone; in summer those rates drop to $69 to $119, still with breakfast (435–646–2900, 800–234–9003).

If you prefer even more peace and quiet, then the Grand Summit Resort in the Canyons might suit you. A four-diamond property with outdoor heated pool and slope-side location, it also has its own children's program (details under Children's World). Also on the slopes is the Sundial Lodge; both properties offer family-friendly options from studios to multi-bedroom condominiums, underground parking, and a Mountain Concierge at the ticket windows to answer all your questions. If the Canyons is your choice, call Central Reservations at (866) 604–4171 to help you plan. Deer Valley is the third area—see that entry for details.

Dining: With one hundred–plus restaurants and bars, it's impossible to list them all. Be aware that in summertime, dining is more limited, so be sure to check before you bounce out to eat as disappointed taste buds can ruin your disposition. Your taste buds can really get a workout in the Village. Try the Continental cuisine at Adolf's or the

Riverhorse on Main Café, with live entertainment; both are local favorites. Chimayo is imaginative Southwestern with a French technique, and Wahso offers Asian grill, with that same French influence, in a setting reminiscent of 1930s Shanghai. Mikados for sushi, Grappa for the feel of a Tuscan farmhouse, and Zoom, Robert Redford's restaurant in the train depot station, are all delightful diversions. Kids like Hot Harry's Burritos, Main Street Pizza and Noodles, and often the Corner Café and Yarrow Social Club have specials. Kristi's Café is open daily year-round for smoothies, coffee, pastry, and gourmet picnic baskets. More summer dining options (and winter too) are listed in the Deer Valley entry. At the Canyons, lunch at Lookout Cabin, a sit-down venue with great views; Dreamscape Grill; or Doc's at the Gondola, all in winter. Have an elegant meal at the Cabin Restaurant or breakfast year-round at First Tracks Café, both in the lobby of the Grand Summit Hotel. Also year-round, the Island Café features Caribbean-style cuisine; it's located in Canyons Village. You probably need at least one trip to Park City to figure out all your favorite places!

Children's World: As with lodging and dining, a wide variety of options exists with programs for children. Comprehensive, in-one-spot winter and summer programs are found at Deer Valley; see the previous entry for details. At the Canyons, the Perfect Kids ski school (435–615–3449) uses a proven method to teach children either the rudiments or the fine points of skiing. Programs run from 9:15 A.M. to 3:15 P.M. but can be extended (8:00 A.M. to 4:30 P.M.) at the Day Care Center. Canyon Cubs for two- and three-year-olds combines day care with beginning skiing and snow play; $170 per day includes everything. Canyon Cats allows children ages four to six to enjoy an entire day of mostly skiing; depending on weather and each individual child, indoor games and care are also provided. Cost is $106 for lessons and lunch only and $122 adds equipment and lift. Ages seven to twelve, the Canyon Carvers, tackle the mountain on skis or snowboards; cost is $122 for lessons and lunch; $138 with equipment/lift. For ages six weeks to six years, the Little Adventures Children's Center (866–604–4170, 435–615–8036), a state-licensed Day Care Center in the Grand Summit Resort, has toys, books, and various age-appropriate activities. In summer, they accept children from six weeks to twelve years old. The center operates from 8:30 A.M. to 4:30 P.M.; the cost is based on age. Winter rates for six weeks to two years are $82 for a full day with lunch, $62 for a half day; for ages two to six years, the cost is $75 for a full day with lunch and $55 for a half day. One-hour private skiing lessons are $125. In summer, ages six weeks to two years are $50 for a full day, $30 for a half day; two- to five-year-olds are $48 and $30; six- to twelve-year-olds pay $45 with lunch, $40 without, or half days for $30 with lunch and $25 without. Activities vary by age groups and might include hiking, gondola rides, arts and crafts, and swimming or water play.

Parents love for their children to have fun, and sometimes to share that fun. Park City offers lots of activities tailored specifically for kids. Depending on the time and length of your visit, Arts-Kids, Inc. (435–615–7878) offers two art-in-nature camps for ages eight to twelve, sampling photography, mask making, poetry, break dancing—even field trips and the Alpine Slide. The Black Diamond Gymnastics & Sports Center (435–615–1800) has Monday through Saturday classes in gymnastics, trampoline, and tumbling for all ages, one year to adults. With twenty-five years of experience, the Norwegian Outdoor Exploration Center (435–649–5322, 800–649–5322) offers summer youth camps for ages six to seventeen years. Their credo,

"Simply stated, we take people outdoors and have fun."

Recreation: The Visitor's Bureau boasts that "Nobody does winter like Park City." That could be so. Especially now, with the addition of Olympic Park, activities seem almost unlimited. With an average of 355 inches of snow annually, a ski season from mid-November to late April, and 2,200 acres of skiable terrain, including ninety-three runs and bowls, fourteen chairlifts, and 3,100 vertical feet, Park City is one of the largest Rocky Mountain ski resorts. Whether you ramble down gentle slopes past old mining buildings, take on the moguls between groves of aspen, or get knee-deep in powder, plenty of variety will keep you happy. There's even night skiing and riding, if you just can't get enough of the slopes. Wolf Mountain is another whole mountain just down the road. Skiing of all types—downhill, cross-country, helicopter, and snowcat; snowboarding, the jumps, luge, and bobsled run at Olympic Park; snowmobiling, hot-air ballooning, tubing, snowshoeing, ice-skating, sleigh rides—is anything missing? Indoors, there are day spas, fitness and health clubs, and massage. Year-round, a ride on the Heber Valley historic railroad along lakes and canyons, following the Provo River, is an exciting trip.

In summertime, the clean mountain air, the plentiful wildflowers, and the great outdoors beckon you. Hiking, horseback riding, mountain biking, tennis, racquetball, golf, and bicycling are favorite warm-weather activities. Park City Mountain Resort has a mile-long listing of adventures for all ages, from the Little Miners Park with rides for the wee ones to alpine slides, the legacy launcher (four—count them—four trampolines to bounce among), diggler scooters, a climbing wall, and the ZipRider, designed to strike fear into the hearts of all but the most extreme. Covering a distance of 2,300 feet with a vertical drop of 550 feet, 110 feet above the ski runs at speeds of up to 60 mph, it's the longest in the world. Tamer, but also fun is the diversion of a stroll along Main Street; shops, restaurants, and a lively atmosphere are entertaining. And Salt Lake City is less than 40 miles away, a good day trip. The Children's Museum of Utah is found here; it's a "hands-on, minds-on" place to explore, create, and imagine, and delightfully interactive.

P.O. Box 39
1310 Lowell Avenue
Park City, Utah 84060
(435) 658–5560, (800) 222–PARK (7275)
www.parkcitymountain.com

SNOWBIRD SKI AND SUMMER RESORT
Snowbird, Utah

Snowbird, along with Alta, have been named the #1 Ski Resort in the U.S. by *Skiing* magazine for three years running. Snowbird's diverse terrain includes some of the most challenging skiing in the world. Yet surprisingly, the size of its intermediate,

novice, and beginner areas is greater than the total terrain of many notable resorts. Every night more than half the slopes and trails are groomed, paving the way for beginner and intermediate skiers, while leaving the rest for those who seek the light, dry Utah powder. Whatever your proficiency and desire, Snowbird accommodates you with more than 2,500 acres of wide-open bowls, gladed tree runs, steep chutes, nightly groomed trails, and cruising boulevards. From the 500 acres of terrain on Mineral Basin to the terrific novice and intermediate terrain off the Baby Thunder Chair, you'll be amazed by the sheer excitement of skiing the "Bird."

Here are a few more facts about Snowbird: a vertical rise of 3,240 continuously skiable feet; average annual snowfall of 500 inches; yes, 500 inches, and it's that "dry" Utah powder known worldwide; the longest descent, Gad Valley, at 3½ miles; the longest designated run, Chip's Run, at 2½ miles. Snowbird enjoys one of the finest ski seasons in the world. Beginning in mid-November, the ski season regularly extends through mid-May. In fact, skiers have even been known to celebrate the Fourth of July on the slopes.

Snowbird offers ideal family vacations. According to *Skiing* magazine, "Snowbird has come up with what might be the best family ski value at a major ski area." The resort has also been awarded the Family Channel's Seal of Quality. Family Travel Forum selected Snowbird as one of the Top Ten Getaways for Tiny Travelers.

Accommodations: A cozy slopeside pedestrian village, Snowbird harmonizes fittingly with the rugged, natural beauty of Little Cottonwood Canyon. And everything at the resort—accommodations, restaurants, shops, skiing, and activities—is within easy walking distance.

Snowbird has three distinctive condominium properties: the Inn, the Lodge at Snowbird, and the Iron Blosam Lodge. Each offers homelike features, such as fireplaces and kitchens; pools, saunas, exercise facilities, and other services are included or easily accessible. Snowbird's flagship accommodation, the Cliff Lodge and Cliff Club, offers easy ski-in, ski-out access along with North America's foremost Persian and Oriental rug collection. Three restaurants, two lounges, and the world-class Cliff Spa and Salon make it the perfect place to retire after an exhilarating day on the slopes.

Winter rates for a room in the lodge range from $189 to $389; summer rates drop to $79 to $169. One-bedroom condominiums with full kitchen are $279 to $569; two bedrooms are $409 to $869; summer rates are lower. Call Central Reservations at (800) 453–3000 to help find the best accommodations for your family.

Dining: The dining at Snowbird is diverse, with over ten restaurants and lounges to please a variety of tastes and styles. Snowbird dining offers everything from Niçoise-style striped sea bass to mountain-grilled burgers to coconut beer-battered shrimp. The Aerie Restaurant is Snowbird's flagship of fine dining. Try the Lodge Bistro for cozy dinners, buffet, and the wonderful view from the Atrium, or great steaks at the Steak Pit. Casual dining is found at the Birdfeeder, the Keyhole (Mexican), and Wildflower (Italian); and families enjoy the Forklift for breakfast and lunch, and, of course, Pier 49 Sourdough Pizza. The Rendezvous serves burgers and sandwiches and Superior Snacks is just that. Children's menus are available at all sit-down restaurants. Find après-ski at the Aerie Lounge, Keyhole Cantina, Wildflower Lounge, or Lodge Bistro Lounge; nightlife with weekly jazz at the Bird; and live music, dancing, pool, and thirteen TVs at the Tram Club.

Children's World: From family ski zones to the Mini Mining Town kids trail, Snowbird is certain to please young skiers. And remember, children under twelve ski free. Up to two children twelve and under ski the chairs free on Snowbird only; tram upgrades are complimentary for nightly rate lodging guests. Snowbird's youngest guests, six weeks to three years old, are well cared for in a safe, fun environment at Camp Snowbird, a state-licensed child-care facility where an open-door policy allows parents to drop in, with picture ID, of course. Registration is required at least two weeks in advance; a credit card is required. A full day is from 8:30 A.M. to 4:30 P.M. and costs $84 in value season; $90 regular. Value season dates vary between November and April. Call for details: (801) 933-2256. Half days cannot be reserved, but are sold daily if space is available.

Day Care Camp for ages three to twelve includes snow play, arts and crafts, table games, and free play; lunch and snacks are included. A full day is $74; half day, morning or afternoon, is $54 in value season; $80 and $60 regular season. When kids also take a ski lesson, the cost is $95.

SMILE stands for Snowbird Mountain Integrated Learning Experience, and it's what happens at the ski school as kids gain confidence and skills on the mountain. For three-year-olds, Chickadees has just the right mix of one-hour lessons each session, snow and indoor play. Fee of $95 per half-day session includes lunch and equipment. For Kinderbirds, ages four to six, the cost is $75 for a half day; $135 for a full day with lunch and supervision. It meets from 9:15 to 11:30 A.M. and 12:45 to 3:00 P.M. Seven- to twelve-year-olds join Mountain Adventures for fun in developing their skills on either skis or snowboards. Grouped by age and ability, the challenges are shared with peers. A full day from 9:15 A.M. to 3:00 P.M., including lunch, is $90; afternoon only (12:45 to 3:00 P.M.) is $56. Snowbird is a Snow Monsters resort, so kids can expect to bump into them around the school (www.snowmonsters.com).

Wednesday and Saturday nights the Kids Club is open from 6:30 to 10:00 P.M. for kids ages four to six. Admission to the "nightclub" is $30 ($40 on Saturday) and includes dinner, entertainment, and craft projects. Adventures After Dark takes seven- to fifteen-year-olds out and about; even the most blasé are excited by the Zip Rider, snowshoe treks, pool parties, tubing, action movies, or ski and snowboard jaunts. Times and cost are the same as above. Babysitting in your room is available at $15 per hour with a three-hour minimum.

Summer brings different activities for Camp Snowbird (ages four to twelve, $50, $40 for second child). Kids explore the canyon with nature hikes and science experiments; work on sports skills and arts projects; and swim every day. Children are divided by age into groups of eight to ten campers. Open early June through late August, from 8:30 A.M. to 5:00 P.M.; all days must be preregistered ($25 fee) and campers get a T-shirt and water bottle. Drop-ins pay an additional fee of $50.

Recreation: Snowbird's Mountain Host program offers free guided skiing tours every day to acquaint guests with the runs and lifts best suited to their skiing abilities. All you need is a lift ticket and a smile to join the group and get better acquainted with the incredible mountain. Snowbird and Little Cottonwood Canyon neighbor Alta offer one lift ticket for both resorts. Made possible by Snowbird's second Mineral Basin chairlift, the Alta-Snowbird ticket provides two of the world's top resorts in one day of skiing.

Almost as famous as the snow, and every bit as great, is the ski school. More than 300 professional instructors offer all-day or by-the-hour private and group lessons. Or, if you want to take your vacation to new heights, try one of Snowbird's specialized seminars that address the specific interests and needs of women, seniors, snowboarders, and experts.

The Activity Center will fill you in on all that goes on: ice-skating, tubing, snowshoe-ing, and luging. Children must be twelve to book the luge sleds on Tuesday, Thursday, and Saturday evenings on Chickadee. Want to be the first to make tracks in all that powder? For $25 extra, expert skiers take the first tram with experienced guides, and history is made. Also on the agenda are night skiing, summit snowmobiling, backcountry tours, swimming, and hot tubs to warm you up after all that snow. Cliff Spa at the Cliff Lodge has a staff of forty just waiting to pamper you. Evenings are filled with après-ski, live music, free ski and snowboard movies, or adventure lectures.

In summer the focus of activities is still on the great outdoors. Snowbird has tennis courts on-site; an extensive program is found at the Snowbird Canyon Racquet and Fitness Club, a short drive away, which offers ten indoor and thirteen outdoor tennis courts, racquetball and squash, yoga and kickboxing, along with aerobics classes and a weight room. Golf is less than fifteen minutes away at the championship Old Mill golf course designed by Gene Bates. Another six courses are within a thirty- to forty-five-minute drive.

Try the Oriental rug tours, stargazing, and murder mystery dinner theater; or spend the day pampering yourself at the Cliff Spa. Offsite, you can visit the Winter Sports Park, tour Antelope Island, check out downtown Salt Lake City, or shop in Park City.

P.O. Box 929000
Highway 210 Little Cottonwood Canyon
Snowbird, Utah 84092
(801) 742–2222, (800) 232–9542
www.snowbird.com

VAIL/BEAVER CREEK RESORTS
Vail, Colorado

Lots of folks talk of Vail and Aspen in practically the same breath. Granted, several similarities between the two come to mind: Both rank right at the top in excellent skiing, both are high in the Rockies west of Denver, both are chic and sophisticated, and to both have been appended newer developments that are upscale and family friendly— Beaver Creek at Vail and Snowmass at Aspen.

Unlike Aspen's history as an old mining town, Vail grew up in the 1960s. The modern-day careful planning and systematic development based on European resorts give Vail its atmosphere; it is a well-laid-out, Alpine-style village designed with the pedestrian in mind (it's nice that so few cars spoil the scenery). Actually, there are three village areas at the base of Vail Mountain—Golden Peak, Lionshead, and Vail Village—each with its own lodging, restaurants, and facilities, and each within walking distance of base lifts. In practical terms, though, since each abuts the next, most folks think of the tripartite as one friendly town. Over the past ten years, Vail Resorts has spent $125 million improving Vail Mountain. Vail Village and Lionshead are now receiving the same attention. Construction began in spring 2005 with new lodging at Gore Creek Place and in Lionshead, The Arrabelle at Vail Square, a luxury RockResort. A new skier bridge connecting the mountain and the square is complete, and additional plans for the plaza include more shopping and dining, a larger ice-skating rink, and spiffy new facilities for skiers plus enhanced streetscapes and landscaping—Vail is on the move, and calling it Vail's New Dawn.

Beaver Creek is just 10 miles farther down the road. Opened in 1980, Beaver

Creek, too, has been planned around a pedestrian village; in addition to the accommodations in the village, lodges and condominiums are tucked among the grand spruce trees on the mountain. Shuttle-bus lines service the Vail Valley, within each village and between mountain bases. A year-round resort area, the Vail Valley also boasts of its summer beauty and offers art and music festivals, hiking, mountain biking, and more from June through October.

Accommodations: Lodging at Vail can be right at the mountain base a couple of skips from the chairlift and dripping with amenities, or back a few paces and not so loaded with extras, or most economically, a shuttle ride away. Of course, these options are reflected in the rates. Vail Valley's Lodging Quality Assurance program is designed to provide guests with just that: information and quality assurance. A Platinum rating represents the finest accommodations; Gold is upscale, inviting, and stylish; Silver offers comfortable accommodations; and Bronze is acceptable, with no frills. The LQA ratings are for the rooms themselves, not location, costs, or amenities. Vail/Beaver Creek Central Reservations at (800) 525–2257 can help sort it all out for you. The Lodge at Vail is the only ski-in, ski-out hotel in the village itself; additional Gold properties include Lionshead Inn, Lodge Tower, Lion Square Lodge, Manor Vail, and Christiania. Vail Visitor Services at (800) 525–3875 also can assist with reservations and information or go to www.vail.com.

With deluxe accommodations and a car-free village, Beaver Creek is a favorite of families. The Park Hyatt, Trappers Lodge, the Inn at Beaver Creek, the Pines Lodge, and Beaver Creek Lodge (all suites) are all beautiful ski-in, ski-out village-based properties. The Park Hyatt offers Camp Hyatt, their own daily, year-round child-care program for ages three to twelve (970–949–1234). The Ritz Carlton also has their own program for children, called The Ritz Kids (970–748–6200), for ages five through twelve. The Charter at Beaver Creek and loads of condominiums and town homes offer a wide range of lodging and amenities. Nearby Arrowhead and Bachelor Gulch also offer ski-in, ski-out options. Beaver Creek supplies complimentary shuttle service between areas. Call (800) 427–8308 or (888) 830–7669, or visit www.beavercreek .com for more information and reservations.

Winter is divided into value season (late November to December 21 and again in April), regular season (January 5 to mid-February), and high season (Christmas and mid-February to early April). Summer rates can be as much as 50% lower than winter rates. Discounts for children are just about universal and package plans are often a good value. The "Travel Deals" section of www.vail.com offers guests lodging discounts, and more than 150 properties in the Vail Valley are listed with Vail/Beaver Creek Central Reservations at (800) 427–8308.

Dining: Hungry for a hamburger? Eager to savor a juicy steak? Or is Mexican fare your idea of the perfect après-ski dinner? In the Vail Valley all this is possible, plus Italian, Chinese, French, German, and, of course, American food. With more than 110 restaurants and bars, there are lots of choices. Many restaurants are right in the lodges, such as the Lodge at Vail, Lion Square Lodge, the Landmark, and the Charter at Beaver Creek. Others are in the villages at the base of the lifts or in the pedestrian areas. Larkspur, at the base of Golden Peak, is listed by USA Today as a "don't miss while in Vail."

More restaurants are on the mountains and not just quick, cafeteria-style mountainside rest stops: Some hit gourmet standards. Whenever weather permits, outdoor barbecues are planned at the midmountain points. Many of the restaurants have children's menus—just ask.

Children's World: Vail and Beaver Creek both have similar high-quality programs for children. Prices and hours may vary slightly, and reservations are highly recommended for both. At Beaver Creek and at Golden Peak in Vail, the Small World Play School entertains little ones two months to six years old from 8:00 A.M. to 4:30 P.M. daily. The toddlers and preschoolers enjoy games, songs, crafts, and indoor and outdoor play in a colorful nursery/schoolhouse atmosphere. Separate playrooms for ages two to eighteen months, nineteen to thirty months, and preschoolers offer closer supervision. The cost varies by season: from $79 to $89 at Vail, and from $89 to $99 at Beaver Creek. Beaver Creek has half-day sessions from noon to 4:00 P.M. ($69 to $76). At Vail, afternoon child care from 2:00 to 4:30 P.M. costs $26 to $36. For $18 additional Vail offers a thirty-minute ski/snowplay program for toddlers twenty months and older. For more information, contact Small World at Vail at (970) 479–3285 or Beaver Creek at (970) 845–5325.

For guests only, the Park Hyatt at Beaver Creek has its own Camp Hyatt children's program for ages three to twelve with activities offered daily from 9:00 A.M. to 10:00 P.M. Indoor and outdoor play (nonskiing) are featured and kids can attend for an hour, the evening, or an entire day. The price is $13.00 per hour; lunch or dinner is $5.00 additional. Spring and fall, Camp Hyatt is available but "on-call" and reservations must be made twenty-four hours in advance (970–949–1234, www.beavercreek.hyatt.com).

Youngsters ages five to twelve years staying at the Ritz Carlton can join the Ritz Kids, a daily program in winter and summer season. Hours are 8:00 A.M. to 4:00 P.M., with full-day sessions for $125, mornings only at $60, and afternoon with lunch is $75. From 4:00 to 6:00 P.M., the club shows complimentary movies (a nice break for parents!) and then Kids Night Out runs from 6:00 to 10:00 P.M. with dinner included for $75. Kids have a great time with the themed activities such as talent shows or secret agents. A nice bonus is socializing with Bachelor, the dog. Children under five are welcome to join the sessions with an adult or babysitter, at half price. Children may also attend for hourly sessions ($18) when the activities are on-site (970–748–6200, www.ritzcarlton.com/resorts/bachelor_gulch/).

The Children's Ski and Snowboard Center operates out of three locations—Lionshead, Golden Peak, and the Village Hall at Beaver Creek (convenient no matter where you're staying!) and divides children into groups (three- to six-year-olds and six- to twelve-year-olds for skiing and up to fourteen for snowboards) for daily lessons from 8:00 A.M. to 4:00 P.M. Both groups have some indoor activities as well as skiing; the older children's schedule concentrates more on skiing. At Vail, programs are $95 to $107, depending on the season, and include lesson and lunch. Lift tickets are $15. Snowboarding lessons are available for ages seven to fourteen; cost is the same. At Beaver Creek, programs are $105 to $125. More information on both children's programs is available at (970) 476–3239 (Vail) or (970) 845–5464 (Beaver Creek). Teens can meet new friends, explore the mountain, and perfect their ski and snowboard skills at Vail. Lesson only $90 or $100; lesson/all mountain $118 or $128. Too cool.

Adventure Zones are special areas on the slopes designed just for kids. Chaos Canyon has bumps, jumps, twists, and tunnels. At others, an old fort, a tepee village, and ancient Indian burial ground await exploration. On Wednesday and Thursday, Night Owls provides a supervised evening of fun at Adventure Ridge. Seven- to twelve-year-olds enjoy dinner and activities atop Vail Mountain from 4:30 to 8:30 P.M. during regular season ($60).

In summer Small World Play School is at Beaver Creek only and starts at two months of age with infant and toddler programs, and special minicamp programs for four- and five-year olds. Hours are Monday through Friday from 8:30 A.M. to 4:30 P.M.

The town of Vail has many programs for youths, open to all. Camps operate from the Golden Peak Children's Center, Monday through Friday, from mid-June to mid-August. The Pre-Kamp for ages thirty months to pre-kindergarten balances the desire for fun with the limits on "little legs and spirits." A 5:1 ratio ensures individual attention, and it's structured around a storybook theme, with a different story each week. Hiking, gondola rides, tours of local businesses, and arts and crafts fill the day from 8:00 A.M. to 5:00 P.M.; the cost is $62 daily or $290 for five days.

Camp Vail, for ages five (and entering kindergarten) to twelve, runs from 7:30 A.M. to 5:30 P.M. and utilizes the whole Vail Valley for fun. Enthusiastic young counselors guide kids in a variety of activities that they can often choose, and Wednesday is a wild card, break-out day. Ratio is 10:1 and the cost is the same as Pre-Kamp. Campers participate in caving, orienteering, swimming, golf, fishing, and climbing as well as art, drama, and nature discovery. Call (970) 479-2290 for details.

At Beaver Creek, Discovery Camp ($80) is for ages five to seven; and Adventure Camp ($90) for ages eight to twelve. Pony rides, canoeing, panning for gold, river rafting, mountain biking, ropes course, and miniature golf are some of the activities, all geared toward each age group. Field trips and special evening activities are also planned. Camp runs Monday through Friday, 8:00 A.M. to 4:30 P.M. For a true Rocky Mountain adventure, the 5-Star Camp ($95) for ages five to twelve, with age restrictions on some activities, does more unusual activities such

as kayaking, rock climbing, Jeep tours, horseback riding, or go-karts. Call (970) 845-5464 for details and reservations.

Recreation: The name of the game is skiing, and the Vail Valley has all the ingredients for an excellent ski holiday. In the middle of the White River National Forest, Vail Mountain rises to 11,570 feet; at Beaver Creek the summit is 11,440 feet. The vertical drop is more than 3,450 feet at Vail and 4,040 feet at Beaver Creek. An average annual snowfall between 300 and 350 inches (and an artificial snowmaking system) accounts for a season lasting from late November to mid-April.

Vail and Beaver Creek skiable terrain totaling over 6,900 acres (lift tickets for the two mountains are interchangeable) provides variety for all levels of skiers, from gentle beginner slopes to challenging intermediates to exciting mogul and bowl skiing. Vail's Blue Sky Basin provides a unique wilderness ski experience, featuring 645 acres of natural, gladed terrain in two world-class bowls. At Vail the runs are ranked 28% beginner, 32% intermediate, and 40% advanced; at Beaver Creek the breakdown is 34% beginner, 39% intermediate, and 27% advanced.

So that you can cut tracks through the Rocky Mountain powder in style, a very large ski school (1,200 instructors!) can assist you. In addition to the typical group and private lessons for all ability levels, the Vail/Beaver Creek Ski School offers free classes with videotaped analysis and high-powered workshops in mogul and powder skiing. Meet the Mountain introductory tours are scheduled daily; this is a morning ski tour with guest-services staff who acquaint you with the area's history and topography. Or enroll in lessons in cross-country skiing, which is so refined here that distinctions are made between backcountry skiing, telemark skiing, and track skiing.

Other wintertime sports include ice-skating at Dobson Ice Arena, Black Family Rink in Beaver Creek, or Nottingham Lake; snowmobiling at Piney Lake; and ice-fishing. Snowcat tours to above 10,000 feet offer spectacular views, and if you can walk, you can snowshoe, for an up-close view of winter. The Colorado Ski Museum is here, or relax in one of the three cinemas. An evening outing in a horse-drawn sleigh may be the right way to finish off a perfect day, or enjoy a brisk horseback ride in the snow. Indoor evening entertainment includes nightclubs and movie theaters; favorite haunts for kids are the video arcades and the Vail Youth Center.

Even after the last skier comes down the mountain in late spring, fun in the Vail Valley continues. As in the winter, summertime activities focus on the beautiful outdoors. Hiking through stands of aspens along the trail systems up Vail Mountain and Beaver Creek Mountain, biking on paths through wildflowers, and fishing in mountain streams get you back to nature. Ride horseback at Eagle Ranch, Beaver Creek Stables, and Piney River Ranch, or muster your courage for river rafting.

Vail Valley has eleven golf courses, and more on the way. Some are public, some private or semi-private, and some are connected to various lodging in the Valley. You're sure to find the one that's just right for your skills. With 300 days of sunshine each year, tennis shines here. Free courts at Golden Peak, or for a little Mozart with your game, schedule one of the Ford Park courts at concert time. Target Tennis is a new teaching concept practically guaranteed to improve your game. Fancy a spa experience? There are at least ten in the area, including the natural Yampah Spa and Vapor Caves in nearby Glenwood Springs. And Beaver Creek hosts weekly rodeos—great fun for the whole family.

Summer Adventure Ridge starts with a scenic ride on the Eagle Bahn Gondola to the Ridge, where you can spend the entire day. In addition to laser tag, trampoline, orienteering, hiking, disc golf, sledding, guided tours, and mountain bikes, the kids can even hunt for buried bones at the Dino Dig. Admission pass includes lunch at Talon's Deck (adults $40, children five to twelve $35). Open select dates June to September. The Discovery Center, at the top of the Eagle Bahn Gondola, teaches about our environment through fun, interactive displays and nature hikes. Cultural events are plentiful: the Arts Festival in June, Vail Valley Music Festival all summer, International Dance, and the Vail Jazz Festival in August. At Beaver Creek, the Vilar Center for the Arts has children's theater, stand-up comedy, Broadway shows, and musicals. Free movie nights for kids twelve and under, plus costume contests add to the fun. Sunday afternoons, Vail Valley chefs demonstrate their skills.

Hot summer nights come alive at Vail Valley—actually, the entertainment is hot, not the weather. Hot summer nights concert series are on Tuesday night, with covered seating and picnics allowed. Gondola rides are free on Friday after 5:00 P.M. to Eagle's Nest on the top of Vail Mountain; drink specials, games, free live music on the deck, and the best sunset views are all here. Add piano bars, live music venues, sports bars, and dance clubs to the mix; and for the younger crowd, Twenty Below offers pool, foosball, music, and movies. All in all, Vail/Beaver Creek is a tasty resort!

Vail, Colorado 81658
(800) 525–2257, (800) 525–3875
www.beavercreek.snow.com
www.vail.snow.com

WEST

California
Idaho
Nevada
Oregon
Wyoming

THE ALISAL GUEST RANCH AND RESORT

Solvang, California

Okay, so cattle ranches are not the first thing that comes to mind when you think of Southern California or Solvang. Nevertheless, it is the West, and at least one does exist. In the Santa Ynez Valley of southern California is a real working cattle ranch—the Alisal (from the Chumash Indian word meaning "grove of sycamores"). Some things just don't change—cattle have been grazing here for almost 200 years, and century-old sycamore trees line the private entrance road. Sixty years ago the current owner's father, a cattleman himself, decided to open the ranch to guests. Today visitors enjoy the atmosphere of an active ranch with the facilities of a resort on this 10,000-acre spread. This is California, after all, so one would expect golf, tennis, first-class accommodations, fine dining, and wine tasting, along with horses and wranglers. And that indeed is what the Alisal delivers. Named a Family Resort of the Year by *Family Circle; Sunset Magazine* also ranked it one of the "50 Best Dude Ranches in the West." Only forty minutes from Santa Barbara and two hours from Los Angeles, the Alisal is a welcome haven to harried city-dwellers that is open year-round.

Accommodations: Decorated in classic California ranch design, seventy-three cottages accommodating up to 200 guests are clustered near the swimming pool and tennis courts or overlooking the golf course. Either studios or two-room suites, all have a wood-burning fireplace, covered front porch, flower gardens in front, and refrigerators. There are no in-room telephones or television—how relaxing! Suites offer a sitting room and soaring ceilings. Based on double occupancy and a Modified American Plan, studio rates are $435 daily; two-room suites are $490 to $550. Children two and under stay free, ages three through six are $50, and six years and older are $80. Cribs are $15 per night. There's a two-night minimum, and Saturday check-ins are not allowed. Weekdays between early September and early June, a Round-Up vacation package is offered. For the price of a room, the Alisal includes unlimited golf, horseback riding (two-hour rides), tennis, and fishing for two people. The package is also available weekends from November through March.

Dining: The Ranch Room serves breakfast from 7:00 to 10:00 A.M. (a lavish buffet or a la carte) and gourmet dinners from a five-item menu that changes every evening. Dinner is a dress-up affair; jackets are required for gentlemen sixteen and older (ties optional), and ladies and children dress appropriately for fine dining. Parents with small children are encouraged to have dinner at 6:30 P.M., before the peak hours of 7:15 to 8:15 P.M. Alisal requests that children's behavior be monitored, especially at meals. In all fairness, they request the same of people with cell phones! Lunch is not included in the room rate but can be ordered from the Chuckwagon Grill (poolside snack bar) and at the Ranch Course Grill (open from 11:00 A.M. to 2:00 P.M.) on the golf course. The River Grill is open daily for lunch, and light fare is available from 3:00 to 5:00 P.M. You may also order a box lunch. In summer you can saddle up early for a breakfast ride to Adobe Camp or enjoy a haywagon ride to your breakfast. Try the seafood barbecue at the lake or a Cal-Mex barbecue at the rodeo arena in the evening. Saturday brings an all-ranch barbecue at the pool lawn. The Oak Room Lounge, an inviting room with a large fireplace, is decorated with warm colors, rustic Western artifacts, and Native American-style rugs. Open at 4:00 P.M., cocktails and complimentary appetizers are served and stories of the day's activities are shared. It's adults-only after 9:00 P.M., with live entertainment and dancing that begins at 6:30 P.M. During the summer and holidays, the Waggin' Tongue Lounge by the pool is open daily from 11:30 A.M. to 4:00 P.M. and reopens at 8:30 P.M. after the Saturday night barbecue. The General Store is happy to deliver snacks, beverages, wine, beer, and other goodies to your room.

Children's World: All summer long and at holiday times, counselors conduct an active schedule of arts and crafts, scavenger hunts, volleyball, hikes, croquet, and other outdoor games.

From age seven and up, children can participate in horseback riding on the trail rides ($40 for one hour) or in private lessons. Younger children get corral rides and equestrian-care lessons ($20). Everyone learns more about ranch animals at the on-site petting zoo. Children's golf and tennis lessons are also available. Tennis lessons are given for ages five to fourteen, twice a week for a half hour ($10). Young Tigers golf lessons are also twice a week for a half hour ($35) for ages seven to sixteen. Children love the private lake, where they can participate in fishing, boating, or canoeing ($25 to $38 per hour). Summer evenings may include campfires with sing-alongs and stories, which are always better at the lake setting. A Family Rodeo is staged weekly in the summer—this is every kid's dream of being a cowboy come true. After watching wranglers perform, they get to participate in branding (on leather or wood), roping, and rodeo-style games; a Western barbecue completes the evening.

The arts-and-crafts room is open daily year-round from 9:30 A.M. to 5:30 P.M., where activities are ongoing. One-hour activities such as disc golf, chalk art, relay races and lawn games, dodge ball or kick ball, face painting, and various water games are scheduled during the day—children can drop in and out as they are interested in the activity.

L'il Wrangler Club has morning and afternoon sessions for children ages four to ten, Monday through Friday; cost is generally $25 to $35 per session. There's a price reduction for two children. Activities last for three hours and include indoor and outdoor fun. Ages four to six are grouped together, as are ages seven to ten, and may have the same activity, such as Fish Fun, but each suited to their age; e.g., the older children will go boating on the lake while younger ones fish from the shore. Wild, Wild West, Dinosaur Days, Olympics, and Wacky Water Days are some of the other themes. Kiddie Korral is the ranch's program for children ages three to five and is offered Sunday through Friday from 6:00 to 9:00 P.M. for dinner and evening fun ($25 per child). Kids ages six to ten have their nature cookouts, a pool bash, barbecues, and movies from 6:00 P.M.

'Tweens (eleven to twelve years old) share some things, like movies, but have their own dinner activities at the Chuck-wagon Grill, lake, or Adobe Camp as well. Late night they may have bingo, talent shows, country dancing, or an adventure at the Adobe Camp. The summertime activities for teens involve their favorite things: eating, music, movies, and sports. Teens have their own section of the weekly barbecue dinner events, plus off-property movies, late-night campfires, or movies at the ranch.

During the winter, the arts and activities room is open from 10:00 A.M. to 4:00 P.M., but supervision is intermittent. Golf, tennis, and horseback-riding lessons fill in the other times. Children's and family activities are scheduled on holidays, but less frequently than in the summer. Check the daily program. Some are complimentary, others have a fee, such as archery (two hours, $25 per person), creative beading (cost varies), or guided mountain biking ($30 with bike rental).

Recreation: Most recreational activities at Alisal have fees. Family Times allow sharing of two-hour nature walks, archery, a ropes course, and crafts such as tie-dye and creative beading. Evening entertainment begins at 8:30 or 9:00 P.M. Family bingo, talent night, storytelling, country dancing, and more are offered. 'Tweens and teens have their own programs. Kids and family activities are pretty much nonstop from early morning to late night, with lots of choices.

Be sure to saunter over to the barn to be matched with the perfect mount for the twice-daily trail rides ($65 per two-hour ride). A breakfast ride is offered three times a week in summer, twice a week during the rest of the year. On summer evenings (Tuesday and Thursday) extend the day with evening rides from 5:00 to 7:00 P.M., or participate in the weekly summer rodeo. More than 50 miles of trails meander through oak and sycamore groves in the rolling hills and along the lake. Wranglers are happy to share a bit of advice about riding, information about the ranch, or maybe even some tall tales along the way.

Trading trails for tees, the gently rambling fairways of two eighteen-hole golf courses are graced with eucalyptus as well as oak and sycamore trees and occasionally a deer or two. Each of the two championship golf courses, the River Course and the Ranch Course, has distinct characteristics shaped by its unique terrain. The driving range, putting green, and practice trap can keep you so busy you'll ride off into the sunset on a golf cart rather than a horse! The resident pro and the pro shop can help

with anything from lessons to new equipment. On the tennis courts (seven in all, located in one of the most scenic areas of the ranch) you're likely to find a good game from 8:00 A.M. to 5:30 P.M., or the resident pro conducting private and group lessons.

If your interests are more wet-and-wild, you might swim in the large outdoor heated pool (certain times for adults only) or head to the lake and hop aboard a sailboat, rowboat, paddleboat, canoe, or kayak ($25 to $50). Even beginners find lots of enjoyment in the sailing and fishing lessons offered. The spring-fed lake—man-made, but mature and encompassing one hundred acres—is stocked with bass, bluegill, and catfish, much to the delight of every angler. A "catch and release" policy protects the fish.

Mornings bring yoga, Pilates, and aqua exercise for those energetic people over sixteen. After riding, golfing, playing tennis, swimming, sailing, and fishing, you can always jog, bicycle, join a guided nature walk, play volleyball, badminton, horseshoes, shuffleboard, croquet, or boccie ball, or take on the new challenge course. Tired yet? Indoors you might play pool or table tennis in the recreation room or relax in the adults-only library with a good book or board game by the fireplace. Be sure to save energy for the evenings, filled with square dancing, cookouts, and movies as well. Every summer Wednesday brings a country fair and rodeo. And strolling through the quaint town of Solvang is always a treat. You are in wine country, so enjoy a tour of the vineyards, a little wine tasting, and the spectacular beauty of the Santa Ynez Valley.

1054 Alisal Road
Solvang, California 93463
(805) 688–6411, (800) 4–ALISAL
www.alisal.com

COFFEE CREEK RANCH
Trinity Center, California

Coffee Creek Ranch, Northern California's only three-diamond dude ranch, is located approximately 300 miles north of San Francisco. Surrounded by National Forest and the Trinity Alps Wilderness Area, the ranch covers 367 acres along Coffee Creek and is home to wranglers and dudes alike. In 1877, Old Charley Henseley staked three claims along Coffee Creek; in 1900 he lost them all in a poker game to Ben Pinkham for $1.00. Mrs. Pinkham started a boarding house for the miners, and it all began then, evolving into a dude ranch in 1946. In 1966 the original ranch house burned completely; built in 1899, Oak Grove Cottage is now the oldest building on the ranch and is currently being restored. The ranch has been in the Hartman family since 1976, being handed down to the next generation, current owner/managers Alicia and Shane Ryan.

Whether you are an old pro at horseback riding or a greenhorn mounting up for the first time, the ranch hands will ensure that your horse and your excursion match your abilities. You can roam this territory all day long or ease into your new cowboy lifestyle more slowly with a half-hour lesson or a two-hour trail ride. Copper Creek Ranch is open from Easter to Thanksgiving.

Accommodations: The sixteen cozy, secluded cottages (one or two bedrooms) are scattered among the trees. Rustic on the outside, all modern and cozy on the inside, each cottage is decorated according to its brand; Circle B for instance has butterflies, bears, and Bigfoot. Spring and fall are geared toward adults; kids are welcome, although there's no specific program or activities for them. In summer, however, families rule. One-week stays are required, beginning on Saturday. Per-person rates for a one-bedroom are $1,075 for adults ($967.50 for ages fifty-five and up, a nice touch), teens are $1,005, children three to twelve are $955, and the under-three set is $300. Cribs, playpens, and highchairs are complimentary. Satellite TV in the main lodge only. The rates increase by only $10 to $20 per person for two-bedrooms, so book early! Rates include your private cabin in the woods, daily maid service, three meals daily, all activities and entertainment, the children's program—just about everything except horseback riding, which has extra fees in the summer. A two-hour ride is $40, breakfast and picnic rides are $45, half-day is $50, all-day is $85, gymkana is $25, and the overnight pack trip is $150. Now, here's the real deal: A weekly rate of $350 gives you all rides (at least four hours daily) and the overnight trip! Junior riders, ages six to eleven, receive one complimentary lesson. Friday is departure day, and the horses' day off.

Dining: Recognizing the healthy appetites that fresh air and exercise can generate, the main dining room serves up hearty, nutritious meals with fresh fruit and vegetables, Black Angus beef, and homemade bread from old family recipes. Outdoor barbecues and poolside cookouts are friendly evening events; Mexican and Italian buffets please everyone. For an adventure, ride out to a cowboy breakfast or a picnic on the trail. Beer and wine are served in the Pony Room.

Children's World: In the summer months the youth program, a complimentary service operating from 9:00 A.M. to 5:00 P.M., Saturday through Thursday, attracts children ages three to seventeen. On its fun-filled schedule are archery, nature walks, pedalboating, gold panning, games, and crafts. Ages three to five are designated Cowboys and Cowgirls, and get free pony rides, playtime with the Corral Critters (rabbits, lambs, pigs), lawn games, and story time; and just wait to hear your child tell about feeding the ducks and geese! Junior Wranglers, for ages six to eleven, branch out into canoeing, swimming, and fishing in the pond, and one free riding lesson. Bronc Busters (twelve- to seventeen-year-olds) get to do it all plus their own special roping lessons, overnight campout, orienteering, rifle and trap shoot instruction, plus hiking to the lake. Although there's no formal program in the evening, counselors are generally present at the evening family activities. For children under three, the weekly rate includes babysitting while you're out on the trail. If additional babysitting is required, you can make arrangements for $6.25 an hour.

Recreation: Saddle up and head into the wilderness for an all-day or a two-hour ride. You'll venture up into the mountains and through the wooded landscape along a clear fresh stream; maybe you'll spot a deer or a bear. Even "dudes" will soon experience the friendly spirit of a trail ride.

Try your hand at fishing; you've a choice of stream, river, pond, lake, or wilderness—fly-fishing or bait casting. The locals say that Coffee Creek yields up some mighty fine trout, so an afternoon with rod and reel may turn into a fresh-fish supper. If fishing's not for you, how about panning for gold in the creek? Perhaps you'll test your keen eye on the archery or rifle range. Hiking trips are an option, and mountain bike trails run through the wilderness area. When not out and about, enjoy the heated swimming pool, volleyball, shuffleboard, basketball, or pedal boating. Doing a lovely bit of nothing is also an option—just let the mountain air work its magic.

Evenings are lively at the ranch, with more activities than days of the week. Hayrides, bonfires, dancing, bingo and talent shows, karaoke and a live band, and even a rodeo liven things up after dark.

HC 2, Box 4940
Trinity Center, California 96091
(530) 266–3343, (800) 624–4480
www.coffeecreekranch.com

HYATT REGENCY LAKE LAS VEGAS RESORT, SPA AND CASINO
Henderson, Nevada

In this twenty-one-acre gloriously natural setting of mountains, desert, and lake, it's hard to believe you're only 17 miles from the glitz and glitter of the Las Vegas Strip. It's also just a short day trip to Lake Mead, Hoover Dam, Red Rock Canyon, and the Valley of Fire. Who says you can't have everything? Reflecting the best desert architecture, the Moroccan flavor is apparent in the high arches and deep loggias, the

grilled ironwork, and the relaxed, open feeling engendered by mountains in the desert. Comfortably terraced into the hillside, Hyatt Lake Las Vegas rates a Mobile four-star, AAA Four-Diamond ranking.

Accommodations: The 493 guest rooms and 47 suites reflect the open-air style of the Mediterranean, and most have views of the lake, mountains, or golf course. The theme is Moroccan and features imported furnishings;

most rooms have small balconies and all have refrigerators. A real pleasure is that the windows actually open, so you can enjoy the wonderfully clear desert air. Rates range from $129 in mid-June (low season) to $399 in January to April (high season). Families can upgrade to an Alcove suite for $100 or an executive one-bedroom suite for an additional $175. A resort fee of $15 per room per night covers incidentals. As always with Hyatt, if you desire a second room, there is a 50% discount, based on availability. Family Fun Experience also offers special options for families such as kids eat free, water toys, and nonmotor watercraft included. A four-night minimum is required; rates begin at $125 per night.

Dining: Japengo, the showcase restaurant, features a full sushi bar (rated best in the valley by *Zagat*), a presentation kitchen where you can watch the culinary artistry, and a menu inspired by the Pacific Rim and exotic Asian flavors. Inspired by the Moroccan tradition of cooking in an earthenware pot, Café Tajine, open for breakfast, lunch, and dinner, serves New American cuisine with an international flavor. Dine indoors or out, with the ever-present scenic views. The poolside Sandsabar & Grill keeps you well fed and watered. The twenty-four-hour Marrakesh Express is the place to have that special coffee, shop for the unusual delicacy to take home or enjoy in your room, or indulge in a late-night dessert in the desert. Catch your favorite midday game or have a nightcap at the Baraka Bar, inside the Baraka Casino; or people-watch, as a change from the scenery, while sipping a drink at the Arabesque Lounge in the lobby. Restaurants have a children's menu in the summer or during promotions only.

Children's World: The Moroccan theme of Camp Mud Castle fits right into the desertlike environs. Open daily year-round, hours are from 10:00 A.M. to 5:00 P.M. and again from 6:00 to 10:00 P.M. for an evening session. Advance reservations are required. As with other Hyatt Camps, a good-size room is dedicated to camp activities that are diverse, and directly related to the unique aspects and location of each property. Petroglyph art, hula hoop and limbo, sundown fishing, a trip to the "swimmin' hole," summer toad and lizard hunts, and playground free time are just some of the things youngsters do here. Evenings bring stargazing and a starlight dinner along with games, movies, drumming, and karaoke contests. Planned for ages three through twelve, the cost is $27 for 10:00 A.M. to 1:00 P.M. or 2:00 to 5:00 P.M. sessions; or $40 until 2:00 P.M. with lunch. The evening session is also $40 and includes dinner. And when they say "daily," they mean "daily"—kids even have their own New Year's Eve gala party!

Recreation: Being ranked twenty-eighth in *Golf Digest's* "Top 75 Golf Resorts in America" apparently isn't sufficient for this resort. Aiming to be a golf mecca, in addition to the two Jack Nicklaus Signature Golf Courses, they've completed the Falls, a course designed by Tom Weiskopf, with dramatic elevation changes from desert to mountainous landscapes. The Falls has been voted "Best New Upscale Public Course" by *Golf Digest* and one of the "Top Ten You Can Play" by *Golf Magazine.* All the courses take advantage of the dramatic desert scenery and the largest privately owned lake in Nevada; the Falls even overlooks the famous Las Vegas Strip, seen in an amazing natural setting. Reflection Bay Golf Club is home to the Nicklaus/Flick Game Improvement School if your game needs a boost. Master plans for the resort include up to six golf courses, so stay tuned.

The heart of the resort is the 320-acre lake, with 10 miles of shoreline and beaches for water play and sunning. Take a spin in a paddleboat or kayak, sail, relax, and go fishing in an electric boat or rent a bicycle and ride along the lakeshore.

The daily Spa Moulay membership is included with the resort fee, so take advantage between 6:00 A.M. and 9:00 P.M. You'll find nine treatment rooms to pamper you (extra cost for treatments). After a workout at the fitness center, two outdoor pools beckon you to relax in the tented cabana shaded by palm trees. The children's pool with water slide and sandy "beaches" keeps youngsters happy for hours. Sport Court is the place to play volleyball, short court tennis, or basketball; a putting green, croquet, and horseshoes while away an afternoon. A complimentary bird-watching backpack sends you off with binoculars and an identification book, while a stargazing kit shows you planets and stars.

The Baraka Casino is European-styled, with gaming tables and, of course, slot machines. The difference here is that it includes scenic views from the two-story windows, unique to casinos in this area. If you want more and bigger, a complimentary shuttle will take you to the Strip. Actually, during the day, and in small doses, Las Vegas is an exciting place for kids too. The various hotels outdo each other for exciting attractions: Walk under and around lions in a glass den at MGM Grand, acrobats fly through the lobby at Circus Circus Adventuredome; an outside roller coaster circles New York–New York; at the Luxor, learn about ancient Egypt through IMAX movies and ride an elevator almost sideways to the top of the pyramid; knights joust at the Excalibur; Atlantis falls at Caesars; and the waters dance to music at the Bellagio—the list goes on and on. This is just a sample, so you see why making several trips is not a bad idea.

Closer to home you'll find MonteLago Village, connected to the resort by walkways and water taxis, and offering dining, shops, and entertainment along the water's edge. Reminiscent of an ancient Mediterranean village, you can stroll the narrow shaded streets or shop on the two-level bridge as if you were promenading on Florence's Ponte Vecchio in Italy.

---

101 Montelargo Boulevard
Henderson, Nevada 89011
(702) 567–1234, (800) 233–1234
www.lakelasvegas.hyatt.com

THE INN OF THE SEVENTH MOUNTAIN
Bend, Oregon

A vacation in the woods and mountains of the great Pacific Northwest, the serenity of hiking in the forest, and the excitement of exploring the Deschutes River whisk you away from city life and everyday routines. The Inn of the Seventh Mountain, located on the sunny side of the Cascade Mountains of central Oregon, is a year-round family resort that boasts a cool forest setting and warm hospitality. Nearby Mount Bachelor is the seventh peak in the chain of mountains running south from the Columbia River and the border with Washington State, hence the name. The resort aims to be "a place where you can interact with nature in a hundred different ways, and interact with your family in the only way that really matters." Encircled by peaks, lakes, and meadows, set in the midst of tranquil beauty with all the necessary amenities, the resort makes it easy to accomplish that goal.

Accommodations: You can choose from a variety of accommodations, from a room to a three-bedroom villa; 180 units are spread throughout twenty-three buildings. Rates vary from $89 to $309, depending on size and season. The highest period is mid-June though August and winter holidays; other periods are lower. Room rates begin at $89; one-bedroom suites are $139 to $189; two-bedrooms are always $259; and three-bedrooms are $229 to $309. Specials are always changing, but as an example, the Whitewater Summer Family Getaway includes two nights' lodging in a one-bedroom condo, breakfast, dinner, and rafting for four. Packages start at $549 and include tax. Hang on, 'cause that's a good deal! Most of the rooms have a private balcony; the condominium units have one to three bedrooms, fireplace, kitchen, and balcony. The architecture is modern yet rustic, and natural-wood facades blend well with the wooded landscape. Condominium decor includes rich textures and earthen colors, brick tiles, and folk art. Improvements are ongoing and the inn has renovated "everything but the scenery."

Dining: Award-winning chef Christopher Berning has joined the inn and opened a new restaurant, Seasons, open daily for dinner. Using local products, the menu is quintessential Pacific Northwest, creatively prepared. Smoked mussels steamed in Oregon chardonnay, or a grilled Black Angus tenderloin served on smoked salmon and morel mushroom ravioli with grain mustard demiglace is just a small sample of what awaits your taste buds. Big Eddy's Café and Provision Company is open all day for breakfast, lunch, dinner, and light snacks. Rimrock Pub is open nightly for drinks and socializing.

Children's World: In addition to individual babysitting, which the staff can help you arrange, events are scheduled all day long for your child's enjoyment. In summer and winter the recreation office publishes a flyer, *This Week at the Inn,* to help you keep track of all the activities. From Memorial Day to Labor Day, Christmas, and spring break, Kids' Quest is a supervised play program for children ages five to twelve. A daily charge of $40 covers lunch, arts-and-crafts classes, movies, and more from 9:00 A.M. to 4:00 P.M. each day. Half-day programs are also available for $15 each session; from 9:00 A.M. to noon and 1:00 to 4:00 P.M. Evening programs are available on demand, with a minimum number of participants.

Your child might also participate in a tennis clinic, take a hayride or a sleigh ride, search out treasures on a scavenger hunt, or take a field trip. There are also two playgrounds and a wading pool and two swimming pools for water recreation.

In winter Mount Bachelor Ski School offers day care and ski/board lessons for children.

The West Village Lodge at the base of the mountain has a day-care center for little ones six weeks to ten years old; age-appropriate activities such as crafts, videos, story time, and circles are planned from 8:30 A.M. to 4:30 P.M.; 7:30 A.M. to 4:00 P.M. on weekends. Daily rates are $45 for children thirty months and older; twenty-nine months and younger is $50. An hourly rate (limited space) is $13, with a two-hour minimum. Children may bring their lunch, or box lunch is available for $5.00, and parents are welcome to eat with their children. For an additional $25, Snowplay is a one-hour introduction to skiing that can be added for three-year-olds. For children four and over, Mountain Masters combines day care and a half-day lesson for $105 not including rentals. Mountain Masters for ages four to twelve is $79 for a full day with lunch; $59 for a half day (two-hour lesson). Rentals are $14.00 and lunch for a half-day session is $5.00. Children are grouped by age, ability, and sport—either skiing or snowboarding. A Guaranteed Kids Package for ages six to twelve ensures beginners learn everything they need to start riding the lifts and enjoying the mountain. An all-day program includes morning and afternoon instruction, lift ticket, and lunch for $79. Children are grouped by age and ability.

Recreation: The recreation department at the inn plans activities for every member of the family, concentrating on water sports, swimming, tennis, and raft trips on the river in the summer; and ice-skating, cross-country skiing, and sleigh rides in the winter. Wintertime also means the thrill of downhill skiing at nearby Mount Bachelor, only 14 miles from the inn.

In summer you just have to discover the beauty of the Deschutes River. Take a relaxing canoe ride and get back to nature, or join a moonlight raft trip. For more daring souls, there are guided white-water raft trips through the rapids. If you prefer to take in the scenic river from land, horseback riding is a great alternative; group trail rides run along the river and into the Deschutes National Forest. The National Forest is also a picturesque haven for hikers and joggers. For the fisherman, the recreation office arranges trips to the favorite spots with a naturalist guide. For a rock-climbing challenge, Smith Rock State Park is one of the best places in the West. Golfers enjoy that the inn is next door to Widgi Creek, one of central Oregon's most popular courses.

Back at the inn, take a dip in one of the two pools, rent a bicycle, play a good game of tennis on one of the four Plexipave courts (group clinics and private lessons are offered), work out in an aerobic-exercise class at the nearby Athletic Club, try your talents in an arts-and-crafts class, go in-line skating, or get lucky in a bingo game. The rec office organizes all sorts of ball games— softball, volleyball, football, and soccer. Join a hayride, complete with a stop for a marshmallow roast, play table tennis, take in a poolside movie, or head to the video-game room. Then relax in the sauna or one of the hot whirlpool baths.

The Oregon High Desert Museum, just 6 miles south of Bend, discloses the natural and cultural history of this region. The museum makes for a fun as well as educational afternoon.

This part of Oregon experiences beautiful Indian summers, so activities continue well into the fall. During the winter months special treats include ice-skating, sleigh rides, cross-country skiing (with lessons for novices), and horseback riding through the snow-covered landscape.

The inn is the closest lodging facility to the Mount Bachelor ski resort (800–829–2442, www.mtbachelor.com) and provides daily transportation to the mountain base. With 3,365 vertical feet, seventy-one runs, 3,683 skiable acres, and plenty of dry powder (an average of 350 inches yearly), Mount Bachelor means excellent downhill skiing for all levels of ability. You'll also find snowboarding, cross-country and telemark skiing, snowshoeing, tubing, and more. The five lodges at the mountain have restaurants for breakfast, lunch, snacks, and cocktails; ski shops; and the ski school, which offers group lessons for all ranges of expertise as well as private lessons. The season is long here, attracting many visitors late into spring.

18575 Southwest Century Drive
Bend, Oregon 97702
(541) 382–8711, (800) 452–6810
www.seventhmountain.com

LA COSTA RESORT AND SPA

Carlsbad, California

Everyone should have at least one spa experience in their life. La Costa is a luxurious resort, a serious spa, and somewhat of a legend. In fact, it was the first establishment to revive the spa regimen as Americans became more health-conscious in the 1960s. Today you can pursue a program of exercise and sound nutrition, redefining your lifestyle after years of sedentary executive matters; or you can indulge in a program of sheer pampering, relieving the stress and tensions of the everyday world.

Located in Carlsbad, just thirty minutes north of San Diego and ninety minutes south of Los Angeles, La Costa enjoys lovely Southern California weather and a picturesque setting of rolling hills. The 400 lush green acres of this four-diamond resort provide an oasis of relaxation.

Accommodations: Four hundred seventy-four guest rooms and suites are all decorated in a Spanish style, and situated around courtyards, near the tennis facilities, adjacent to the spa, and along the golf courses. Rates are $210 to $300 for a standard plaza room, $260 to $350 for deluxe rooms, $335 to $425 for spa rooms, and suites range from $385 to $475. Children under eighteen staying in their parents' room are free; cribs are provided without charge. Packages can provide a savings. For example, Legoland is just minutes from the resort and has partnered with the hotel to provide plaza accommodations, breakfast, and tickets to Legoland. The package is for two adults and one child; extra children are $45 each. Be sure to inquire about the spa, golf, and tennis package plans. A $20 per night resort fee is assessed for incidentals.

Dining: Just because this is a spa, don't expect diets and tasteless tofu. Oh, no. Dining here is gourmet and still healthy. Legends California Bistro features classic California cuisine, along with vegetarian selections from the Chopra Center. It's open daily from 6:30 A.M. to 9:00 P.M.; 10:00 P.M. on weekends, when a jazz trio plays. Dine indoors or out in the California sunshine. At the Marketplace you'll find your Starbucks morning coffee, TCBY treats, and an Internet cafe, if you need a technology fix. Fire and water combine nicely in the Bluefire Grill; fountains, a fireplace with handblown glass wall, and grills set the stage for scrumptious dining at lunch and dinner. If you choose the outdoor patio, another firepit warms and cheers you. Start lunch with warm duck confit with poached pears, or maybe one of the sandwiches that take three lines of the menu to describe. Free-range meat, coastal specialties, and fresh vegetables are the base, while California is the inspiration. Saturday evenings, the telescope is set up for stargazing, and the Sunday Champagne Brunch is also here, complete with live music. Fresh juice drinks, smoothies, and light, healthy food are served at the Spa Café for an after-treatment treat. Weather permitting, weekend lunches and drinks are served poolside at the Splash Bar & Café.

Children's World: Camp La Costa is active year-round and operates from 9:00 A.M. to 4:00 P.M. daily. For three- to twelve-year-olds, the fun includes golf and tennis lessons, swimming, kite flying, and arts and crafts. Kids not only enjoy themselves, they often learn something too, as they experience the surroundings in imaginative and entertaining ways. Weekly themes set the stage, whether it's Star Struck, Time Travel, Under the Big Top, Story Book, sports, science or adventure, or Culture Shock, experiencing what it might be like to live in other countries. The fee is $50 for a full day, $35 for the morning session (9:00 A.M. to 1:00 P.M.), and $30 for the afternoon (1:00 to 4:00 P.M.). Lunch is available for $6.50. If less time is desired, the hourly rate is $10. On Friday and Saturday nights camp take over with dinner and entertainment from 6:00 to 10:00 P.M.; the fee is $45 a night. Individual babysitting can be requested through the concierge.

Recreation: La Costa's spa awards are many: Top Ten recognition from *Condé Nast Traveler, Travel + Leisure, Zagat Survey,* and *Spa Finder;* Top 50 Golf Courses from *Golfweek* and *Links Magazine;* and for tennis, the top 100 resorts in the world from *Racquet* magazine and the Top 50 Tennis Resorts from *Tennis* magazine. The spa programs and facilities are extensive. Facials from deep cleansing to mud packs, massages of the shiatsu and Swedish variety, herbal wraps, body scrubs, exfoliation, aromatherapy, reflexology, and hydrotherapy baths are just some of the methods utilized to revive weary guests. Athletic Club facilities include swimming pools, a weight room, a cardiovascular room, Pilates, spinning, and a jogging track. You can join one of the many exercise classes offered throughout the day or, with an exercise physiologist, you can devise a personalized fitness program. Individualized analysis also extends to dietary counseling and menu planning. This is, after all, California, and some of the special lectures and workshops include Tai Chi, Intuitive Solutions, Goddess Retreat (for women only, of course),

or Creating a Life Plan. Check to see if there's something of interest to you during your visit.

The Chopra Center is a unique place for healing and deep rejuvenation. Yoga and meditation are offered, along with Ayurvedic treatments and three- to five-day programs. Deepak Chopra, a Western-trained physician from India, has done much to introduce principles of the ancient Indian health system to the West. Ayurvedic refers to the "knowledge of life" and has been practiced for over 5,000 years.

Golf enthusiasts find their exercise on the two eighteen-hole championship courses. At the Golf School the latest technology is used to scrutinize and improve your game. Tennis players have twenty-one courts at their disposal and can choose grass, clay, or hard-court surfaces. Clinics are held daily, and private instruction is easily arranged. The golf and tennis pro shops offer a wide range of equipment and apparel. Croquet, bicycles, and five heated swimming pools complete the picture of exercise potential at La Costa. Rejuvenation potential is unlimited.

San Diego is a paradise for children; among other attractions are Birch Aquarium, San Diego Wild Animal Park, Seaworld Adventure Park, and the famous San Diego Zoo. Old Town San Diego and Carlsbad, or Village by the Sea, are day excursions the entire family will enjoy. Legoland is just minutes away, and irresistible for kids (and many adults!).

2100 Costa del Mar Road
Carlsbad, California 92009
(760) 438–9111, (800) 854–5000
www.lacosta.com

MONTECITO SEQUOIA RESORT

King's Canyon National Park, California

How about vacationing with Earth's largest living thing? No monsters or even whales here, we're talking about the giant sequoia trees. Set on forty-two acres within the Giant Sequoia National Monument, the Montecito Sequoia Resort is in partnership with the Sequoia National Forest to protect these incredible trees and give people a chance to play and appreciate nature in this wonderful area. Between King's Canyon and Sequoia National Parks, the resort sits at 7,500 feet elevation, on Lake Homavalo. Not only do they have a children's program, they cover the entire gamut from toddlers to seniors. Yes! Parents, this is your chance. Be honest, now. Sometimes, as you send your precious child off to frolic and play all day, don't you wish you could go to camp too? Is there maybe just a tinge of envy, a nostalgic remembrance of summer days of your own youth, when nothing stretched before you but time and fun? Well, rejoice! Montecito Sequoia has over thirty varied activities and programs for everyone! This resort epitomizes our philosophy of family travel—time together and time apart. Kids and parents can join each other's activities or do their own, or both.

Be sure to fill your gas tank in Fresno or Visalia as no gas is available near the parks. Stop at the park's Lodgepole Visitor Center on your way up and brush up on your Sierra Nevada and sequoia natural history, see the Crystal Caves, and take the short drive to visit The General Sherman and the General Grant Giant Sequoia Trees—the earth's largest tree and the official Christmas Tree of America. Then on to the resort for a rollicking good time and quintessential camp fun. The resort is open 365 days a year and is uniquely beautiful in each season. Rated one of the Top Ten Family Resorts in the country by *Travel Smart* newsletter and *Family Travel Forum,* it has also been featured in *National Geographic Traveler, Travel + Leisure,* and *Food & Wine* magazines.

Accommodations: Approximately 206 guests can be accommodated. Four lodges contain thirty-six hotel rooms with private baths that can accommodate two to eight people; three two-room suites suit larger families. All rooms have either king- or queen-size beds and deluxe bunks, with daily housekeeping included. For the really hardy, there are five lakeside cabins (propane heating) and eight mountain-view cabins (wood-burning stoves). Decor is comfortable and similar to hotel rooms— except—the two bathhouses are nearby. Right, no facilities in the cabins.

From late-June until Labor Day, High Sierra Family Camp is in high gear, with three-, four-, six-, and eight-night camp sessions available. A six-night all-inclusive package in the cabins is $882 per adult, $845 for teens, $798 for youths two to twelve years, and $121 for infants under two years. Package cost in the lodge is $992, $961, $929, and $121. In summer, one-night stays are allowed only on Saturday; rates are $130 to $160. Summer Family Camp rates include all meals, the children's programs, and most activities for the entire family (horseback riding and waterskiing are extra). Fall rates include lodging, buffet meals, evening activities, and snacks available twenty-four hours daily. Rates are $125 per adult per night in the lodge and $105 in the cabins; ages four through six are $59 and children two through four are $20 each per night, in either accommodation. Stay mid-week, and you may have three nights for the price of two. From mid-November, a two-night minimum is required in winter. Winter Week-ender packages are from $145 per adult per night in the lodge, $115 in the cabins; ages four through sixteen are $65 each and children one through three are $16 per night. Rates include all meals, snacks, and the children's program for ages four to eleven. There's no program for the under-three set. Spring again includes all meals and some evening activities; rates for a three-night package are $250 per adult in the lodge, $210 in the cabins; youths from four to sixteen are $130 in either accommodation.

Dining: Guests consistently rave about the food at the lodge. Award-winning Chef Eric Cook and his staff take care to prepare only the freshest and finest selections and the choices available are impressive. California cuisine, vegetarian specialties, and kid-friendly dishes are all part of the package. Mothers especially are delighted to dine so well, with no cooking or dishes! Meals are hearty, and served buffet-style. Breakfast choices include eggs and cereal, along with waffles, pancakes, bacon, and sausage. Fresh fruit is served at every meal. Lunch offers not only sandwiches and salads, but hot entrees as well. Dinner features fresh vegetables, a salad bar, and choice of several delicious entrees. And guess what? Dessert is available from lunchtime on into the evening, along with hot soups and soft ice cream! Good thing there's all those activities. And heaven forbid anyone should ever be hungry; fruit, cereal, snacks, and do-it-yourself sandwiches are available twenty-four hours daily in the main lodge, along with hot and cold beverages, including Starbucks coffee.

Children's World: Separate programs divided by age for Minnows (two years), Tadpoles (three and four years), and Chipmunks (five and six years) have two adventure cabins and two play yards, a gymnastics area, and their own space on the lake. Summer activities include pony rides, dock fishing, insect safaris, kiddie Olympics, swimming, artistic fun, boating, and more depending on age. In winter, it's for ages four to eleven years for two hours in the morning and two hours in the afternoon; there's snow play, snowshoeing, skiing, and indoor activities. Montecito Sequoia's philosophy is that learning is fun, and children love to learn. The summer programs for youths and teens are always "free choice" where kids tell the counselors what they want to do—their favorite activity or stay with the group. When they do, they are then fully committed to the activity and get excited about it, regardless of age. Age groups are Marmots (seven to eight years), Bobcats (nine to ten years), Cougars (eleven to twelve years) and Bears (thirteen to seventeen years). All have separate leaders and KILTS (teens in training for leadership) who help with choices. Parents may join at times, and evening activities are for everyone. A typical day includes the morning Pow Wow planning, four activity sessions, the evening program, and nightly campfire.

Recreation: As we stated in the beginning, summer has about thirty-five listed activities, and in winter, count on at least twenty. Most recreation is included in the rates; there are additional charges for horseback riding, mountain bikes, and waterskiing; instruction and guided tours outside of summer camp are extra, but very reasonable. Children's programs are always included in the rate, when they're offered (summer and winter). Forests, lakes, and mountains provide the backdrop for learning and fun. Waterskiing, wakeboarding, canoes, paddleboats, sailboats, stream and lake fishing, the swimming pool, and hot tub are starters for water experiences. Twenty horses and two teaching arenas, scenic trail rides, hiking, and mountain biking range over the mountain; at the resort try archery, trampolines, tennis, a golf cage, fencing, a rock climbing wall, and the rifle range. The list just goes on and on. In summer, some activities are weekly, like the Artist of the Week program which teaches watercolor and oils; and there are once-a-week "happenings" like carnivals and fort building. Evening activities have something for the whole family to share and have fun: games, karaoke, night hikes, and stargazing an amazing sky, Casino Night, movies, and theme nights. Traditional camp activities for adults, even grandparents, are as exciting as for the kids. Whatever your skill level, the staff is ready and able to instruct and help. Winter brings snowshoeing, dog-sledding, tubing, ice-skating, snow bikes, skiing, and snowboarding. Montecito Sequoia has been voted the number two cross-country ski resort, with 82 kilometers of trails.

8000 Generals Highway, Box 858
King's Canyon National Park, California
93633
(559) 565–3399, (800) 843–8677
www.montecitosequoia.com
www.mslodge.com

NORTHSTAR-AT-TAHOE
Truckee, California

Tahoe has long been known for the clear deep waters of a 200-square-mile lake, the majestic mountain peaks of the Sierra Nevada, and its proximity to the entertainment and nightlife of Nevada casinos. Northstar-at-Tahoe enables vacationers to partake of all of these. Open year-round, it is a 2,420-acre mountain resort just 6 miles from Lake Tahoe that offers winter and summer family sports activities. Lake Tahoe straddles the California/Nevada state line and at 6,223 feet is the largest alpine lake in North America. It is the second deepest lake in the U.S. (1,645 feet at its deepest point) and so clear you can see a dinner plate at 250 meters. And who do you suppose figured out that if you were to tip Lake Tahoe over, the water would be 14.5 inches deep over all of California?

With the Nevada state line only 7 miles away, side trips to gambling casinos are manageable excursions for grown-ups. But it's not all about glitz. Northstar has long received accolades as one of the top family ski resorts in the United States. *FamilyFun,* *Ski Magazine, Child* magazine, and *Family Life* magazine have all recognized Northstar for its family programs and children's ski and snowboard school. The resort was featured as a top family destination on NBC's *Today Show.* Northstar is dedicated to the environment, and their mission is to treat it with respect. The championship golf course is a certified Audubon Cooperative Sanctuary, and the resort promotes environmental planning, water quality management, and revegetation practices. Northstar participates in Sustainable Slopes, an environmental charter for ski areas.

A new project, The Village at Northstar, with phase one due in December 2005, will combine lodging, shopping, strolling, and dining in a village ambience with lots of new retail stores, a Mexican restaurant, a family-style gourmet pizzeria, a fine dining venue, and everyone's favorites, an ice cream parlor and chocolatier. A new, high-speed quad chair lift is already in place; with the high-speed gondola, you'll get there in half the time. For the 2005–2006 season, lifts are being rerouted to open more intermediate runs. Phase two, due in 2006, will add more shops and 192 condominium units. So right now, there's a lot of redoing and renaming going on, but it's all for a better mountain.

Accommodations: The lodging facilities include hotel-type rooms, condominiums ranging in size from studios to four-bedroom units, and three- to six-bedroom homes. With the exception of the lodge rooms, all have a fully equipped kitchen and fireplace; many units have a private balcony overlooking the wooded landscape and the mountains. The wooden facades and rustic designs of the buildings blend well with the natural setting.

Village rooms are $129 to $145 in summer, $209 to $255 in winter. Two-bedroom condominiums are $225 to $255 in summer, $319 to $439 in winter. The Ski Trails lodging is closest to the slopes; ski-in, ski-out on-trail condominiums range from $245 to $329 for a one-bedroom and $345 to $439 for a two-bedroom. Rates do not include a $5.00 per night resort fee. Cribs are provided at no additional charge. Package plans are available throughout the year and provide a savings. For example, Stay and Golf Free begins at $59 per person. The on-site transportation system is complimentary for Northstar guests. Guests also have complimentary access to the Swim and Racquet Club with swimming pools, fitness center, tennis courts, and outdoor hot tubs. A Teen Center is located here as well.

Dining: The six restaurants at Northstar mean time off for the family cook. True North is Northstar's new signature restaurant, reflecting their commitment to the environment. Casually elegant, dinners feature all-natural meats, sustainably caught or farmed seafood, and fresh organic produce; even the decor reflects earth tones. The Martis Valley Grill is open holiday weeks in winter, and daily for breakfast, lunch, and dinner in summer months. Themed family-style buffets (Italian, Southwest, Mediterranean, etc.) are offered. A pizzeria operates in winter only for pizza, soup, and salad bar. You can use the on-mountain pizza phone to call in your order, then ski down to eat.

The two winter restaurants on the mountain are the Lodge at Big Springs, open for breakfast and lunch, and the Summit Deck and Grill, open for lunch. Each offers an informal atmosphere and allows skiers to get back on the slopes quickly. The Summit Deck is really that—set at 8,600 feet on top of Mount Pluto, it has wonderful views of Lake Tahoe and the Pacific Crest from the outside deck. However, to dine here you must be able to ski or ride intermediate runs. And in winter "the party's at the Alpine Bar"; live music, a sports bar with multiple TVs, appetizers, and a full bar tempt skiers off the slope at day's end.

In summer the Turn, at the golf course, has patio dining for lunch and afternoon snacks. Or call your order in while teeing off at the ninth hole, and pick it up as you play through. The Village Food Company, in the Village Mall, is open year-round; with a deli, gourmet groceries, espresso bar, and video rentals, it also provides the supplies for a picnic or snacking in your condo.

Children's World: The Minors' Camp Child-Care Center is fully licensed and accepts children as young as two years old (must be toilet trained). In the winter it is open daily from 8:30 A.M. to 4:30 P.M. Under the guidance of an experienced staff, two- to six-year-olds paint, learn songs, listen to stories, play in the snow, and take walks; with snacks and a hot lunch, the full-day fee is $75; afternoons are $38. The day-care center suggests that children ages four to six who are willing would benefit from participating in the award-winning Startykes program at the Ski and Snowboard

School. It's designed for this age group, and engages children fully and enjoyably into their first ski experience. At three years little ones can join the Minors' Camp Ski and Snowplay program; in addition to the non-skiing activities, these children receive one and a half hours of ski instruction during the day. The fee for child care plus skiing (equipment included) is $85 a day. Five- to six-year-olds with some skiing experience receive two and a half hours of ski instruction in addition to indoor activities at a daily rate of $95. The learn-to-ski programs are offered on weekends and holidays.

Ski and *Family Life* magazines rank Northstar's kids' ski and snowboard school as one of the best in the nation. The ski and snowboard school is separate from the Minors' Camp program, and the teaching area is at midmountain. Startykes have all classes outdoors on the snow, but with lots of breaks, snacks, and variety to keep children interested and energized. StarKids, skiing or snowboarding for ages seven to twelve, groups children by age and ability, and offers something for everyone. Classes for StarTykes run from 10:00 A.M. to 3:00 P.M.; StarKids go until 3:45 P.M.; full-day classes include lunch for both groups; half-day classes do not. Cost is the same for both groups; full day including lift ticket, lesson, rental, and lunch is $99; half day is $79 for lift ticket, lesson, and rental. An all-day adventure for StarKids offers Action Zone and tubing in the morning and lift, lesson, rental, and lunch in the afternoon for $99. Register early, as availability is limited for this activity. If your children need lessons only, the full day costs $88; $44 for a half day. On all programs, even Minors' Camp, holiday prices are $2.00 to $8.00 higher.

Star Parks are six terrain parks for kids, just their size and designed with jumps, bumps, and secret snow play areas to kick off skis or boards and just play. Patrolled by ski patrol, they're close to main runs as well. Look for star prints on the trail map. Another special thing: Mommy, Daddy, and Me is a free program (except Saturday) for ages three to four and their parents, when trained instructors teach you how to teach your kids.

The highlights of the Minors' Camp summer program (mid-June to Labor Day) for children ages two (must be toilet trained) to ten are swimming lessons, nature walks, tennis, arts and crafts, science, and junior ropes course. Day camp is normally in session Monday through Saturday from 9:00 A.M. to 5:00 P.M. Some field trips/activities may have extra charges or may not be appropriate for children under five years old, so do call ahead. Parents or guardians must remain on Northstar premises while children are enrolled in Minors' Camp and are given pagers. The summer camp is suspended until the new Village opens, and should be operational by summer 2006. Call for prices and hours.

Recreation: For downhill skiing at Tahoe, you can look forward to 2,280 vertical feet. The Northstar Village is at the base of Mount Pluto, which rises to a summit of 8,600 feet. There are seventy runs and seventeen lifts, and locals boast of sunshine 80% of the season. The ski school, with its 200–plus instructors, offers lessons for beginners through experts to help all visitors meet the variety of this mountain. Fifty kilometers of groomed trails attract cross-country skiers; lessons, guided tours, and snowshoe rentals are available at the Nordic Ski Center. The Action Zone is the spot for tubing and snow toys, such as the snowscoot, the skifox, and the snowbike—you figure them out, please.

Après-ski activities may mean taking a sleigh ride or a trip to the Swim and Racquet Club, where you'll find saunas, spas, an adult lap pool, a fitness center, and a teen center, or enjoying a stroll through the Village, which houses shops, restaurants, and bars.

During the summer other activities lure visitors outdoors to the sunshine and clean mountain air. Northstar fully promotes the concept of "recess"; that precious time dedicated to the sole purpose of running around outside and playing that unfortunately is disappearing from our too-busy lives. Well, here's your chance to bring it back. Enjoy golf on an eighteen-hole course that wanders over meadows, past mountain streams, and through groves of tall pines and aspens. The Golf Course Clubhouse includes a pro shop and a restaurant. To work on improving your game, check with the resident pro for tips, or practice solo on the driving range and putting green.

At the Swim and Racquet Club, play tennis on one of the ten courts, take a swim in the adult lap pool or junior Olympic-size pool, or just soak up the sunshine on the poolside deck. No one over six years old is allowed in the Kiddie Pool, and families have their own hot tub, one of three. A fitness center is open to guests fourteen and older. The Arcade and Youth Center is a favorite place for kids to "just hang" and have some fun. Foosball, table tennis, and video games—plus the usual suspects of TV and vending machines. June through August, Northstar has teen and children's two-day golf clinics for kids ages six to sixteen, as well as Junior Tennis Camps, rated as a best value.

The Adventure Park offers challenge and junior ropes course, outdoor climbing wall, and orienteering courses. Off-road all-terrain vehicle (ATV) tours get down and dirty for those over sixteen. The latest addition, summer Action Zone, features bungee trampolines, a mountain bike park, and basketball shoot and shower: a timed shoot by which the loser gets soaked. The Northstar stables provide well-groomed horses for riding the mountain trails and offer lessons and guided trail rides. Hiking and biking are also favorite sports in High Sierra country. Take a scenic chairlift ride, and bring your bike along. For adventures in boating and fishing, the clear blue waters of Lake Tahoe await you. And music fills the air every summer Sunday afternoon with free outdoor concerts. The Lake Tahoe Shakespeare Festival begins in July.

P.O. Box 129
Truckee, California 96160
(530) 562–1010, (800) GO–NORTH
(466–6784)
www.skinorthstar.com,
www.northstarattahoe.com

THE RANCHO BERNARDO INN
San Diego, California

Good news, weary travelers. It is still possible to vacation in the classic style and relaxed atmosphere of an old California ranch. Set in the San Pasqual Mountains of Southern California, the four-diamond Rancho Bernardo Inn is just thirty minutes north of San Diego. Here, on 265 acres, the inn revives the elegance and charm of the early rancheros' way of life, capitalizes on the California sunshine and balmy weather, and adds fine sporting facilities as well—all to provide the perfect holiday for you. Conferences and meetings are popular here; family activities tend to center around weekends and high summer. The inn is open year-round and is a member of Preferred Hotels Worldwide. The inn has received the AAA Four Diamond award for twenty-eight consecutive years, as well as the Mobil four-star rating, and is one of *Zagat*'s top 100 hotels and resorts.

Their mission is simple: Treat each guest as a lifelong friend.

Accommodations: As you might expect of an old California ranch, the architecture reveals a Spanish influence reminiscent of the area's heritage. The eight red-tiled haciendas house 287 rooms and suites. These are decorated in warm earth tones, highly polished wood, and hand-picked antiques and local art. Every room has a patio or private balcony with valley, garden, or golf course view. Suites offer wood-burning fireplaces and adjoining court-yards. Room rates range from $239 to $299; suites from $309 to $578. Stay and Play packages (based on double occupancy) from $318 to $453 include deluxe room accommodations and your choice of one "play" option (golf, massage, tennis, or local San Diego attraction admission) per person for each night of your stay. Breakfast and dinner may be added to any stay. Children sixteen and under stay free in parents' room; cribs are provided at no charge.

Dining: El Bizcocho is the elegant French restaurant of the inn. This mission-style dining room is open for evening dinner and Sunday brunch; jackets are requested for gentlemen. With consistently high ratings from *Zagat,* one critic calls it "a circus of the senses." More casual and open for breakfast, lunch, and dinner, the Veranda Bar and Grille will lure you with its fresh seafood dishes, such as tiger shrimp Provençale and classic California grill cuisine. Alfresco dining was meant for San Diego's several hundred days of sunshine. The Sports Grill serves sandwiches and snacks on its patio, near the ninth hole. On Wednesday, complimentary tea, tasty sandwiches, and pastries in the Music Room make a perfect afternoon interlude to tide you over between a lovely lunch and a delicious dinner. For aperitifs and evening entertainment, La Taberna features a piano soloist or dancing.

Children's World: Camp RBI is an active, fun-filled camp offered on holiday weekends throughout the year: Easter, Memorial Day, the Fourth of July, Labor Day, Thanksgiving, and Christmastime; it is also in operation some weekends from mid-July to mid-August. Minimum age is four years, and there's really no maximum; some activities are planned for older children and teens as well. Kids have their own clubroom filled with toys, books, and games and a craft station where wild animal masks, hand puppets, or windsocks can be done as creatively as imaginable. Between 9:00 A.M. and 9:00 P.M., children share age-appropriate outdoor activities like basketball, swimming, biking, tennis, soccer, relay races, scavenger hunts, and dance contests. Indoor activities such as games, movies, storytelling, and crafts are also scheduled. A full-day session includes lunch, dinner, and a souvenir craft; half-day sessions are also available. Cost is $40 for a half day or $65 for the full day. Each session has a major theme, often connected to the holiday. Teens have their own lounge, filled with Nintendo, Play Station, music, and movies. It's a great place for them to gather and act nonchalant.

Excel is the place for children ages six to thirteen to learn the basics or prepare for competition in golf, tennis, and swimming or participate in team sports like volleyball and soccer. For a day or a week, the time is filled with professional instruction, a little pool time, and a box lunch, plus a T-shirt. Video reviews at the end of the day further develop skills. Excel operates Monday through Friday from 9:00 A.M. to 4:00 P.M., mid-July through mid-August; cost is $65 per day or $40 per half day. On all programs, a discount is offered for the second child in a family.

Recreation: Golf and tennis players are well cared for at Rancho Bernardo. Oaks North, three nine-hole executive courses located ten minutes away, will whet your appetite for the eighteen-hole championship resort golf course. Planted with sycamore, eucalyptus, pine, and olive trees, the lush green fairways roll down the foothills to the valley. With resident pros, individual and group lessons, clinics, tournaments, a driving range, and a well-stocked pro shop, you've got every chance in the world of polishing your game. If that's not enough, seven more championship courses are within a ten- to forty-minute radius of the inn.

Tennis players are found on the twelve outdoor courts including two stadium courts, four of which are lighted for nighttime play. The Tennis College has a thirty-year history of providing programs to players of all skill levels. Stroke development, teamwork, and strategy are just some of the topics covered in the two- to five-day sessions. Private instruction is also available from the five on-site tennis pros.

When you've run out of energy and are ready to relax, head to the full-service Buena Vista Spa. You can enjoy an indoor or outdoor massage, facial, or other relaxing treatment; have a tempting, healthy spa lunch; and unwind in the steam or sauna room. Stop at the spa or gift shop and take your experience home with one of the spa's exclusive, custom-blended skin- and hair-care products. Have a pleasant dip in one of the two swimming pools, or bicycle and jog around the carefully tended grounds. Because of the sunny Southern California weather, these sports continue year-round. Can't miss your daily workout? Drop by the fitness center, where you can also consult a nutritionist or personal trainer.

All of San Diego's attractions are twenty to thirty minutes away. The famous San Diego Zoo, SeaWorld, the Aerospace Museum, and the Wild Animal Park beckon. Enjoy a picnic in Balboa Park, Legoland, or shop at Horton Plaza, a fabulous "mall" like no other. You can even take a quick trip to Mexico—it's an easy forty-five-minute train ride from downtown San Diego to Tijuana for great bargains.

17550 Bernardo Oaks Drive
San Diego, California 92128
(858) 675–8500, (877) 517–9342
www.ranchobernardoinn.com

SNAKE RIVER LODGE AND SPA
Teton Village, Wyoming

In the early 1800s, a lone trapper named John Colter inadvertently discovered much more than the beaver he was hunting. After wandering in the Northwest Territory for some months, he returned home with tales of vast untouched forests, thermal pools and sulfur springs, of catching a fish in a fresh stream and cooking it in a nearby boiling one. Everyone laughed and dubbed it "Colter's Hell." Then other mountain men found the same phenomena, and gradually, the Jackson Hole valley became the crossroads of the western fur trade. Today, almost 200 years later, this land is protected by Yellowstone and Grand Teton National Parks, and has become the crossroads for travelers searching for grandeur and wilderness, trading their tame existence for adventure, but with comfort and luxury—a far cry from a tent, a few blankets, and a campfire. The Snake River Lodge and Spa is definitely luxurious; a member of Preferred Hotels & Resorts Worldwide, it is also Jackson Hole's first AAA-rated Four Diamond award resort. It is located 50 miles from the south entrance to Yellowstone, 10 miles from Jackson Town Square, and only 1 mile from the southern entrance to Grand Teton National Park.

Accommodations: Completely renovated in 2001, the Snake River Lodge is snuggled into the mountain at the base of the Jackson Hole Ski Resort, with eighty-eight guest rooms and forty-six condominium/suites. The decor is western, the feeling is one of comfort—leather, warm wood, and stone fireplaces. Rooms have many amenities, from plush robes to wireless connections, cable TV, and minirefrigerators. Luxury rooms add a gas fireplace, and executive rooms feature a comfortable sitting area with sofa-bed and a jetted bathtub. Views vary; all standard rooms have a partially obstructed view, while deluxe rooms overlook the village; some rooms have balcony with valley views. Room rates range from $139 to $459; children fourteen years and younger stay free in the same room with parents. Summer and winter are high seasons, when costs are similar. In April and November, much of the area is closed; at the hotel, the restaurant and spa are not operative. General packages begin at $119 in early December, or $289 from June through October. Room and unlimited golf in summer months is $249 per person per day, mid-week. A three-day package including room, a National Park Pass (valid for one year), breakfast for two, and a picnic lunch is $799 in May and September, $1,049 in high summer. Condo/residence suites (two bedroom units with full kitchen and dining area; three-bedrooms add an adjoining luxury queen room) are available both at the hotel and at Crystal Springs Lodge, opened in 2003 and right next to Snake River Lodge. Rates range from $320 to $2,000. Package rates for two-bedrooms begin at $320 to $950 daily depending on season. The lodge is in the heart of Teton Village, but it's still only 20 yards to the lift, so it's ski-in, walk-out access, with heated walkways and hiking trails literally out the back door. Resort fee is 4% of room rate, valet parking is $10 summer and $17 winter; there's also a paid village lot ($10) nearby. The concierge can arrange everything prior to your arrival—groceries, dining, child care, and spa services. Use the online request form.

Dining: The GameFish restaurant features regional favorites for dinner and an expansive breakfast buffet to start your day off right. *Wine Spectator* gave it the award of excellence in 2004, for its extensive wine menu. The Fireside Bar is a great place to unwind, sample a regional beer, and meet friends. The restaurant closes in April and November. One of the pleasures of being in the village is the wide choice of nearby restaurants. Kids like Billy's Burgers for "the best hamburger in Jackson Hole"; Nani's Genuine Pasta House, a comfortably cozy place; and Mountain High Pizza, of course. Lots of restaurants feature steaks, seafood, and game; the Alpenhof Bistro, Blue Lion, Gun Barrel Steak and Game House, Off Broadway Grill, and the Million Dollar Cowboy Steakhouse are good places to begin. Cadillac Grille has been a local favorite for seventeen years and Merry Piglets is the oldest and most popular Mexican eatery. Breakfast and lunch at Jebediah's, microbrews at Snake River Brewery & Restaurant, Austrian specialties at Stiegler's, raw oysters at Rendezvous Bistro, contemporary Asian and Latin and over 900 wine selections at Koshu Wine Bar, and

Sweetwater's lunches at the log cabin—there's something for everyone! For that special night out, try Old Yellowstone Garage or Snake River Grill.

Children's World: Snake River Lodge has come up with an innovative idea—to have a "kid-cierge." They plan to bring local children and guest children together on Saturday morning for a free breakfast and sharing of all the inside information on "kid's stuff" to do in the area. What a great idea! Babysitting can be arranged with the concierge; forty-eight-hour cancellation applies.

The winter and summer programs for children at Snake Lodge utilize the Jackson Hole Mountain Resort facilities at The Kids Ranch. The Cody House is a 106,000-square-foot children's facility housing daycare for ages six months and up, as well as all youth rentals and Mountain Sports School. Fort Wyoming, a western playground, is adjacent, and in winter, a magic carpet and gentle protected slope is perfect for little first-timers.

The Kids Ranch Summer Day Camp operates mid-June to Labor Day from 9:00 A.M. to 4:00 P.M., combining recreation, nature, history, and science. In June, camp is open Monday through Friday, then daily in July and August. For older children, mornings are active, spent hiking from the aerial tram or at the climbing wall; after lunch and free play, science projects and arts and crafts are followed by water play or an afternoon activity. Wranglers are from six months to two years ($80), Rough Riders encompass three-year-olds to kindergarten ($75), and Explorers are first to fifth graders ($75). Teen Extreme is for middle and high school ages ($75). Their activities include mountain biking, rock climbing, orienteering, hiking, environmental education, horseback riding, soccer, kayaking, bungee trampoline, and other outdoor sports. Lunch is included, and multiday rates are available.

In winter, little Wranglers are looked after and entertained with indoor and outdoor play. A licensed child-care facility, lunch is provided but parents may need to bring any special foods. Cost is $100 for full day, 8:30 A.M. to 4:30 P.M.; $85 for morning and $75 for afternoon. Half-day pick-up and drop-off is at 12:30 P.M. For Ski School, a full day is from 9:00 A.M. and pick-up is at 3:15 P.M.; half day is 12:45 to 4:00 P.M. Rough Riders (ages three to six) have small class size with specially trained instructors, lunch, and lesson/lift ticket for $100; half day is $75. With equipment, it's $110 and $90. Little Rippers (ages five to six) have beginner snowboard semi-private lessons with maximum of three children for $175, afternoon only $80; rental is $10 extra. Explorers (ages seven to fourteen) do just that—explore the mountain, scout for moose and eagles while improving their skills on skis and boards. Lesson/lift is $120 or, afternoons only, $100. Rental is $10 more; lesson only is $10 less. Teen Extreme for twelve to seventeen years is a unique skiing/riding program for advanced youths who often ski/board with the Athlete Team. The Terrain Park and Superpipe are perfect for kids to practice as it's not too small and not too big—just right. At all levels, Scavenger Hunts have kids sliding all over the mountain to combine skiing and riding skill building with fun and educational mountain exploration. Ski-cology is an interactive program that combines environmental awareness with ski/board lessons. Kids find secret trails with native plant and animal life—this hands-and-skis-on experience is so much fun, they don't even know they're learning! Special events include Kids Night Out and the New Year's Eve Glo-Worm Parade, a real highlight. Kids Night Out is scheduled on specific dates year-round for ages three to fourteen.

Grouped by age, kids enjoy indoor games, movies, and dinner or maybe ice-skating on the pond or sledding. Sometimes Owlie the owl and Petey the Peregrine falcon come for an interactive demonstration with live birds of prey. From 6:30 to 9:30 P.M., it's $55 per session.

Recreation: At the lodge, the five-story Avanyu Spa offers body and mind restoration; Avanyu is the Tewa Native American name for the mythical water serpent representing the life-giving powers of water, used extensively here. The Fitness Center features Cybex strength training. Indulge and entertain the whole family in the stunning indoor/outdoor swimming pool with cascades of waterfalls, large boulders, warmed walkways, sauna, and hot tubs hidden in caves (open 8:00 A.M. to 10:00 P.M.).

Winter in Jackson Hole means snow, lots of snow—often more than 500 inches in one winter! With three ski areas and some of the most accessible back-country skiing, that's a lot of fun as well. Skiing here can be ranked big (Snow King, vertical rise 1,571 feet, 400 skiable acres), bigger (Grand Targhee, vertical rise 2,400 feet, 2,000 skiable acres), and biggest (Jackson Hole, with a vertical rise of 4,139 feet, 2,500 acres of skiable terrain and 50% expert). Check out each of their Web sites for all the information, and to see which one fits your needs. Snow King has ice-skating and a tube park and there's snowmobiling and snowshoeing in the Parks. Horseback riding is offered at Goosewing Ranch, a year-round guest ranch; half day, full day, and even overnights offered. Dog-sledding combined with swimming and a barbecue lunch? Now that's a new twist! It helps that it's in the Granite Hot Springs area, though. Sleigh rides or a snowcoach tour of Yellowstone put a whole new face on winter.

Summer brings all those wonderful mountain activities of hiking, mountain biking, fly-fishing, kayaking—outfitters throughout the area offer all mountain diversions. And at Jackson Hole Trail Rides, in Teton Village, from June through September, a chance to ride into Grand Teton Park. Other summer "to-dos" include rafting on the Snake River, a hot-air balloon ride, or fishing at Crystal Springs Pond behind the hotel. Snow King Resort at the south end of Jackson has a 2,500-foot alpine slide; ride the chairlift to the top, and they say you control your own speed down. Uh-huh. Next to the slide is Alpine Golf, an eighteen-hole miniature golf course with waterfalls, ponds, and great views. Plus the events in the Parks—for example, Colter Bay Marina in Grand Teton has scenic boat cruises to Elk Island and canoe rentals. Everything around here is scenic, whether it's an adventure on air, land, or water. Redesigned by Robert Trent Jones, *Golf Digest* rates the Jackson Hole Golf and Tennis Club among the top ten resort courses in the nation. Like everything else here, it's very scenic, with views of the snow-capped mountains and water hazards provided by the Gros Ventre River. Movies on the Mountain are family films shown outside on the base of Jackson Hole Mountain Resort. Monday through Saturday for the entire summer, you can witness frontier justice in a shoot-out at Jackson Town Square. The longest-running in the country, it's been happening for forty-five years—I guess justice is kinda hard to come by. Music and arts also fill the summer days and evenings.

7710 Granite Loop Road
Teton Village, Wyoming 83025
(866) 975–ROCK, (307) 732–6000
www.snakeriverlodge.com

SQUAW VALLEY USA
Olympic Valley, California

Squaw Valley—the name itself is synonymous with skiing. From the earliest days (would you believe 1949?), the sunny California weather combined with six high alpine peaks and 4,000 acres of lift-served terrain have made this a world-class ski area. From its beginning in 1949 with one chairlift, a rope tow, and a lodge to hosting the 1960 Olympics, Squaw Valley is now a premier destination resort with year-round recreation and a strong commitment to environmental programs as a member of Sustainable Slopes. Mother Nature deposits an average of 450 inches of snow between mid-November and April, which means upper-mountain skiing into late May. The Sierra Nevada and Lake Tahoe provide a spectacular backdrop, and the vastness of the area contributes to a wide variety of skiing. Squaw Valley is located near the north end of Lake Tahoe.

Accommodations: A central reservation office (800–545–4350) will work with you to find the most appropriate lodging for your family and your needs. Hotels, motels, lodges, and condominiums all have various rates and package plans. Among the closest to the slopes are Squaw Valley Lodge, a ski-in, ski-out condominium ($215 to $1,025); three-day ski packages are available from $414 per person. The PlumpJack Squaw Valley Inn ($199 to $625) is located next to the tram, with sixty rooms and includes a mountain breakfast. The Resort at Squaw Creek, a luxury ski-in, ski-out resort and hotel with a full-service spa, oversize rooms, four restaurants, and an ice rink, sits at the base of the Squaw Creek Lift; rooms are $275 to $3,000. The new Village at Squaw Valley USA offers European-style luxury accommodations at the base of the mountain with easy access to base lifts and village activity. Get a Fourth-Night-Free package starting at $523 per person in a one-bedroom condo. The Olympic Village Inn is a European-style condominium complex about 4 blocks from the base of the mountain; one-bedroom suites, some with fireplaces, are $175 to $395.

Dining: Squaw Valley is certainly the place to eat, drink, and be merry, and choices are plentiful. In the Base Village, the Salsa Bar & Grill has a Southwestern flavor—watch out for those tequila specialties. Start your day off at Wildflour Baking Company for coffee and homemade pastries, Mother Barclay's Café, or grab a bite at the cable car building on your way up. Crepes for breakfast or lunch at Les Crepes de Dion; microbrews and good food (with lots of sunshine vitamin D) at the Sundeck Tavern; and the kids won't be able to walk past Northern Lights, offering ice cream and refreshments. The General Store and Dave's Deli have take-out meals, supplies, and sundries; Mountain Nectar offers smoothies, bagels, wraps, and panini sandwiches; while pizza at Le Chamois has been a tradition for thirty years. Many of the hotels and lodges have fine dining restaurants; and new additions in the Village are PlumpJack Balboa Café, with classic American brasserie fare and take-out, and the upscale High Sierra Grille. To "eat raw at Squaw," stop by Mamasake Sushi Bar. See what other wonderful places your family will discover.

Gold Coast, at the top of the Funitel, has a food court on the lower level, and the Crossroads Café on the upper level with wraps and salads and a wonderful view from the outside deck. The Mermaid or Waterfall Bars may call you over for a short stop at day's end. As always, many eateries close or have limited hours in spring and summer, so do check beforehand.

On the mountain, the Sunset Dinner at Alexander's ($25 per person) is delightful. Ride the Cable Car to High Camp, winter and summer, and savor views of the valley and Lake Tahoe with your three course dinner. The Terrace Bar & Deli also offers panoramic views, lunch, and a place to relax at day's end. The Poolside Café, overlooking Lagoon & Spa, has a fun kids' menu, soup-and-salad bar, and hot sandwiches; eat indoors or on the open sundeck. In summer the poolside barbecue and umbrella bar really shine.

The casinos and showrooms of Nevada are readily accessible for dining and evening pleasures. If you want to stay in the neighborhood, however, try the après-ski at Bar One, Le Chamois, or the Plaza Bar, where you'll find entertainment after a strenuous day of skiing.

Children's World: SquawKid's Children's Center is 12,000 square feet of comprehensive programs, all for kids ages three to twelve. KT the Bear presides on most days, to the delight of little ones. Adjacent to the lifts at the base of the mountain, it's designed to be a one-stop center for families with everything kids need and special parking. Parents can even buy their own lift tickets there to save time. Squaw Valley no longer has a daycare program for toddlers. Snow Cubs is a ski-snowplay program for three- and four-year-olds, and includes one-hour ski lesson, arts and crafts, using snowshoes, a walk around the village, and active play. Snow Sliders, for ages four to six, enhances learning and keeps kids smiling. The full-day program includes several hours on the snow, snack, and lunch; a new magic carpet lift helps with tired little legs. This is a physically

demanding program, and if youngsters choose not to ski in the afternoon, they may join the snowplay, movies, and other activities with the Snow Cubs. Junior Mountain is for ages seven to twelve, with more focus on safety, skill development, and skiing etiquette—and still keeping the kids smiling. The Snowboarding program for ages six to twelve has the same goals. For all programs, nonholidays, the cost is $89 for a full day and $69 for a half day. Holiday times go to $119 for all day, and $89 for a half day. All children receive lesson and all-day lift ticket; lunch is included in the full-day session. Sessions run from 8:30 A.M. to 3:45 P.M.

While summertime has no organized children's programs, many events and activities are planned for kids and families. Old West Weekend, Village Movie Nights, Sunday Family Kite Flying, and Hiking with a Ranger are just a few.

Recreation: The definite wintertime focus of Squaw Valley is skiing and nowadays, snowboarding. Squaw Valley receives 450 inches of snow every year—that's over 47 feet! One of the unique aspects of skiing here is that one wonders, where are the trails? Squaw Valley has thousands of acres of open bowl skiing rather than traditional trails. Instead of trails being rated, the lifts are rated beginner, intermediate, and advanced based on the type of terrain they serve. Add this to sunny California days, and you can see the attraction. Squaw Valley has three dedicated terrain parks and two half-pipes, plus a 525-foot super-pipe—enough to keep huckers and jibbers happy.

Imagine yourself on an uncrowded run. The sun is shining and you kick up some powder as you stop to check out the scenery. Take off your goggles and look out over glistening white snow to the blue waters of Lake Tahoe. Seventy percent of the runs are for beginner/intermediate skiers. Moreover, Squaw Valley is one of those rare places where this group is not confined to the lower elevations but can ski all day above 8,000 feet in the sunny, sheltered bowls. The vertical drop is 2,850 feet, and challenging slopes for expert skiers are not lacking, as the 1960 Winter Olympics were held here. In fact, Squaw Valley considers itself the birthplace of the American Extreme Skiing Movement. Squaw's six peaks are interconnected by thirty-three lifts that include a 110-passenger cable car, a 28-passenger Funitel (the first of its kind in North America), four high-speed detachable quads, and three 6-passenger chairs. The ski school organizes classes and clinics for all levels, from beginners to racing competition. A special timed race course allows skiers to perfect their racing styles (and keeps them off the regular slopes!). High Camp is the base for night skiing and riding under the stars, the most extensive at Lake Tahoe. Your day or afternoon lift ticket is valid.

Cross-country skiing, offered at the Resort at Squaw Creek, augments the snow diversions of Squaw Valley; the Olympic Ice Pavilion and snow tubing round it out. The Ice Pavilion also operates in summer, if you find yourself pining for winter sports.

In the summertime the cable car operates for scenic tours, hiking, swimming, full-moon hikes, stargazing, mountain biking, and many more events. The High Camp Bath & Tennis Club has a spectacular mountain location at 8,200 feet, surrounded by the beauty of the Sierra's peaks. The Headwall, on the mountain, offers wall climbing, bungee trampolines, and a new experience that promises a thrill, the Skytrek. Climb up a tree, and then trek among the treetops through a series of twenty-five platforms connected by cables, bridges, and zip lines. Tennis, fishing, biking, horseback riding, and nature trails are popular pastimes. Golf is top-notch here, with an eighteen-hole Robert Trent Jones Jr. course that weaves its way through mountains and meadows. Swimming pools, exercise spas, and racquetball/squash courts round out the pleasures.

P.O. Box 2007
1960 Squaw Valley Road
Olympic Valley, California 96146
(530) 583–6985, (800) 403–0206
www.squaw.com

SUNRIVER RESORT

Sunriver, Oregon

Nestled in the pines between the towering Cascade Mountains and the high desert, Sunriver Resort encompasses 3,300 acres on the dry side of the Cascade Mountains and enjoys nearly 300 days of sunshine each year. This four-diamond resort has earned numerous awards including *Condé Nast Traveler's* "Top 50 Ski Resorts in North America," *Family Circle's* Top 10 Vacation Destinations, and "#1 Family

Resort in the Northwest" from *FamilyFun* magazine; at least eight golf awards including top one hundred golf resorts in the world and one of the one hundred best women-friendly courses, plus dining and wine awards. It's a unique blend of natural beauty, resort comforts, personal service, and great recreation that makes for a memorable vacation. Sunriver offers three championship golf courses and one of the most complete lists of recreational activities to be found, including organized children's, teen, and family programs. In the winter enjoy world-class skiing at nearby Mount Bachelor. Sunriver Resort has its own shuttle to the mountain that will have you on the slopes within minutes.

Accommodations: Accommodations at Sunriver Resort include deluxe rooms and suites, featuring stone fireplaces and private decks; the suites accommodate two to six people and have a kitchen and dining/living room. River Lodges are close to the main lodge and offer great views; four two-story buildings house deluxe rooms featuring Northwest decor. Lodge Village rooms and suites are also just steps from the Sunriver Lodge and underwent a $3-million renovation in 2005. Summer rates range from $199 to $219 for rooms and $259 to $299 for suites in Lodge Village; River Lodges are $279 to $309 and suites are $500. Higher rates apply on weekends. Winter rates at Lodge Village average $155 (room) to $288 (suite). Winter packages are available; inquire for details. Guests at Sunriver enjoy access to the resort and club membership privileges for golf, fitness center, and dining.

Approximately 270 private homes and condominiums can be rented on a short-term basis. With one to five bedrooms, these can easily sleep up to ten people comfortably. All include a well-equipped kitchen, living and dining areas, and fireplace; some have hot tubs and deck. They are strategically located along the golf course, tucked in among the pines, facing the Cascade Mountains, or overlooking the Deschutes River. Prices for a two-bedroom range from $179 to $279 per night, size and season being the determining factors; summer and Christmastime are the high seasons. The architecture is warm and rustic, modern yet compatible with the surroundings, and individually decorated by owner's taste. For homes and condos a two-night minimum and a one-time cleaning fee are required.

Dining: The Meadows at the Lodge specializes in Northwest cuisine and is open for breakfast, lunch, and dinner daily. Enjoy great views and an imaginative children's menu. The Merchant Trader Café, located on the lower level of the lodge, features snacks and lighter fare for breakfast and lunch, and is open daily. As the name suggests, while you dine you can shop the unique merchandise here. In summer, dine outdoors and enjoy dinner and live music on weekends. The Grille at Crosswater Club is open during the summer months for lunch and dinner, and has limited winter hours. A private club atmosphere, it's open to resort guests and members only.

In addition, Sunriver's Village Mall has a number of restaurants and a grocery store. Whether you cook in or dine out, the variety from quick sandwiches to gourmet fare satisfies almost any mood. For late-night fun, the Owl's Nest Pub in the lodge offers cocktails nightly and live entertainment every Friday and Saturday night.

Children's World: Fort Funnigan gives children ages three through ten a chance to develop new skills and friendships as they create, discover, and experiment in Sunriver's unique environment. Each session revolves around a theme, and includes nature study, adventure, crafts, and games. Sample themes are junior detective, pirates of the high desert, fish and fun, rodeo, or twistin' tropics. Details of all programs can be found on Sunriver's Web site, along with a helpful parent handbook. Fort Funnigan operates daily except Sunday from mid-June through Labor Day, and on holidays and weekends throughout the year. Spike, the porcupine mascot, hangs out daily at Fort Funnigan; he often makes surprise appearances at other events, and has his own "room" on the resort's Web site. Costs are $65 for a full day, 9:00 A.M. to 4:00 P.M. with lunch. Half days are $35 (9:00 A.M. to noon or 1:00 to 4:00 P.M.) and are available on Monday, Wednesday, and Friday.

Evening programs are also themed— kids enjoy clown school, south of the border, weird and wacky science, Oregon Trail campout, and safari expeditions. Monday and Friday evening sessions are 5:00 to 9:00 P.M. with dinner for $40; and Tuesday, Thursday, and Saturday from 6:00 to 9:00 P.M. without dinner for $30. No night programs on Sunday or Wednesday.

Guided Adventures is designed for preteens and teens (ages eleven through fifteen) and is held during the summer months. On Monday, Tuesday, Wednesday, and Friday from 9:30 A.M. to 3:30 P.M., activities are geared toward the more independent and adventurous nature of this age group. Prices vary according to the scheduled activity: Wrangler Day features horsemanship and trail rides ($60); Challenge Yourself ($50) is safe but thrilling and involves ropes, cables, tall trees, bikes, and more; an excursion to the top of Mount Bachelor via chairlift, a day playing on glaciers, and hiking back down the mountain ($50); and River Adventure, bike riding and canoeing along the Deschutes River ($50). Also on Friday night is Cosmic Bowling from 9:00 P.M. to midnight in Bend ($35). Kids are advised to bring their bike, helmet, and lunch every day.

Teens ages thirteen to nineteen have their own summer schedule, generally two to three hours in the afternoon and evening (much their preference!). Monday is Night Spiker Volleyball, with the unique effect of black lights and neon body paint ($20.00);

Tuesday is indoor rock climbing in Bend ($45.00); Wednesday is dodgeball at the resort ($5.00); Thursday is white-water rafting ($45.00); and Friday is cosmic bowling 'til midnight in Bend ($35.00). Often a dance is scheduled weekly. During the rest of the year, loose activities are offered for teens, such as dances or pizza parties.

In addition, youth summer activities include bicycle riding, swimming lessons, canoe or white-water raft rides, games, and tennis. The resident naturalists at the Sunriver Nature Center introduce children to the magic and mystery of the local environment and animals; the Nature Center is open year-round.

In winter the rink at the Sunriver Village Mall makes a great spot for ice-skating. Wintertime also means that all the services of Mount Bachelor are available. Mount Bachelor offers state-licensed daycare beginning at age six weeks, from 8:30 A.M. (7:30 A.M. on weekends) to 4:00 P.M. Cost is $45 for children thirty months and over, $50 for twenty-nine months and under; an hourly rate of $13 per hour with a two-hour minimum is based on space available (800–829–2442). Lunch is $5.00 or children may bring their own. Snowplay, a one-hour introduction to skiing, is available for three-year-olds for $25 additional. Children four and over have Mountain Masters/day-care, a combination day-care and half-day ski lesson, for $119 with lunch and rentals; recommended for ages four to six and new to skiing. Mountain Masters (levels 1–5) for ages four to twelve for beginners is grouped by age, ability, and sport (ski or snowboard). The same is true for Mountain Masters (levels 6–9) for ages seven to twelve. On-snow time is 9:00 to 9:45 A.M.; pick-up at 3:00 P.M. Cost is $79 for lessons and lift ticket, full day;

$59 for half day (10:00 A.M. to noon or 1:00 to 3:00 P.M.); rental equipment is $14. For more details, please see the information on Mount Bachelor Ski School for kids, under the listing for the Inn of the Seventh Mountain, or go to www.mountbachelor.com.

Recreation: The Sage Springs Spa and Club is the venue for Sunriver's golf and tennis. With fifty four holes of outstanding championship golf, set amid rivers, meadows, wetlands, pine forests, and spectacular Cascade Mountain views, the Sunriver golfing experience offers incredible variety. Crosswater was designed by Robert Cupp and John Fought and offers play exclusively for resort guests and Crosswater Club members. It is designated a certified Audubon Sanctuary. The Woodlands was designed by renowned architect Robert Trent Jones Jr., and consistently ranks among the top twenty-five resort courses nationwide. The Woodlands' tree-lined fairways, seven lakes, and strategically placed sand traps have earned Sunriver Resort the distinction of a *Golf Magazine* Silver Medal Award. The Meadows, playing to more than 7,000 yards, has four sets of tees, meticulously prepared bent grass greens, and spectacular Cascade Mountain views; it is also home to the Sunriver Resort Golf Learning Center. No wonder *Golf Digest* rates the golf resort as one of "America's 100 Greatest."

Tennis at the Sage Springs Spa is a year-round sport with three indoor courts and five outdoor courts. Indoor court fees are $24, and you can stay after your game for the steam room or hydrotherapy spa. Outdoor court fees are $10, and another twenty-seven courts are to be found scattered throughout the Sunriver Community. If your serve or backhand needs some polishing, you can always sign up for lessons. Sunriver Resort offers their own year round tennis program.

Two swimming centers are operated by and open to the community; each has a heated Olympic-size pool, a diving pool, and a wading pool, providing plenty of variety. The south pool also has a water slide and hot tubs. The Lodge Village pool and three outdoor spas are for guests only.

The Deschutes River provides hours of enjoyment for fishermen, who snag brookies, rainbows, and German browns. The Sunriver Marina offers canoe, raft, and kayak float trips down the scenic and calm Deschutes. Marina staff will pick you up downriver and bring you back to the marina; the trips are offered mid-April to mid-October, weather permitting. For the more adventurous, local outfitters offer half-day and full-day white-water rafting trips down more turbulent portions of the Deschutes, leaving from the resort daily during the summer months.

For landlubbers in your party, just about any type of rental bikes are available for excursions on the 30 miles of paved paths; guides at the Sunriver stables are ready to show off the scenery in rides along the river; the wilderness beckons interested backpackers. Trails past meadows and through the woods await joggers and nature lovers. Surrounding Sunriver Resort is the Deschutes National Forest, offering additional opportunity for back-to-nature serenity and elbow room. The Sunriver Nature Center, a private, nonprofit organization, has been offering extremely comprehensive, very reasonably priced programs for more than twenty-five years. Many nature walks, lectures, and programs are free; there are also archaeology tours, combined biking/bird-watching excursions, spelunking in Lava River Cave, and much more. See galaxies, nebulas, and all of space at the Sunriver Nature Center & Observatory; a nature trail and botanical garden provide earthly fun and learning.

Sage Springs Club and Spa features spa services and hydrotherapy spas; a fitness club with extensive classes in yoga, aerobics (water and other), Pilates, and more; and personal trainers who are available to help with your regimen. The indoor tennis center is here as well.

Sunriver Village has restaurants and interesting shops and boutiques. The Sunriver Music Festival takes place in August; orchestral programs are presented in the Great Hall, originally constructed as an officers' club when what is now Sunriver Resort was Camp Abbot, a training center for the Corps of Engineers during World War II. The Great Hall is composed of 511 logs, totaling 150,000 board feet of lumber and is the only original building that remains. Completely restored to its original beauty, it serves as Sunriver's most popular entertainment venue.

Lots of activities are available for families from the fairly sedate Art in the Afternoon to the challenge ropes course. Art in the Afternoon, daily from 1:00 to 3:00 P.M., offers the joy of creating art, a different medium every day: ceramics, body art, candles, tie dye, soap making. Children must be accompanied and prices vary. Black light volleyball is another event the entire family can enjoy (age eleven and older, $20). The Fun Runs and Youth Triathalons are three or five miles, and you can walk as well. For ages ten and up, the challenge ropes course involves zip lines, a trapeze, cables, and trees ($50 per person).

The High Desert Museum, 8 miles from the lodge, is a terrific educational introduction to the cultural and natural history of the Northwest, and a big attraction for kids and adults alike. The otter pond, where you can watch playful otters, is a favorite highlight, as is watching the birds of prey in action.

At Sunriver you'll find a dozen ways to enjoy winter. Mount Bachelor (800–829–2442, www.mtbachelor.com) is one of the West's top-rated ski areas. You'll find breathtaking views, plenty of deep powder, and slopes to challenge skiers and snowboarders of all abilities—from beginners to Olympic champions. You can head cross-country on miles of groomed forest trails or break your own path through snowy meadows. Trek the mountain outback by snowshoe, snowmobile, or dogsled, or take a leisurely tour in a horse-drawn sleigh. And at day's end back at the resort, slip into a steaming outdoor spa for a relaxing soak.

1 Center Drive
P.O. Box 3609
Sunriver, Oregon 97707
(541) 593–1000, (800) 801–8765
www.sunriver-resort.com

SUN VALLEY

Sun Valley, Idaho

Just saying "Sun Valley" calls to mind fantastic downhill skiing, beautiful powder, and gorgeous sunshine. Located in south-central Idaho, Sun Valley is a Tyrolean-style village perched high in the Sawtooth·Mountains. With a ski season that runs from late November to early May, spectacular scenery and mountain air, Sun Valley is indeed a skier's paradise. In 1935 the Union Pacific Railroad sent Count Felix Schaffgtosch to search for the perfect spot for a grand American resort to draw rail travel west. After months of finding nothing that met his strict criteria, he happened upon Ketchum, an old mining town in central Idaho. His response? "This place combines more delightful features for a winter resort than anyplace I have ever seen in Switzerland, Austria, or the U.S." Averell Harriman, then chairman of the railroad, determined to build a resort worthy of the majestic setting, and Sun Valley was born in 1936. Instantly successful, European nobility and Hollywood royalty flocked to the new resort, creating the first destination resort in America. That standard of excellence and style continues today, as families from around the world continue Harriman's vision of "roughing it in style." Sun Valley introduced the world's first chairlift and began the long-running affair between Americans and skiing.

You won't need your car at Sun Valley, as it's a walking village. Even the condominiums are close, but if they seem too far, just hop on the complimentary bus. Continuous round-trips to Dollar and Bald Mountains are offered by both the resort and KART, the Ketchum Area Rapid Transit; service is free throughout the Wood River Valley.

Accommodations: The historic, original Sun Valley Lodge provides upscale lodging and fine dining in an imposing four-story hotel. Each of the lodge's 148 rooms and suites has a French Country decor with marble-appointed baths. The Sun Valley Salon & Day Spa, massage center, heated swimming pool, and bowling alley are located here. Room sizes vary, and Family Suites are one option with three beds in one and a half rooms with one and a half baths. July and August are the highest season and rates range from $199 to $469; winter rates drop slightly to $179 to $429; spring and fall are even lower. The chalet-style Sun Valley Inn is set in the midst of the village and contains meeting spaces, rooms, and suites. There are workout and laundry facilities, open to all resort guests, and the super-heated Inn Pool for year-round swimming in the crisp mountain air. Summer rates are between $239 for a standard room and $299 for a suite; $129 to $219 in winter. Deluxe condos are located near the lodge and inn; rates range from $199 for a studio to $449 for a two-bedroom. Standard condos form a horseshoe around the village, all within a ten-minute walk of the inn or lodge; rates range from $179 to $289. Both include daily maid service, fully equipped kitchens, and spacious living areas. There is no additional charge for cribs, and children stay free in the room with parents. Ages fifteen and under ski free—one child per adult, with purchase of adult lift ticket.

Dining: Thirteen restaurants at the resort please almost any mood from fancy to family-style. Though many families cook meals in their condominium units, occasional nights dining out mean a real vacation for the family chef too!

The Lodge Dining Room, open for dinner and Sunday brunch, combines excellent service, fine dining with a French flair, and live music in an elegant setting. Also in the lodge, Gretchen's is open for breakfast, lunch, and dinner with a warm, family atmosphere. In summer enjoy the gourmet buffet on the terrace overlooking the famous outdoor ice rink.

In the village, Konditorei and Sun Valley Deli have sandwiches, pastries, and ice cream; kids love the Bald Mountain Pizza and Pasta. The Ram Restaurant at the Inn is open evenings only for steak, seafood, and fondues.

On the mountain, Sun Valley's owner considers "Baldy" a "regal mountain, wearing a crown with three jewels"—the award-winning day lodges of Warm Springs, Seattle Ridge, and River Run Lodges. Cluster stations ensure that your food is fresh and prepared exactly to your order—baked potatoes, soup, salad, and grills are above-average mountain fare. Lookout at the top of the mountain is cafeteria-style; Roundhouse is more intimate with seating around a four-sided fireplace—it's the first original day lodge. Dollar Cabin suits youngsters just fine and offers their all-time favorites of hot dogs, hamburgers, and fries.

In winter, for an unusual adventure in dining, take a horse-drawn sleigh ride to a rustic cabin nestled in the woods; at the Trail Creek Cabin, enjoy prime rib or Idaho trout near a warm fire. Après-ski haunts include the Duchin Lounge, in the lodge, known for its "HBR" (hot buttered rum) and a favorite for socializing, live music, dancing, and entertainment. The Boiler Room, open only in winter, most evenings features aprés-ski entertainment and early evening performances of live comedy or music. *Forever Plaid,* a family musical, generally plays once a week. First-run movies show in the Opera House in winter and summer.

Children's World: While Mom and Dad are schussing down Bald and Dollar Mountains, children are not left out of the fun in this winter wonderland. At Dollar Mountain, the Sun Valley Ski and Snowboard School starts three- and four-year-olds in Tiny Tracks introductory classes for $50 for an hour. Dollar Cubs, for four- and five-year-olds (level 2), and Dollar Bears, for ages six to twelve (with ability levels 1 to 4), enjoy a full day of supervised activity (8:30 A.M. to 4:00 P.M.) with four hours per day of skiing instruction for $95. Consecutive day rates are lower. Snowboard clinics for ages seven to twelve are also at Dollar Mountain; same hours and rates apply. All rates include supervised lunch but not lift tickets, and children may ride the lift alone. For the six- to twelve-year-old intermediate to expert skier or snowboarder (levels 5 to 9), Bald Eagles ski clinics strengthen technique and provide the proper amount of challenge. From 8:45 A.M. to 3:45 P.M., classes and sign-up begin and end at River Run Plaza Children's Center.

The licensed Sun Valley Playschool in the village entertains nonskiing little ones six years old and younger, including infants. The school has games, toys, arts and crafts, and a nap room for tots who grow weary of all the excitement. There are opportunities for ice-skating and an outdoor playground for romping in the snow. Rates are the same as in summer.

In summertime Playschool activities for the six-and-under group turn to swimming, arts and crafts, paddleboating, hayrides, and walks around the village. Summer hours are Monday through Saturday from 8:30 A.M. to 4:30 P.M. Rates are for a full day or half day and depend on age: six months to two years, $90/$64; non-potty-trained toddlers, $68/$54; potty-trained and older children, $59/$49. Pony rides and hayrides are $13.50.

For youngsters ages six to fourteen, from mid-June through early September, the day camp can be enjoyed on a weekly or daily basis. Fishing clinics, hayrides, paddle-boating, swimming, ice-skating, and lift rides fill the days. Some activities are extra, such as horseback riding or barbecue ($14). Full day is $59.00, half day is $49.00, and lunch is $7.00.

Recreation: Suitable terrain for all levels of skiers is provided at Sun Valley. With its wide-open spaces and gentle trails, Dollar Mountain (628 vertical feet), known as "the finest teaching mountain in the world," is favored by beginners and those who want a few warm-up runs. Bald Mountain, with 3,400 vertical feet, is a challenge and caters to intermediate and expert skiers. Combined, these mountains offer seventy-five runs, nineteen lifts, and 2,054 skiable acres. Sun Valley prides itself on lots of good skiing from well-groomed terrain to unpacked powder and short lift lines—the combination every downhill skier seeks. A complimentary bus service operates continuously throughout the day, shuttling guests to the base of both mountains.

The Nordic and Snowshoe Center grooms 40 kilometers of well-marked trails for cross-country skiers through aspen trees, along the creek, and over sloping meadows. There are also 8 kilometers of designated snowshoe trails. Sun Valley was a pioneer in providing Nordic skiing specifically for children. Machine-set tracks designed for a child's stride cover 3 miles of the Nordic Ski Center and in some places parallel adult tracks, allowing an easy family cross-country-skiing experience. Backcountry skiers can tour the mountain from yurt to yurt (Siberian-style huts), finding a warm, welcoming meal and bed at each.

Private and group lessons are available in both downhill and cross-country skiing at beginner, intermediate, and advanced levels. At the ski shops you can rent equipment or purchase all the accessories necessary for either undertaking. With indoor and outdoor rinks, another favorite wintertime sport has become a year-round one here. Ice skates can be rented, and just behind the lodge is an Olympic-size skating rink where such greats as Sonja Henie, Peggy Fleming, and Dorothy Hamill have practiced. Saturday night ice shows are presented throughout the summer, and have been a tradition for over sixty-five years.

Another year-round activity is swimming; there are two glass enclosed indoor heated pools (one at the lodge and one at the inn), one outdoor Olympic-size pool, and a kiddie pool. Relax in the sauna or the Jacuzzi, or make an appointment with the masseur in the lodge to ease your overworked muscles. The game room in the lodge offers pool tables, video games, and bowling alleys; or perhaps you'd like to take in a movie at the Opera House. The shops in the village might tempt you with their selections of books, gifts, fashions, jewelry, pottery, and toys.

Summer brings music festivals, parades, antiques and crafts fairs, bicycle races, and much more. Tennis and golf enthusiasts are in their heyday, for there are eighteen outdoor tennis courts, as well as clinics and private lessons with video-taped analysis. An eighteen-hole championship golf course, redesigned by Robert Trent Jones Jr., rolls over gently sloping terrain. Two nine-hole courses provide another option. At the pro shop, you can arrange for lessons and pick up extras in equipment and clothing.

Fishing in Silver Creek makes a pleasant afternoon for novice fishermen as well as experienced anglers; Sun Valley Lake is stocked with trout. The mountain trails are open to you for horseback riding and hiking in the wooded wilderness; chairlifts give access to "Baldy's" Summit. Trap and skeet shooting (instruction available) are also popular with summer visitors. Take a rowboat or paddleboat out on the lake, line up rentals at the bike shop, or plan a whitewater raft trip. Whether winter or summer sports beckon you, you'll be captivated by the majestic mountains and the warm, friendly atmosphere of Sun Valley.

1 Sun Valley Road
Sun Valley, Idaho 83353
(208) 622–2001, (800) 786–8259
www.sunvalley.com

THE WESTIN
MISSION HILLS RESORT
Rancho Mirage, California

Palm Springs is another name associated with Hollywood stars and elegant living. Its prestigious neighbor, Rancho Mirage, is newer, but making its own name as "the Playground of the Presidents." Set on 360 acres next to the Mission Hills Country Club, the Westin welcomes guests to the California desert. The lush landscaping and verdant golf courses belie its desert location, but the surrounding mountains and canyons, which reflect the sun and shadow and the clear starry nights, are stark and wondrous reminders of what lies beyond the resort's boundaries.

Shopping and art galleries vie with golf as diversions, and natural sightseeing is varied. Indian Canyons have indigenous flora and fauna in dramatic contrast to the rocky gorges and barren desert; Joshua Tree National Park's 8,000 acres encompass some of the most interesting geological displays in the California desert; and the Living Desert's magnificent botanical gardens provide a fascinating and educative journey. Palm Canyon Drive and El Paseo have all the glitz and glamour you might crave. Casinos, hot mineral springs spas, and shopping are pleasant diversions.

Accommodations: Southwestern adobe mixed with classic Moroccan design provides a distinctive architectural achievement. Blue domes reflect the cloudless skies; warm brown arches repeat themselves down a long pathway, framing the desert palms and mountains. The 512 guest rooms are scattered in sixteen lowrise pavilions interspersed with meandering walks, gardens, lagoons, and waterfalls. Guest rooms are of generous size, and most feature a private patio or balcony. Westin has become noted for their "heavenly beds and baths." February to April is the high season, when rooms range from $199 to $450; from June through mid-September, the rates drop to $99 to $209. Check for specials during summer; for example, a room rate of $199 includes a $200 certificate at the spa. Not a bad deal. The remaining months are a midrange of $149 to $365. December 25 to January 31, rates are highest. Children under eighteen stay free in their parents' room. Often there are specials for families, too; for example, children stay, play, and eat free. In deluxe accommodations, children twelve and under eat free from the children's menu, and play tennis free after 2:00 P.M. Or Westin Fun, where two children join the Westin Club and eat free.

Dining: Bella Vista features Mediterranean cuisine and is open for breakfast, lunch, and dinner. Typically Californian, it blends a sunlit atrium with palm trees. Indoor/outdoor dining is available; with views of waterfalls and colorful gardens, it hardly seems like the desert. If you can't tear yourself or your kids out of one of the three swimming pools, La Paloma, Las Brisas, and Las Hadas serve light poolside snacks and drinks; Caliente is the poolside cabana area. When the ice cream urge strikes, go Someplace Else—that's the name of the resort's ice cream parlor, you know. For evening cocktails the elegantly casual Lobby Lounge offers drinks and a tapas menu. Sit inside or on the patio with its circular firepit. Westin has prepared a nice list of family restaurants in the area for those who want to venture out.

Children's World: Westin Kids Club is a basic program at Westin resort properties, designed to make family travel safe, convenient, and enjoyable. Children get special age-appropriate gifts upon check-in; parents get a safety kit, if desired (electric-outlet covers, adhesive strips, ID bracelets, and local emergency numbers); and the room is ready with cribs, potty seats, or bed rails if needed. Jogging strollers, high chairs, and bottle warmers are complimentary, meals can be ordered in advance from a children's menu so that they are ready upon arrival at the restaurant, and a lot of information about local things of interest to families is available. An in-room "Story Line Program" delivers different bedtime stories via speakerphone. It's a really comprehensive approach, and during the summer special rates and "Kids Eat Free" promotions are generally available.

The Cactus Kids program for ages four to twelve bills itself as "the coolest thing in the desert." Operating daily year-round from 8:00 A.M. to 5:00 P.M., it costs $40 per four-hour session (8:00 A.M. to noon and 1:00 to 5:00 P.M.) or $12 per hour. Lunch is additional. Reservations are requested at least one day in advance, and the program will be run for even one or two children. Activities include arts and crafts, volleyball, lawn games, movies, nature walks, and bicycle riding.

Recreation: Two championship golf courses, two practice ranges, and six greens and sand traps keep golfers happy. The Pete Dye Resort Course has his trademark deep bunkers and undulating fairways, while the Gary Player Signature Course is a mosaic of waterfalls, ravines, and lakes. Take lessons from the resident pros, or sign up for a Golf Digest School. Play tennis in the cool of the evening on the seven lighted tennis courts, or join the Reed Anderson Tennis School. Forget something? The pro shops have everything you need. Las Brisas is the largest of the three swimming pools; it was made to resemble the surrounding canyons and has a 60-foot water slide, two whirlpools, and spacious sundecks. Treat yourself to massage, herbal wraps, and facials at the new Spa at Mission Hills; work out at the fitness club; or follow a more leisurely pace with traditional lawn games such as croquet and shuffleboard.

If you need more action, Oasis Waterpark is nearby as well as Camelot Park, where you can enjoy miniature golf, bumper boats, go-carts, or batting cages. Take the Palm Springs Aerial Tramway 8,516 feet to the Mountain Station for a bird's-eye view, and hike through Mt. San Jacinto Wilderness State Park. Weather permitting (meaning when there is snow), Nordic skiing operates from November to April. At the opposite end of the environmental spectrum, explore the desert by four-wheel drive with experienced guides who can show you the secret life of the desert, or have a real Old West experience in a two-hour covered-wagon tour. As a contrast to all this nature, any teenagers in your party might gravitate toward the Palm Desert Town Center, the area's largest indoor shopping mall. Palm Springs and El Paseo shopping are just minutes away.

Also in the vicinity you'll find the Children's Discovery Museum of the Desert, the Uprising Outdoor Adventure Center, the Desert Museum and the Living Desert, Moorten Botanical Gardens, and the wineries of Temecula Valley. Indian Canyons make an interesting hiking excursion, and Joshua Tree National Park (100 miles), with its fascinating trees and vegetation is a good, but long day trip.

71333 Dinah Shore Drive
Rancho Mirage, California 92270
(760) 328–5955, (800) WESTIN–1
www.westin.com

CANADA

Alberta
British Columbia
Ontario
Quebec

DEERHURST RESORT

Huntsville, Ontario

The Muskoka region is Ontario's most popular holiday area. With its clear lakes and beautiful woodlands, it attracts visitors in summer and winter. Deerhurst Resort encompasses 800 acres on the shores of Peninsula Lake and allows guests to experience all the beauty of the area. And yes, there are still deer at Deerhurst.

The original lodge at Deerhurst was opened in 1896 by Charles Waterhouse, with just eighteen guest rooms. Three generations of Waterhouses oversaw the expansion of the property and today it is one of the largest resort complexes in Canada. In 2002 it was voted the "Best Summer and Winter Resort in Ontario" by e-kidstoronto.com; and the *Toronto Sun* readers' survey has voted it the "Best Resort in Ontario" for the past three years. It's a place where families can share the fun together as well as share the stories about their own adventures.

Deerhurst is 2½ hours by car north of Toronto, or only forty minutes by air from Toronto to the resort's private airstrip.

Accommodations: Today's accommodations are a far cry from the lodge rooms (without baths) of the early days. At that time accessible only by steamboat, the first guests paid $3.50 per person for a week's lodging, with three meals daily! Today, low-rise accommodations for 425 guests are located throughout the resort's landscaped acres. The guest rooms and suites are well appointed and comfortable and are grouped in condominium-style buildings with views of the lake, woods, pools, and golf course. Rates include complimentary access to a wide array of leisure activities, and are higher in summer. A variety of styles suit every need. For families, the Sports Villas are quite popular; a separate sitting area, kitchenette, and patio or balcony allows for more space. Deluxe and Luxury suites have full-size stove and refrigerator. Groceries are obtainable in Huntsville, 13 kilometers from the resort. Low-season rates at the Sports Villas start at C$169 and go to C$369 in July and August. Since standard rooms are C$139 and C$319, the villas are an excellent value. Rates are C$309 to C$619 for a deluxe two-bedroom suite. A daily resort fee of C$7.00 per room provides parking, shuttle service, fitness center, squash, tennis, racquetball, swimming pools, whirlpool and saunas, hiking/biking trails, and children's playroom. In summer, it covers golf putting and practice area, canoes, kayaks, windsurfers, and water trampolines; in winter, cross-country skiing, ice-skating, and tubing. Children under eighteen stay free when occupying their parents' room.

Dining: In the Eclipse Restaurant, no less than eight chefs display their talents with regional bounty; venison, fresh fish, wild mushrooms, and wild berries are often featured in creative dishes. The cuisine is matched by the decor of lake and trees viewed through huge picture windows and set under soaring Douglas fir ceiling beams. Open for breakfast and dinner, it's all family friendly. The signature restaurant, Steamers, is pure Canadian, with intimate dining rooms in a romantic log house atmosphere designed for adult dining. Open seasonally. The Pub at the Pavilion is casual and well suited for families; soups, sandwiches, pastas, and salads are typical fare here, served all day, from 11:00 A.M. to 11:00 P.M. The Poolside Deck, with views of the lake, serves barbecue favorites in the summer; a golfers lounge is also available for all-day summer dining.

A Modified American Plan is available for adults only. This includes a buffet breakfast and three-course table d'hôte dinner or a la carte selections from the three resort restaurants. Cost is C$59 per person per night and must be purchased for each day of your stay. There is no meal plan for children, but children's menus are available in the Pub and the Eclipse Dining Room.

Just off the lobby, the Landing Lounge is a good place to meet, unwind, and start the evening. Deerhurst keeps reinventing the critically acclaimed nightly entertainment, which in its twenty-fourth year is also Canada's longest-running stage show. This lavish performance of music, dance, and exciting visuals is where Shania Twain started performing, so who knows what future superstar you may see? CW's Lakeside Bar & Dance Club, open seasonally in the original lodge by the lake, is the place to end the evening with DJ, dancing, laser lights, and arcade. Speical shows are performed three times a week including "Rock 'n' Roll Party" and "Saturday Night Fever."

Children's World: Daily through the summer season and school holiday periods, and on Saturday throughout the year, Deer Club operates from 9:00 A.M. to 5:00 P.M. Children ages four to twelve swim, hike, make crafts, and enjoy the playground. The fee is C$45 for a full day (including lunch) and C$25 for a half day. Younger children, ages eighteen months to four years, join the Bambi Club, which has its own premises especially suited to little ones. The cost is C$65 full days and C$35 half days. Full day includes lunch for children on regular solid food.

Recreation: The eighteen-hole Deerhurst Lakeside Golf Course was built in 1966 and redesigned in 1988 with many enhancements. Built in 1991, the top-rated Deerhurst Highlands is a magnificent eighteen-hole course winding atop a ridge above the lake, resulting in a combination of challenging play and beautiful scenery. Highlands Course is included in *Golf Digest*'s Planet Golf rankings of the best courses in one hundred nations, along with being the only Ontario resort course to be in the top twenty list of Canadian courses. A driving range, practice tees, and target greens make up the seven-and-a-half-acre instructional facility. A team of professionals direct private lessons and group clinics.

The Pavilion, a complete sports complex, consists of two indoor tennis courts, a racquetball court, three squash courts, a fitness room, two pools, and a whirlpool. Also available here is an Aveda Concept Spa, where you can relax in the steam and sauna rooms or schedule a massage, facial, body wrap, or hair-styling service.

If you prefer to exercise in the open air, three more swimming pools await you, and eight more tennis courts are outdoors (tennis lessons are available). Water sports on the lake abound: sailing, waterskiing, kayaking, fishing, and sailboarding. And don't forget you can hike and jog along the nature trails in the beautiful Muskoka Woods. Horseback riding or a horse-drawn carriage or hayride lets the horse exercise and you simply enjoy, while mountain biking puts you back on the pedal.

Included in the accommodation rates are tennis, squash, racquetball, the swimming pools and beach, hiking trails, and the fitness room. In summer, canoes, kayaks, pedal boats, sailboats, and sailboards are all complimentary to guests. Four lakes mean over 60 kilometers of waterways to explore, and replica boats tour where grand steamships used to travel. Waterski or fish for lake trout and northern pike. Or just sit by the water and take it all in.

Something is scheduled just about every hour from 8:00 A.M. until 2:00 in the morning. Start the day with power walks, yoga ($5.00), or aquafit in the pool ($5.00); then try basketball, road hockey, or volleyball; junior golf lessons ($20.00) or tennis lessons ($25.00); watercolor and funky folk art ($15.00 to $36.00); and all kinds of dance, such as adult ballroom ($30.00), Dance! Dance! for ages three to eight ($28.00), and Hip Hop for nine- to fourteen-year-olds. Afternoon and early evening are for family activities such as Kids R Krafty ($5.00), stuff a teddy bear (price varies), build a birdhouse ($12.00), nature hikes, and treasure hunts. After dinner, a guided sunset canoe trek, family movie, teen movie, or bingo may beckon, wrapped up with a beach bonfire and marshmallows. Set one evening aside for the musical review, and another for the magic show, and at least one party night at CW's Lakeside Bar and Dance Club, to put all those dance lessons to use.

In winter, cross-country ski trails and equipment, outdoor ice rink and skates, hockey and broomball equipment, and snow tubing, plus indoor racquet sports, pool, and fitness room are complimentary to guests. Deerhurst is the gateway to over 2,000 kilometers of groomed trails and is right on the Trans Ontario Provincial trail system that connects the entire province, so snowmobilers are in snow heaven. Just next to the resort is Hidden Valley Highlands, open on weekends for a little taste of downhill skiing and snowboarding on eight slopes and thirty-five acres of runs. Group sleigh rides or a spin in an old-fashioned cutter will have everyone singing "Jingle Bells." For something a little more unusual, try dogsledding.

1235 Deerhurst Drive
Huntsville, Ontario
Canada P1H 2E8
(705) 789–6411, (800) 461–4393
www.deerhurstresort.com

FAIRMONT CHATEAU LAKE LOUISE

Lake Louise, Alberta

The Fairmont Chateau Lake Louise is located 100 miles west of Calgary in spectacular Banff National Park. Banff National Park was the third in the world, and the first in Canada, founded in1885 after the accidental discovery of a hot springs on Sulphur Mountain. Starting out as a 26-square-kilometer reserve, it is now 6,641 square kilometers of incredible beauty, part of the UNESCO Rocky Mountain World Heritage Site and the most visited park in Canada. Glaciers, snowcapped peaks, meadows of mountain flowers, wilderness, wild creatures, and the impressive Icefields Parkway make this area well worth many visits.

Is there anyone who has not seen an aerial photo of an amazingly colored lake surrounded by mountains, always with that stunning castle-like structure in the foreground? The Fairmont Lake Louise is generally referred to as the "Diamond in the Wilderness." Views from the hotel across this magnificent glacier-fed lake are truly breathtaking, as the eye takes in the expanse of the lake's turquoise water, the blue ice of the Victoria Glacier, and the majestic peaks of the Canadian Rockies that form the Continental Divide. The mountains provide excellent opportunities for skiing in winter and endless exploration into the wonders of nature in summer. Luxurious and inviting, the elegance of another era blends with the natural wonders that surround you. The resort is open all year.

Accommodations: Original accommodations on this site, built in 1890 by the Canadian Railway, were rather modest, welcoming a mere dozen adventurous guests at a time and during summer only. Following two devastating fires, which left only the Painter wing standing, the main structure of the current hotel was built in 1925. An additional wing was created as part of a C$65-million renovation in the late 1980s. From the elegant lobby to the helpful staff, careful attention to the needs of guests is evident everywhere. The resort's 489 rooms, ranging from standard bedrooms to suites, are all comfortably and pleasantly decorated. Carved wood, curved lines, an Alpine flavor, a hint of a splendid past—it's all here. Some even offer the luxury of a private Jacuzzi. Rooms facing the lake are preferable, but it's difficult, if not impossible, to find a bad view anywhere. Rates for a standard mountain view room begin at C$249 in winter, and rocket to $699 in summer. Children under eighteen are free in parents' room. Packages run the gamut from a simple bed and breakfast to all-inclusive. All package rates are per person, per day, based on double occupancy. The Bed-and-Breakfast package is offered year-round, and is just that; rates start from C$126 in winter and C$266 in summer. The Chateau Experience package combines indulgence with activities; rates of C$312 in winter and C$452 in summer include breakfast and dinner, a guided adventure activity, afternoon tea, and a thirty-minute spa treatment per person. Winter ski packages including tri-area lift tickets begin at C$360 with breakfast and

parking. Rates are dependent on occupancy at Fairmont, so use these as a guide.

Dining: The Fairmont prides itself on a truly unique Canadian cuisine. For fine dining at its best, the gracious and elegant Fairview Dining Room presents a lovely selection of Alberta beef, Tataki of Bison, and lamb and fish dishes as well as a wine list of over 400 labels from around the world, including wonderful British Columbia wines. Old-world tradition prevails at the Walliser Stube with a classic Swiss menu featuring their famous fondue. In summer, dine in the grand manner in the opulent Victoria Room where table-to-ceiling windows overlook lush flowers and the blue, blue lake. Stone fireplaces and wooden beams enhance the setting. Get an early start on your day at the Poppy Brasserie, or stop by for lunch or dinner (7:00 A.M. until 8:30 P.M.)—delicious international specialties are the order of the day. The Chateau Deli is open twenty-four hours a day and you can leisurely eat there or get it to go. Want a gourmet lunch to go or have a craving for a decadent dessert in the middle of the night? This is the place for you. Afternoon Tea in the Lakeview Lounge is a nice tradition, and not at all stuffy. A pot of specially blended tea, sparkling wine, exquisite finger sandwiches and pastries—ummm, quite civilized. At the other end of the day, sink into the throne-like chairs of the Lakeview Lounge and revel in the glacier, forested slopes, and other glorious views while you sip a sunset. Step through the doors of the Glacier Saloon and into the Old West. Shoot a game of pool, dance to live music, and meet and mingle; pub meals, light snacks, après-ski, and a patio in summer. Warmth and hospitality are what's really served throughout the hotel.

Children's World: A staff-supervised children's playroom is available daily in ski season, on weekends only at other times, including summer. Here kids from age three can do crafts, watch movies, play games, or (literally) hang out on the climbing wall. A C$10-per-day fee applies. Open from 9:00 A.M. to 10:00 P.M., parents may leave their children for a maximum of four hours while they pursue other activities within the hotel; they cannot, however, leave the grounds, as this is not licensed day care. At other times, babysitting can be arranged; rates are C$12 per hour for up to two children. A nice touch is that all sitters have undergone the Royal Canadian Mounted Police security check. Yes, the "Mounties" do still exist!

Five minutes away at the Lake Louise ski area, winter children's programs begin with day care for the wee ones to school age (C$39 for full day and $25 for half day) and Kinder-ski for ages three and four. Chocolate Moose Park combines indoor and outdoor fun; one-hour ski and play is C$15; morning and afternoon ski and play is C$25. Combined with day care, the cost is C$36 and C$46. Kids Ski for ages five to twelve explores the mountain and increases skill through fun and games. Snowboarding is for ages seven to twelve; both groups have instruction in small groups divided by age and abilities. A full day is C$69 with lift for either program.

Recreation: Lake Louise boasts 4,200 skiable acres, with over 113 marked runs, the longest of which is 8 kilometers (5 miles). Forty-five percent of the runs are intermediate, 30% are expert. A nice feature is that every chair lift has an easy and a more difficult way down, opening the mountain to all levels of ability. With a vertical rise of 3250 feet and a top elevation of 8,650, the annual 200-inch snowfall is respectable. Whether on a long run from the top of the mountain or in the middle of acres and acres of open bowls, everyone in the family will find his or her favorite terrain.

Cross-country skiing is a big feature at the Fairmont, with a wide variety of pictur-esque trails leading right from the hotel.

Ice-skating on Lake Louise, snowshoeing, dog-sledding, and horse-drawn sleigh rides add action to the wintertime picture. Evenings are filled with star-gazing and sto-ries by the fireplace. The resort has an indoor swimming pool, a hot tub, and a well-equipped exercise room; visit the spa for a variety of therapeutic treatments.

In May, the resort sponsors a wine and food festival. In summer, the Lake Louise Gondola and Interpretive Center does truly special programs. Ride to an elevation of 6,850 feet where two ecosystems meet and the Rockies are spread before you in a majestic panorama as you learn about griz-zly bears in their own habitat. Excursions that range from four to eight hours, with pro-fessional mountain guides, reveal the nature and history of the Canadian Rockies in a national park that is home to elk, bighorn sheep, moose, and mountain goats. Canoe-ing on the lake and biking the many trails open up to visitors the natural splendors of this region. Every imaginable mountain sport, winter or summer, is here. Torchlight dinners on the mountain, soaking the day away in the mineral hot springs, or heli-skiing the glacier—Lake Louise guarantees to live up to your expectations or gives you a "snow-cheque" to return. *SKIING* magazine voted Lake Louise number one for scenery and number two for value in all of North America in 2002. And the wonders of a great national park surround you; in Banff, don't miss the drive through the Bow Valley, or a day trip on the scenic Icefields Parkway.

---

111 Lake Louise Drive
Lake Louise, Alberta
Canada T0L 1E0
(403) 522–3511, (800) 441–1414
www.fairmont.com/lakelouise/
www.skilouise.com
www.canadianrockies.net

FAIRMONT LE CHÂTEAU MONTEBELLO

Montebello, Quebec

You don't have to travel all the way to Europe for a vacation in a French château. Voilá! The Fairmont Le Château Montebello is a luxury resort in a peaceful woodland setting located on the shores of the Ottawa River between Montreal and Ottawa.

Built of over 10,000 massive cedar logs by a team of craftsmen in 1930, Fairmont Le Château Montebello served as an exclusive private club for forty years. In 1970 it became a resort open to the public year-round, and last year celebrated its seventy-fifth anniversary. Today the Château's old-world charm and contemporary elegance come together as a lovely holiday destination, with the distinction of being one of the world's largest log structures. Le Château Montebello is a CAA/AAA Four Diamond resort with a five-star rating from Quebec Lodging. Awards are almost too numerous to list—in 2005, *Travel + Leisure*'s top 500, and *Condé Nast Traveler*'s Gold List for two years running; in 2004, perhaps most important as the praise comes from readers, the resort received Reader's Favorites status in *Departures, Condé Nast Traveler*'s Reader's Choice award as one of the top ten Canadian resorts, and as the number one family-friendly resort in Canada in *Travel + Leisure*'s Family Reader's Poll.

Accommodations: The central log chateau shelters all 211 guest rooms and suites, combining rustic elegance with a Swiss chalet–inspired decor. Guests can gather around the huge six-sided fireplace sitting in the center of the soaring three-story atrium for warmth and socializing. The chateau has four wings radiating from the center, affording the guest rooms views to the river, gardens, and forest. Yield manage-ment is the rule for rates at most Fairmont hotels. This means that rates depend more on availability than season—room rates seem to range from C$215 to C$309 in general. However, if occupancy were low, rates could drop. Between the end of May and late September, Family Fun two-night packages start from C$400 per night (two adults, two children under twelve; inquire for rates on teens) and include lodging, daily buffet breakfast and dinner, bike rental, miniputt, a pontoon boat cruise, half-day canoeing at Fairmont Kenauk, and the Children's Activity Program. With a minimum three-night pack-age, the rate drops to C$355 and includes even more "goodies." With any stay, a chil-dren's rate of C$36 for ages four to twelve includes buffet breakfast and dinner, wel-come gift, three hours of children's program or day care, evening films, crafts and other activities. Promotion is good daily in sum mer, and on weekends at other times of the year. This is a great deal, as the children's program alone is C$35. Bed-and-Breakfast packages start from C$227 per night based on double occupancy. Children eighteen and under stay free in the room with parents.

Dining: For dinner, Aux Chantignoles is the rustic yet gourmet dining room of the resort. Menu items such as rack of caribou with juniper berries enhance the feeling of a hunting club; the French flavor shows in the cassoulet of snails. The breakfast buffet gives a jump-start of energy to your day; this is also the venue for the Sunday brunch. The Golf Club Terrace is popular for light lunches; a food cart makes the rounds of the greens if you just can't wait. The Igloo Bar is a summer restaurant for outdoor barbecues, ideal for lunch or dinner. The

Bistro-Bar la Seigneurie is the place for gathering at the end of an active day; enjoy cocktails at the bar, "pub grub," or a light repast at one of the small tables or the central gazebo-like area while kids are entertained with video games and pool tables; a house band plays on weekends.

Rue Notre-Dame, where the hotel is located, has many popular eateries. Try the charming Café Terrasse la Lanterne, an ivy-covered roadside inn in Montebello's commercial district with river views and delectable desserts. For lunch, Le Bistro feels like dining at a friend's home; Le Zouk Resto-Pub is a rustic looking joint that's a favorite with locals and tourists alike. At night, the bar is a favorite hangout. For international dining, Le Mar-Lyn, in a beautiful old home, is great for romantic dinners while Le Pot au Feu serves up an eclectic and creative menu in a homey ambience.

Children's World: Daily during July, August, and school holidays, fun rules at the Children's Activity Center, from 9:00 A.M. to noon and evenings from 7:30 to 9:00 P.M. Appearances by Monte the Beaver create even more excitement. Year-round, the program operates only on Friday and Saturday evenings, Saturday from 9:00 A.M. to noon, and Sunday from 9:00 A.M. to 1:00 P.M. Outdoor activities such as hiking and group games are mixed with toys, games, and arts and crafts based on the ages and number of children in the program. The program, for ages three to twelve, is included in the Summer Family Fun package; otherwise, cost is C$35 per session. Outside of regular program hours, day care or babysitting is available at an hourly cost of C$9.00 for one child, C$10.00 for two children, with a three-hour minimum.

Recreation: Le Château Montebello is quite proud of its golf course, ranked as Quebec's second toughest by *Canada Golf Magazine*. It features a wide range of difficult holes and natural obstacles, so golfers need to be alert with a few tricks in their bag. The golf school provides lessons and organizes clinics. At the Health Club and Sports Complex, you can work out in the exercise room, play squash or tennis, swim laps in the indoor pool, or relax in the saunas or whirlpools. The outdoor pool is a beautiful setting for relaxing, sunning, and swimming. Referee the kids in volleyball and badminton games, then round up the whole crew for bike riding or miniputt. Other activities include water sports, cruises, jet-skiing, and horseback riding.

The Ultima Spa offers professional services, including full-body massage, facials, body wraps of mud or algae, body exfoliation and polishing, and therapeutic baths using either relaxing pine and rosemary milk or stimulating mineral salts. What a treat after a full day of activity!

The whole family can discover the beauties of Fairmont Kenauk, a 100-square-mile plant and wildlife preserve within 6 miles of the resort, with scores of activities—birdwatching, picnics, hikes with or without a naturalist, mountain biking, or fishing. Explore White Fish Lake by rowboat or canoe, float down the Kinonge River, or rent a motorboat at the marina. It's a great place to laze away summer days enjoying nature. Omega Park provides a slightly different approach to nature. Drive along a 10-kilometer road through 1,500 acres of a woodland corral where native animals small (raccoons, wild boar, and deer) and large (bison, black bears, and wild sheep) roam free. Don't forget your camera! About 10 miles west of Montebello is the Plaisance Waterfall, cascading more than 200 feet within the Papineau-Labelle Wildlife Reserve; a great spot for a picnic and hike.

Snow brings enchantment to the woods and hills and is the focus of wintertime fun. The familiar activities of ice-skating, ice-fishing, sleigh rides, and snowmobiling compete with the more exotic: dogsledding, curling, snowshoeing, broomball, and deck hockey. More than 27 kilometers of cross-country ski trails beckon, or you may prefer just a walk in the snow and curling up with a good book in front of the huge six-sided fireplace in the château.

392 rue Notre-Dame
Montebello, Quebec
Canada J0V 1L0
(819) 423–6341, (800) 441–1414
www.fairmont.com/montebello/

FAIRMONT
LE MANOIR RICHELIEU
Charlevoix, Quebec

In Quebec's Charlevoix County, near Quebec City, the mountains and forests stretching along the great St. Lawrence River create a vista of magnificent scenery and quiet charm. In this rural area, where farming and agriculture are part of daily life, Fairmont has created a historically splendid resort, blending the quiet charm of the countryside with the sophistication of a three-star, four-diamond resort. The hotel is the recipient of *Condé Nast Traveler*'s top seventy-five hotels in North America and is on the Gold List of World's Best Places to Stay. Tourism in Charlevoix dates back to 1761, when sports-men came for the salmon fishing and wilderness. The original Le Manoir Richelieu was built in 1899, atop a cliff overlooking the majestic St. Lawrence River. Destroyed by fire in 1928, it was rebuilt in the style of a French castle, and opened again in 1929. A $140-million renovation and expansion was completed in June of 1999, bringing the hotel back to its original glory.

The Charlevoix region was granted status as a World Biosphere Reserve by UNESCO in 1988, and is the first biosphere reserve to be populated in the world. Within its boundaries are historical gardens, art gal-leries, a marine museum and eco-center,

and many working studios for pottery, papermaking, and fabrics; an amazing vari-ety of wildlife also calls this area home.

Accommodations: Comfort and luxury are offered by 405 guest rooms and 17 one- and two-bedroom suites, and kids love the idea of staying in a castle. Summer is high season, when a Fairmont room with garden view is C$269, river view is C$319. Those same rooms in winter are C$149 and C$189; and in spring the rates drop even more. Children under eighteen stay free in the room with parents. A summer family fun package includes breakfast and dinner, miniputt, a horse-drawn carriage ride, bike rental, tennis, and the kids' club; rates vary according to number and ages of children.

Dining: For fine dining, the four-diamond restaurant Le Charlevoix, overlooking the St. Lawrence, showcases antiques, local art, and fresh produce from the region. Le Saint-Laurent, the hotel's main dining room, is open for breakfast and dinner, and is famous for its buffet. Also overlooking the river, fresh fish and grilled specialties will tempt you. Families enjoy Le Bellerive, with a relaxed bistro atmosphere, which serves a casual menu and light buffet. In summer dine alfresco on the sunny terrace. For a romantic evening, the French cuisine at L'Auberge sur La Cote in nearby La Malbaie is a favorite of townsfolk. Sip a cocktail at La Brise Lobby Bar or stroll over to the Bar Le Marie-Clarisse or Salon Murray at the Casino.

Children's World: The "Club des amis," or Friends' Club, is just that, a friendly place for children to gather. A membership card and surprise gift is given when registering. In summer the club operates daily from 8:00 A.M. to 10:00 P.M. for ages four to twelve. Fees are C$12.00 per hour (C$6.00 each additional child) or C$75.00 for the entire day (C$60.00 for second child, C$50.00 for the third), including meals. Daytime (8:00 A.M. to 5:00 P.M.; C$60.00) and evening (5:00 to 10:00 P.M.; C$55.00) sessions are also available. Children participate in aquatic games, swimming, sports, arts and crafts, treasure hunts, and nature excursions. A mini-cinema for kids has shows from 7:00 A.M. to 8:00 P.M., with popcorn. A giant beanbag and children's playground are always popular.

In winter, weekends for kids begin at 5:00 P.M. Friday and continue almost nonstop until noon on Sunday. Friday and Saturday nights until 10:00 P.M. and all day Saturday are filled with the same pursuits as summer, plus the outdoor thrill of snowshoes, ice-skating, and sledding. Babysitting is available for C$6.00 per hour with a three-hour minimum.

Recreation: Golf at the Fairmont Le Manoir Richelieu began in 1925, when President William Taft opened the eighteen-hole course. At the turn of this century it was named "Canada's Golf Resort of the Year" by *Canada's Golf Ranking Magazine,* and was listed one of *Golf Magazine's* Silver Medal Resorts in 2002. As well, at least three public courses are nearby, so golfers can't get complacent. At the resort itself, enjoy saltwater swimming indoors or out, a wading pool, and water volleyball and basketball. A

game room provides evening entertainment for the family. An evening spent at the Casino de Charlevoix, next door to the hotel, may be rewarding—if your luck holds. Horseback riding with gorgeous views, pony rides for the youngsters, and carriage rides at sunset are found at the equine center. Tennis, aqua-aerobics, hiking, a fitness room, and mountain biking will keep you in shape while a whirlpool soothes you at the end of it all. Lawn games and French Bowl are delightful ways to pass an afternoon. AmeriSpa can pamper you with twenty-two treatment rooms, and even a seven-day rejuvenation.

Winter snows bring wonderful outdoor opportunities such as sleigh rides, dogsledding, ice-fishing, horseback riding, and all those sports that require snowshoes, skates, or cross-country skis. Plus you can give the traditional Canadian sport of broomball a whirl. The Multi-Sports Center can arrange it all. Snowmobiles are so popular that the resort provides parking, if you want to bring your own! Skiers have a choice of Mont Grand-Fonds (15 kilometers from the hotel) with a 335-meter vertical drop and cross-country skiing; or Le Massif, at 770 meters (2,536 feet) the highest vertical drop east of the Canadian Rockies, with an average snowfall of over 250 inches (80 kilometers away). The hotel has shuttles to both ski areas.

For foreigners, shopping at the hotel or nearby local craft shops and art galleries can be a bargain with the exchange rates and tax regulations. The Route des Saveurs (Flavor Trail) showcases the region's excellent products: lamb, migneron cheese, and mini-vegetables. The circuit includes restaurants that use regional products in their cuisine; and also a tour of the farms that produce them. It's an authentic glimpse into another way of life, and a great way for kids to make the connections with where food originates other than the grocery store. The Park of Hautes-Gorges-de-la-Riviere-Malbaie follows the Riviere Malbaie as it winds through some of the most extraordinary valleys between the highest cliffs east of the Canadian Rockies. Here you can participate in biking, canoeing, hiking, and kayaking; or the more sedate can enjoy a glass-bottom boat cruise. A cruise to the mouth of the St. Lawrence to witness migratory whales is a thrilling experience for all; between June and October at least six species of whales also visit. Charming villages dot the coastline. The Tourism Office (800–667–2276) has loads of information.

---

181 rue Richelieu
Charlevoix, Quebec G5A 1X7
(418) 665–3703, (800) 257–7544
www.fairmont.com/richelieu

GRAY ROCKS RESORT
Ville de Mont-Tremblant, Quebec

Just 75 miles northwest of Montreal, in the Laurentian Mountains, you will find a charming four-season, four-star lakeside family resort with a French flavor. Right in the middle of French-speaking Canada, Gray Rocks welcomes American visitors and both French and English are spoken here routinely. You might choose to take the opportunity to brush up on your French, but rest assured that your interests uttered in English in the dining room, on the tennis courts, or during a ski lesson will be well received with warm French-Canadian hospitality.

Since its beginning in 1906, Gray Rocks has developed into a renowned ski, golf, and tennis resort with hotel and condominium accommodations for all tastes. The hotel sits on the shores of Lac Ouimet. Gray Rocks's own ski mountain, Sugar Peak, rises right behind the hotel; beautiful views of Mont-Tremblant are also impossible to miss. Golf was the first sport in this area, followed by skiing. Today recreational pastimes also include tennis, water sports, horseback riding, mountain biking, or nature hikes.

Accommodations: Fifty-one lakeside rooms with private balcony are available in the hotel's Pavilion and Chalet Suisse; fifty-four regular rooms have lake or mountain views; rooms and suites have various bed arrangements. Fifty-six one-, two-, and three-bedroom condominiums are tucked in among the trees ¾ mile from the hotel, with free shuttle-bus service. As usual, rates depend on the size of the accommodation, the number of people, the location, and the season. Children five years and under receive free lodging and meals; six to ten years receive 45% off double occupancy rates; and eleven to seventeen receive 35% off double occupancy rates. Gray Rocks has multiple seasons: spring (end of May to early July), regular (July and the last week of August), summer (most of August), fall (early September to early October), and winter (which is even more complicated!). Hotel package rates are per person, per night, and include access to indoor pool and exercise area, private beach, nonmotorized watercraft, social programs in the evenings (seasonal), and a full hot and cold buffet breakfast and dinner daily; condominium rates are per unit, per night and are without meals. Hotel rates range from C$99 to C$139 in spring and fall; C$119 to C$159 in regular season; and C$129 to C$169 in summer. Condominium spring and fall rates are C$159 to $239; $199 to $359 in regular season; and C$239 to C$479 in summer. If you're renting a condo and want a meal plan, it's C$55 for adults, C$45 for ages eleven to seventeen, and C$35 for ages six through ten. Under-fives always eat free.

In winter guests enjoy a getaway similar to the summer hotel package, with free skiing at Gray Rocks or nearby sister resort Mont Blanc. The package is for one night's lodging (two days), dinner and breakfast, access to the pool, and social entertainment. Regular season rates range from C$155 to C$205 per person, and children's rates apply. This package is for hotel guests only. Condominium rates during regular season range from C$268 to C$469 per unit per day, with no extras.

The most popular winter package is the all-inclusive ski or snowboard week from Sunday to Saturday morning. You will enjoy six nights of lodging; eighteen full-course meals; twenty hours of ski instruction or ten hours of snowboard instruction with the renowned Snow Eagle Ski School; video critique; seven-day lift ticket; races and awards; complete social program for adults, teens, and children; and access to the fitness center with indoor pool. In the regular season, the package is C$1,454 to C$1,851 per person based on double occupancy. Condominium rates are C$1,543 to C$2,699 per unit per week (six nights, seven days), again with no extras. To add the Ski Week amenities to the condos, but no meals, adults pay C$325, and children ages three through seventeen are C$280; under-fives still eat free. Note that value season rates are generally C$100 to C$350 per person less than regular season rates for the Ski Week package; and C$385 to C$685 less for the condominiums. Holiday season, when rates are the highest, incorporates Christmas, Presidents' Week, and some March dates. Skiing can be an affordable sport, after all. And Gray Rocks is family friendly both winter and summer.

Dining: The main dining room, with its fireplace and picture windows overlooking scenic Lac Ouimet, provides a pleasant ambience during meals. Continental and French-Canadian cuisines are featured; four-course table d'hôte dinners and lavish breakfast buffets keep guests satisfied. Cozy lounges with fireplaces and lake views are perfect to relax and mix with old and new friends; the Thirsty Eagle Bar, with a circular fireplace, has evening entertainment in season. In summer, twice weekly barbecues are scheduled on the outdoor patio. There's also a cafeteria at the Chalet Lucile Wheeler, located midmountain and accessible by car, shuttle bus, or skis. Both golf courses have a club house with snack bar and lounge area.

Children's World: In summer during July and August, the daily children's activity program is in high gear. Youngsters join other children their own ages for supervised morning and afternoon events. Preschoolers ages three to five head to the playground, go on treasure hunts and hayrides, or frolic on the private beach. Kids ages six to nine go swimming and horseback riding, try their talents in arts and crafts, and join hayrides. Preteens (ten to twelve) and teens (thirteen and older) enjoy volleyball, tennis, hiking, canoeing, sailboarding, fishing, and various excursions. For all children ages three to five, the cost is C$35 per child per day and includes lunch. The 8:30 A.M. to 3:30 P.M. programs are included for hotel guests ages six to seventeen as part of the package. Camp is available to condominium guests' children for C$35. Day care for ages six months to two years is also offered, and promises "vigilant supervision and experienced staff"; the ratio of children to supervisor is 2:1 and cost varies from C$17 per hour, C$40 for a half day, and C$65 for a full day with lunch. Private babysitting may be arranged, with a three-hour minimum.

Junior Golf clinics run Monday through Friday, for a total of ten hours. The teaching ratio is 5:1 and the fee is C$195. Junior tennis clinics are offered for ages five to ten and eleven to fourteen; C$15 per one-hour session, Monday through Friday. For more serious aspirations, the one- or two-week resident Junior Camp programs in golf and tennis will definitely improve skills.

In winter Gray Rocks's philosophy is to put children on skis as much as possible. Given that the resort's own gentle mountain is just out the back door, this philosophy is easily practiced. The children's ski classes are divided along age lines as well as ability; heaven forbid your first-time thirteen-year-old skier should be in a class with four-year-olds! Camaraderie in a peer group is important in the learning experience. Children and teens can also meet their friends in a variety of après-ski activities, such as cookie baking, face painting, treasure hunts, arts and crafts, table tennis tournaments, parties, movies, water polo, and sleigh rides or bingo with Mom and Dad. You want to have some fun with your kids, too!

Day-care service is also available in winter for ages six months to two years as well as private babysitting. Snow Eaglets combines day care and snow play with an introduction to skiing. Three-year-olds spend one to two hours (as tolerated) in outside play and ski familiarization; four- and five-year-olds have more stamina and therefore more ski time. It's very personalized for your child's abilities and desires. Daily rates are C$60 for a full day with lunch, and C$35 for a half day; C$285 for a five-day week includes 8:30 A.M. to 4:00 P.M. daily, with lunch. In addition, Monday evening from 5:00 to 6:00 P.M., children gather while parents have wine and cheese; and again from 6:00 to 10:00 P.M. on Friday, for the awards and ski dinner. On the mountain an exclusive snow park for beginners is close to the day lodge and children's services and is kept secure with an easy-ride "magic carpet" lift and fenced outdoor play area.

The Junior Ski and Snowboard weekly program is designed for ages six to thirteen; it's included with hotel vacation packages, C$285 for condo guests. Two-hour ski lessons in the morning and afternoon (snowboarding is morning only), plus the special evening hours, have kids schussing down the slopes by the end of the week.

Recreation: Think of Gray Rocks as a university for sports. Its qualified ski, golf, and tennis instructors combine expertise with a sincere enthusiasm for teaching. Improvement of skills and self-confidence go hand in hand, and both are better achieved with ample doses of encouragement and humor. More than 250,000 ski-weekers have enjoyed Gray Rocks's unique teaching methods in a safe, uncrowded ski environment.

The Snow Eagle Ski School has a fine reputation (rated by *Ski* magazine as one of the top-ten ski schools in North America) and more than fifty years of experience. The resort boasts a number of third-generation families who have learned to ski on these slopes and continue to return for their winter holidays. Though Gray Rocks has a modest 620-foot vertical drop, there's variety and, if not long, then challenging runs. Snowmaking facilities cover 95% of the slopes, ensuring a ski season from Thanksgiving through early April. Mont-Tremblant ski resort is less than 5 miles from Gray Rocks, so intermediate and advanced skiers can seek additional challenges there. The ski boutique can meet your needs for rentals, repairs, fashions, and accessories. Cross-country skiing is a growing favorite at Gray Rocks. Nearby Domaine St. Bernard offers well-maintained trails through the woods, next to the river. A tour around the area is a lovely way to spend a winter morning, and a sleigh ride with the kids caps off a perfect day.

Summertime opens another whole realm of outdoor sports and activities. There's a private sandy beach along a section of the lake. This is Canada, but summers are hot, so swimmers will be happy. The complete marina near the beach offers opportunity for canoeing, sailboarding, sailing, taking out a paddleboat, or enjoying an afternoon of fishing.

A classic eighteen-hole golf course (La Belle) will take you through lush fairways over diverse terrain framed by the rugged beauty of the Laurentians. Three learning holes are reserved for Eagle Golf Academy players. The combination of time-proven teaching strategies and small class ratios helps players take strokes off their game and turns newcomers on to the joys of the sport. Gray Rocks recently opened an eighteen-hole championship course (La Bête) designed by renowned golf architect Graham Cooke. The course winds its way along Devil's River, offering superb views of the surrounding mountains. With bent grass tees, greens, and fairways, four sets of tees to choose from, and eighteen distinct and challenging holes, you will leave knowing you have played one of Canada's best courses. In fact, it was voted the best family golf resort in Quebec by *Golf Ranking Magazine.*

Tennis buffs enjoy the largest outdoor complex in Canada with twenty-two Har-Tru courts (ten near the hotel and twelve at the golf club). Tennis lessons with videotaping can help you isolate the improvements necessary for a good game. Gray Rocks's golf and tennis academies offer acclaimed two- and five-day clinics.

Jogging along the lake or hiking and horseback riding in the hills are excellent ways to explore the countryside and revel in the clean mountain air. You can enjoy a nice afternoon next to the beach playing lawn games, or get in shape at Le Spa fitness center. Le Spa features an indoor swimming pool, an exercise room, hot tubs, a sauna, and a professional massage service. Many activities are offered free of charge; some, such as golf, tennis, and horseback riding, carry additional fees.

Family activities are many at Gray Rocks. Visiting the playground, sharing the putting green or croquet, evening barbecue and bonfire, bingo, karaoke night, and hay (or sleigh) rides are just some of the ways families share fun.

2322 reu Labelle
Ville de Mont-Tremblant, Quebec
Canada J8E 1T8
(819) 425–2771, (800) 567–6767
www.grayrocks.com

SEVERN LODGE
Port Severn, Ontario

Severn Lodge is beautifully located in the midst of the Georgian Lakelands of Ontario, only 90 miles from Toronto. Georgia Bay forms the northeastern part of Lake Huron and is named in honor of England's King George IV. The area's piney woods, fine fishing, and clear waters attract many vacationers. The geographic features of the Cambrian Shield area where the lodge is located are unique. Spectacular rock formations created during the Ice Age, granite outcroppings, windswept pines, and hardwood forests dot the many islands and inlets. And the Severn Lodge, on the shores of Gloucester Pool, adds to the natural features with its warm pride of being "owned and operated by the same family, for families, since 1937." Severn Lodge is a special place, where the everyday hustle and bustle quiets, and one has time to breathe the fresh air, relax, and do as much or as little as you want. Set in a sheltered cove, the resort encompasses one hundred acres of waterfront property, with over 2,000 feet of private shoreline. The lodge is open from mid-May to mid-October only.

Accommodations: Severn Lodge dates back to the late 1800s. Its early-twentieth-century ambience remains preserved in the many white clapboard buildings, log crisscross railings, and cobblestone sidewalks. All accommodations and facilities, however, are very modern.

Grouped in about a dozen individual buildings surrounding the main lodge and set among the trees and along the lake, the accommodations are in three styles. Hotel-style rooms have two double beds with a view of the waterfront; family-size rooms are one large room with two sleeping areas separated by a dividing wall and a sitting area with sofa bed; and two-bedroom units offer more privacy. Three different rate groups reflect location and different amenities. Two- to seven-day packages are fully inclusive and include lodging, baggage handling, two or three meals daily (according to the season), the children's activity program, evening entertainment, and use of the recreation facilities. Children's rates are based on age and some weeks during summer (June especially) are designated "kids free" (under twelve) and 50% off for teens. Stays for children two and under are always complimentary. Adult rates are per person and range from C$209 to C$398 for spring and fall (two to three days). Seven days in July and August run C$979 to C$1,193 for adults, up to C$569 for ages two to twelve, and teens are C$339 to C$679. Cottages

and suites are located both on-site and off-site, about five minutes by boat or car from the resort. These rates are per unit, and include the deluxe recreation package but no meals or daily maid service. Weekly rates range from C$1,629 to C$2,179. Remember, that's less in U.S. dollars, depending on the current exchange.

Dining: The charming, elegantly rustic dining room has a wood-beamed ceiling and many large windows that capture the views. The Canadian cuisine is accompanied by freshly baked breads and pastries. Severn Lodge has a reputation for delicious foods, and children always have special choices (including vegetables and fruit), and even their own summertime buffet. A weekly excursion takes all the children to a nearby island for a picnic. Some summer days feature a poolside barbecue with grilled foods; you can dine either inside or outside. Usually you have four or five choices for dinner; one night each week there's a barbecue, another may be a deluxe buffet. Fresh, high-quality, healthy foods are always used, and vegetarians are not forgotten. Picnic lunches can be prepared for guests who are off hiking or canoeing during the midday meal.

Children's World: The summer activities program seems to combine the best of all worlds, flexibly structured yet with lots of freedom. Children gather after breakfast, break for lunch with parents, and after that, they're off again until about 5:00 P.M. Daily from mid-June to Labor Day the camp includes hikes, crafts, volleyball and baseball games, swimming, diving and boating lessons, picnics, and movies. Add waterskiing, Indian Night, Talent Night, a Fish Derby, corn roasts, and bonfire sing-alongs and you know you have happy kids. No additional charges are applied for these events, and children of all ages are welcome to participate.

Every effort is made to include even very young guests, but a supervised toddler activity program also provides pint-size fun, with specially designed indoor and outdoor play areas for two- to four-year-olds. The program is complimentary and includes arts and crafts, sand-castle building, and other beach and playground activities. This program runs daily, and kids eat most meals with their parents. The lodge staff can also arrange an individual babysitter for an extra cost. Favorites among the younger set are the sandy beach; the playground, with its swings, slide, sandbox, and climbing equipment; and the dock, for "just fishin'." The Junior Program (ages five to eight) has supervised activities around themes of history, culture, or nature. Kids are kept busy with fishing derbies, waterskiing and tubing, island picnics, and scavenger hunts. Ages nine to twelve are in the Youth Program, filled with age-appropriate fun, and teens have just what they like—many things to do and not too much structure. Programs for older children are daily in high summer, but all ages eat most meals with parents; occasionally a pizza party or picnic is scheduled "for kids only."

Recreation: Severn Lodge also knows that creating family memories is an important part of the vacation. Lots of family activities such as picnics, canoeing the coves, horseback riding, and just exploring can be fit into the flexible schedules of the kids' program. Evening entertainment in the Regatta Room is geared toward all ages, and often includes children. Severn Lodge is really a family operation, and programming is eclectic and interesting. Sometimes it may be a nature "show and tell," where a local expert with reptiles or falcons will come, bringing "friends" to demonstrate their stories. Or an early "explorer" will land on the lakeshore during the bonfire, and tell stories about the early days of discovery. There's a sense of camaraderie about Severn that makes a memorable vacation.

Water sports are an important part of Severn Lodge. Wonderful swimming can be had either in the lake or in the heated swimming pool; perhaps you'd like to try the whirlpool spa at the deepwater dock. Maybe you would prefer to stay on top of the water in a fishing boat reeling in walleye, bass, muskie, and northern pike. Also on top of the water (with any luck, you will stay on top) is the waterskiing instruction offered several times a week. Free use of the lodge's sailboats, paddleboats, kayaks, and canoes can make an afternoon lazy or exciting, depending on your skill. The resort has a unique collection of antique runabouts and motor launches. Rental fees are charged on a daily or weekly basis for outboard boats, motors, and Jet-Skis; the lodge offers island cruises aboard the 37-foot vintage 1922 mahogany motor launch for an extra charge.

On land you can jog or hike on the trails around the lodge's one hundred acres, explore on mountain bikes, or play a game of tennis. The recreation building, with its library and large stone fireplace, is quite inviting if relaxing is a favorite pastime; here you will find table tennis, a wide-screen TV, card and board games, and a pool table.

Nearby sightseeing (15 to 20 miles) takes you back in history; Sainte-Marie among the Hurons, a Jesuit Mission, and the Huron Indian Village are reconstructions of seventeenth-century settlements. You will also find horseback riding, golf, live theater, museums, casino gambling, and fabulous shopping in nearby lakeside villages. Canada's Wonderland, a major theme park, is one hour away.

Box 250, 116 Gloucester Trail
Port Severn, Ontario
Canada L0K 1S0
(705) 756–2722, (800) 461–5817
www.severnlodge.on.ca

SUNSHINE VILLAGE

Banff National Park, Alberta

High in the Canadian Rockies in Banff National Park is Sunshine Village, one of the best ski destinations in Canada. Perched along the Continental Divide, the peak elevation at Sunshine is 9,200 feet. Located only 85 miles west of Calgary and just 5 miles from the town of Banff, Sunshine is a three-mountain ski resort, Goat's Eye, Mount Standish, and Lookout, constantly being improved. Back in the '20s and '30s, Banff was a summer destination. Those skiers that did come were usually from Europe, and were referred to by the locals as "those people with wooden heads and feet to match." Most had to ski over from Banff—hardly a day trip!

In summer White Mountain Adventures in Canmore provides day trips only, starting you out on the mountaintop for hiking and mountain pleasures. Follow the clearly marked trails on your own, or take a free interpretive walk led by experts. Uncrowded and incredibly scenic, Sunshine Village is a good example of man and nature in harmony.

Accommodations: The Sunshine Inn, constructed in the 1960s and '70s, is still the only on-slope accommodation in the Canadian Rockies; it's right in the middle of the ski area, at an elevation of 7,200 feet with access via gondola. A three-story complex consisting of eighty-four rooms and suites, the inn affords its guests ski-in, ski-out access and a chance at making those coveted "first tracks." Accommodation options include rooms and suites in the main hotel and older terrace rooms in an adjoining wing. Terrace rooms have separate sleeping areas with doors, but showers only and no TV; inn rooms have full bath and TV, a queen, and sofa bed. Rates include lift tickets, and children six and under always stay and ski free. Children over six pay

C$25. In value season, standard inn rooms begin at C$310. Check in on a Sunday and stay five nights for special rates that include lodging, lift tickets, four hours daily ski lessons, and some evening activities. Cost for a five-night ski package in a terrace room is C$2,150, C$1,750 in a standard inn room, and children over six pay C$225. Festive and Powder seasons are more expensive.

Getting to the inn is easy. Check in at the base area, take the gondola to the village, and start skiing. Your bags will magically arrive at your room, and your car will be parked. If you arrive outside of gondola hours, you'll have the thrill of taking "Sunshine Suzy," a cross between an SUV and a tank. She's also available for a fee if you want to escape the mountain at an odd hour, say for an evening in Banff. In the world's longest and fastest gondola, the trip takes twelve minutes; gondola hours begin at 8:00 A.M. and weekday closing is at 5:30 P.M., 7:00 P.M. on Saturday, and 10:30 P.M. on Friday and Sunday. If you want to ski Sunshine but don't fancy staying on the mountaintop, central reservations has options in Banff.

Dining: Three locations on the mountain offer amenities. The mountaintop village, where the inn is located, has the largest selection with six restaurants, bars, and lounges. The inn's dining room, the Eagle's Nest, offers fine dining, from rack of lamb to fantastic sirloin steak. The Chimney Corner is a lounge offering cocktails, well-priced food, and entertainment in the evenings. In the Daylodge, the Deli and the cafeteria-style Alpine Grill offer soup and sandwiches; the new Mad Trappers Saloon, located in the original 1928 Sunshine Lodge, is the place to go for lunch, drinks, and après-ski. Goat's Eye is the midstop; the gondola connects to the village at the top and the base area. Goat's Eye Gardens has hot food and drinks as well as snacks, beer, and wine. The gondola base area is where you first arrive, and has a great restaurant. The Creekside Bar and Grill has just about everything—a to-go breakfast so you can hit the slopes early, sandwiches and pizza for lunch, plus a full sit-down menu and at the end of the day, an après-ski bar.

When you feel like escaping the mountain, nearby Banff has one hundred–plus restaurants, many of them family-friendly. Joe Btfsplk's Diner is a 1950s-style diner complete with jukebox, neon, and red vinyl booths; what better than a burger and a shake, unless it's homemade meatloaf and apple pie. Casual dining on hearty, traditional Italian food is the order of the day at the Old Spaghetti Factory where portions are so large you might consider sharing. In an original 1928 building, Melissa's has served Alberta steak and a great kid's menu for over twenty-seven years—locals say the breakfast is *huge*. Craig's Way Station has an extensive menu, with specials for kids, including fourteen different chicken dishes. Have breakfast here at any time of day, with fireplace and view.

Children's World: Day care and children's ski schools are in the village at the base of the Clock Tower, where children are carefully supervised in a variety of programs. Be sure to check exactly what is included in the five-day packages, as you may want to adjust the kids' programs to fit what is complimentary into a coherent day for your youngster. Tiny Tigers Daycare is a safe, licensed facility for ages nineteen months to six years, with indoor and outdoor play, lunch, and snacks. Cost is C$30 for a half day, C$55 for a full day. Five full days are C$233. Three- to five-year-olds have all the advantages of day care, plus one hour of skiing in the morning and afternoon—it's popular, so reserve early. Cost is

C$49 for a half day, C$78 for a full day, and C$323 for the five-day package.

Children from six to twelve years old have the Kids Kampus program where laughter and play go hand-in-hand with learning to be better skiers or riders. A full day is C$85 and a five-day package is C$350, both including lunch. An introductory program for first-timers (ages six to twelve) provides everything needed to get kids started enjoying the snow with skis or boards. A full day is C$130; add-on days are also available. We all know that different ages have different notions about what's fun. Sunshine Mountain Riders for thirteen- to eighteen-year-olds knows what this group wants. Small teams spend the day exploring the mountain with peers, grouped by age and ability; lunch and easy socializing included for C$89 daily or $374 for five full days.

Recreation: Sunshine Village is located on the Continental Divide, where you can ski the provinces of both British Columbia and Alberta off the same run. The top elevation at Sunshine is almost 9,000 feet and the base elevation is 5,440 feet, yielding skiers more than 3,500 vertical feet. Mother Nature drops more than 10 meters (33 feet) of snow here each year, which results in good skiing from mid-November through the end of May. Of the 101 named runs currently open, 55% are intermediate; the remainder are split evenly between beginner and expert. Many of the runs are above the treeline, giving skiers that top-of-the-world feeling. Sunshine Village boasts North America's largest new ski terrain, Goat's Eye Mountain (elevation 9,200 feet), offering extreme-expert-only (Double Black Diamond) chutes and glades, runs, and free fall with an 83-degree pitch. Two snowboarding parks (one half-pipe and one terrain park) keep snowboarders happy.

When not skiing, you may want to pursue less rigorous activities in the family games room or relax your weary muscles in the sauna or the Sunshine Inn's giant outdoor hot pool, rated Canada's best by *Ski Canada* magazine. Mad Trapper's is the gathering place to down a few and grab a bite, to trade mountain adventures and tall tales of the trails, and to make new friends from all over the world.

Box 1510
Banff, Alberta
Canada T0L 0C0
(403) 762–6500, (877) 542–2633
www.skibanff.com

WHISTLER/BLACKCOMB
Whistler, British Columbia

If you're lucky enough to hear the whistling call of the indigenous marmots, you'll easily recognize how Whistler Mountain got its current name. Originally known as London Mountain, on the old Caribou Gold Rush Trail, this area saw its first settlers in 1914, an adventurous couple who built a fishing lodge on the shores of Alta Lake. Though still attracting fishermen in the summer, Whistler is famous today as an outstanding ski destination. The village has a permanent population of approximately 10,000 people.

Skiers first schussed these slopes in the mid-1960s, and the early 1980s witnessed considerable expansion and development, primarily the opening of Blackcomb Mountain. The two mountains, Whistler and Blackcomb, are serviced by three base facilities. In the Coastal Mountains, Whistler/Blackcomb is just 75 miles north of Vancouver.

Here's just some of what people are saying about Whistler: *Ski* magazine calls it the number one ski area in North America and the "#1 Dream Vacation Destination"; the *Daily Telegraph* has rated it the number two ski resort in the world. It has the longest ski season in Canada; and in North America boasts the most skiable terrain (more than 7,000 acres), the greatest lift-serviced vertical (5,280 feet), the most slopeside accommodations, and the most qualified ski instructors. *Family Travel Forum* rated it the Top Family Getaway and it was *BC Parent's* Families Favorite Ski Resort. It garnering fifteen new awards in 2005, including best mountaineering, best late season resort, *Condé Nast's* Hot List, best new expert terrain. And finally, *USA Today* called Whistler one of the top ten places to chill while enthusiasts ski. Whew, that's a lot of mountain! Better go soon and beat the crowd, as Whistler has been chosen as the site of the 2010 Olympics and Paralympics games. Whistler will host the Alpine, Nordic, Sliding, and all Paralympic events, while Vancouver will host the ice events, freestyle skiing, and snowboarding. The Olympics Information Center is near the marketplace in the village.

Accommodations: Hotels and condominiums are found throughout Whistler Resort in all price ranges. In 2003 five Whistler hotels were named on the *Condé Nast* reader's poll of the top fifty ski resorts in North America: the Westin Resort (#1), the Fairmont Château Whistler (#2), the Pan Pacific Lodge (#8), the Summit Lodge (#13), and the Delta Whistler Resort (#17) all garnered acclaim. *Condé Nast* in 2005 named the Westin Spa and The Vida Wellness Spa at the Fairmont Château Whistler as top resort spas. A Four Seasons hotel and resort opened in 2004 in the Upper Village; 2005 will bring the London Mountain Lodge, twenty-five log cabins on ten acres of the western shore of Nita Lake. The larger facilities are the Fairmont Château Whistler at the base of Blackcomb, with ski-in, ski-out convenience, 550 units, indoor and outdoor swimming pools, a health club, and indoor tennis courts; the Delta Whistler Village Mountain Suites, an all-suite facility; and the Westin Resort, one of the locations for day-care facilities and child care with ski-in, ski-out options and 419 suites, in the heart of the village. Midsize properties are the Marriott Residence Inn, with 184 units slopeside on Blackcomb Mountain, or the Crystal Lodge in the village, with 134 rooms. For condominiums, consider Stony Creek, Glaciers Reach, and Aspens; smaller complexes such as the Hearthstone Lodge, Powderview, Whistler Resort and Club, or Whiski Jack Condos might also be the perfect choice for your family. Contacting Central Experience at (800) WHISTLER is the first step in sorting out all these choices. Tell them your priorities and they'll help find the perfect lodging for your family. You might want to consider one of the available packages, or book a "hot deal" online. Inquire about the PEAK rating system to help with consistent, reliable information.

Most everything is within easy walking distance, and pedestrian-only spaces means real freedom of movement and less worry about the children. Upper Village is located at the foot of Blackcomb Mountain—here you'll find the chairlift, and in summer, the Farmer's Market and Kid's Adventure Zone. It's a short five-minute walk to Whistler Village. The Whistler Activity Centre at the Conference Center is a good resource for maps, activities, tours, restaurant recommendations, and information. Hours are 9:00 A.M. to 5:00 P.M. daily. The free Village Shuttle runs from 8:00 A.M. to midnight daily, and makes a loop from Marketplace (Village North) to the Upper Village—the front of the bus says Village Shuttle, so you can't miss it.

Dining: With almost a hundred restaurants and cafes, you'll never have trouble indulging your palate's whim, whether you crave French, Italian, Japanese, Mexican, Thai, or Greek cuisine or even fast food. Five restaurants on Whistler and eight on Blackcomb serve hearty soups and stews, burgers, pizza, waffles, sushi, quiche, and pasta to skiers reluctant to leave the slopes for very long. Christine's at the top of Blackcomb Mountain lets you enjoy fine dining in your ski boots, with a view as superb as the menu. At Blackcomb Base II, 18 Degrees Below is the breakfast and lunch spot for teens, with their kind of food—burgers, fries, and pizza. Blackcomb has several log cabins scattered around the mountainside with tasty treats like waffles or barbecue. A special evening snowmobile adventure to the Crystal Hut for a cheese fondue makes a nice family memory. The Dubh Linn Gate Pub at mountains' base is an authentic Irish Pub, perfect for day's end. In a ski resort known for fine dining, The Bearfoot Bistro is not just a meal but an experience—five courses served with five different wines. Some of the restaurants favored by families are Black's Restaurant, The Old Spaghetti Factory, Monk's at Blackcomb, Dusty's at Whistler Creek, and the Keg Steakhouse. Caramba, Earl's, the Mongolie Grill, Milestones, and Wildwood are more family favorites. Après-ski is also family-friendly here; children of all ages are welcome until 7:00 P.M., so you can enjoy a drink with friends while the kids have hot chocolate.

Children's World: Whistler Kids has 500 instructors dedicated to making the mountains a kids' playground. The instructors are highly trained ski and snowboard professionals, specializing in kids' needs. Teaching more than 140,000 kids every winter, Whistler Kids is Canada's premier recreational operation for children. No wonder the kids keep bringing their parents back!

Whistler Kids offers a broad range of programs catering to kids as young as three months; kids first take to skis at three years. Daily rates for full-day day care at three locations are C$98 and ski programs for three- to four-year-olds are C$103 with lift and lesson; five- to six-year-olds are C$99 for lesson and lift, either ski or snowboard (available for ages six and up only). Seven- to twelve-year-olds can choose ski or snowboard programs for C$121; and Ride Tribe! for ages twelve to eighteen gives them lots of action and informal lessons with no standing around (C$134). Twelve-year-olds can choose either Whistler Kids or Ride Tribe. If time permits, consider one of the Adventure Ski Camps, available at all levels. Packed with fun activities, kids stay with the same group and instructor, building friendships and confidence and increasing learning and skills. Two-day camps run on the weekend, three-day camps from Monday to Wednesday, and five-day camps are Monday through Friday.

Saturday Night Out from 6:00 to 10:00 P.M. is for kids ages five to twelve and gives everybody a break. The mountain and the village are the stage for themed nights with dinner and experiences they can't wait to tell you about (C$45). On Thursday, mid-December to mid-March, weather permitting, Whistler Kids Jib Sessions provides an evening introduction to tricks and jibs on the Magic Carpet and Magic Chair (ages five to twelve, minimum Level 3 ability). From 5:30 to 9:30 P.M., kids should be ready to jump, jib, jive, and have dinner too!

But Whistler is not just about winter. Unlike most ski resorts, Whistler has children's programs year-round. In the spring, programs are daily from late April to late June, for ages eighteen months to twelve years. Running from 9:00 A.M. to 4:00 P.M., activities are similar to the summer, with two age groups (eighteen months to four years and five to twelve years). Cost is C$79 including lunch and snacks; half day is C$45. Fall is a similar program but details were not available at press time. The Sports Center, Meadow Park, and the Whistler community also have summer camps and activities for children and families. Late June to Labor Day, daily summer programs for children are packed with activities that build skills and self-confidence and are just plain fun. Located at various venues throughout Whistler, there's something for kids eighteen months to seven years. From 9:00 A.M. to 4:00 P.M., ages eighteen months to four years go on nature walks, visit the fire hall and puppy day care, and have games and nap time (C$83 all day; C$45 half day). Five- to seven-year-olds also do nature hikes, plus gondola rides, swimming, Frisbee golf, arts and crafts, and outdoor games. Cost is the same, C$83 full day with lunch and snacks; C$45 for morning only. Two- and three-day pricing is in place for July and August.

For eight- to twelve-year-olds, the Mountain Bike Program is a comprehensive, skill-based program allowing specific progression. Daily or two- and three-day camps go from beginners level through trials park, descents, and trail rides for intermediate and advanced riders. Cost depends on equipment needed, and ranges from C$83 for full day including lunch to C$122 adding bike and safety equipment.

MY Youth Centre allows twelve- to eighteen-year-olds their own space with all their favorite things, like DVDs, Nintendo 64, air hockey, pool, and table tennis, for only C$5.00. Open Wednesday, Thursday, Friday, and Saturday from 2:00 or 3:00 P.M. until 8:00 P.M. (10:00 or 11:00 P.M. on weekends), it's also the center for some planned events such as hikes and overnight excursions. Teens have their own Web site at www.whistleryouthcentre.com.

Recreation: Get introduced to Whistler/Blackcomb in free morning or afternoon guided tours and you'll begin to appreciate the mountains. More than 200 trails, twelve bowls, and three glaciers provide all the variety any skier could hope for. Choose chutes filled with powder, steep runs through trees, broad trails perfectly groomed, or mogul monsters. The average annual snowfall of 360 inches is complemented by sophisticated snowmaking capabilities. Both mountains open in late November, and skiing continues to late April on Blackcomb and to mid-June on Whistler. Blackcomb opens again in mid-June for glacier skiing through August for those who can't get enough of winter. Both mountains average 55% intermediate terrain; Blackcomb has about 5% more expert trails.

When taking a break from skiing, try ice-skating, snowshoeing, and snowmobiling, or organize a sleigh ride. Cross-country skiers take to the 10 miles of track-set trails through the forest and valley. Or try indoor rock climbing. Summer or winter eco-tours are available. For just a little less strenuous exercise, visit one of the many spas, or stroll through the village to discover its over 200 shops.

Summer or winter, family activities abound. It would take pages and pages to begin to outline all there is to do at Whistler/Blackcomb; we encourage you to check the extensive Web site so you can find your favorites and plan ahead. Especially for the ski and ride programs in winter and adventure camps in summer, advance reservations are a must.

In summer golf is a premier sport, with four eighteen-hole courses, each with fine credentials. The Whistler Golf Course was designed by Arnold Palmer, and the Château Whistler Course was designed by Robert Trent Jones Jr. Jack Nicklaus was responsible for Nicklaus North, which opened in 1994, and the Big Sky Golf and Country Club was designed by Robert Cupp.

Hiking and biking across the Alpine terrain are favorites with summertime visitors. Whistler's intent is to become a mountain biking mecca, and they are well on their way. For family fun, the Meadow Park Recreation Center has an indoor pool outfitted for kids, an outdoor playground and waterpark, and an indoor ice rink for those who miss winter. Adventure Zone is one of those places where you can do everything—wall climbing, minigolf, luge, trapeze, kiss-the-sky trampoline, and horseback riding. Zipline Ecotours gives a twist to outdoor adventure where you spend two and a half hours flying through the trees over a series of cable cords and suspension bridges with a bird's-eye view over gaping gorges and rushing rivers. The five lakes provide fishermen, swimmers, and boaters with ample fun. Two movie theaters, art galleries, a museum, an art studio with fun workshops, and three Internet cafes may draw you indoors for a while. A variety of festivals and special events are available throughout the year, and actually, more visitors arrive in summer.

Tourism Whistler
4010 Whistler Way
Whistler, British Columbia
Canada V0N 1B4
(604) 664–5625, (800) 944–7853
www.whistlerblackcomb.com
www.mywhistler.com

INDEXES

Alphabetical Index of Resorts

Weekapaug Inn, Weekapaug, Rhode Island, 26

The Westin Mission Hills Resort, Rancho Mirage, California, 228

Whistler/Blackcomb, Whistler, British Columbia, Canada, 249

Wild Dunes Resort, Isle of Palms, South Carolina, 65

Resorts by State/Province

UNITED STATES

Alabama
Marriott's Grand Hotel Resort, Golf Club & Spa, Point Clear, 92

Arizona
The Arizona Biltmore, Phoenix, 132
Enchantment Resort, Sedona, 137
Hyatt Regency Scottsdale Resort at Gainey Ranch, Scottsdale, 142
Los Abrigados Resort and Spa, Sedona, 146
Tanque Verde Ranch, Tucson, 148

California
The Alisal Guest Ranch and Resort, Solvang, 196
Coffee Creek Ranch, Trinity Center, 199
La Costa Resort and Spa, Carlsbad, 205
Montecito Sequoia Resort, King's Canyon National Park, 207
Northstar-at-Tahoe, Truckee, 209
The Rancho Bernardo Inn, San Diego, 212
Squaw Valley USA, Olympic Valley, 218
The Westin Mission Hills Resort, Rancho Mirage, 228

Colorado
Aspen/Snowmass Village, Aspen, 156
Breckenridge Ski Resort, Breckenridge, 162
The Broadmoor, Colorado Springs, 166
C Lazy U Ranch, Granby, 169
Club Med/Crested Butte, Crested Butte, 172

Keystone Resort, Keystone, 175
Vail/Beaver Creek Resorts, Vail, 190

Florida
Amelia Island Plantation, Amelia Island, 70
The Breakers, Palm Beach, 73
Cheeca Lodge and Spa, Islamorada, 78
Club Med/Sandpiper, Port St. Lucie, 83
Hawks Cay Resort, Duck Key, 86
Marco Island Marriott Resort, Marco Island, 91
The Resort at Longboat Key Club, Longboat Key, 94
South Seas Resort, Captiva Island, 96
Sundial Beach Resort, Sanibel Island, 98
TradeWinds Island Resorts/Island Grand, St. Pete Beach, 100

Georgia
Callaway Gardens, Pine Mountain, 75
The Cloister, Sea Island, 80
Jekyll Island Club Hotel, Jekyll Island, 88

Idaho
Sun Valley, Sun Valley, 225

Illinois
Eagle Ridge Inn and Resort, Galena, 104

Maine
Sugarloaf/USA, Carrabassett Valley, 22

Maryland
Hyatt Regency Chesapeake Bay, Cambridge, 53

Massachusetts
The Lighthouse Inn, West Dennis, 8

Michigan
Grand Traverse Resort and Spa, Acme, 108
The Homestead, Glen Arbor, 112
Grand Hotel, Mackinac Island, 118
Mission Point Resort, Mackinac Island, 119
Shanty Creek, Bellaire, 123

Minnesota
Grand View Lodge, Nisswa, 110

CANADA

Alberta
Fairmont Chateau Lake Louise, Lake Louise, 234
Sunshine Village, Banff National Park, 247

British Columbia
Whistler/Blackcomb, Whistler, 249

Ontario
Deerhurst Resort, Huntsville, 232
Severn Lodge, Port Severn, 244

Quebec
Fairmont Le Château Montebello, Montebello, 237
Fairmont Le Manoir Richelieu, Charlevoix, 239
Gray Rocks Resort, Ville de Mont-Tremblant, 241

Children's Programs by Season

As an aid in planning your vacation, resorts are listed according to when the children's programs operate: Daily Year–Round, Summer, or Winter. Some resorts, such as ski areas, may be listed under both Summer and Winter. Many resorts may also have children's programs during other times of the year; for example, major holidays or year-round on weekends. We have marked these resorts with an asterisk (*) to indicate that there is more available than just summer or winter; check the entries for details. It is always safest, however, to contact the resort to ensure that the children's program is running when you want it. Please note that other resorts not listed are considered family-friendly but have limited or no supervised children's programs: The Arizona Biltmore, El Monte Sagrado, Highland Lodge, and Ludlow's Island Resort. Again, please see resort descriptions for details.

DAILY YEAR-ROUND PROGRAMS

Amelia Island Plantation
The Breakers
Cheeca Lodge and Spa
Club Med/Sandpiper
Enchantment Resort
Grand Traverse Resort and Spa
Hawk's Cay Resort
The Homestead, Virginia
Hyatt Regency Lake Las Vegas Resort, Spa and Casino
Hyatt Regency Scottsdale Resort at Gainey Ranch
Hyatt Regency Tamaya Resort and Spa
La Costa Resort and Spa
Marco Island Marriott Resort
Marriott's Grand Hotel Resort
The Resort at Longboat Key Club
Rocking Horse Ranch
South Seas Resort
Sundial Beach Resort
Tanque Verde Ranch
TradeWinds Island Resorts/Island Grand
Vail/Beaver Creek Resorts
The Westin Mission Hills Resort
Whistler/Blackcomb

SUMMER PROGRAMS

*The Alisal Guest Ranch and Resort
Angel Fire Resort
Aspen/Snowmass Village
The Balsams Grand Resort Hotel
The Bishop's Lodge Resort and Spa
Breckenridge Ski Resort
The Broadmoor
*C Lazy U Ranch
Callaway Gardens
*The Cloister
Coffee Creek Ranch
Deer Valley Resort
*Deerhurst Resort
*Eagle Ridge Inn and Resort
Fairfield Sapphire Valley
*Fairmont Le Château Montebello
*Fairmont Le Manoir Richelieu

Flathead Lake Lodge
*Flying L Guest Ranch
Golden Acres Farm and Ranch
*Grand Geneva Resort
Grand Hotel
Grand View Lodge
Gray Rocks Resort
*The Greenbrier
*The Grove Park Inn Resort and Spa
High Hampton Inn & Country Club
*The Homestead, Michigan
*Hyatt Regency Chesapeake Bay
*Hyatt Regency Hill Country Resort
The Inn of the Seventh Mountain
Jekyll Island Club Hotel
Keystone Resort
*Kiawah Island Golf Resort
Killington Ski and Summer Resort
Kingsmill Resort
The Lighthouse Inn
The Lodge of Four Seasons
Los Abrigados Resort and Spa
Mission Point Resort
*Mohonk Mountain House
Montecito Sequoia Resort
Mountain Sky Guest Ranch
Mount Snow
The Mount Washington Resort at Bretton
    Woods
Northstar-at-Tahoe
Park City Mountain Resort
*The Rancho Bernardo Inn
Ruttger's Bay Lake Lodge
*The Sagamore
Scott's Oquaga Lake House
*Seabrook Island Club
Severn Lodge
Shanty Creek
*Skytop Lodge
Smugglers' Notch Resort
Snake River Lodge and Spa
Snowbird Ski and Summer Resort
Stratton Mountain Resort

Sugarloaf/USA
*Sunriver Resort
Sun Valley
*Tan-Tar-A Resort
The Tides Inn
The Tyler Place Family Resort
Vail/Beaver Creek Resorts
Weekapaug Inn
Wild Dunes Resort

WINTER PROGRAMS

Angel Fire Resort
Aspen/Snowmass Village
The Balsams Grand Resort Hotel
*Big Sky of Montana
The Bishop's Lodge Resort and Spa
Breckenridge Ski Resort
Club Med/Crested Butte
Deer Valley Resort
*Fairmont Chateau Lake Louise
Gray Rocks Resort
The Inn of the Seventh Mountain
Keystone Resort
Killington Ski and Summer Resort
Montecito Sequoia Resort
Mount Snow
The Mount Washington Resort at Bretton
    Woods
Northstar-at-Tahoe
Park City Mountain Resort
Shanty Creek
Smugglers' Notch Resort
Snake River Lodge and Spa
Snowbird Ski and Summer Resort
Squaw Valley USA
Stratton Mountain Resort
Sugarloaf/USA
*Sunriver Resort
Sunshine Village
Sun Valley
Taos Ski Valley
Vail/Beaver Creek Resorts

ABOUT THE AUTHORS

JANET TICE grew up in Oklahoma, then spent just as many years in Manhattan. Always a gypsy (although her mother denies it), she considers herself a citizen of the world. Schooled at the University of Oklahoma, with a Master of Science degree from the University of New York, her background in psychiatry prepared her for over twenty-five years in the travel business, which she claims is just another kind of craziness. Proud mother of Fabiana, for many years her inspiration and best field agent, she was a proponent and practitioner of family travel long before it became fashionable. She founded and directed Families Welcome!, a tour company for families, from 1986 to 1995. Currently living in North Carolina, her heart is really in the Southwest.

JANE WILFORD was born and reared in New Orleans, Louisiana. She earned a Bachelor of Arts degree in Art History and History from Duke University and a Master of Science degree in Library Service from Columbia University. After living for several years in New York and London, she currently resides in Connecticut with her husband, D. Sykes Wilford, and sons, Sykes and Paul, and daughter, Sarah. The Wilford family travels extensively throughout the United States and Europe.

HELP US KEEP THIS GUIDE
UP TO DATE

Every effort has been made by the authors and editors to make this guide as accurate and useful as possible. However, many things can change after a guide is published—establishments close, phone numbers change, facilities come under new management, and so on.

We would love to hear from you concerning your experiences with this guide and how you feel it could be made better and kept up to date. While we may not be able to respond to all comments and suggestions, we'll take them to heart and we'll also make certain to share them with the authors. Please send your comments and suggestions to the following address:

The Globe Pequot Press
Reader Response/Editorial Department
P.O. Box 480
Guilford, CT 06437

Or you may e-mail us at:
editorial@GlobePequot.com

Thanks for your input, and happy travels!